Knowledge Management and E-Learning

IT MANAGEMENT TITLES
FROM AUERBACH PUBLICATIONS AND CRC PRESS

The Executive MBA in Information Security
John J. Trinckes, Jr
ISBN: 978-1-4398-1007-1

**The Decision Model: A Business
Logic Framework Linking Business
and Technology**
Barbara von Halle and Larry Goldberg
ISBN: 978-1-4200-8281-4

The SIM Guide to Enterprise Architecture
Leon Kappelman, ed.
ISBN: 978-1-4398-1113-9

Lean Six Sigma Secrets for the CIO
William Bentley and Peter T. Davis
ISBN: 978-1-4398-0379-0

**Building an Enterprise-Wide Business
Continuity Program**
Kelley Okolita
ISBN: 978-1-4200-8864-9

Marketing IT Products and Services
Jessica Keyes
ISBN: 978-1-4398-0319-6

**Cloud Computing: Implementation,
Management, and Security**
John W. Rittinghouse and
James F. Ransome
ISBN: 978-1-4398-0680-7

**Data Protection: Governance, Risk
Management, and Compliance**
David G. Hill
ISBN: 978-1-4398-0692-0

**Strategic Data Warehousing: Achieving
Alignment with Business**
Neera Bhansali
ISBN: 978-1-4200-8394-1

**Mobile Enterprise Transition
and Management**
Bhuvan Unhelkar
ISBN: 978-1-4200-7827-5

The Green and Virtual Data Center
Greg Schulz
ISBN: 978-1-4200-8666-9

The Effective CIO
Eric J. Brown, Jr. and William A. Yarberry
ISBN: 978-1-4200-6460-5

**Business Resumption Planning,
Second Edition**
Leo A. Wrobel
ISBN: 978-0-8493-1459-9

**IT Auditing and Sarbanes-Oxley
Compliance: Key Strategies for
Business Improvement**
Dimitris N. Chorafas
ISBN: 978-1-4200-8617-1

**Best Practices in Business Technology
Management**
Stephen J. Andriole
ISBN: 978-1-4200-6333-2

**Leading IT Projects:
The IT Manager's Guide**
Jessica Keyes
ISBN: 978-1-4200-7082-8

**Knowledge Retention:
Strategies and Solutions**
Jay Liebowitz
ISBN: 978-1-4200-6465-0

The Business Value of IT
Michael D. S. Harris, David Herron,
and Stasia Iwanicki
ISBN: 978-1-4200-6474-2

**Service-Oriented Architecture: SOA
Strategy, Methodology, and Technology**
James P. Lawler and H. Howell-Barber
ISBN: 978-1-4200-4500-0

Service Oriented Enterprises
Setrag Khoshafian
ISBN: 978-0-8493-5360-4

Knowledge Management and E-Learning

Edited by

Jay Liebowitz, DSc and Michael S. Frank, PhD

CRC Press
Taylor & Francis Group
Boca Raton   London   New York

CRC Press is an imprint of the
Taylor & Francis Group, an **informa** business

AN AUERBACH BOOK

Auerbach Publications
Taylor & Francis Group
6000 Broken Sound Parkway NW, Suite 300
Boca Raton, FL 33487-2742

© 2011 by Taylor and Francis Group, LLC
Auerbach Publications is an imprint of Taylor & Francis Group, an Informa business

No claim to original U.S. Government works

Printed in the United States of America on acid-free paper
10 9 8 7 6 5 4 3 2 1

International Standard Book Number: 978-1-4398-3725-2 (Hardback)

Library of Congress Cataloging-in-Publication Data

Knowledge management and e-learning / edited by Jay Liebowitz and Michael S. Frank.
    p. cm.
   Includes bibliographical references and index.
   ISBN 978-1-4398-3725-2 (hbk. : alk. paper)
   1. Knowledge management. 2. Computer-assisted instruction. 3. Distance education.
I. Liebowitz, Jay, 1957- II. Frank, Michael S.

   HD30.2.K6368425 2011
   658.3'12402854678--dc22   2010032000

Visit the Taylor & Francis Web site at
http://www.taylorandfrancis.com

and the Auerbach Web site at
http://www.auerbach-publications.com

From Jay ... To the Liebowitz–Zeide families and all
my students and colleagues worldwide.

From Michael ... To my wife, Jennifer, and my sons, Aidan and Darren,
all of whom have changed my life immeasurably for the better.

Contents

SECTION III   KM AND E-LEARNING: CASE STUDIES

SECTION IV   KM AND E-LEARNING: INDUSTRY PERSPECTIVES

Preface

This work embraces two heretofore distinct fields of study, knowledge management and e-learning. In order to understand the impetus to link these two fields by a common thread, it is necessary to understand the two fields and the focus of each.

Knowledge management (KM) has developed as a field from its roots in data and information management. Organizations became aware of the need to store and retrieve knowledge that would be indispensible to their overall functions. The explosion of knowledge brought about by the technological revolution, particularly in the past decade, brought to light how much information was available on almost any given topic and that the traditional repositories for such knowledge (file cabinets, for example) were insufficient for storing knowledge.

It was alarming to realize that within the past 15 years more information could be stored on a single desktop computer or a mobile handheld device than an entire organization might be able to store anywhere prior to that time. While data retrieval might be enhanced by technology, the fact is that such retrieval can only occur with an organization's ability to access and be aware of the repositories that exist to serve the organization's purposes in the future.

Moreover, aside from their need to use current and stored knowledge, many organizations, willingly or not, have become the developers and dispensers of new knowledge. This historical anomaly occurs in light of the individual's ability to instantly access a plethora of information that relates directly or tangentially to one's inquiries. This linkage and the serendipitous search-outcome effect allow new ideas and thoughts that lead to innovation to occur on a regular basis. The result of these events is that the new knowledge becomes part of the repository and knowledge base of the organization.

Much has been written in the field of knowledge management. The body of that literature suggests the KM embraces a process of creating, acquiring, capturing, aggregating, sharing and using knowledge to enhance organizational learning and performance. Many definitions and philosophical positions emerge in the dynamic field of knowledge management. The common thread running through that field ultimately returns to the aforementioned factors in one way or another.

It is only natural that the evolution of knowledge management would find its way into the university setting. After all, correctly or not, universities were seen, and perhaps still are seen, as the primary creators and dispensers of knowledge. Whether this remains true in the wake of a technological cataclysm will be debatable. On the other hand, the university remains front and center in the dispersion of information to society writ large both for practical and theoretical reasons.

Increasingly, universities are expanding their e-learning capabilities to serve larger populations of students or students whose expectations embrace modern technology and who expect, perhaps even demand, a modernized educational experience built on the latest technology and "social networks." Clearly, Starbucks aside, the coffee house or local pub has been supplanted by the laptop and Blackberry. The future for such devices, even within their social network settings and functionalities, remains both vast and unknown.

So, against this background, the editors attempt to bring the two fields together. This book, as far as the editors know, is the first venture into that unknown territory. Surely, distance learning has been in existence for centuries. The most common form of distance education likely remains various forms of correspondence. Much later (the 1980s), the videoconference emerged using, at first, one-way and later two-way communication, and it became popular in both classrooms and corporations. Of course, the emergence of the Internet and digital technologies forever changed the world in unforeseen ways.

Revolutions can occur unexpectedly. The editors of this book both work for University of Maryland University College (UMUC), which is the largest public university in the United States. Founded in 1947, most of the growth that catapulted the university to its present size was unplanned, particularly in the early stages circa 1995. In 1995, a few courses were put online. The online environment in that decade was the clunky command-driven DOS-based platform.

What the faculty observed was that online classes began to fill at four or five times the rate of their face-to-face sisters. The more classes that went online, the faster they filled.

Several inquiries revealed that the vast majority of students who were enrolling online lived less than a few miles from a campus location. By 2010, the university had a four-fold increase from 1995. Today, 29 of 32 undergraduate degrees, 15 masters' degrees and one doctorate are offered online.

The point of the aforementioned discussion is that much of the early planning was more or less just-in-time planning. The infrastructure that the university operates today, as discussed below, in the early stages of growth, was unforeseen. At the time the online revolution started, there was not a strategic design. Rather, the push for more and more online courses and supporting technology came from the students. This push resulted in a morass of structural and functional changes that should prove of interest to the reader.

The change in structure and function led to two looming issues facing all providers or potential providers of distance education: (1) changing the culture of their current delivery system providers and (2) understanding the economic model of e-learning. These issues beg for the use of knowledge management principles presented in this book. These principles, which are provided throughout this book, should serve scholars and practitioners who seek to make use of the techniques, tools, and implementation guidance presented herein.

The support of online education requires a huge financial and faculty commitment. The financial commitment is unusual because the financial cost of the commitment is funded from an operating budget largely to support the learning platform and ancillary student services. Traditional universities still expend funds to construct new buildings. Those funds are from a capital budget. Understanding the difference in these two budget models explains the difference between those who will be successful and those who will not in future large scale e-learning ventures.

E-learning commitment extends to providing a deep array of support services to enrich the e-learning environment. Technical support is essential, as is a substantial library data base and research assistance. There must be the ability to train faculty and provide services to support their teaching and their development in an e-learning environment. Mechanisms for testing, adapting, and deploying new technology are necessary. Given the interplay among all these components of the e-learning process, a knowledge management system of superior scope and depth must be an essential part of the process.

Often, gaining faculty commitment means a change of culture. Certain myths associated with e-learning must be abolished: e-learning is inferior to face-to-face learning; e-learning is severely limited in terms of the subject matter that can be taught; e-learning and rampant cheating run hand-in-hand. In fact, UMUC's studies show no difference between e-learning and face-to-face courses learning outcomes. UMUC offers every array of technical and non-technical courses online. So, subject matter is not a barrier in terms of what can be taught. On the matter of cheating, anyone who has attended a large public university where class size is often in the hundreds can attest to the possibilities that the person taking the test may not be the person enrolled in the course. Moreover, many new technologies have identification features and ease of deployment; thus, the matter of the potential to cheat in an e-learning environment will be resolved by technology before large traditional public universities can solve the potential to cheat in their large face-to-face classes. Student and faculty engagement and satisfaction are the same in face-to-face classes as in e-learning courses. Therefore, we conclude that the future is bright for the continued expansion of e-learning. But, that expansion can only occur within the context of a superior knowledge management infrastructure.

This book sheds light on the potential synergies between e-learning and knowledge management. It is divided into four parts: (I) Setting the Stage, (II) Methodologies and Techniques, (III) Case Studies and Applications, and (IV) Industry Perspectives. The 19 chapters are written by some of the leading authorities from 8 countries in the fields of knowledge management and e-learning. The editors greatly appreciate their invaluable contributions, as well as the wonderful support from our publishing editor, John Wyzalek, the production coordinator, Jennifer Ahringer, and the project editor, Andrea Demby at Taylor & Francis. Our students and colleagues at UMUC deserve heartfelt thanks as they allow us to be creative and innovate along the way. To give back, we are donating all book royalties to UMUC to support graduate student and faculty research. And, certainly, without our families' support while we "went upstairs to work on the book," this volume would never have been possible.

Enjoy!

Michael S. Frank, PhD
Jay Liebowitz, DSc
Co-Editors

About the Editors

Dr. Jay Liebowitz is the Orkand Endowed Chair of Management and Technology in the Graduate School of Management and Technology at the University of Maryland University College (UMUC). He previously served as a professor in the Carey Business School at Johns Hopkins University. He was recently ranked one of the top 10 knowledge management researchers/practitioners out of 11,000 worldwide. At Johns Hopkins University, he was the founding program director for the Graduate Certificate in Competitive Intelligence and the capstone director of the MS-Information and Telecommunications Systems for Business Program, where he engaged over 30 organizations in industry, government, and not-for-profits in capstone projects.

Prior to joining Hopkins, Dr. Liebowitz was the first knowledge management officer at the NASA Goddard Space Flight Center. Before NASA, Dr. Liebowitz was the Robert W. Deutsch Distinguished Professor of Information Systems at the University of Maryland-Baltimore County, professor of Management Science at George Washington University, and chair of artificial intelligence at the U.S. Army War College.

Dr. Liebowitz is the founder and editor-in-chief of *Expert Systems with Applications,* an international journal (published by Elsevier), which had about 1,600 paper downloads per day worldwide last year. He is a Fulbright Scholar, IEEE-USA Federal Communications Commission Executive Fellow, and Computer Educator of the Year (International Association for Computer Information Systems). He has published over 40 books and myriad journal articles on knowledge management, intelligent systems, and IT management. His most recent books are *Knowledge Retention: Strategies and Solutions* (Taylor & Francis, 2009) and *Knowledge Management in Public Health* (Taylor & Francis, 2010). He has lectured and consulted worldwide. He can be reached at jliebowitz@umuc.edu.

Michael S. Frank, PhD, serves as vice provost and dean of University of Maryland of University College's Graduate School of Management and Technology. His service with the graduate school includes chairing the Information Technology Systems Department and General Management Programs Department.

Before coming to the graduate school, Dr. Frank held executive level positions in the private and public sectors for many years. As an executive vice president for a large Maryland financial institution, he supervised several hundred people, drafted strategic and business plans, oversaw reorganizations and staffing, and controlled approximately $1 billion in assets. Prior to that he was the human resource director of one of Maryland's largest jurisdictions, where he directed all human resource and collective bargaining activities for over 4,000 employees.

Dr. Frank is the recipient of numerous official commendations, a leadership award, UMUC's highest teaching excellence award (the Drazek Award), and several professional awards, including a Professional Writers Award from the International Personnel Management Association, and a Sustained Outstanding Quality Award from the National Capital Area's Management Association. His teaching, research, publication, and consulting interests reside in the fields of human resource management, organization theory, technology issues, and e-learning. He can be reached at mfrank@umuc.edu.

List of Contributors

Ulrich Bernath, PhD
Ulrich Bernath Foundation for
  Research in Open and Distance
  Learning
Oldenburg, Germany
and
Adjunct Professor
University of Maryland University
  College
Adelphi, Maryland

Joseph Betser, PhD
Senior Project Leader for Technology,
  Strategy, and Knowledge
The Aerospace Corporation
El Segundo, California

Francisco J. Cantu, PhD
Professor and Dean of Research and
  Graduate Studies
Tecnologico de Monterrey
Monterrey N.L., Mexico

Jason C.H. Chen, PhD
Professor, Management Information
  Systems
School of Business
Gonzaga University
Spokane, Washington

Donna J. Dennis, PhD
President, Leadership Solutions
  Consulting, LLC
Princeton, New Jersey

Michael S. Frank, PhD
Vice Provost and Dean
Graduate School of Management and
  Technology
University of Maryland University
  College
Adelphi, Maryland

Yolanda Heredia, PhD
Professor and Dean of the Graduate
  School of Education
Virtual University, Tecnologico de
  Monterrey
Monterrey N.L., Mexico

Li-An Ho, PhD
Associate Professor, Department of
  Educational Technology
Tamkang University
Tamsui
Taipei County, Taiwan

Tim Howell
Consultant and Former International
  Space Station Engineering and
  Manufacturing Manager at
  Rocketdyne
Santa Clarita, California

Thomas Hülsmann, PhD
Program Coordinator
MDE Center for Lifelong Learning
  (C3L)
Carl von Ossietzky Universität
  Oldenburg
Oldenburg, Germany

Gwo-Jen Hwang, PhD
Distinguished Professor, Department
  of Information and Learning
  Technology and Dean
College of Science and Technology
National University of Tainan
Tainan City, Taiwan

Mary Key, PhD
President
Key Associates, Inc.
Tampa, Florida

Allison Kipta
Customer Trainer Staff
Lockheed Martin IS&GS Security
Westminster, Maryland

Charles S. (Steve) Knode, PhD
Collegiate Professor and Program
  Director
Chief Information Officer Program
University of Maryland University
  College
Adelphi, Maryland

Jon-David W. Knode, DCD
Assistant Professor of Business
  Administration and Marketing
Reeves School of Business
Methodist University
Fayetteville, North Carolina

Jay Liebowitz, DSc
Orkand Endowed Chair in
  Management and Technology
Graduate School of Management and
  Technology
University of Maryland University
  College
Adelphi, Maryland

Binshan Lin, PhD
BellSouth Corporation Professor
Louisiana State University in
  Shreveport
Shreveport, Louisiana

Catherine Lord
Senior Strategy Consultant
IBM Software Group
Victoria, British Columbia, Canada

Stephen Miller
Associate Provost
Information and Library Services
University of Maryland University
  College
Adelphi, Maryland

Jürgen Moormann, PhD
Professor of Banking and Head of
  ProcessLab
Frankfurt School of Finance
  & Banking
Frankfurt am Main, Germany

Stephan Poelmans, PhD
Hogeschool-Universiteit Brussel
dep. Handelswetenschappen
Brussels, Belgium

Enrica Porcari, PhD
First CIO and CGIAR ICT-KM
   Program Lead
CGIAR c/o Bioversity International
Rome, Italy

Stella Porto, DSc
Professor and Director, Master of
   Distance Education & E-Learning
Graduate School of Management and
   Technology
University of Maryland University
   College
Adelphi, Maryland

Claudine SchWeber, PhD
Professor and Program Director
Doctor of Management Program
Graduate School of Management and
   Technology
University of Maryland University
   College
Adelphi, Maryland

Theodore E. Stone, PhD
Professor and Director of Academic
   Technology
University of Maryland University
   College
Adelphi, Maryland

Heather K. Tillberg-Webb
Office of Learning
Johns Hopkins Carey Business School
Baltimore, Maryland

Frederik Truyen, PhD
Dienst Informatieverwerking
Faculteit Letteren
Leuven, Belgium

Antoniette (Toni) S. Ungaretti, PhD
Assistant Dean and Director
Office of Learning
Johns Hopkins Carey Business School
Baltimore, Maryland

Jan Vanthienen, PhD
Professor and Microsoft Research
   Co-Chair
Katholieke Universiteit Leuven
Leuven, Belgium

Christine Walti, MDE & MSW
Anne Arundel Community College
   and
University of Maryland University
   College Graduate School of
   Management & Technology
Annapolis, Maryland

Minhong Wang, PhD
Director
KM & EL Lab
and
Co-Editor-in-Chief of *KM & EL: An
   International Journal*
Faculty of Education
The University of Hong Kong
Hong Kong, China

Stephen J.H. Yang, PhD
Co-Editor-in-Chief of *KM & EL: An
   International Journal*
Distinguished Professor and Associate
   Dean of Academic Affairs
National Central University, Taiwan
JhongLi City, Taiwan

KM AND E-LEARNING: SETTING THE STAGE

I

Chapter 1

The Synergy between Knowledge Management and E-Learning

Jay Liebowitz and Michael S. Frank

Contents

Introduction

Both fields, knowledge management (KM) and e-learning, seem to be evolving over the years. KM, although coined in the early 1980s, deals with how best to leverage knowledge internally and externally in order to stimulate innovation, build a sense of community, preserve the institutional knowledge base, and promote internal and external organizational effectiveness. Although collaboration and integration seem to be the buzzwords being used in KM circles, the next phase of KM will highlight continued use of Web 2.0 and social networking tools and their capabilities, as well as borrow from complementary sets of approaches in order to better integrate KM within the daily working lives of the employee. Similarly, e-learning has been around for years, with the Sloan Consortium first launching the major

3

e-learning initiatives at universities over 17 years ago. According to the most recent Sloan Consortium International Conference on Online Learning (October 2009), there are about 4 million persons getting their degrees online with about a 20% growth rate. Corporate universities as well are actively pursuing e-learning for further training and educating their employees.

As these two fields further develop, synergistic relationships should increase between KM and e-learning. Some of these relationships are quite evident. For example, both disciplines deal with knowledge capture, sharing, application, and potentially knowledge generation. Both the disciplines of knowledge management and e-learning have important technological components to enhance learning. Both disciplines ultimately contribute to building a continuous learning culture, whether knowledge-enabled or learner-enabled. Similarly, both disciplines can be decomposed into learning objects for ease of knowledge retention and transfer. And both knowledge management and e-learning are maturing to the point where there are numerous journals and associated communities that deal with KM and e-learning—including the international journal *Knowledge Management and E-Learning*, which has recognized the importance of the synergy between the two disciplines.

So, what are the inferences one can draw from the foregoing description of the state of the disciplines? To unravel that question, one must become familiar with some of the work that has attempted to associate these two disciplines. Then, one can speculate as to where a merger of these disciplines may lead in terms of both theory and practice.

Background Literature on the Synergy between KM and E-Learning

While there has been a paucity of papers written on the synergy between knowledge management and e-learning, a few scholars have made the attempt. Chunhua (2008) discusses e-learning as a new approach to KM. In his paper, the synergies are shown as using e-learning as a tool to help internalize tacit knowledge; using e-learning as a way to acquire knowledge; and applying e-learning to promote knowledge sharing. E-learning in this regard can be seen to be part of organizational learning in which KM plays a role in the knowledge acquisition, sharing, and application phases as well.

Lamont (2003) observes and discusses that e-learning has not reflected a strategic, enterprise-wide vision, but has more of a tactical and departmental focus. KM, on the other hand, reflects a more strategic view of the organization. According to Lamont, some scholars and practitioners see e-learning migrating to become a part of KM; others see KM as a tool to be used in an e-learning process. Certainly, reusable learning objects (or knowledge objects) allow learning content to be chunked into smaller units whereby learning management systems can provide support for the use of these learning objects in the development of courses (Lamont, 2003). Companies too, such as Cisco, have committed to using reusable learning objects over the years.

KM portals can be used also as gateways to e-learning. E-learning has been mainly static content, but KM has the potential to make it a more dynamic process, whereby integrating e-learning and KM will bring the learning experience closer to the job (Lamont, 2003).

Wild et al. (2002) developed a framework for e-learning as a tool for KM. They claim that "many corporations are discovering that e-learning has many of the same attributes as basic knowledge management processes and thus can be used as a tool for knowledge management" (p. 372). Further, they indicate that e-learning creates a growing repository of knowledge that, through tailored knowledge management processes, can personalize the learning experience. E-learning can assist in the "dissemination and applying knowledge acquired" process associated with the KM value chain.

Barker (2005) advocates KM for e-learning whereby effective KM exists within the context of ongoing educational processes, arguing that this can lead to growth economies and more stable societies based on knowledge-sharing principles. Other scholars have focused on the more narrow concepts of e-learning as they relate to KM. Lytras et al. (2005), for example, guest-edited a special issue on "Knowledge Management Technologies for E-Learning" in the *International Journal of Distance Education Technologies* and discuss the importance of learning objects that possess tacit knowledge characteristics. Mouzakitis (2009) at the 2009 World Conference on Educational Sciences discusses the following advantages of using e-learning in training activities: cost-effectiveness; productivity improvements; faster learning; better retention; customer satisfaction and employee increased satisfaction; and facilitation of self-paced learning.

Chen and Hsiang (2007) studied the importance of developing a knowledge community through e-learning as a critical element in implementing KM policy. E-learning, they argue, should help nurture a learning organization and foster a corporate culture based on knowledge sharing (Chen and Hsiang, 2007). Further, they observe the complementary roles of KM and e-learning through the following critical success factors for knowledge community-based e-learning: participation of key personnel in the development of a knowledge strategy; procedural design needs to complement current work and help to establish a loop of knowledge sharing; learner-focused technology; knowledge community involvement to complement company business goals; new business strategies and marketing; establishment of a culture of learning; providing concrete rewards for goal achievement; providing ample learning time and space within the company; and establishing mutual trust between members of a team. Taken together, a culture of knowledge sharing combined with or enhanced by e-learning will develop (Chen and Hsiang, 2007).

Other researchers have demonstrated how combining KM and e-learning through the use of intelligent systems increases organization performance. Del Peso and De Arriaga (2008) discuss intelligent e-learning systems through automatic construction of ontologies. This process allows automatic updating of the knowledge bases used in intelligent e-learning systems to increase interoperability and communication among knowledge bases. Lau and Tsui (2009) discuss how the integration of KM within an e-learning environment can provide a learning grid that enables the learner to identify the correct learning objects associated with the learner's context, needs, and preferences (Lau and Tsui, 2009). Shaw (2009) shows that tools such as knowledge maps can improve one's e-learning performance. Knowledge maps are similar to concept maps in showing visualized concepts, knowledge, and relationships (Shaw, 2009). In terms of improving e-learning performance, Ho and Kuo (2009) display through their research that organizations can improve adult workers' e-learning outcomes by facilitating positive computer attitudes.

Still others have looked at the influence of culture on e-learning and KM. Lee et al. (2009) studied learners' acceptance of e-learning in South Korea. Aside from the implementation of the educational model to address the learner's needs and educational objectives, the success of e-learning, according to Lee et al. (2009), was determined by instructor characteristics, teaching materials, perceived usefulness, playfulness, and perceived ease of use. These characteristics seem to be consistent with the research on e-learning in other countries. Olaniran (2009) explores culture relating to e-learning, concluding that attention to the cultural needs of users is crucial for e-learning success. Moreover, he argues that a failure to recognize cultural learning differences will lessen the effectiveness of e-learning.

A Framework for Studying the Integration of KM and E-Learning

From Bransford's work (1998), a framework for studying the integration of knowledge management and e-learning can be positioned around the intersection of three components: knowledge-enabled, learner-centered, and community-accessed. Knowledge-enabled refers to the KM part of the equation in terms of having the right knowledge available at the right time and place for the learner. Learner-centered refers to the focus being on the learner with the various teaching paradigms being adapted to the learner's style. Community-accessed, the third component, is a combination of both KM and e-learning. This refers to the ability to learn from others through a community of interest. A community of interest brings social networking characteristics to KM (i.e., the "connection," people-to-people approach) and to e-learning (i.e., using technology to reach out to the communities for learning). The intersection of these three components is the core of where knowledge management and e-learning meet.

Let us look further at each of these three components since they are critical to an understanding of current and future trends. The knowledge-enabled component allows the learner to access the right knowledge to facilitate personal decision making. In Liebowitz's (2008, 2009) and Nevo and Chan's (2007) work, they identify important characteristics of KM system success factors. These include ease of use, value and quality of the knowledge, system accessibility, user involvement, integration, top management support/commitment, project manager and team skills, incentives, interpersonal trust and respect, reciprocity, shared values, and convenient knowledge transfer mechanisms. KM usually involves people, process, and technology. The people component deals with how best to build and nurture a knowledge-sharing culture. The process component refers to how to embed knowledge management processes into the daily work lives of the employees. The technology component refers to creating a unified knowledge network as an enabler to integrate across isolated islands of knowledge (i.e., functional silos or stovepipes in organizational parlance). Knowledge-enabled thus means that the learner should have developed a knowledge base through formal training and education or through experiential learning and have the ability to reach out to other sources, whether knowledge repositories, experts, or practitioners in the field, to bring the relevant knowledge to bear on a particular issue at hand. Liaw et al. (2010) and Wang and Haggerty (2009) broaden the discussion to include knowledge transfer in virtual settings. Their collective works, respectively, show that mobile learning can support individual KM. They further report that optimal knowledge transfers can be achieved only by individuals with the right personal capabilities and skills for virtual work.

The learner-centered or learner-centric component of the triad discussed above has an e-learning flavor in which the paradigm shifts from directed learning to facilitated learning. In this sense, learning becomes more "individualized," and "on the fly" or "just-in-time" learning becomes the norm (Connolly, 1998). This may account for the findings of Ambient Insight (2009) that 12 million students now take some or all classes online, and the trend line projects that there will be 22 million online students by 2014. There are various benefits to this form of virtual learning: greater flexibility for employee and company; enhanced peer-to-peer interaction; more one-on-one interaction with instructor; greater access to experts through technology; and expanded time period, allowing for more individual reflection. An e-learning approach can take advantage of coaching and facilitated learning by building online knowledge repositories, such as lessons learned and best practice systems. Expert systems that allow the capture of expertise in a well-defined area so that knowledge is at the fingertips of the learner are enabled. Thus, the synergy between KM approaches and e-learning becomes apparent. The collective intelligence of the learner can be amplified by taking knowledge and internalizing it with KM systems such as best practice systems, expertise locator systems, e-mentoring, and others described in the various chapters that follow.

The third framework component is community access. In today's culture and lexicon, by this we mean social networking sites, Web 2.0 tools, online communities, chat rooms, and the like, the learner's knowledge base is broadened and enhanced through interactions with others. One might argue that such interaction is a form of "strategic intelligence" in terms of improving the organization's strategic decision-making capability through KM, business intelligence (BI), and competitive intelligence (CI) (Liebowitz, 2010). KM and BI focus on the internal intelligence of the organization, while CI examines the external intelligence factors that affect the organization. BI may include some KM-related approaches, such as data mining, to identify hidden patterns and relationships in the organization's databases. CI deals with building a systematic program for collecting, analyzing, and managing external intelligence (e.g., competitors, environmental conditions, etc.) toward improving the organization's decision-making ability. The intersection of KM, BI, and CI forms "the strategic intelligence" of the organization. Thus, the community-access component of the framework described earlier allows the learner to enhance personal intelligence, as well as build organizational strategic intelligence.

What Research Lies Ahead for the KM/E-Learning Linkage

A common linkage between KM and e-learning is the use of learning/knowledge objects. According to the Web-Based Training Information Center (WBTIC, 2009), the trend that will have the biggest impact on online learning in the coming years is learning objects. The goals of learning object design are (WBTIC, 2009)

- Reusability: Learning content is modularized into small units of instruction suitable for assembly and reassembly into a variety of courses.
- Interoperability: Instructional units that interoperate with each other regardless of developer or learning management system.
- Durability: Units of instruction that stay the course and ever evolving delivery and presentation technologies without becoming unusable.
- Accessibility: Learning content that is available anywhere, any time—learning content that can be discovered and reused across networks.

By packaging these learning objects within e-learning, online learning can become more powerful and agile. If some of these learning objects are actually "knowledge objects," whereby the learner has access to interactive pools of knowledge, then the learner can augment personal knowledge through these knowledge bases for a deeper understanding of specific knowledge. For example, at Tsinghua University in China, the Digital Teaching Reference Book System was constructed by using knowledge objects for the microstructure of digital resources (Zhang and Li, 2006). The creation and reorganization of knowledge objects serve as the knowledge elements in teaching reference materials (Zhang and Li, 2006).

Another area of research to couple KM and e-learning is through the incorporation of dynamic knowledge features into the learning management system. For example, "dynamic" knowledge objects could be infused into e-learning to push appropriate information or knowledge to the user as needed. This "just-in-time" approach facilitates the learning process through the currency of knowledge that is being enhanced. Intelligent agents (know-bots) could also be used to dynamically assess what the learner is working on during the e-learning experience in order to build a dynamic, extensive user profile. In addition, text summarization technologies could be used to summarize conference and discussion threads for ease of understandability. Thus, future research and practice will involve the application of intelligent systems, artificial intelligence, and virtual reality technologies to enhance the learner's online experience.

Another important area for coupling KM and e-learning is to better capture, share, and leverage knowledge for e-learning modules (Saxena, 2007). Intelligent tutoring systems might be used to augment student and professor online interactions. Intelligent tutoring modules could determine the level of student understanding as the student proceeds through the online course, and they could direct the learning strategies accordingly to supplement the professor's interactions with the student. Knowledge taxonomies and ontologies, such as those developed through Stanford University's public domain ontology building tool, Protégé, could also be created to allow a stronger shared vocabulary and understanding between the professor and the student.

In the years ahead, KM and e-learning will play synergistic roles, as discussed throughout these book chapters. Applying complementary sets of approaches in each field will ultimately enable reciprocal development. The journey looks exciting on the path to inquiry and wisdom.

References

Ambient Insight (2009), The US Market for Self-paced eLearning Products and Services: 2009–2014 Forecast and Analysis Report (Sam Adkins, Chief Research Officer), Seattle, WA.

Barker, P. (2005), "Knowledge management for e-learning," *Innovations in Education and Teaching International*, Vol. 42, No. 2, Routledge, May.

Bransford, J. (1998), "Designing environments to reveal, support, and expand our children's potentials," *Perspectives on Fundamental Processes in Intellectual Functioning* (S. Sloraci and W. McIlvane, Eds.), Ablex Publishing.

Chen, R. and C. Hsiang (2007), "A study on the critical success factors for corporations embarking on knowledge community-based e-learning," *Information Sciences*, Vol. 177, Elsevier.

Chunhua, Z. (2008), "E-learning: The new approach for knowledge management," *2008 IEEE International Conference on Computer Science and Software Engineering Proceedings*, IEEE Computer Society.

Connolly, C. (1998), "Developing Learner-Centric Content: White Paper," Empower Corporation, http://www.managersforum.com/other/LearnerCentric%20learning.htm.

Del Peso, J. and F. de Arriaga (2008), "Intelligent e-learning systems: Automatic construction of ontologies," *Current Themes in Engineering Technologies* (ed. by S. Ao, M. Amouzegar, and S. Chen), American Institute of Physics.

Ho, L. and T. Kuo (2009), "How can one amplify the effect of e-learning? An examination of high-tech employees' computer attitude and flow experience," *Computers in Human Behavior Journal*, Elsevier, doi:10.1016/j.chb.2009.07.007.

Lamont, J. (2003), "Special section: E-learning world: Bridging the worlds of e-learning and KM," *KMWorld*, Vol. 12, No. 2, Information Today Inc., February.

Lau, A. and E. Tsui (2009), "Knowledge management perspective on e-learning effectiveness," *Knowledge-Based Systems Journal*, Vol. 22, No. 4, Elsevier, May.

Lee, B., J. Yoon, and I. Lee (2009), "Learners' acceptance of e-learning in South Korea: Theories and results," *Computers and Education Journal*, Vol. 53, Elsevier.

Liaw, S., M. Hatala, and H. Huang (2010), "Investigating acceptance toward mobile learning to assist individual knowledge management: based on activity theory approach," *Computers and Education*, Vol. 54, Elsevier.

Liebowitz, J. (Ed.) (2008), *Making Cents Out of Knowledge Management*, Scarecrow Press/Rowman & Littlefield, Maryland.

Liebowitz, J. (2009), *Knowledge Retention: Strategies and Solutions*, CRC Press, Boca Raton, FL.

Liebowitz, J. (2010), "Strategic intelligence, social networking, and knowledge retention," *IEEE Computer*, IEEE Computer Society, February.

Lytras, M., A. Naeve, and A. Pouloudi (2005), "Special issue: knowledge management technologies for e-learning," *International Journal of Distance Education Technologies*, Vol. 3, No. 2, Idea Group Publishing, April–June.

Mouzakitis, G. (2009), "E-learning: The six important 'Wh...?'", *Procedia Social and Behavioral Sciences* 1, Elsevier.

Nevo, D. and Y. Chan (2007), "A Delphi study of knowledge management systems: Scope and requirements," *Information and Management Journal*, Vol. 44, Elsevier.

Olaniran, B. (2009), "Discerning culture in e-learning and in the global workplaces," *Knowledge Management and E-Learning: An International Journal*, Vol. 1, No. 3, University of Hong Kong.

Saxena, A. (2007), "Knowledge management and its applications in distance education," *Turkish Online Journal of Distance Education*, Vol. 8, No. 4, October.

Shaw, R. (2009), "A study of learning performance of e-learning materials design with knowledge maps," *Computers and Education Journal*, doi:10.1016/j.compedu.2009.08.007, Elsevier.

Wang, Y. and N. Haggerty (2009), "Knowledge transfer in virtual settings: The role of individual virtual competency," *Information Systems Journal*, Vol. 19, No. 6, Blackwell, November.

Web-Based Training Information Center (WBTIC) (2009), "Learning Objects: Trends," http://www.wbtic.com/trends_objects.aspx.

Wild, R., K. Griggs, and T. Downing (2002), "A framework for e-learning as a tool for knowledge management," *Industrial Management and Data Systems Journal*, Vol. 102, No. 7, Emerald.

Zhang, C. and L. Li (2006), "Digital teaching reference book service: A case study on knowledge-object-based microstructure of digital resources," *International Information and Library Review Journal*, Vol. 38, No. 3, Elsevier, September.

Chapter 2

Knowledge Management and the Mega-University: Engagement of the Adult Learner in the Post-Gutenberg Academy

Theodore E. Stone

Contents

Introduction

In Plato's allegory of the cave, he described a world in which slaves were chained in a cave facing a back wall. From the moment of their birth, unable to turn their heads, all that the slaves knew of reality was from the shadows cast on the cave wall by a light shining from behind. All the slaves would know of a cup, for example, would be the shadow of the cup cast on the wall. For the slaves, the cup's shadow would be what was real about the cup, not the object casting the shadow, which would have been incomprehensible to them. Thus, argued, Plato, all that is perceived as reality is a mere shadow of a Greater Reality.

Plato used this allegory to describe the role of the philosopher in seeing beyond mere facts and observations, and detecting patterns of information that bring about a deeper understanding within a body of knowledge. In the 21st century, the modern discipline of knowledge management plays a role that is similar in many ways. Toward this end, knowledge management for organizations often focuses on two key elements:

- The belief that organizations must access and collect knowledge that reflects strategy, policy, and practice at all levels of the organization
- The belief that the organization performs better when it is able to connect its intellectual assets—both explicit and tacit knowledge (Barclay and Murray, 1997)

Certainly there is a third and crucial aspect of knowledge management in a knowledge-based society: organizations gain value through the creation and dissemination of new knowledge, which includes contextualizing that new knowledge in the framework of that which is already known, whether that be a business process (e.g., customer service) or a business strategy (e.g., future markets).

The role of the 21st century university is at the forefront of all these areas: the creation of new knowledge, the contextualization of the new knowledge in a knowable framework, and the dissemination of that new knowledge. This central role of the university in a knowledge-based society intersects with supporting all members of society, at all levels, helping them become life-longer learners. As one educator has noted, the "changing conditions of modern life—the speed of technological change, the globalization of culture and economics, the increasing social and ethnic diversities of all communities ... require a renewed commitment to lifelong learning within institutions of higher education" (Walshok, 2001). The demand for accessible lifelong education by the adult learner who requires anytime-anywhere access to higher education has intersected with another interesting trend in higher education: the emergence and rise of the mega-university.

Mega-Universities

Mega-universities are institutions that are largely distance education enterprises, support open enrollment/open admissions practices, and typically enroll 100,000 or more students (Daniel, 1998). These universities largely serve the academic needs of working adults. While the early mega-universities asserted that research might be a fundamental value of their institutions, they evolved to be largely teaching institutions, as full-time staff at these universities tend to be small in relation to the size of their student body:

> A research tradition takes time to establish and in its first decade each mega-university had to focus single-minded on creating a large and novel teaching system. Furthermore the number of full-time academic staff in each mega-university (except China's) is tiny in relation to the study body and small in relation to the institutional budget. (Daniel, 1996)

The past decade has also seen the rapid rise of the for-profit mega-universities, mainly in the United States. The rapid growth of these institutions has been driven through the growth of online learning, with $2 billion in annual revenue earned by for-profit institutions for their online programs by the year 2004 (Blumenstyk, 2005). These institutions are almost exclusively teaching institutions with little or no research activities, and the populations they serve are largely working adults. As will be discussed later in this chapter, a key motivation for adult learners to engage in study at a university is because of the need to acquire skills and credentials to maintain their employment, advance in their employment, or seek a new career path. So, understanding the motivation of the adult learner can also provide insight into best practices for engaging the adult learner to interact with the institution in a different role and capacity, from a knowledge management perspective.

By redefining the role of the adult learner in the university, mega or otherwise, and through engagement at a level meaningful to the adult learner, the mega-university's role can be transformed through directly engaging the adult learner as a full member of the academic university through the creation and dissemination of new knowledge. This is not a new idea, but in fact a very old one. And it is an idea that has come full circle in many ways. This chapter will examine a model for the development of universities from a technological perspective, from the pre-Gutenberg era to the post-Gutenberg era. Examined in this context will be the needs and motivation of the adult learner in the context of the post-Gutenberg age of mega-universities. Finally, an example of authentic learning engagement for the adult learner will be examined in this context.

The Evolution of the University

For those academicians who do not work or live in Europe, visiting the old, traditional universities is a delight. For example, in England, visiting Cambridge or Oxford, one is immediately struck by the rich history of the campuses. Walking through these campuses, one can only imagine what life was like for scholars who came to study at one of the original four black-robed professions: law, medicine, education, and divinity (the traditional robes have remained to this day with three out of four of these professions.) At the center of these campuses, or at least near the center, was the library. This should not be surprising. In the era of university education before the invention of movable type by Johannes Gutenberg, most people did not own books; it would have seemed like an extravagant luxury. So the university library was the only place to find scholarly texts—the medieval equivalent of a knowledge management system.

Scholars of this era would go to the library for three key reasons: to read books; to copy books (in scriptoria); and, perhaps most importantly, to write books and leave them behind in the library for others to read. It would be interesting to have a discussion with a scholar of that era on the notion of intellectual property rights in publishing. Clearly, the idea of writing a scholarly book as a vehicle to generate revenue simply would not have existed.

The key point here is the involvement of the student in the knowledge management process at the university. The student arrived at the university not to merely attend classes and earn a diploma—the student would be expected to participate in a material and substantial way.

The Gutenberg Era (1450–1992)

The emergence of the movable type press in the 1450s changed everything. The scriptoria were no longer needed. Scholarly texts could be duplicated and disseminated with more ease, more rapidity, and at a much lower cost. Scholars could own books and develop small personal libraries if they desired.

Almost at the same time as the invention of movable type in Central Europe emerged from Italy an invention of a very different sort was introduced to Europe: double-entry bookkeeping, and the introduction of the classic elements of capitalism—investment, profit and loss.

Scholarship (and ultimately knowledge management at the university) in the age of Gutenberg found itself at the junction of these two trends. With owners of printing presses making investments in the publishing of scholarly works, there was the added expectation of profit by those who took the financial risks to publish the work. Added to the challenge of peer review was the challenge of return on investment for the disseminating publishers of the work. Today, it is common to hear scholars joking about needing to ask permission to cite their own work since they signed away the rights to their publishers.

In the United States, the university of this era came into full bloom with the emergence in the mid-19th century of the land grant university. Originally developed to promote best scientific practices in the field of agriculture, the land grant universities greatly expanded access to higher education for the citizenry. It also led to the expansion of university credentialing of professions that previously were not viewed as university fields. Today, for example, at University of Maryland University College, there are 32 undergraduate degree programs and 14 master degree programs. Quite an expansion of fields of study from the four black-robed professions in the Middle Ages!

Changing Role of the Learner

From a knowledge management perspective, the role of the learner in this era also shifted somewhat. Professionalism in most fields demands that learners develop mastery of broad content areas. A certified public accountant is expected to know not only the differences between managerial and financial accounting, but is also expected to be well versed in the rapidly changing fields of accounting information systems and tax law. In recent years, with the rapid expansion of knowledge and information in particular fields, learners often have found themselves as consumers of information; that is, attaining mastery of a field of knowledge in order to be certified or credentialed in that field by the university. Because of the vast amount of knowledge to be acquired, student-scholars have been less and less engaged as partners in the creation and dissemination of new knowledge.

Because of the differences in student engagement at different universities, in 1970, the Carnegie Commission on Higher Education developed a classification of differences between institutions of higher learning (The Carneige Foundation for the Advancement of Teaching, n.d.) The Carnegie classification provides ratings for criteria such as size; residential or nonresidential campuses; for-profit or not-for-profit institutions; mostly part-time student body or mostly full-time; professions-focused curricula or arts and science focused; comprehensive or research institutions, etc.

The potential for changing the level and quality of engagement for learners and the contribution they could make, particularly for adult learners, changed radically and sharply in 1992 with the development of the World Wide Web and the Mosaic browser, the first widely disseminated browser for the then-nascent medium.

The Emergence of the Post-Gutenberg University

Similar to how transformative movable type was in the 1450s, the World Wide Web and its easy access through a browser has begun to transform how students in the university could create and interact with new knowledge and how such knowledge is managed and disseminated. Scholars could publish and disseminate new content and knowledge, liberated from the requirements for investment, and concerns about profit and loss. One of the first published examples of this was by educator Ben Shneiderman. In 1993, Shneiderman immediately saw the potential for engaging his graduate computer science students in constructing new knowledge. He challenged his students to create knowledge resources to be read and used by others in the field. (Shneiderman, 1994) Shneiderman wrote

> The students were required to construct an online *Encyclopedia of Virtual Environments (EVE)* within 7 weeks. They coordinated their efforts, defined the audience to be undergraduate computer science students, identified 40 topics, and wrote them in a common style and level. Then the 24 students worked together in nine teams to create term-length research projects with algorithm development or human factors studies. The multimedia results were published online in Mosaic in our own *Journal of Virtual Environments (JOVE)*.

Shneiderman went on to report that two students found the course too intense and dropped it, but others reported that they "felt that this course was a unique and exciting experience that changed the direction of their professional work and personal goals."

In many ways, Shneiderman's early experience with the nascent World Wide Web was a demonstration of the engaging power of learners creating something real and substantial, not only developing something of value to them, but something that would be of value to others. In this context, the post-Gutenberg university brings learner engagement, at the graduate level, full circle to experiences in the pre-Gutenberg university where students were much more directly involved in the creation, replication and dissemination of knowledge. Though Shneiderman attributed the success in part to the collaborative experience of the students in creating knowledge resources of value, it also should be considered that adult learning theory can explain how graduate-level students would be motivated through publishing, electronic or otherwise, as part of their academic experience in the university.

Adult Learners

Adults come to the university for a variety reasons—sometimes for personal enrichment, but mostly to gain a professional competitive edge. Whether it is finish a degree program that was begun but never completed or to earn new credentials, adult learners are often concerned with keeping their job, seeking a promotion at their work place, or entering a new career. A U.S. Department of Labor report estimated that adult learners over the age of 24 comprise about 44% of the U.S. postsecondary students, and millions more could improve their economic lot by gaining academic credentials. This is in view of the fact that traditional universities have policies that are primarily directed to traditional university students in the age range of 18–22 years old (Kazis et al., 2007).

The Labor Department report notes that there are a number of barriers to adult learners at most universities because of the adult learners' need for focusing on careers, their family responsibilities, the scheduling of courses, the need to travel to distant campus to attend classes, and the cost of attending courses. The mega-universities have found a niche in serving adult learners by addressing several of these concerns. For example, University of Maryland University College (UMUC) has become the largest online public university in the U.S. largely by serving the needs of the adult learner. In the 2007 academic year, 85% of the enrollments were fully online, accounting for more than 193,000 seats in classes (UMUC Office of Institutional Planning, Research and Accountability, 2009). The admissions policy of mega-universities tends to be open, as a means of making the university more adult-friendly. It is assumed that adults may have a several-year gap from their last academic experience, whether coming to the university for the first time or returning to complete a degree and/or earn a new one. As an example, with UMUC's admission policy, most applicants who have a high school diploma or the equivalent can be admitted and register for undergraduate courses. And in most cases, neither transcripts nor test scores are required at the time of admission (UMUC School of Undergraduate Studies, n.d.)

In addition to open admissions, another of the mega-university's defining criteria is the practice of distance education, with distance education delivery of courses being a primary mode of providing academic programs by the institution. During the 1980s and 1990s, in several cases governments worldwide sponsored the creation of these institutions as a means of providing accessible education at a scalable cost (Daniel, Mega-Universities and Knowledge Media: Technology Strategies for Higher Education, 1996). But it also met the requirements of adult learners who needed flexibility in their schedules because of obligations to job and family.

This notion of flexibility for the adult learner is echoed in the Department of Labor report referenced earlier when it is noted that

> Over 80 percent of potential students over 25 years of age reported they would consider an on-line program .... The increased interest by adults is most likely attributable to the flexibility and convenience offered by on-line programs. For example, students do not need to live near a college campus or commit the time to commuting, parents can complete coursework while their children are asleep without paying for childcare, and workers with unpredictable schedules can complete their coursework at a different time each week. (Kazis et al., March 2007)

Characteristics of the Adult Learner

Though career promotion and job security are central motivations for the adult learner, it is worthwhile to examine other motivational factors of the adult learner as well. Aside from career security or career advancement, other motivational factors might include the following:

■ Social relationships—Joining an academic community and attending classes, whether face to face or online, is an opportunity to network and make professional connections.

■ External expectations—Especially in knowledge-based or knowledge-rich organizations, workers are expected to demonstrate that they are life-long learners.

■ Social welfare—Adults, especially civil servants and government workers, are often motivated to improve their knowledge set though a sense of community service.

■ Stimulation and cognitive interest—Adults will also attend academic programs, such as language classes, simply for personal enrichment. (Westover, 2009)

The great challenge for the mega-universities that serve the adult learner is to design academic curricula that are able to build on the rich knowledge that adult learners bring into the academy. In fact, it cuts to the heart of the matter on multiple levels. The mega-universities that offer online instruction are generally well equipped to deliver content to the learner (which would be sufficient if adult learners were merely empty receptacles to be filled with knowledge) and to measure the level at which the learner successfully achieved the predicted outcomes. What is less clear is how the adult learner is able to contribute back to the institution toward creation and dissemination of new knowledge in his field of study. Creating such an academic environment that engenders a more bidirectional interchange of knowledge between learner and academy not only would progressively support the institution in following best practices in adult learning, but could also be an evolutionary step in the role of the mega-university in its management of knowledge. In this context, it is germane to consider the characteristics of the adult learner.

The characteristics of the adult learner have been articulated by Malcolm Knowles and expanded on by Stephen Lieb (Lieb, 1991). They include the following:

■ *Adults are autonomous and self-directed.* As learners, adults are driven by internal needs and desires. This includes contextualizing their experience as an adult university student into a schema of what they need to acquire in terms of knowledge and skills and in terms of what they can contribute.

■ *Adults have accumulated a foundation of life experiences and knowledge that may include work-related activities, family responsibilities, and previous education.* This life experience has the potential of being contributed into the collective knowledge pool of the university. Consider, for example, rapidly evolving fields such as data or network infrastructure security. A practitioner in the field (who is also an online student earning a graduate degree) has much to contribute to the university's knowledge of the state of practice in the field.

■ *Adults are goal-oriented.* Adult learners return to the university to achieve something substantial, something tangible. Of course, that usually means being conferred a degree. But a new diploma is really a means to an end, which is often advancement and recognition as a leader in the field. Engaging these learners by recognizing and incorporating their contributions into the knowledge matrix of the university can motivate the adult learner beyond merely earning a degree and awarding them the status of being intellectual peers in an academic community.

■ *Adults are relevancy oriented.* Working adult learners are not likely to have much patience for being treated as though they were just receivers of knowledge, learning for learning's sake. As working adults, they have specific problems to solve in their work environment, and they are looking for real, practical solutions they can apply. This principle might also suggest that working adults in the learning environment may have less patience for simulations and virtual reality as well. Clearly, in professions where students can cause harm while learning (such as piloting aircraft or nursing), simulation and virtual reality become an important step in the application of newly acquired knowledge and skills. However, for working adults with professional experience in their fields, virtual reality encounters, such as scenarios in an environment such as Second Life, may appear to lack relevance.

■ *Adults are practical, focusing on the aspects of a lesson most useful to them in their work.* As noted earlier, working adults who take courses at the university have immediate and practical needs for acquiring knowledge and skills. A well-designed class ought to have a feedback mechanism to determine what those needs are, and for discovering how working adults are applying the newly acquired knowledge in the workplace to meet those needs. This feedback loop thus becomes an instrumental branch of the university's knowledge management system in that particular field.

■ *As with all learners, adults need to be shown respect.* But particularly with working adults, showing respect means recognizing what adult learners as scholars and practitioners in their field can contribute back to the academy as they earn their degree. It also suggests that the relationship between the adult learner and the academy could and should exist post graduation.

Engaging Learners in Knowledge Construction and Publication

Engaging the adult learner in constructing, honing, and publishing new knowledge in their professional fields seems to align positively with almost all the characteristics of the adult learner. Only 18 years after the creation of the World Wide Web, it is not unusual for university-level classes to build in components of Web publishing into the course. An undergraduate agriculture class recently at the University of Missouri in Columbia had students publish essays to the class course management system to see if peer review in this Web-based environment would improve the quality of writing (Motavalli et al., 2007). Though the author reported success, it does not match the adult learning characteristic of being relevant; rather, it is an academic classroom exercise since the writing was merely a classroom activity; it was never intended to be viewed as a professional publication outside of class. In another case, researchers looked at how student learning might improve by having university students engage as a group in constructing a Wiki-based document in a statistics class. Once again, the exercise was academic and short-lived. While students showed evidence of being engaged in terms of classroom involvement, there were no measurable improvements on student outcomes when compared to a control group (Neumann and Hood, 2009).

In both of these examples, the Web-publishing exercises were academic, limited to the classroom, presumably short-lived (in that it appears that the writing created by the students would not be accessible after the semester ended) and, thus, a low-stakes exercise for the student outside of the class.

But what if the stakes were raised for the students by engaging them in creating professional work to be disseminated outside of the classroom experience?

Student Engagement as Scholars and Authors

The idea was put to a test in the fall of 2009 at University of Maryland University College (UMUC) with graduate students at the completion of their academic program: given the possibility of having their final product selected for publication in a book, would students voluntarily (and for no extra credit) submit a specially rewritten version of the capstone project? The study took place in two sections of the capstone class in the Master of Education (M.Ed.) program in Instructional Technology. This is an advanced degree program that focuses on integrating technology in the pre-K-12 schools to strengthen teaching and learning. In the capstone course, students pursue independent projects in a learning environment (often where they are working or teaching) and are expected to bring to their capstone project the best practices in curriculum design, as well as to identify appropriate educational technology for achieving specific and measurable learner outcomes. It should be noted that most students in the course sections were working full-time in addition to pursuing their M.Ed. degree in an online program.

The primary deliverable for the capstone course was a portfolio, written in five chapters, on the student's applied research project in the field of Instructional Technology. Students were also given the option of rewriting the content of their portfolio into a 20- to 25-page paper to be considered for publication as a chapter in a book. Students were told that submission of the paper for consideration of publication was strictly voluntary, would not be graded, and would not be considered as extra credit toward the grade. Not only that, the selection of the papers for chapters would be selected by an editorial board of faculty in the department. The purpose of the book was to highlight best practices in the rapidly changing field of instructional technology. Students were told that the book would also be used as a reference in future classes and to help to codify the "school of thought" at the university in this field.

Among the enrollees who completed the course, 64% of students from both sections of the course submitted papers to be considered for publication. Compared to earlier class interactions, student involvement in the class online discussions seemed more focused and meaningful. In the course evaluation, one student commented that among the strongest elements of the course was "the possibility that the project [would] be published and the implementation of the project to a be a subject that really be used in class [that the student is teaching] and for professional development." The positive student response seems to be rooted in several of the criteria for adult learner characteristics: relevance, practical focus of the project, and respect for the student as an equal in the academy. Another comment from the course evaluations said that there was "room for the course to be adapted to the student's needs and interests. The project assigned was directly related to who I am as a teacher." And still another comment from the course evaluations on the possibility of publishing: "This is a great course, and I recommend that more opportunity for publication be offered. In any course, publishing is a real motivator. I would love to have my project or any of my papers made good enough to publish. Thank you for the opportunity to have my capstone published."

There are several astonishing things about these course evaluation comments, not the least of which was that the mere possibility of the work being reviewed for publishing appears to have aligned perfectly with the goals of the student as adult learner, even though it was a voluntary activity to submit a paper to be considered, and even though it was not for a grade or extra credit. Even more important, if working adults, as practitioners in their professional fields, contribute articles and chapters to faculty peer-reviewed journals and books at their university, then a critical event occurs. That is, the currency of the professional activities of the adult learner are filtered through a faculty peer-review process in the academy and *the adult learner is able to make a relevant and substantial contribution to the knowledge base of the university as a peer of the university's academic community*. This is good from a knowledge management perspective for the university, and it is good from an adult-learning perspective for the student.

This also suggests that the role of the university library becomes more central to the academic identity of the university, since it is the organization within the academic framework best suited for the categorizing and contextualizing university-produced knowledge. Here again, the roles of the library and the librarian at the academy come full circle as well with the assumption of a more central role in the knowledge creation and management of the institution.

The irony should not be lost: in the age of the post-Gutenberg academy, with its unlimited publishing potential of electronic media on the World Wide Web, even the hint of publication in a book or a journal provides motivation for the adult learner. From a knowledge management perspective, which suggests that meaningful knowledge can only exist in a context, this makes perfect sense if one considers adult learning behavior and the need for relevance and substance on the part of the learner.

Publishing as Adult Learner Behavior and Knowledge Management

In past semesters for this online capstone course, students have been encouraged to self-publish their applied research portfolios on the Web as a way of disseminating the research they conducted for the culminating activity of their academic program. Publishing on the Web does not seem to motivate the learner as much as the mere possibility of having a paper considered for publication in a book. The following may explain why:

1. *Self-publishing on the World Wide Web does not contextualize the work.* With billions of pages of information on the World Wide Web, and self-publishing freely available to anyone with a Google or Yahoo account, self-publishing of student work lacks context and meaning. Publishing work in the context of the academy where it is peer reviewed and contextualized by an editorial board of faculty peers allows the work to be understood meaningfully.

2. *Publishing in printed volumes enables the adult learner to disseminate effectively from a career perspective.* As has been discussed, adult learners are largely concerned about jobs and careers—the ability to keep employment in a difficult job market; the ability to be promoted; or the ability to shift careers. Showing a prospective employer a research project that was published on a student-produced Web site will not be as meaningful or informative as providing the employer a copy of a university peer-reviewed journal which contains an article on the student's research, so that the project could be seen in the context of articles by other students from the program. This also contributes to the emergence of the "school of thought" associated with a particular academic program at the university. For the mega-universities, this might mean that the schools of thought emerge as much from the learners' work as they would from the faculty in a traditional research university.

3. *Sharing expertise and mentoring others is an adult activity.* Ultimately, the sharing of knowledge, and the training and development of other professionals, is an adult activity since it advances knowledge in a professional field. Publishing, similar to presenting at a professional or academic conference, is evidence of a type of leadership in a chosen profession.

4. *Publishing invests the adult learner in the academy.* Mega-universities, in general, and online universities, in particular, have struggled with the ability to create a sense of academic community among their learners beyond the mere

transactional sense of students attending classes to earn a degree. For adult learners, contributing substantially to the university's knowledge base in a professional subject and being recognized as a peer in the academy can be foundational to the learner forging a lifelong relationship with the institution—a role that should be important to both parties in an era that encourages lifelong learning in the workforce.

Conclusion

As comprehensive teaching institutions, the mega-universities are largely focused on professional education for working adults, often delivering that education through e-learning techniques. Learners in this context are sometimes viewed as customers or consumers of professional knowledge at the academy. Their relationship with the university is largely a transactional one. For tuition and fees, students gain attendance in classes that lead to a certificate or diploma. This is something the mega-universities do well, in general, as they provide professional education opportunities to working adults.

At the graduate level of study at these institutions, learners often already work professionally in the fields they study at the university. Because of this, their capacity to contribute to the state of the art of the university's knowledge base in their subjects could be substantial, particularly in rapidly changing fields such as computer science, healthcare informatics, instructional technology, and biotechnology, to name a few. Creating systems to engage students in contributing to the university's knowledge base both motivates the adult learner and enriches the university.

In many ways, this thinking brings the post-Gutenberg university full circle back to the pre-Gutenberg university in terms of engaging the best of the students to create new knowledge, or at the very least, to become partners in the academy with the dissemination of knowledge of the academy. From a knowledge management perspective, this could be a key evolutionary component of the mega-university, where knowledge management intersects with e-learning in the 21st century.

References

Barclay, R. O., and Murray, P. C. (1997). What is Knowledge Management? (Knowledge Management Associates) Retrieved December 1, 2009 from Knowledge Praxis: http://www.media-access.com/whatis.html.

Blumenstyk, G. (2005, January 7). For-profit education: Online courses fuel growth. *The Chronicle of Higher Education, 51* (18), p. A11.

Daniel, J. (1998). Knowledge media for mega-universities: scaling up new technology at the Open University. *Continuing Higher Education Review, 62* (1), 16–27.

Daniel, J. (1996). *Mega-Universities and Knowledge Media: Technology Strategies for Higher Education.* London, U.K.: Kogan Page Limited.

Kazis, R., Callahan, A., Davidson, C., McLeod, A., Bosworth, B., Choitz, V. et al. (March 2007). *Adult Learners in Higher Education: Barriers to Success and Strategies to Improve Results.* U.S. Department of Labor, Employment and Training Administration, Office of Policy Development and Research, and Jobs for the Future. Washington, DC: U.S. Department of Labor.

Lieb, S. (1991). Principles of Adult Learning. Retrieved December 24, 2009 from University of Hawaii Honolulu Community College: http://honolulu.hawaii.edu/intranet/committees/FacDevCom/guidebk/teachtip/adults-2.htm.

Motavalli, P., Patton, M., and Miles, R. (2007). Use of Web-based student extension publications to improve undergraduate student writing skills. *Journal of Natural Resources and Life Sciences Education, 36* (1), 95–102.

Neumann, D. L., and Hood, M. (2009). The effects of using a wiki on student engagement and learning of report writing skills in a university statistics course. *Australasian Journal of Educational Technology, 25* (3), 382–398.

Shneiderman, B. (1994, April 12). Education by Engagement and Construction: Can Distance Learning be Better than Face-to-Face? Retrieved December 22, 2009 from HIT Lab, University of Washington: http://www.hitl.washington.edu/scivw/EVE/distance.html

The Carneige Foundation for the Advancement of Teaching (n.d.). Carnegie Classifications. Retrieved December 27, 2009 from The Carnegie Classification of Institutions of Higher Education: http://classifications.carnegiefoundation.org

UMUC Office of Institutional Planning, Research and Accountability. (2009, October 5). Fiscal Year 2009 Fact Sheet. Retrieved December 24, 2009 from UMUC Office of Institutional Planning, Research and Accountability : http://www.umuc.edu/ip/factsheet-09.shtml

UMUC School of Undergraduate Studies. (n.d.). Applying for Undergraduate Admissions. Retrieved December 24, 2009 from UMUC School of Undergraduate Studies: http://www.umuc.edu/studserv/ugp_ss/ugpapply.shtml

Walshok, M. L. (2001). Thinking more strategically about funding lifelong learning programs. *Conitnuing Higher Education Review, 65* (1), 77–88.

Westover, J. H. (2009). Lifelong learning: Effective adult learning strategies and implementation for working professionals. *International Journal of Learning, 16* (1), 435–443.

Chapter 3

Global Trends Affecting Knowledge Management and E-Learning

Catherine Lord

Contents

The Global Workforce Is Growing ... Up

One of the greatest resources of the 21st century is our global supply of talent and labor. During the next decade, we will be challenged to find new and smarter ways to work to ensure a lasting economic revival for an increasingly urban global population. Aligning supply and demand will require a fresh understanding of these workers — where they live, their age, and their skills.

We also need to examine trends in structural or social units that people work within to help them perform their tasks or make meaningful decisions so that we can predict shifts in the transfer of knowledge or learning of new skills.

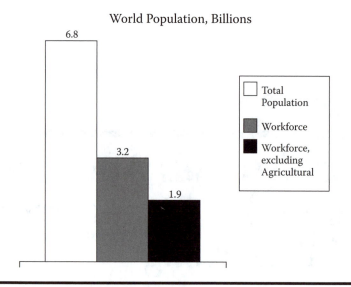

Figure 3.1   World population (billions).

To lay the foundation for a glimpse into this near future, we need to take a look at key trends that are shaping the global workforce today. In the decade from 2010 to 2020, several disruptive forces will operate to create a climate of change in the way we work. These changes fall into three areas: demographic, economic, and technological.

To put today's workforce into perspective (see Figure 3.1), the current world population is 6.8 billion people in total; there are about 3.2 billion people in the workforce, or 1.9 billion if agricultural workers are excluded (Central Intelligence Agency, *The World Factbook*, 2009).

By 2050, the United Nations organization (2009) predicts that the population will reach 9 billion with very little change coming from mature economies. They noted that the net population of mature economies would actually decrease in size if it were not for migration. On the other hand, developing countries will increase by 1.1 billion people over age 60, plus 1.2 billion people of working age. The United Nations also found that overall, the population is aging — with growth tripling among those 60 years of age and older and quadrupling among those 80 years of age and older.

Given this massive workforce tilting we are about to see from mature to emerging economies, it really does become critical that we challenge our assumptions about the workforce, many of which were derived from studies and observations in the West.

One way to predict this workforce of the future is to take a closer look at the G-20 countries. There is very sound rationale for this — according to the G-20 organization (G-20, 2009), they collectively represent two-thirds of the world's population, 80% of world trade, and about 90% of the global gross national product. The G-20 workforce is an important indicator; it includes the vast majority of the world's "information workers," and it also provides a more balanced view across developing economies. This includes millions of workers who consider mobile technology to be their primary form of communication and interaction for dialogue that is not "face to face."

The G-20 workforce is also interesting in that it includes very large virtual workforce units that collaborate multinationally across different types of infrastructure or even across geographies with varying access to electrical power.

Ensuring adequate supply and demand in the global workforce will require new levels of flexibility and creativity. At a policy level, the International Labour Organization (ILO) is a significant force in creating recommendations for developing and maintaining jobs, covering issues from labor migration to education. One of the changes they recommend is a shift from our current three-tier education structures (primary, secondary, and tertiary) to one of life-long learning in order to avoid critical pockets of skills shortages. The G-20 and the ILO have been working in concert on many policy issues, and according to an ILO press release (September 18, 2009), they estimated they were able to save from 7 to 11 million jobs in 2009.

Literacy is another variable that may need to be accommodated; while the average literacy percentage of the G-20 countries is on par with the global rate, at 82% (Central Intelligence Agency, *The World Factbook*, 2009), there are scenarios where information must be shared with customers, patients, or citizens and businesses across literacy levels. Microlending is a good example where it is not always possible to communicate with e-mail and computers when text-to-speech service on mobile devices is required in a local dialect.

Another policy area with regards to the workforce of the future is the area of language and culture. To this end, the United Nations Educational, Scientific and Cultural Organization (UNESCO), has provided an updated framework (2009) to reflect the way we measure and view the impact of culture in a way that is more inclusive of developing nations and modern social networking and digital media. Another potential area of change is the way we handle language issues; while English is a major transactional language, it is not always the best choice for expression of culture, creativity, and innovation for all people, and we are likely to see a shift toward more content being translated *into* English rather than *from* English as is the case today.* In other words, we are encouraged to think of ways to enhance and stimulate multicultural input rather than try to work towards a "uni-culture."

Recent papers (Olaniran, 2009) stress this theme in the context of e-learning in the global workplace or in education, having found that certain cultural heritage elements must be preserved in the learning experience rather than trying to distill everything down to a global universal level in order to prevent psychological barriers that can be just as powerful as geographic barriers (Olaniran, 2009).

---

* UNESCO (2009) found that 55% of material translated was from English into other languages.

The End of the Homogeneous Workforce

We noted earlier that the global workforce, excluding agricultural workers, was 1.9 billion workers. Almost three-quarters of these service and industry workers, 1.4 billion people in all, are in the G-20 countries.

In 2010, this group is collectively much more familiar with technology than they were at the alleged "Y2K" inflection point in 2000. In 2010, three out of ten G-20 workers will have been born after 1980 and will have grown up using the Internet, iPods, or mobile phones. They are likely to be more comfortable sending text messages than telephoning. In just ten more years, this group will swell to *more than half* of the entire G-20 workforce in their twenties and thirties.

Many of these workers born post-1980 will meet the criteria for being described as "digital natives" (Palfrey and Glasser, 2008); not only "born digital" but also having developed habits such as maintaining a digital identity, multitasking, or consuming and creating digital content, among other characteristics.

At the other end of the scale, workers 60 years old and over are also a growing force with newer trends toward full-time, rather than part-time employment as in the past (Bureau of Labor Statistics, 2008).

In more developed economies, participation of women in the workforce is increasing at three times the rate of men through 2020 (ILO, 2009). Some countries are postulating that this shift toward equal numbers of women and men in the workforce will lead to increasing "feminization" of workforce culture, which is linked to concepts such as "work-life balance" and more relational or humanitarian type of work (Hofstede, 2004). In developing countries, male–female participation is fairly stable and equal.

Altogether, the result will be a very different workforce from the one we have known. To summarize this massive shift, the ratio of working-age persons in less developed versus developed economies leaps from 2:1 to 5:1 from 1980 to 2020 (United Nations, 2008) ranging across four generations of workers.

Where Did All the Workers Go?

Today's workforce is more likely to migrate to address pockets of skill shortages in certain regions. The result is that workers and, as we will see shortly, customers and partners, are far more likely to stretch across geographic, age, and cultural boundaries than they have ever in the past.

To illustrate this more clearly, let us divide our G-20 countries into two groups. The first group consists of mature economies and includes developed nations as well as major trading partners that have some reciprocity of labor or free trade; the remaining countries, emerging economies, constitute the second group. Thus, we will divide the G-20 for the purpose of comparison as follows:

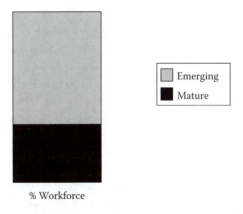

% Workforce

Figure 3.2   Global workforce (Nonagricultural 2009).

Mature: European Union, NAFTA (US, Canada, Mexico), Australia, Japan
Emerging: "BRIC" (Brazil, Russia, India, China), Argentina, South Africa, Indonesia, Turkey, South Korea, and Saudi Arabia.

Using this classification, one-third of the global workforce (see Figure 3.2) is in mature economies, and two-thirds are in emerging economies.

Between 2010 and 2020, the G-20 workforce will see a net increase of a quarter of a billion workers, with a mere 3% net going into the mature economies' workforce given the large waves of retirement and changes in fertility rates. A full 97% of the net new workers will stream into the emerging workforce, based on calculations of urbanization and growth in economically active populations (United Nations, 2009).

This view does not take into account other nascent shifts; the workforce in emerging economies may become even larger again due to "outflows of talent" from the West (*Harvard International Review*, Spring 2009)* where Western-educated professionals return to their native homelands for several reasons. Their home countries can now offer opportunities they could not in the past, and they have developed a sufficiently rich entrepreneurial culture. These "returnees" also miss their families or their culture, and their need to move away from home is diminishing. Many emerging economies provide incentives to woo these professionals back home.

---

* Vivek Wadhwa of Harvard and Duke Universities, AnnaLee Saxenian of University of California at Berkeley, Richard Freeman of Harvard University, Guillermina Jasso of New York University, Gary Gereffi of Duke University, and Ben Rissing of the Massachusetts Institute of Technology, with financial support from the Kauffman Foundation, conducted a 3-year study of over 1000 foreign students and over 1000 returnees as well as in-country research in China and India to quantify and explain the phenomenon of returnees.

Historically, countries that have had a higher percentage of post-secondary education have had an advantage in weathering skill shortages, but with increased urbanization and migration we are likely to see this gap narrowing. One exercise is to superimpose the average number of years of education over the urban growth rates and we can see this gap may be just over 2 years apart between our two G-20 groups, or hardly enough to claim a significant advantage going forward. Either way, with lifelong learning coming into vogue coupled with the fact that many jobs can be now be outsourced (Friedman, 2005, 2006, 2007) or expatriated, there is an increasing decoupling of citizenship and delivery of labor. This is also evident at the individual level with the portion of the workforce that roams freely to where the work is, known as "digital nomads" (Makimoto and Manners, 1997; Berreby, 1999).

The next great shift is driven by global economics: where are the products and services destined for what these workers are contributing to? In other words, where are the customers or people these workers will serve?

Increasingly, the majority of customers will be in the East, not the West. The rise of the middle class in Asia versus the West has been illustrated as a major shift (Bhalla, 2009), with the recognition that "middle class" is a global designation of discretionary income, as a percentage. After food and shelter, expenditures move toward items such as education, clothing, appliances, and cars.

In 1980, twice as many consumers were in the West as were in the East; goods and services were tailored to these Western tastes in everything from refrigerators to cars or shoes or soft drinks. By 2006, this has more than reversed; with three times as many consumers in Asia as in the West, primarily due to China's fourfold increase in middle class from 1990 to 2005, and this trend will continue with a fourfold increase in India's middle class from 2005 to 2015, doubling again by 2025 (*The Economist*, February 2009). Established Western brands are increasingly partnering with China and India brands to adapt to local markets; and in turn, these new ventures sell into Africa and emerging markets. We can picture this as a wave that continues across many other emerging economies.

Can we begin to imagine how many products and services need to be redesigned for different cultures, tastes, or price points? How many service calls will be placed from new customers in Asia or Africa? All of this will drive further migrations of jobs or talent along with retraining to improve collaboration and knowledge transfer in an increasingly diverse workplace.

Globally Linked Economy, Globally Linked Workforce

Just as global and national governments have come together to stabilize the economy since 2008, we can expect them to play an increasing role in shaping the workforce over the next decade. Stimulus funding in 2009 and beyond will continue to directly target certain industries from automotive to textiles, and other policies will target migration, remissions of foreign workers to their families "back home," education, and microfinance.

More people are already taking notice of the impact of changes in Asia's foreign investment and energy policies and how they indirectly impact job markets in the West. These include some fairly dramatic shifts in private ownership and foreign ownership, impacting many areas from automobiles to insurance. Others are surprised to learn of the transfer of ownership of some well-known Western brands to the East, along with new hybrid West–East brands or new joint ventures in everything from cars to refrigerators.

Ripples are increasingly being felt in the workplace, and it is not uncommon to have 24-year-old merchandisers in Asia working with 50- or 60-year-old engineers in Germany on products designed by digital natives on the American West Coast, with research supplied from academia. It is quite likely that our definition of "coworker" will have shifted significantly by the end of this decade.

One other trend that is impacting the location of workers is an increase in the number of professionals that are being sent out by emerging economies to search for fuel for their country's burgeoning middle class — whether the search is for oil or for land for biofuels — this can involve a broad range of occupations. Many managers from China in their 30s and 40s are routinely posted abroad to countries including Africa and Russia, joining the traditionally Western "expat" club.

Won't Technology Make it all Easier?

In the "good old days" of the personal computer era, software was developed that allowed people to create and share information in a fairly homogeneous way. Standards were created to make it easier to broker information between different systems as needed. While standards will continue to be important, this next decade is also viewed by many in the information and communications technology (ICT) sector as the end of the "one size fits all" era (Forrester Research Inc., 2009) based on studies on information workers in the United States.

As we move forward into an era of social, rather than personal, computing and communication, there will be some major technology changes that will dramatically increase the number of possible combinations of how information can be created or consumed. These include cloud computing and "green" technology plus a much richer range of connected devices, many of these from the consumer market.

Cloud computing has been defined by the National Institute of Standards and Technology (NIST) as follows:

NIST's v15 (2009) draft defines cloud computing as

> a model for enabling convenient, on-demand network access to a shared
> pool of configurable computing resources (e.g., networks, servers, storage,

applications, and services) that can be rapidly provisioned and released with minimal management effort or service provider interaction.

(Mell and Grance, 2009, p. 1)

Cloud computing will have a major impact on the workforce in terms of ubiquity and reach. "The cloud" can span across many different types of networks, such as broadband, cellular, or new wireless sensor networks such as Zigbee, as well as across multiple organizations with a common mission. New scenarios will be possible that will make it easier for workers to remain in the context of their business process or learning environment.

Information technology is also becoming "greener," with larger data centers becoming the norm rather than server farms. This will also create new opportunities for partnering with greater agility, whether this is across businesses of all sizes and academia, or profit and nonprofit. The workforce will also become more interconnected, with different motivations.

The number of device types will explode in this coming decade as part of our connected experience to information. By 2012, for every personal computer (PC) that ships, whether it is a laptop, desktop, or server, there will be twice as many alternate devices that ship. The PC as we have known it since the 1980s will give way to more situational devices. Of these devices, six out of ten shipping in 2012 will be smartphones, two out of ten will be mobile Internet devices (MIDs) such as personal music players, Internet tablets, ebook readers, digital photo frames, personal navigation systems, gaming handhelds, or media phones. One out of ten devices will be a netbook or a smartbook depending on the processor, and one will be a different emerging Internet device altogether such a digital sign; set top box; a monitoring device for homes; health, automotive, or appliance consoles; or even a wearable computing item for security, health, and entertainment.* In addition to these five classes of devices, the workforce will also use landline or IP-PBX telephony, basic mobile phones, and fax machines to communicate.

By 2020, new device shipment rates will have left their mark through replacement of aging units, and a plethora of devices will be used in performing tasks as well as for personal use. They will reach workers at home, in their vehicle, and in public environments. Access to information and the ability to communicate will become more universal for the globally distributed workforce.

---

* The total number of device shipments by 2012 was calculated to be 1.3 billion units in total, with 32.9% being traditional computers (servers, desktops, and laptops) and 67.1% being alternate devices. Of these alternate devices, 60.4% were calculated to be smartphones, 20.3% were calculated to be mobile Internet devices (MIDs), 11.1% were netbooks or smartbooks, and 8.2% were calculated to be other devices. Calculations were created and normalized with multiple sources including inStat, iSuppli, Gartner Group/AMR Research, as well as production data by manufacturer type and/or processor chip type for 26 device types.

Not all devices or networks will meet privacy requirements in all situations — many transactions or exchanges cannot be conducted over public channels. A mobile text message may be acceptable for a reminder or to provide a delivery date, but not for financial or medical data.

The quality of service of the Internet varies across these different geographies, notably, outside of large urban areas, where workers may live or travel to. Work will need to travel equally well over cellular or wireless local networks, such as in a hospital. The type of media that can be used over a 2G network is very different from media that can be used over a 3G or 4G network, again illustrating that "one size will not fit all."

Unified communications (UC) technology will also have a tremendous impact on the workforce of the future. Unified Communications is defined as the forms of call, multimedia, and messaging technologies that are controlled by an individual for business and social purposes (IEC, 2007). Examples of increasing ubiquity of UC technology include instant or short messaging (IM, SMS, or MMS) and voice or video over Internet such as Skype or YouTube. The increasingly ubiquity of being able to exchange presence information or collaborate and interact with data online is allowing us to increase the speed of exchanging knowledge and information.

This will raise additional security concerns where business records or compliance factors require an official record or "rollback" to provide an audit trail of what information was provided to whom. This is also a consideration for organizations that allow the use of "free" online or mobile applications for everything from chat to sharing files or creating content. In many cases, an organization will have a policy forbidding the use of public instant messaging, and they may block this traffic at the network level, but they may not be able to block use from an iPhone or Dopod over a cellular network.

Remote access is also cultural to some degree. Many emerging economies do not routinely provide remote access to corporate systems as they do in the West. Such access would be considered a privilege according to one's role, and not a right as in the West.

When designing knowledge and learning systems for the future workforce, we should also consider access from mobile networks. From an access point of view, in 2008 there were three times the number of mobile subscribers as there were either landline or Internet subscribers worldwide (ITU, 2008).

Culture Matters

Work scenarios of 2020 will be increasingly diverse; they will involve increasingly distributed teams that are also more likely to be situational. For example, a team may form to open new stores in Nairobi and then disband, or a factory may need to be relocated to a more plentiful source of water.

How then should we define "co-workers" in the future? Will they be joint partners, academia, or outsourced talent?

One of the key trends in the field of human resources is that organizations will begin to harness and manage internal and external talent, and we can expect to see some innovative decoupling of the workforce from the organization itself. New business models are emerging that will also shift our definition of what a workforce is. One example is found in the music industry, where some innovative artists have found that they can crowdsource the producer role. Rather than hiring producers, they can sell "producer points" via crowdsourcing. This new shared ownership pool determines the title, song tracks, mix, album covers, tours, and so on. They also can collectively share in the returns. The workforce that we have known in the past is likely to be treated more as a resource, perhaps more like how capital is handled. It may be borrowed, loaned, and invested.

As we start to imagine the myriad of combinations — mixing age, skills, location, education — we begin to wonder what else do we need to look at? Are there any patterns that have emerged? In Asia, the average worker is between 25 and 35 and increasingly will be considered a "digital native." They might not have a Facebook profile or be in LinkedIn, but may be very connected on Kaixin, Xiaonei, or Orkut. They prefer voice or texting to e-mail. They are unlikely to have more than ten years of experience, and they belong to many communities. At first glance, an average Asia worker pattern appears very similar to that in the West, and it appears that collaboration should be "second nature." Collaboration styles are a result of age, language, and culture. But is this true?

This brings us to a final area of observation: the cultural work style. Many organizations are familiar with more explicit cultural aspects such as the things we can see, the proper greeting style or dress, but less familiar with implicit cultural nuances such as individualism, sense of urgency, and formality.

In one culture, individualism is highly prized, and a high contributor of knowledge capital would be rewarded with a personal "five-star" ranking. In another culture, it is more important to belong to a business unit with very high key performance indicators (KPIs), indicating that "my division is the best." The very unit of work "ego" will vary by culture.

Sense of urgency is a more subtle variable between cultures. As an example, if someone in Germany asks a question, they may mean "please give me the most thorough and precise response"; whereas someone in China running a busy 24-hour factory cannot afford any downtime, means "please give me the fastest answer." We can imagine the inner dialog that occurs when someone expecting a thorough response is given a quick response with few details, or conversely when someone takes 2 days to reply when you were hoping for an immediate answer!

Some work cultures are very formal in nature and very hierarchical. Workers in the West tend to have much more autonomy and unstructured environments compared to Eastern counterparts with a solid regimen of weekly reports presented to authorities or posted on a bulletin board.

Other cultural attributes are related to risk-taking and uncertainty or thinking long-term versus short-term (Hofstede, 2004). If we avoid making judgments based on our own cultural bias, then neither is right nor wrong. They are just different.

Some of the other intangible cultural aspects (see Figure 3.3) include visual or verbal communication cues, social practices or values regarding education, personal aspirations, and so forth. The 2009 UNESCO Framework for Cultural Statistics has updated their 1986 codification of the implicit cultural attributes such as values, emotions, and beliefs to be more inclusive of developing countries, and has also updated some of the explicit cultural attributes to reflect new expressions of culture in technology, such as Web portals, wikis, audio, and video works and social networks. All of this is vital to understand if we are to promote peace and security as well as universal respect as noted in the UNESCO charter (UNESCO, 2009).

As discussed at the beginning of the chapter, scenarios that require new creative thought or improved communication and decision making can harness some of the implicit cultural issues and treat them as valuable assets. Increasingly, organizations are recognizing that they are more than just "nice-to-haves" that make working or learning more pleasant, but they can translate into economic impact by increasing motivation, reducing conflict, and enhancing decision making. Leaders who understand these variables will be able to manage them and increase the effectiveness of their teams and better meet the needs of the people they serve.

With this backdrop for the next decade, we can anticipate many shifts in the workforce — while individual countries will continue to address their unique workforce and employment issues — and there is much we can accomplish collectively in order to work smart together more effectively.

Figure 3.3 Cultural diversity. Selected words related to the UNESCO report on cultural diversity. (Image courtesy of http://www.wordle.net/.)

References

Berreby, D. (1999). The Hunter-Gatherers of the Knowledge Economy: The Anthropology of Today's Cyberforagers. *Strategy and Business*, published July 1, 1999/Issue 16. http://www.strategy-business.com/article/19461?gko=cadd5.

Bhalla, S. (2009). *The Middle Class Kingdoms of India and China* to be published by the Peterson Institute for International Economics, Washington, DC, in 2009/2010, as referenced in Special Report: The New Middle Classes in Emerging Markets: "Burgeoning Bourgeoisie." *The Economist*, February 2009.

Bureau of Labor Statistics. (2008). Spotlight on Statistics: Older Workers—Are There More Older People in the Workplace? July 2008. United States Department of Labor, referenced online at http://www.bls.gov/spotlight/2008/older_workers/ as at December 31, 2009.

Central Intelligence Agency. (2009). *The World Factbook*. Online Publication as at December 31, 2009, available at https://www.cia.gov/library/publications/the-world-factbook/index.html.

Friedman, T.L. (2005). *The World is Flat: A Brief History of the Twenty-First Century*. New York. Farrar, Straus and Giroux.

G-20. (2009). About G-20, referenced online as at December 31, 2009 at http://www.g20.org/about_what_is_g20.aspx.

Hofstede, G., and Hofstede, G.-J. (2004). *Cultures and Organizations: Software of the Mind.* New York: McGraw-Hill, 2004.

International Engineering Consortium (IEC) (2007) Definition of Unified Communications. http://www.iec.org/online/tutorials/unified_comm/.

International Labour Organization (ILO) http://www.ilo.org/global/About_the_ILO/Media_and_public_information/Press_releases/lang--en/WCMS_113989/index.htm.

International Telecommunication Union (ITU). (2008) http://www.itu.int/ITU-D/ict/statistics/at_glance/KeyTelecom99.html.

Makimoto, T., and Manners, D. (1997) *Digital Nomad.* New York. John Wiley & Sons. West Sussex, U.K., New York.

Mell, P., and Grance, T. (2009). National Institute of Standards and Technology (NIST), NIST Definition of Cloud Computing v15. Dated 10-7-09 as available online as at December 31, 2009 at http://csrc.nist.gov/groups/SNS/cloud-computing/.

Olaniran, B.A. (2009). Discerning culture in e-learning and in the global workplaces. *Knowledge Management and E-Learning: An International Journal (KM&EL)*, Vol. 1, No. 3 (2009) http://www.kmel-journal.org/ojs/index.php/online-publication/article/view/7.

Palfrey, J., and Glasser, U. (2008). *Born Digital: Understanding the First Generation of Digital Natives*. New York: Basic Books, A Member of the Perseus Books Group.

UNESCO. (2009). UNESCO Framework for Cultural Statistics. Montreal, Quebec. Canada. Referenced online as at December 31, 2009 at http://www.uis.unesco.org/template/pdf/cscl/framework/FCS_2009_EN.pdf.

United Nations. (2008). Press Release: 2008 Revision of World Population Prospects, March 11, 2009 http://esa.un.org/unpd/wpp2008/pdf/WPP2008_PressRelease.pdf.

United Nations. (2009). Online Database: UN Population Data. Referenced as at December 31, 2009 at http://esa.un.org/unpp.

UNESCO. (2009). World Report, Investing in Cultural Diversity and Intercultural Dialogue. October 2009. Available online at: http://portal.unesco.org/culture/en/ev.php-URL_ID=39891&URL_DO=DO_TOPIC&URL_SECTION=201.html.

Wadhwa, V., Saxenian, A., Freeman, R., Jasso, G., Gereffi, G., and Rissing, B. (2009). An Outflow of Talent: Nativism and the US Reverse Brain Drain. *Harvard International Review*, Spring 2009.

KM AND E-LEARNING: METHODOLOGIES AND TECHNIQUES

II

Chapter 4

Assurance of Learning: Demonstrating the Organizational Impact of Knowledge Management and E-Learning

Antoniette (Toni) S. Ungaretti and
Heather K. Tillberg-Webb

Contents

Introduction

The wise see knowledge and action as one.

—Bhagavad-Gita

The fields of knowledge management (KM) and e-learning (EL) have gradually converged as the technological solutions to facilitate both processes have become more sophisticated and interactive ("KM and e-learning: a powerful combination," 2003). The value proposition of KM has shifted from local to centralized, decentralized, and finally evolutionary sharing of knowledge among employees (Bonifacio et al., 2008). Similarly, EL has developed from a process focused on distributing information and knowledge to one that deeply engages learners in sophisticated interactions through communities that transcend geographic barriers. The result is an unmistakable growing relationship between KM and EL to address needs through knowledge sharing and learning.

Instead, the underlying distinct epistemological frameworks of these two domains persist in keeping these fields disjointed (Schmidt, 2005). KM relies on a framework of "sharing" and "transfer of knowledge"; whereas e-learning is the development of an individuals' knowledge, competencies, and attitudes or dispositions through a pedagogically designed learning process delivered via multimedia technology (Clark and Mayer, 2007). Rather than serving as differentiators, these epistemologies might more appropriately be viewed as reciprocal perspectives on a common entity. The lens for this convergence is a systemic perspective on learning through which both of these fields are viewed as essential components of learning, with assurance of learning driving the impetus for either. Through the lens of learning, both the increased interaction of KM and EL and the unique theoretical foundations of each become complementary in the achievement of identified learning goals.

Both KM and e-learning professionals strive to change behavior, increase content knowledge, and impact organizational effectiveness. However, evaluation is focused on the inputs related to processes, products, and systems used to manage knowledge and deliver content. Adding assurance of learning to these two frameworks as described in our model shifts the focus to a more systemic view of the impact on knowledge transfer, learning, and the impact of the facilitation of these two processes on the organization as a whole. Without a mechanism in place to measure the impact of initiatives on individual learners and the collective impact on the organization, achieving the desired institutional transformation will be challenging. The pressure to view knowledge and learning systemically will require a focus on the techniques and capacities of KM and EL to support the achievement of learning outcomes and the ability of organizations to adjust rapidly to shifting information landscapes in the face of significant challenges to (1) create and nurture a knowledge-sharing culture; (2) support learners in adapting to change; (3) design training and development to achieve the mission and advance competence; (4) design education to prepare students to achieve success; (5) develop learners to ask appropriate questions; and (6) provide needed relevant information just enough, just in time.

Towards a Unified View

KM (the *what* and the *how*) and e-learning (the *how, where,* and *when*) become more robust with the addition of assurance of learning: the *why*, the *how we know,* and the *guidance for next steps.* Integrating these related but distinct domains with an assurance of learning perspective broadens the focus from where is the knowledge and how is it preserved, shared, distributed, and captured to what is learned, how we know it has been learned, what difference does it make, and how this informs future action.

The Dynamic Learning System (DLS) introduced in Figure 4.1 conceptualizes the commonalities in the value chains of each of these domains and analyzes the systemic impact of merging these models into a unified value chain that promises to continually assess and improve the impact of learning and knowledge creation activities. By describing the impact and emphasis of Assurance of Learning (see Figure 4.1; AoL value chain) and analyzing the gaps in the literature on KM and EL in the areas of assessment and evaluation, this DLS model presents an opportunity to bridge the intentions of these areas and demonstrate value creation to a learning organization.

Assurance of Learning (AoL)

AoL describes a systemic, intentional process that identifies desired learning and provides a process to measure its achievement and the improvement of both the learning and the process to attain it. This process has a number of different names such as *learning outcomes assessment* (American Public University System, 2009; Kuh and Ikenberry, 2009; Nusche, 2008), *assessment* (Association of American Colleges and Universities, 2009; Michlitsch and Sidle, 2002), the *outcomes assessment* movement (AACSB, 2007; Astin, 1991; The Association to Advance Collegiate Schools of Business, 2009), *assessing student learning* (Middle States Commission on Higher Education, 2006), as well as *assurance of learning* (Marshall, 2007; May and Tidwell, 2007; The Association to Advance Collegiate Schools of Business, 2009; Zhu and McFarland, 2005). This chapter uses the term *assurance of learning* over the more commonly used term, *learning outcomes assessment,* to indicate that this process is systemic and multidimensional—not limited to assessment of learning outcomes. This learning assurance system encompasses a broader feedback loop that simultaneously ensures learning and impact at the individual, group, and

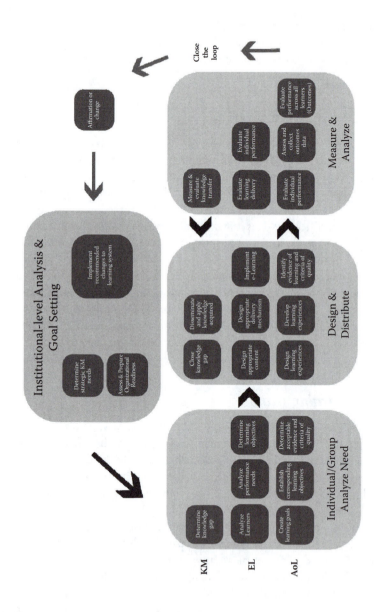

Figure 4.1   Dynamic Learning System Model.

institutional levels. It ensures that the identified learning goals are being most effectively addressed by current processes and components at all levels.

Viewing learning as part of a system has developed over the last half century. Early educational theorists first wrote about instructional *systems*, with evaluation and feedback as critical components of these systems in the 1960s (Shrock, 1995). Glaser and Cox (1968) pushed educational assessment toward a new type of test, criterion-referenced, that focused on learning outcomes rather than on the traditional norm-referencing of educational tests in the 1960s. Outcomes analysis has been an integral aspect of instructional design as part of learning program evaluation (Dick et al., 2001; Gagne et al., 1992). However, emphasis has been on front-end analysis of learner and task analysis, with evaluations focusing on individual performance and evaluation of the delivery mechanism and materials to impact the discrete instructional goals rather than organizational performance. Wiggins and McTighe (2005) introduced the concept of backwards design, which is similar to an instructional design process, but with additional emphasis on designing assessment criteria early in the design process.

Defining Learning

Learning is a phenomenon in which a new behavior or piece of information is incorporated by an individual in a way that results in a change of their conceptual knowledge or practiced behaviors. Piaget (1970) defined learning as the equilibration that results from the mutual interaction of accommodation (a change in schema or mental constructs based on experience) and assimilation (the integration of experience into schema or mental constructs). Thus, learning is constructed in an active process by the individual. Argyris and Schön (1978) proposed that learning takes place only when new knowledge is translated into different behaviors that are replicable. For Kolb (1984), learning is the process whereby knowledge is created through the transformation of experience. As described in the instructional design literature, "Learning is ... a unique product 'constructed' as each individual learner combines new information with existing knowledge and experiences" (Dick et al., 2001, p. 22).

A Focus on Learning Outcomes

The challenge of assuring learning is defining what constitutes successful learning. In definitions and descriptions of learning, two meanings emerge that Klein (1998) characterizes as (1) the acquisition of skills or *know-how* (the ability to produce some action) and (2) the acquisition of *know-why* (the ability to articulate a conceptual understanding of the experience) (p. 42). By stating learning goals and objectives at a macro (organizational) and micro (instructional) level prior to conducting the instructional program, measurement of "successful learning" becomes possible. "Learning outcomes refer to the personal changes or benefits that follow as a result of learning," (Nusche, 2008, p. 7) whether those results were intended or not. Learning outcomes can be psychomotor, cognitive, attitudinal/affective, procedural (applied), perceptual, or metacognitive (Dick et al., 2001; Gagne et al., 1992). While knowledge management has typically focused on tacit and explicit knowledge, but less on explicit skill development, and e-learning has typically emphasized job-based skills that can be measured in performance, the learning needs of organizations are more substantial than these frameworks can accommodate.

With rapid advances in new technology, it has become critical for learners/workers to ask compelling questions and to shift their view of learning as not the "study of facts" but "asking questions" (Barak and Rafaeli, 2004). The central role of professional development in learning organizations is shifting to one where learners engage in learning experiences that run the gamut from discrete skills to applied knowledge and higher-order problem-solving. Determining learning outcomes in higher-order skill learning scenarios is more challenging, and capturing measures of this type of learning is critical to demonstrating its impact on the organization. While traditional assessment has been used to determine the impact of instructional practice for individual learners, new movements in analyzing learning, such as assurance of learning through learning outcomes and assessment, have become imperative in professional education environments such as medicine (Handfield-Jones et al., 2002) and business (Marshall, 2007; Zhu and McFarland, 2005).

Growth of Assurance of Learning Movement

Traditional views of evaluation either analyze the functioning of a learning management program or conceptualize learning outcomes as a phenomenon that happens for an individual student. Assurance of Learning places the focus on continuous improvement, which must be demonstrated via measurable results and impact on the learning community. Assurance of Learning requires "operationalizing learning goals by specifying measurements that assess achievement on those goals" (Ammons and Mills, 2005, p. 2). As a movement, it strives to compensate for the lack of attention to output in traditional evaluation of learning. It measures the success of education and training programs by capturing data on what learners know and can do as a result of an educational implementation and gauges their competency. This requires a shift from "providing instruction" to "producing learning" (Barr and Tagg, 1995), or focusing on outputs over inputs.

AoL ensures that organizations engaged in this process demonstrate the impact of their KM and EL programs. Developing an Assurance of Learning/outcomes assessment plan requires engaging stakeholders, connecting assessment to valued goals and processes, creating a written plan, timing assessment to coincide with other critical process, and building a culture based on evidence (Banta et al., 2009).

Higher Education

Beginning with the recommendation from *A Nation at Risk* "...that schools, colleges, and universities adopt more rigorous and measurable standards," (National

Commission on Excellence in Education 1983) a continuously evolving and growing movement of accountability has altered the American educational landscape. The Spelling Report recommended that "… higher education must change from a system primarily based on reputation to one based on performance" (2006). In 2008, the Association for American Colleges and Universities and the Council for Higher Education Accreditation issued a statement that "each college and university should gather evidence about how well students in various programs are achieving learning goals across the curriculum … The evidence gathered through this process should be used by each institution and its faculty to develop coherent, effective strategies for educational improvement" (p. 2).

Meanwhile, key accrediting bodies in higher education have responded to the calls for accountability and modified their standards to emphasize the need to assess student learning outcomes as is evident in regional accrediting body standards (Advanced, 2006; Middle States Commission on Higher Education, 2006) as well as professional education organizations such as business, education, and medicine (Accreditation Council for Graduate Medical Education, 2009; National Council for Accreditation of Teacher Education, 2008; The Association to Advance Collegiate Schools of Business, 2009). Standards require not only the traditional analysis of inputs such as number of faculty and facilities, but also of outputs, including evidence of student learning and the use of that evidence to improve the learning experiences within the program and the school.

Corporate Sector

The corporate sector has witnessed a similar trend of increased accountability through opportunities such as the Baldrige National Quality (2009), which provides a dynamic systems perspective with feedback from measurement and analysis to enhance management performance. Kaplan and Norton's (2001) *Balanced Scorecard* is a dynamic system of information regarding performance in key metric areas aligned with an organization's vision and strategies. The ISO 9000 (2009) quality management systems certification includes among its principles employing a consistent organization-wide approach to continual improvement of the organization's performance and establishing goals to guide, and measures to track, continual improvement. Despite the importance of evaluating the effectiveness of learning programs, only about one-third of corporate educational initiatives evaluate the outcomes of their programs (Strother, 2002).

Knowledge Management (KM)

KM is a process of creating, acquiring, capturing, aggregating, sharing, and using knowledge, wherever it resides, to enhance organizational learning and performance (Becerra-Fernandez and Sabherwa, 2008; Boomer, 2004). Barker (2005) and Becerra-Fernandez and Leidner (2008) describe a hierarchy of complexity with *knowledge* (that which enables actions and decisions) at the highest level, *data* (collected observations and facts) at the lowest level, and *information* (processed and analyzed data) at the middle level.

The question of how to best define knowledge is the center of lively epistemological debate (Shin et al., 2001). However, there is agreement that knowledge can be classified into tacit knowledge and explicit knowledge. Tacit knowledge is subconsciously understood and applied, difficult to articulate, developed from direct experience and action, and usually shared through highly interactive conversation, storytelling, and shared experience. Explicit knowledge is consciously understood and can be more precisely and formally articulated; it is readily codified, documented, transferred, and shared (Becerra-Fernandez and Sabherwa, 2008; Barker, 2005). KM involves the management of the relationship between tacit—the know-how possessed by individuals—and explicit knowledge—the systemically documented know-how that becomes available to everyone in the organization (Ruggles, 1999).

The ultimate goal of KM should be to convert tacit knowledge to explicit knowledge to transform the capacity of individuals within the organization to use information strategically and apply higher-order thinking to an informed decision-making process. Nonaka and Takeuchi (1995) in a study of successful Japanese companies (i.e., Honda, NEC, and Fujitsu) describe four types of knowledge creating processes—*socialization, externalization, combination,* and *internalization*—to ultimately inform decision making (Choo, 1998). KM has adopted communication and collaboration solutions to address the unique challenge of articulating, sharing, and leveraging tacit knowledge (Mihalca, 2008).

Ho (2009) suggested that the goal of KM is to deliver the right knowledge to the right members at the right time so that they can take the right actions and improve performance (O'Dell and Grayson, 1999; Milton et al., 1999). The fast pace of today's world requires that attention not just be on supply-side KM, the existing organizational knowledge, but also on demand-side KM, the development of new knowledge, for organizations to remain competitive (McElroy, 2003). Drucker (1993) noted that KM is different from general management activities in its focus on the perspective of knowledge and its intent to apply this knowledge in a systematic and organized manner to create additional knowledge. Weggeman (1997, cited in Wild et al., 2001) defines the knowledge value chain as four successive constituent processes: determine strategic KM needs, determine knowledge gap, close the knowledge gap, disseminate and apply knowledge acquired, and measure and evaluate knowledge transfer (Figure 4.1; see KM value chain) critical to assurance of learning.

Technology Relationship

Mihalca et al. (2008) and Schmidt (2005) suggest that though KM is rooted in the field of management studies, it is closely integrated with information and communication technologies as the technology is needed to support KM, and KM is the rationale for the technologies' existence. Becerra and Sabherwa (2008) note the pivotal role of enabling technologies that support computer-based simulations, discussion groups, videoconferencing, and management information systems as well as social supports such as professional development, face-to-face meetings, and collaborative work. Willett (2001) suggests that "knowledge reciprocity" (p. 255) is becoming part of the culture of knowledge-intensive organizations.

Boomer (2004) cautions that KM is not about the technology systems that implement it but rather about the processes people use to capture knowledge. For example, the Internet and other collaboration technologies enable organization-wide socialization that has merged KM and OL (Becerra-Fernandez and Sabherwa, 2008, p. 33). McAfee (2006) notes that social media (wikis, blogs, and tweets) are shifting knowledge-based organizations from hierarchical structures to interdependent knowledge communities. Sabry and Barker (2009) note the critical importance of *interactivity* in the design of effective learning systems in organizations. KM has forayed into concepts such as "communities of practice" with initiatives such as Collaborative Methodology, where horizontal networks are created to cut across hierarchical and isolated organizations to allow professionals to share and 'harvest' best practices (Bate and Robert, 2002). Becerra-Fernandez and Sabherwa (2008) describe this evolution in their article addressing the relationship of KM and OL.

Limitation of KM

Adrian Snook (Lelic, 2001) observed that throughout specialist KM publications *knowledge* appears to be recognized as the key to organizational effectiveness. He also observed that the words *skill* and *competence* appear to be absent. Snook contends that in fact what organizations ultimately need is not knowledge but rather competent employees with the right combination of skills and the underlying knowledge needed to competently complete their jobs. Furthermore, he comments that persons facing daunting development challenges require carefully designed learning experiences based on sound pedagogical principles by instructional experts with practice activities and assessments crafted to both develop and test competence.

Mihalca et al. (2008) and Schmidt (2005) suggest that the language of KM is somewhat "naïve" because it views knowledge almost as a tangible item to be developed, captured, distributed, etc., as reflected in the extensive use and focus on learning objects that can be compiled into a "corporate memory" (Schmidt, 2005, p. 204). The KM literature addresses knowledge flow, content, and context but does not mention the role of the learner in constructing a unique mental construct of the knowledge and the impact of that learning on KM effectiveness.

A Constructivist Perspective

KM facilitates and supports the sharing of both explicit and tacit knowledge through the creation of learning objects or through communication and collaboration interactions. Schmidt (2005) suggests that the KM field does not fully appreciate its primary role to facilitate goal-oriented *learning* in organizations—that understanding how *learning* takes place is critical to its effectiveness. Furthermore, learning is not just the transfer of knowledge but rather an active process of each individual constructing unique understandings, skills, and attitudes.

To explain, constructivist theory approaches learning from a genetic epistemologic orientation in which the organism—the learner—is engaged in an adaptation process when confronting a new experience. Through this encounter, the learner experiences disequilibrium: a disconnect between current knowledge and experience in comparison to this new situation. The learner engages in a dynamic process with two components: assimilation (applying current mental constructs to the new situation) and accommodation (adjusting current mental constructs to apply to this new situation) and accommodation to new encounters in the environment. This process continues until the learner has enhanced, adjusted, or expanded the current mental construct and has achieved equilibration. The result is a change in the learner or *learning* (Piaget, 1970). Critical to learning success is the perceived value of the required change by the individual that maintains engagement until equilibration has been achieved (Piaget, 1970)—the significance of which can be understood in the effort of teachers and managers to engage students and employees, respectively, in activities to advance learning.

Interestingly, organizational learning similarly connects to the constructivist perspective. Herbert Simon in his classic description of organizational learning describes it as the "growing insights and successful restructurings of organizational problems by individuals reflected in the structural elements and outcomes of the organization itself" (Simon, 1969, as cited in Fiol and Lyles, 1985, p. 803). Mihalca et al. (2008) make an interesting observation by noting parallels between educational systems and KM systems: both involve the creation of useful knowledge from information and/or data found among the intellectual capital available within the organization. Learning consists of the development of insights along with structural and other action outcomes: one aspect consisting of a change in a state of knowledge (not readily observable) and the other of a change more readily observable as a behavioral or organizational outcome (somewhat analogous to tacit and explicit knowledge).

A corporate example that approaches this is in Accenture, which views the KM functions as a six-step process: acquire, create, synthesize, share, use to achieve organizational goals, and establish an environment conducive to knowledge sharing (Meister and Davenport, 2005). Another is Cap Gemini Ernst and Young, which promotes a four-phase KM approach: knowledge generation, knowledge representation, knowledge codification, and knowledge application (Andreu et al., 2004). Aside from a few examples, KM has not fully realized that not just *learning* but how *learning* takes place is extremely important to facilitate goal-focused *learning* in organizations. It is this aspect of managing knowledge that seems to be omitted from the KM literature and is captured with the addition of the AoL perspective on learning.

E-Learning (EL)

EL's roots in the merging of instructional systems design and performance systems technology distinguishes the domain. Though EL can be defined as "the acquisition and use of knowledge distributed and facilitated primarily by electronic means," (Waight et al., 2002, p. 492) there is an implication in using the term that an instructional design process has been implemented to systematically evaluate performance tasks, analyze learners, define behavioral learning objectives, and create a sequence of learning activities planned and designed to best take advantage of human learning capabilities. Also, there is an expectation that multimedia design components take into account usability and visual cognition.

The pedagogical framework of EL has evolved from its early roots in behaviorism in the late 1950s and 1960s to encompass a broader definition of "learning" that includes collaborative and constructivist paradigms of learning, including opportunities for practice with feedback, social collaboration, tailored instruction, simulation, and games (Clark and Mayer, 2007). This expansion has occurred in tandem with increased capabilities in computer systems as well as the recognition of the importance of the social process of learning. EL instruction also entails learners working in a distributed manner, in other words, in different locations or at varying times. Analysis of definitions across government, business, and professional associations demonstrates the common perception across these areas of practice that EL is "anytime, anywhere, cost effective, have a global reach, be just-in-time, allow personalization and improve collaboration and interactivity" (Waight et al., 2002, p. 497).

The roots of EL in programmed instruction, task analysis, and Skinner's theory of reinforcement historically underpin the pedagogical thinking of instructional design and EL (Shrock, 1995). Early computer-based training (CBT) was highly regimented and derived from behavioral principles of learning. They lacked the nuance to assist learner with diagnostic interpretations of wrong answers (Ravenscroft, 2001) and required learners to work in social isolation. Today's EL does presume that materials for learning will be highly scripted with content recorded and delivered for learners; however, opportunities for feedback are also expected.

Because of these characteristics of EL, learners are required to be more disciplined, self-motivated, and self-regulated than in a traditional classroom environment. The well-documented problem of "e-learning dropout" (Clark and Mayer, 2007), ranging from 35% to 80% (Hodges, 2004), indicates that EL requires highly motivated learners and has led to an increased emphasis on teaching presence (Anderson et al., 2001; Garrison, 2007; Shea et al., 2005; Shea et al., 2003) which in self-paced EL might be largely felt in the instructional design of course materials (Tillberg-Webb and Wongtanasirikul, 2006); and social presence (Gunawardena, 1995; Gunawardena and Zittle, 1997; Richardson and Swan, 2003; Rourke et al., 1999; So and Brush, 2008) in highly interactive formats such as facilitated discussions or interactive environments such as wikis and blogs (Beldarrain, 2006).

The EL process is generally tied into institutional or organizational objectives in that materials should be developed based on a job analysis (Clark and Mayer, 2007). In order to maximize transfer of knowledge, a careful needs assessment of expert performance in a given domain is necessary via a task or procedural analysis (Dick et al., 2001, pp. 19–22; Gagne et al., 1992, p. 23; Jonassen et al., 1999). Though the organizational objectives are important here, for example, the ability of a worker to perform at a level that fulfills institutional needs, the performance of individuals within the EL materials is tracked and, ideally, program evaluations are conducted to link the training programs to improved institutional effectiveness.

Instructional design as a foundation for EL implies that the entire set of events and materials that "affect learners" for the purpose of accomplishing "a particular goal of learning" (Gagne et al., 1992) is a process that must be carefully and systematically planned. Objectives of EL are designed as behavioral learning objectives, as there is no teacher to teach per se. At the same time, the ability to provide feedback can be constrained by the available technologies.

Discussion of quality assurance in EL typically focuses on course design and presentation, such as in the EL assessment rubric Quality Matters (2006) or that proposed by Ireland et al. (2009), both of which focus on organization of an EL site, appearance, consistency, appropriate use of tools, learner support, and resources. In contrast, assessment and assurance of learning must address the process of learning by its output and the acquired competencies demonstrated by learners rather than the evaluation of products and individual progress (Barak and Rafaeli, 2004).

Wild et al. (2002) suggest an EL value chain (Figure 4.1; see value chain) with a four-step process that aligns with the Weggeman (1997, cited in Willett., 2001) KM value chain. The first process, *assess and prepare organizational readiness,* corresponds to the first two KM processes, *determine strategic KM needs* and *determine knowledge gap.* The second through fourth processes, *design appropriate content, design appropriate presentation, and implement EL,* correspond to the last two KM processes, *disseminate and apply knowledge acquired,* and *measure and evaluate knowledge transfer.* Figure 4.1 expands these aligned value chains and combines them with that of assurance of learning to create a more robust and dynamic learning system.

Dynamic Learning System Model

Organizations are already, in a sense, learning systems, where the ability of an organization to grow is dependent on collective learning (Nevis et al., 2000). The Dynamic Learning System (DLS) combines the elements of the KM, EL, and AoL value chains to demonstrate the commonalities and power of combining the principles of these domains to build a knowledge/learning organization. Thus, the DLS model incorporates the common elements of the value chains of each of these domains, synthesizing the key value creation to occur in Institutional-level

Analysis and Goal Setting; Individual/Group-Level Needs Analysis; Design and Distribution of Knowledge/Learning; and Measurement and Analysis of Learning/ Knowledge Creation.

The key component of the DLS that is unique is the collection and analysis of learning outcomes data at a unit of analysis above individual learners. "To think of the value chain as an integrated learning system is to think of the work in each major step, beginning with strategic decisions through to customer service, as a subsystem for learning experiments. Structures and processes to achieve outcomes can be seen simultaneously as operational tasks and learning exercises; this holds for discrete functions and for cross-functional activities such as new product development" (Nevis et al., 2000).

KM focuses on organization-level knowledge as implemented by individuals; EL suggests focus on individual learners with an emphasis on impacting the organization; and assurance of learning focuses on the external goals driving the management of data, externalization of tacit knowledge, training of individuals on explicit knowledge, which in turn should develop individuals to make better decisions—in other words—a systemic approach to knowledge and learning. DLS requires an analysis of organizational impact of KM and EL delivery via the additional step of analyzing learning outcomes across a program or organization and recommending changes to the learning system based on outputs.

Though some evaluation is inherent in KM systems, the emphasis is on what is tacit and explicit knowledge and how it will be managed and made accessible: created, organized, shared, preserved, made explicit, gathered, captured, codified, etc. Assurance of Learning (AoL) addresses this from the *why is this important* and *what evidence indicates that it has been learned* perspectives. From this perspective, the driver is not a focus on knowledge itself but the ability of the learner to know what needs to be known and demonstrates that knowing. AoL explicitly provides a framework and a process to identify the level at which the learner knows, what is and is not being learned, progress toward reaching specified goals, and the effectiveness of the approaches used—traditional, project based, EL, etc.—from the perspective of the individual. Moreover, the framework and process transcends the individual to assess this at the project/program/unit/department level, and at the institution/organizational level. AoL addresses this from the *why* and the *how do we know that progress is being made toward identified organizational goals* standpoints— a systemic process of continuous improvement based on clear goals and evidence of achievement with direction on needed improvements.

The convergence of the KM and EL domains has occurred as companies have begun to look at "learning" instead of "training" with education (Ismail, 2001). The overlapping concept of learning objects and a shared obsession between KM and EL to develop optimal systems to label and categorize metadata of learning objects to enhance reusability (Currier et al., 2003) further integrates the fields. Thus, the description of Weller et al.'s (2005) incorporation of interactive, dynamic ICT into an EL experience designed with 155 learning objects so that learners could structure the content in ways that made sense for their learning experience and were also required to communicate and collaborate via blogs, audio podcasting, IM, etc., fits right into the definition of EL while also using some of the same concepts and terminology as KM. To take it a step further and conceptualize Weller's learning design within the DLS framework, if the learning outcomes were measured in not just this instance but in the broader array of instances, those learning outcomes could be used to determine areas that required further development, elaboration, or additional practice for learners.

In order to move to a system that shifts perspective from inputs to outputs, from viewing learners as passive recipients of knowledge to active generators of knowledge ... "who share responsibility in the process, practices of self-assessment and collaboration" (Barak and Rafaeli, 2004, p. 86), a shift in assessment strategies is required and, as Barak and Rafaeli (2004) describe, can encompass strategies such as self-assessment, peer assessment, and achievement assessment.

Future Trends in Assurance of Learning

As the need to ensure successful achievement of learning outcomes continues to impact learning professionals, whether their main focus is KM or EL, several trends will continue to grow in importance:

- Systems that track data collection of learning outcomes and measure success of learning programs as a function of learning outcomes
- Adoption of learning portfolios, especially e-portfolios, to document learner's progress across a program of professional development
- Reporting that illustrates the development of higher-order thinking development, problem-solving ability
- Strategies for evaluating team performance and assessing team-learning outcomes

Incorporating systems for tracking learning outcomes across learning programs first requires levels of communication and collaboration across an institution, which is a time-intensive process. Second, the systems available to track data are either prohibitively expensive or time and financial resource intensive. In terms of technology, some institutions have adapted the use of learning management systems such as WebCT (Motiwalla et al., 2006) or instituted tools such as Blackboard Outcomes Assessment (2009) to track learning outcomes. The selection and integration of technology tools is only one aspect of a larger system that involves communication and consensus at several layers of an organization to select goals and desired learning outcomes.

Tied in with developing systems to track learning outcomes across programs is a renewed interest in learning portfolios, particularly in electronic format. The Accreditation Council for Graduate Medical Education (2009) is piloting the use of learning portfolios to demonstrate learning outcomes. Furthermore, ePortfolios meet the needs of KM, especially in terms of the organization of knowledge and creation of new knowledge, and of EL in that the ePortfolios must be designed with target learning objectives. They also meet the needs of AoL in that the portfolios will demonstrate competency on learning outcomes. A focus on both the selection of appropriate materials to demonstrate learning competencies with ongoing reflection on the learning process (Mason, Pegler, and Weller, 2004) highlights ePortfolios as a learning and assessment tool that facilitates higher-order thinking and metacognitive skill development.

Strategies for evaluating team performance outcomes could be a trend in the future of assurance of learning. As "organizational learning takes place through individuals and the positive and negative outcomes that their members encounter from their behaviors" (Bonifacio et al., 2008, p. 13), measuring the impact of organizational learning systems on individuals and teams is critical and must be more synergistic and nuanced than simply tallying individual learner's accomplishments (Becerra-Fernandez, 2008). New models of demonstrating "learning" that transcend simply measuring individual's accomplishments are required for organizations.

Conclusion

According to Senge (1990), learning organizations are "… organizations where people continually expand their capacity to create the results they truly desire, … where people are continually learning to see the whole together" (3). Combining AoL with KM and EL creates a compelling, robust, dynamic learning systems model that employs the unique elements of each domain to advance the organization through simultaneously addressing individual-, group-, and institutional-level needs. A shift from inputs to a focus on outputs serves to remove hierarchical barriers (often driven by an input orientation) to problem solving or problem synthesis. Multilevel analysis of learning provides not only a measure of individual performance but also insight into needed changes and adjustments required at all levels to optimize impact. A dynamic learning systems approach that combines KM and EL with AoL, and is fueled by measurable evidence that monitors and directs change, creates a gestalt that magnifies the power of the discourse on learning in both the university and the corporation. KM, EL, and AoL together make this possible. Power exponentially increases when these fields are viewed not as silos, as complements, or as one subsuming the other, but as integral components critical to learning.

References

AACSB. (2007). AACSB Assurance of Learning Standards: An Interpretation. Retrieved December 31, 2009, from https://www.aacsb.edu/accreditation/papers/AOLPaper-final-11-20-07.pdf.

Accreditation Council for Graduate Medical Education. (2009). The ACGME Learning Portfolio. Retrieved December 31, 2009, from http://www.acgme.org/acWebsite/portfolio/learn_alp_aboutalp.asp.

AdvancED. (2006). Accreditation Standards for Quality Schools: For Schools Seeking NCA CASI or SACS CASI accreditation. Retrieved December 31, 2009, from http://www.advanc-ed.org/accreditation/standards/advanced_school_standards.pdf.

American Public University System. (2009). Learning Outcomes Assessment. Retrieved December 31, 2009, from http://www.apus.edu/community-scholars/learning-outcomes-assessment/.

Ammons, J. L., and Mills, S. K. (2005). Course-Embedded Assessments for Evaluating Cross-Functional Integration and Improving the Teaching-Learning Process. *Issues in Accounting Education, 20*(1), 1–20.

Anderson, T., Rourke, L., Garrison, D. R., and Archer, W. (2001). Assessing teaching presence in a computer conferencing context. *Journal of Asynchronous Learning Networks, 5*(2), 1–17.

Andreu, R., Lara, E., and Sieber, S. (2004). *Knowledge Management at Cap Gemini, Ernst & Young.* Cambridge, MA: Harvard Business Review Case Study.

Argyris, C., and Schön, D. A. (1978). *Organizational Learning: A Theory of Action Perspective.* Reading, MA: Addison-Wesley.

Association of American Colleges and Universities. (2009). Association of American Colleges and Universities. Retrieved December 31, 2009, from http://www.aacu.org/.

Astin, A. W. (1991). *Assessment for Excellence: The Philosophy and Practice of Assessment and Evaluation in Higher Education.* Westport, CT: Oryx Pr.

Baldridge National Quality Program. (2009). 2009–2010 Baldridge National Quality Program Criteria for Performance Excellence. Retrieved December 31, 2009, from http://www.baldrige.nist.gov/PDF_files/2009_2010_Business_Nonprofit_Criteria.pdf.

Banta, T. W., Jones, E. A., and Black, K. E. (2009). *Designing Effective Assessment: Principles and Profiles of Good Practice.* San Francisco, CA: Jossey-Bass.

Barak, M., and Rafaeli, S. (2004). On-line question-posing and peer-assessment as means for web-based knowledge sharing in learning. *International Journal of Human–Computer Studies, 61*(1), 84–103.

Barker, P. (2005). Knowledge management for e-learning. *Innovations in Education and Teaching International, 42*(2), 111–121.

Barr, R. B., and Tagg, J. (1995). From teaching to learning: A new paradigm for undergraduate education. *Change, 27*(6), 12–25.

Bate, S. P., and Robert, G. (2002). Knowledge management and communities of practice in the private sector: Lessons for modernising the National Health Service in England and Wales. *Public Administration, 80*(4), 643–663.

Becerra-Fernandez, I., and Leidner, D. (Eds.). (2008). *Knowledge Management: An Evolutionary View.* Armonk, New York: M.E. Sharpe.

Becerra-Fernandez, I., and Sabherwa, R. (2008). Individual, group, and organizational learning: A knowledge management perspective. In I. Becerra-Fernandez and D. Leidner (Eds.), *Knowledge Management: An Evolutionary View* (pp. 13–39). Armonk, New York: M.E. Sharpe.

Beldarrain, Y. (2006). Distance education trends: Integrating new technologies to foster student interaction and collaboration. *Distance Education, 27*(2), 139–154.

Blackboard. (2009). Blackboard Outcomes Assessment. Retrieved December 31, 2009, from http://www.blackboard.com/Teaching-Learning/Learn-Capabilities/Outcomes-Assessment.aspx.

Bonifacio, R., Franz, T., and Staab, S. (2008). A four-layer model of information technology support of knowledge management. In I. Becerra-Fernandez and R. Sabherwa (Eds.), *Knowledge Management: An Evolutionary View* (pp. 13–39). Armonk, New York: M.E. Sharpe.

Boomer, J. (2004). Finding out what knowledge management is–and isn't. *Accounting Today*, *18*(14), 9–22.

Choo, C. W. (1998). *The Knowing Organization*. Oxford: Oxford University Press.

Clark, R. C., and Mayer, R. E. (2007). *E-learning and the Science of Instruction: Proven Guidelines for Consumers and Designers of Multimedia Learning*. San Francisco, CA: Pfeiffer.

Currier, S., Barton, J., O'Beirne, R., and Ryan, B. (2003). Quality assurance for digital learning object repositories: How should metadata be created? In *Communities of Practice: Research Proceedings of the 19th Association for Learning Technology Conference* (pp. 130–142).

Dick, W., Carey, L., and Carey, J. O. (2001). *The Systematic Design of Instruction* (5th ed.). New York: Longman.

Drucker, P. F. (1993). *Managing for the Future*. Butterworth-Heinemann Oxford, England.

Fiol, C. M., and Lyles, M. A. (1985). Organizational learning. *The Academy of Management Review*, *10*(4), 803–813.

Gagne, R. M., Briggs, L. J., and Wager, W. W. (1992). *Principles of Instructional Design*. Holt, Rinehart and Winston, New York.

Garrison, D. R. (2007). Online community of inquiry review: Social, cognitive, and teaching presence issues. *Journal of Asynchronous Learning Networks*, *11*(1), 61–72.

Glaser, R., and Cox, R. C. (1968). Criterion-referenced testing for the measurement of educational outcomes. In R. Weisgerber (Ed.), *Instructional Process and Media Innovation* (pp. 545–550). Chicago: Rand McNally.

Gunawardena, C. N. (1995). Social presence theory and implications for interaction and collaborative learning in computer conferences. *International Journal of Educational Telecommunications*, *1*(2/3), 147–166.

Gunawardena, C. N., and Zittle, F. J. (1997). Social presence as a predictor of satisfaction within a computer-mediated conferencing environment. *American Journal of Distance Education*, *11*(3), 8–26.

Handfield-Jones, R. S., Mann, K. V., Challis, M. E., Hobma, S. O., Klass, D. J., McManus, I. C. et al. (2002). Linking assessment to learning: A new route to quality assurance in medical practice. *Medical Education-Oxford*, *36*(10), 949.

Ho, C. T. (2009). The relationship between knowledge management enablers and performance. *Industrial Management and Data Systems*, *109*(1–2).

Hodges, C. B. (2004). Designing to motivate: Motivational techniques to incorporate in e-learning experiences. *The Journal of Interactive Online Learning*, *2*(3), 1–7.

International Organization for Standardization. (2009). ISO 9000/ISO 14000 - Quality management principles. Retrieved December 31, 2009, from http://www.iso.org/iso/iso_catalogue/management_standards/iso_9000_iso_14000/qmp/qmp-6.htm.

Ireland, J., Correia, H. M., and Griffin, T. M. (2009). Developing quality in e-learning: A framework in three parts. *Quality Assurance in Education*, *17*(3), 250-263.

Ismail, J. (2001). The design of an e-learning system Beyond the hype. *The Internet and Higher Education*, *4*(3–4), 329–336.

Jonassen, D. H., Tessmer, M., and Hannum, W. H. (1999). *Task Analysis Methods for Instructional Design*. New Jersey: Lawrence Erlbaum Associates.

Kaplan, R., and Norton, D. (2001). *The Strategy-Focused Organization: How Balanced Scorecard Companies Thrive in the New Business Environment*. Cambridge, MA: Harvard Business School Press.

Klein, D. (1998). *The Strategic Management of Intellectual Capital*. Woburn, MA: Butterworth-Heinemann.

KM and e-learning: A powerful combination. (2003). *E-Content*, *26*(10), 18–22.

Kolb, D. A. (1984). *Experiential Learning: Experience as the Source of Learning and Development*. Prentice-Hall Englewood Cliffs, NJ.

Kuh, G., and Ikenberry, S. (2009). *More than You Think, Less Than We Need: Learning Outcomes Assessment in American Higher Education*. National Institute for Learning Outcomes Assessment.

Lelic, S. (2001). Your say - Knowledge management and e-learning—Inside Knowledge. *Inside Knowledge*, *4*(8). Retrieved January 1, 2010, from http://www.ikmagazine.com/xq/asp/sid.0/articleid.38EE1741-0728-4E67-BB57-5B75D35B100F/eTitle.Your_say__Knowledge_management_and_elearning/qx/display.htm.

Marshall, L. L. (2007). Measuring assurance of learning at the degree program and academic major levels. *The Journal of Education for Business*, *83*(2), 101–109.

Mason, R., Pegler, C., and Weller, M. (2004). E-portfolios: An assessment tool for online courses. *British Journal of Educational Technology*, *35*(6), 717–727.

May, G., and Tidwell, M. (2007). Assurance of learning: Implementing a uniform assessment process across multiple sections of a managerial communication course. In *Proceedings of the 2007 Association for Business Communication Annual Convention*. Presented at the Association for Business Communication Annual Convention, Washington, D.C.

McAfee, A. P. (2006). Enterprise 2.0: The dawn of emergent collaboration. *MIT Sloan Management Review*, *47*(3), 21.

McElroy, M. W. (2003). *The New Knowledge Management*. United States: Butterworth-Heinemann.

Meister, D., and Davenport, T. (2005). *Knowledge management at Accenture*. Cambridge, MA: Harvard Business Review Case Study.

Michlitsch, J. F., and Sidle, M. W. (2002). Assessing student learning outcomes: A comparative study of techniques used in business school disciplines. *Journal of Education for Business*, *77*(3), 125–30.

Middle States Commission on Higher Education. (2006). Characteristics of excellence in higher education requirements. Retrieved December 31, 2009, from http://www.msche.org/publications/CHX06_Aug08REVMarch09.pdf.

Mihalca, R., Uta, A., Andreecu, A., and Întorsureanu, I. (2008). Knowledge management in e-learning systems. *Revista Informatica Economică*, *46*(2), 60–65.

Milton, N., Shadbolt, N., Cottman, H., and Hammersley, M. (1999). "Towards a knowledge technology for knowledge management," *International Journal Human-Computer Studies*, 51, 615–641.

Motiwalla, L., Tello, S., and Carter, K. (2006). Outcome assessment of learning objectives: A case for using e-learning software. In *Proceedings of the Twelfth Americas Conference on Information Systems*. Presented at the Conference on Information Systems, Acapulco, Mexico.

National Commission on Excellence in Education. (1983). *A Nation at Risk: The Imperative for Educational Reform*. Washington, D.C.: National Commission on Excellence in Education. Retrieved December 29, 2009, from http://www.ed.gov/pubs/NatAtRisk/index.html.

National Council for Accreditation of Teacher Education. (2008). Professional Standards for the Accreditation of Teacher Preparation Institutions. Retrieved December 31, 2009, from http://www.ncate.org/documents/standards/NCATE%20Standards%202008.pdf.

Nevis, E. C., DiBella, A. J., and Gould, J. M. (2000). Understanding organizations as learning systems. *Knowledge, Groupware and the Internet, 43.*

Nonaka, I., and Takeuchi, H. (1995). *The Knowledge-Creating Company: How Japanese Companies Create the Dynamics of Innovation.* Cambridge: Oxford University Press.

Nusche, D. (2008). Assessment of Learning Outcomes in Higher Education: A Comparative Review of Selected Practices. OECD Education Working Papers, No. 15, OECD Publishing.

O'Dell, C., and Grayson, Jr., C. J. (Mar/Apr 1999). "Knowledge transfer: Discover your value proposition." *Strategy & Leadership, 27*(2), 10–15.

Piaget, J. (1970). *Genetic Epistemology.* New York: Columbia University Press.

Quality Matters. (2006). The Quality Matters Rubric. Retrieved December 13, 2009, from http://www.qualitymatters.org/.

Ravenscroft, A. (2001). Designing E-learning INTERACTIONS in the 21st Century: Revisiting and rethinking the role of theory. *European Journal of Education, 36*(2).

Richardson, J. C., and Swan, K. (2003). Examining social presence in online courses in relation to students' perceived learning and satisfaction. *Journal of Asynchronous Learning Networks, 7*(1), 68–88.

Rourke, L., Anderson, T., Garrison, D. R., and Archer, W. (1999). Assessing social presence in asynchronous text-based computer conferencing. *Journal of Distance Education, 14*(2), 50–71.

Ruggles, R. (1999). The state of the notion: Knowledge management in practice. *The Knowledge Management Yearbook 1999–2000, 295.*

Sabry, K., and Barker, J. (2009). Dynamic interactive learning systems. *Innovations in Education and Teaching International, 46*(2), 185–197.

Schmidt, A. (2005). Knowledge maturing and the continuity of context as a unifying concept for knowledge management and e-learning. In *Proceedings of I-Know* (Vol. 5). Citeseer.

Senge, P. (1990). *The Fifth Discipline: The Art and Practice of the Learning Organization.* New York: Doubleday.

Shea, P., Li, C. S., Swan, K., and Pickett, A. (2005). Developing learning community in online asynchronous college courses: The role of teaching presence. *Journal of Asynchronous Learning Networks, 9*(4), 59–82.

Shea, P. J., Pickett, A. M., and Pelz, W. E. (2003). A follow-up investigation of "teaching presence" in the SUNY Learning Network. *Journal of Asynchronous Learning Networks, 7*(2), 61–80.

Shin, M., Holden, T., and Schmidt, R. A. (2001). From knowledge theory to management practice: Towards an integrated approach. *Information Processing and Management, 37*(2), 335–355.

Shrock, S. (1995). A brief history of instructional development. In G. Anglin (Ed.), *Instructional Technology: Past Present, and Future* (2nd ed.). Englewood, Colorado: Libraries Unlimited, Inc.

Simon, H. A. (1969). *The Sciences of the Artificial.* MIT Press, Cambridge, MA.

So, H. J., and Brush, T. A. (2008). Student perceptions of collaborative learning, social presence and satisfaction in a blended learning environment: Relationships and critical factors. *Computers and Education, 51*(1), 318–336.

Strother, J. B. (2002). An assessment of the effectiveness of e-learning in corporate training programs. *The International Review of Research in Open and Distance Learning, 3*(1).

The Association to Advance Collegiate Schools of Business. (2009). Eligibility procedures and accreditation standards for business accreditation. Retrieved December 31, 2009, from http://www.aacsb.edu/accreditation/BUSINESS-STANDARDS-2009-Final.pdf.

Tillberg-Webb, H., and Wongtanasirikul, N. (2006). Strategies for building a community of inquiry in asynchronous online instruction. Presented at the International Conference e-learning 2006 at Ramkhamhaeng University, Bangkok, Thailand.

U.S. Department of Education. (2006). A Test of Leadership: Charting the Future of U.S. Higher Education. Washington, D.C. Retrieved December 29, 2009, from http://www.ed.gov/about/bdscomm/list/hiedfuture/reports.html.

Waight, C. L., Willging, P. A., and Wentling, T. L. (2002). Recurrent themes in e-learning: A meta-analysis of major e-learning reports. In *Proceedings from the Academy of human Resource Development Conference* (pp. 491–499). Citeseer.

Weggeman, M. (1997). *Kennismanagement.* Schiedam: Inrichting en Besturing van Kennisintensieve Organisaties.

Weller, M., Pegler, C., and Mason, R. (2005). Use of innovative technologies on an e-learning course. *The Internet and Higher Education, 8*(1), 61–71.

Wiggins, G. P., and McTighe, J. (2005). *Understanding by Design* (2nd ed.). Upper Saddle River, NJ: Pearson.

Wild, R. H., Griggs, K. A., and Downing, T. (2002). A framework for e-learning as a tool for knowledge management. *Industrial Management and Data Systems, 102*(7), 371–380.

Willett, C. (2001). Knowledge sharing shifts the power paradigm. In D. Morey, M. Maybury, and B. Thuraissingham (Eds.), *Knowledge Management: Classic and Contemporary Works.* Cambridge, MA: MIT Press.

Zhu, F. X., and McFarland, D. (2005). Towards assurance of learning in business programs: Components and measurements. *Journal of the American Academy of Business, 7*(2), 69–72.

Chapter 5

A Model for E-Learning and Knowledge Management: The Virtual University at Tecnológico de Monterrey

Yolanda Heredia and Francisco J. Cantu

Contents

Introduction

For the past four decades, the concept of educational technology has been evolving into what it is today. Since the early 1950s, efforts to improve the educational process by using some kind of technology, such as radio, television, or audiovisual media, have been evident. The importance of the components has shifted through the years. In the early 1950s and 1960s, the focus was mainly on the means by which information was sent. During the 1970s, communication theory emphasized the process of sending and receiving information with transmitters and receivers. Later the importance was placed on the learning process. In this sense, educational technology attempts to support and improve the educational process when combining instructional methods that are grounded on a learning theory with new models that are based on information and communication technologies (ICT) (Escamilla, 2003).

In the context of globalization, which is characterized by entwined economies and increasing immigration, a growing need for lifelong education has emerged, especially for people who often were excluded from schools and universities. This new channel allows education to reach people who could not attend traditional campus classrooms. All of these forces stimulate the development of more specific educational models. In the last two decades, many universities have incorporated some kind of distance learning into their teaching–learning process. All these resources seem to benefit the teaching–learning process by reaching a more diverse student body. Hence, new educational models have emerged.

Background

Currently there is an identifiable continuum of educational models stretching from the traditional way of teaching in the classroom to a 100% distance education model,

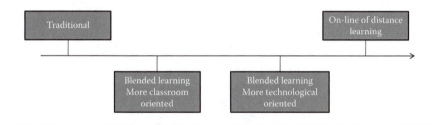

Figure 5.1   Schemes of Educational Models.

through the use of ICTs, as shown in Figure 5.1. First, the traditional way of teaching in a classroom, face to face, is based on a lecture and a chalkboard at the front of the classroom. Distance learning via computer technology today incorporates a learning management system (LMS) or electronic platform. The professor can post syllabi, a calendar, grades, and so forth. The information on the course is static, and requires, as does a traditional class format, a classroom posting. Students can post their homework on electronic platforms, and this is the entire role the platform plays. This simple model is called *Blended Learning* (BL). A further step is a more technology-oriented blended learning in which the professor and his or her students are not in the same classroom; generally, they are geographically distant and use an LMS to post syllabi and a calendar and use all the communication tools of the platforms, but at least two or three times during the semester they attend face-to-face sessions on campus. This model blends the best of both worlds, the virtual and face-to-face. The final online distance education model in which professor and students are far from one another other actually mimics a campus or a classroom. All the course information is posted on the LMS. The students and the professor exchange communications through the LMS platform, since it is the only vehicle that allows them to teach and learn. The professor posts many kinds of learning resources that are available to students at all times. Students and teacher interact frequently on the platform and use other tools to communicate with one another.

Naturally, each model has its own unique character, applied to satisfy specific needs and requirements. Every university creates or modifies the educational model to answer precise student needs in specific social contexts. On the other hand, these models require, in many cases, a clear vision on the part of campus authorities to implement faculty training in the use of the technology, and technical and pedagogical support for these activities. Table 5.1 shows typical faculty and student activities, the type and role of technology employed in the teaching–learning process, and special training requirements to support the LMS for each educational model.

Blended learning is defined as a combination of face-to-face instruction with some elements of the course delivered by technology (Kerres and De Witt, 2003; Osguthorpe and Graham, 2003). There can be many possible arrangements, from the inclusion of more face-to-face components with little technology delivery (such as LMS for syllabi, or e-mail communication between professor and students) to

Table 5.1 Activities and Roles in Educational Models

Model	Professor Activity	Student Activity	Type and Role of Technology	Special Training/Special Support
Traditional Synchronic	Design the course Teach every day course in classroom usually by lecture format Grade student activity Communicate face to face Has office time to attend to students' doubts	Go to classroom during the semester Listen to professor and take notes Do homework individually or in teams Study to take exams	Blackboards (traditional or smart) that help in the classroom process PC's and projector for use by professor in presentations PC's for students to take notes or research information in class	Does not require special training
Blended learning classroom oriented Synchronic	Design the course Teaches every day course in classroom and post syllabus and calendar on LMS Communicate face to face and by e-mail with students Evaluates students' activities Post grades on LMS	Go to classroom during the semester Listen to professor and take notes Review the LMS and get information from it Do homework individually or in teams Send homework by LMS Communicate with professor and classmates face to face and by e-mail Study to take exams Review grades on LMS	Classroom is the center of activity LMS just to publish syllabi, calendar, and grades	Little special training to make use of LMS

Blended learning technological oriented Synchronic and asynchronic	Design the course Post all the course in LMS Communicate by several means (LMS, e-mail, chats) Attend the campus sessions/satellite sessions Evaluates students' activities Post grades on LMS	Review course on LMS Make learning activities individually or in teams Send learning activities by LMS Communicate with professor and classmates by several means (LMS, e-mail, chats) Attend the campus/satellite sessions Take exams in face-to-face sessions Review their notes by LMS	PC, internet, LMS and satellite technology are fundamental to this model Classroom on Campus is necessary Other communication means by internet	Little special training to use of LMS
Online or distance Education Asynchrony	Design the course Post the course on LMS Design learning resources and post them (videos, animations, etc.) Communicate by several methods (LMS, e-mail, chats, mobile means) Teaches on LMS Evaluates students' activities Post grades on LMS	Review course on LMS Perform learning activities individually or in teams Send learning activities by LMS Communicate with professor and classmates by several means (LMS, e-mail, chats) Take exams on LMS Review their notes by LMS	PC, internet, LMS are fundamental to this model Other communication means by internet	Requires training to use LMS as professor and students Need of a support pedagogical team to design, develop the course and resources.

extensive use of technology for face-to-face classes, for example, satellite sessions, and course delivery by LMS with e-learning components. As mentioned earlier, these combinations can be made with several types of technology and used in many different ways, as mentioned above. The main objective of blended learning is to get the best of both methods.

E-learning or distance education usually occurs when professors and students are not in the same place and may be in different time zones. In this sense, communication between them must take place through artificial means, such as printed material sent by mail, telephone, and more recently by ICT. In general, technology allows for both asynchronously and synchronous sessions. To Moore and Kearsley (1996), distance education is planned learning that normally occurs in a place different from the teaching site and, as a result, requires specific techniques of course design, instructional techniques, and methods of communication via electronic and other technology, as well as an infrastructure to support the special organization and administrative arrangements.

It is possible to distinguish three types of education models for distance education: independent study, the remote classroom, and the interactive model based on ICT (Escamilla, 2008). Independent study, based on printed material, is the most "classic" type of distance education technique; it uses printed materials and is known as "correspondent study." Students learn by themselves using the designated material. The material is written as a "guided didactic conversation," so careful reviewing is required since the student is alone with the material (Holmberg, 1998 in Escamilla, 2008).

The second model, the "remote classroom," tries to reproduce from a distance the interactions that occur in the classroom. Generally speaking, this model is a traditional professor is in a classroom and the students utilizing the television or the Internet. Another name for this model is "distributed classroom." It is based on technology that allows for synchronous transmission of material to the student (Bates, 1995; Levenburg and Major, 1998). These models are available only for classes that have such technology. Thus, the instructional design for this model is defined by the available technology and depends more on institutional capacity than on student needs (Heydenrych, 2000).

The third model is based on ICT and uses the Internet exclusively. Materials and communication take place on an LMS. This model is known as online or e-learning. In this model, all the participants are taught in the same context. The communication can be both ways, asynchronous or synchronous. To be successful, this model requires more specific course design and close, guided communication. It can be a constructivist learning environment. These three models are summarized in Figure 5.2

The Education Model at Tecnológico de Monterrey

In this section, we introduce Tecnológico de Monterrey, presenting an overview of the education model on which a description of the institution's e-learning system,

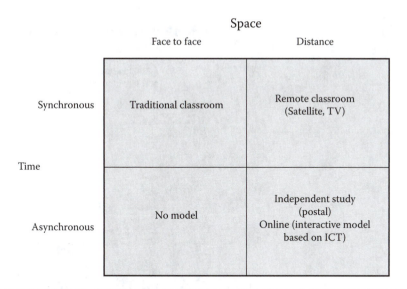

Figure 5.2 Diverse educational models by time or space flexibility.

called the Virtual University, is given in the section titled "The E-Learning Model: The Virtual University."

Tecnológico de Monterrey

Tecnológico de Monterrey was founded in 1943 by Eugenio Garza Sada and a group of businessmen who established EISAC, a nonprofit association to support the institution's operations. Tecnológico de Monterrey is a private institution, independent of and not related to any political party or religious group that operates as an educational institution under the statute of a Free University, granted by a presidential decree. Its mission statement declares that its goal is to prepare people with integrity, ethical standards, and a humanistic outlook, who are internationally competitive in their professional field and, who, at the same time, are good citizens committed to the economic, political, social, and cultural development of their community. Nowadays, Tecnológico de Monterrey is a multicampus university system with 33 campuses throughout the country, as shown in Figure 5.3.

The operation of its campuses is supported by nonprofit, civil associations that are constituted by a group of distinguished leaders who are committed to quality in higher education. Each year, the trustees of these various governance associations meet to establish the goals that guide the decisions needed for achieving the institutional mission, which stresses the development of local communities around the country. In order to raise funds to increase the scholarship program and the investment in infrastructure, Tecnológico de Monterrey organizes national lotteries every year. The institution has achieved recognition for both high academic standards

Figure 5.3   Tecnológico de Monterrey.

and for the culture of entrepreneurship, hard work, efficiency, and responsibility it seeks to instill in its students. These values have motivated alumni from different regions of Mexico to promote the establishment of campuses in their home cities. The institution has accepted the responsibility of responding to the important economic and social challenges of the country's development. Alumni have become directors of successful companies in Mexico and other countries, and an increasing number of graduates are in important positions in government and public service. Thus, Tecnológico de Monterrey is working to become a highly recognized university around the world, for the leadership exercised by alumni in the private, public, and social sectors, and for the research and technology development it carries out to promote a knowledge-based economy by generating incubator and business models, improving public administration and public policies, and creating innovative systems for the sustainable development of local communities.

The Education Model

The education model of Tecnológico de Monterrey focuses on the students and their learning, for which students are held responsible. The professor plays the role of facilitator and guides the students in analyzing problems and discovering relevant knowledge in order to apply it in problem solving of practical situations (Martin, 2002). To achieve these objectives, the education model emphasizes collaborative work and didactic techniques such as problem-based learning, project-oriented learning, and the case-solving method. In this way, knowledge is applied to solve real-life problems; it makes studying meaningful and becomes the object of critical reflection and social commitment. The education model also includes processes that are enhanced by the use of information technologies and telecommunications. Both face-to-face students and online students use computers to do homework assignments, fulfill their learning objectives, and interact with their classmates and professors. The use of computers favors active student participation on the courses, encourages them to assume responsibility in their learning process, and leads to the formation of authentic learning communities. Every semester, symposia and seminars are organized in various academic disciplines to give students the opportunity to learn about the latest trends. These activities, which are a very important part of academic life, help students develop their teamwork and leadership skills. Students take part in the university's social projects, as well as those administered by different organizations within civil society, government agencies, and charitable institutions. The experience obtained this way allows them to become aware of the social reality of other groups, understand the needs of their environment, and apply the knowledge they have acquired by contributing to the country's social and economic development. Through the school's programs, students acquire knowledge and skills to

- Promote the international competitiveness of companies
- Develop business models to compete in a global economy
- Develop business incubator models and networks to contribute to the creation of enterprises
- Collaborate in professionalizing public administration through analyzing and proposing public policies for México's development
- Design innovative models and systems for education, social, economic, and political improvement

The academic programs also encourage students to appreciate a humanistic culture in its diverse manifestations, as well as the historical and cultural identity of the country and its regions. The programs also include reflections on the ethical aspects involved in dilemmas that arise in professional life, as well as activities aimed at developing civic capabilities. Other elements of the education model that reinforce the entrepreneurial culture and encourage technology transfer include business incubators, business accelerators, and technology parks for the creation and attraction of competitive businesses to accelerate regional growth. Through the development and creation of business incubators, high-tech company, and park models for landing companies, new businesses can be set up and jobs generated.*

---

* See http://ruv.itesm.mx.

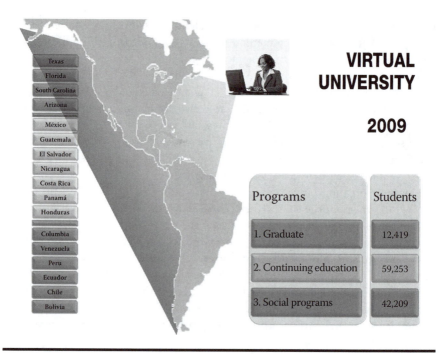

Figure 5.4 Tecnológico de Monterrey's Virtual University.

The E-Learning Model: The Virtual University

The e-learning model at Tecnológico de Monterrey is based on its Virtual University (VU), which has been in operation since 1989. It has become a leading worldwide institution in distance education by offering a variety of online programs. The Virtual University's coverage extends to various Latin American countries and the United States, as shown in Figure 5.4.

The Virtual University offers graduate degree programs, continuing education programs for companies as well as government and nongovernmental organizations, programs for elementary and secondary school teachers, and programs for the development of marginalized communities. In order to do so, it uses learning networks and advanced information and communication technologies.

The E-Learning Education Model

The Virtual University's student-centered education model shifts the emphasis from the teacher to the student as the heart of the learning process. The model enables students to explore and replace the traditional professor's lecture with efficient teaching–learning strategies. The components of the model include the following.

Students

In a student-centered model, students play a more active role and must assume responsibility for their own learning. The advantage student's gain by adopting an active role is the development of new skills, and an increase in their retention capacity. In distance education, the role of the professor is to organize and facilitate the learning process. Professors provide knowledge and design the course contents. Students interact with the professor and their peers, generating new content via research and interaction with classmates.

Self-Directed Learning

Academic activities are carried out by each student, at his or her own personal pace. Self-directed learning promotes an independent kind of learning and allows a student to develop abilities, attitudes, and values that can help them perform better in a global society.

Some of these self-study activities include the following:

a. Reviewing articles and reading material
b. Reviewing links and databases
c. Reviewing contents of the Web page
d. Taking exams
e. Analyzing and reviewing cases, situations, and problems
f. Completing homework assignments

Collaborative Learning

Collaborative learning is a socialization experience that is oriented toward getting students to play an active role in their learning via interaction with the professor and their fellow students, often located in different geographic regions. Collaborative activities include

a. Problem solving
b. Case solving
c. Collaborative activities
d. Exchange of ideas and opinions
e. Carrying out projects
f. Discussion, analysis, and debates

Faculty

Courses are designed by outstanding faculty members who are specialists in the institution's various content areas and are supported by a group of educational technology specialists who enhance materials using various technologies.

Tutoring

The model requires direct monitoring of learning by personal tutors. The tutor is a professor who is a specialist in the field and can facilitate learning and support students during the entire educational process.

Tutoring is provided by both the professor and the tutor, through the following media: interactive forums on the technological platform, e-mail, instant messages, telephone and, on special occasions, by radiochat (voice broadcasting).

Meaningful Learning

Classes promote meaningful learning as students apply their knowledge, skills, and attitudes in a real-world context. Knowledge is applied to solving real-life problems, which makes studying meaningful and becomes the object of critical reflection and social commitment. Everything learned has an impact on students' development and as individuals and in the workplace.

Course

The course content is provided online in a manner that facilitates learning over the Internet. The courses encourage research and information queries using digital libraries and other databases. Course design offers flexibility in time and space, so students can work at their own speed.

Teaching Techniques

The education model centers on the use of advanced teaching techniques that help students to learn collaboratively through problem solving and case analysis, as well as project design.

Information Technologies

The model requires the use of a technological platform and diverse information technologies to provide students with a space for interaction, querying, and learning. The VU's educational model promotes meaningful learning using technologies in a learning environment. As a result, students develop new and useful skills and knowledge for their personal and professional life. This is achieved by

- Teamwork
- Technology utilization
- Cases, problems, and solution generation
- Information search and analyses

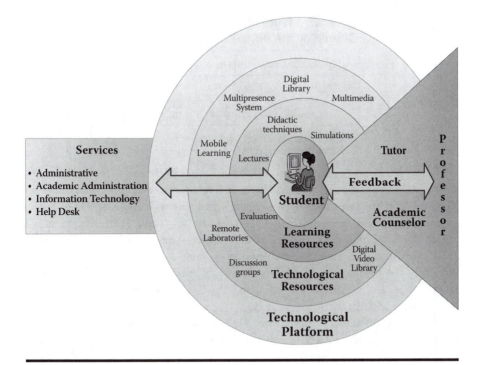

Figure 5.5   Elements of the e-learning course delivery process.

Blackboard

Blackboard, used in many universities, is a flexible, proprietary LMS platform. It contains basic functions to create the documents for the administration of a course. It is based on Web technologies and has the following characteristics:

- It offers the possibility of applying Web-based systems that help design a course creatively and that use electronic resources to support learning.
- It is governed by international standards (IMS) for content development.
- It allows for synchronic and nonsynchronic communication.
- It is easy to use and does not require extensive training.

Figure 5.5 summarizes the main elements of the e-learning model developed at the Virtual University over the years.

The E-Learning Programs

The e-learning programs offered by the Virtual University follow the education model described in the section titled "The Education Model at Tecnológico De Monterrey" and in the subsection titled "The E-Learning Education Model." There

Table 5.2 Types of e-Learning Programs Offered by the Virtual University

• Undergraduate courses
• Graduate programs
• Continuing education programs
• Social development programs

are four types of programs, as shown in Table 5.2. The Virtual University does not award undergraduate degrees. However, undergraduate courses are given online. The VU's graduate degree programs focus on the areas of business, engineering, information technologies, public management, the humanities, and education. The continuing education programs are offered to companies and the government for professional training and skill development in employees. The social programs are offered by Tecnológico de Monterrey and the Virtual University in alliance with federal, state, and municipal governments in rural areas for basic training and the development of skills by their residents.

The following statistics pertain to 2009: 17,330 undergraduate students were taking online courses; 12,419 students were enrolled in graduate programs; 59,253 employees took continuing education programs; and 42,209 people benefited from courses in social program courses.

The e-learning graduate programs offered through the Virtual University are displayed in Table 5.3. These programs are in the areas of business, information technologies, engineering, public management, and the humanities.

The e-learning graduate programs in education offered through the Virtual University are shown in Table 5.4. There are three master programs, with various specializations, and a research PhD program in educational innovation.

A Knowledge Management Model for E-Learning

This section outlines the main components of a knowledge management (KM) model that is under development to support the e-learning model at Tecnológico de Monterrey's Virtual University. This model is at the core of a research project at Tecnológico de Monterrey (Cantu and Heredia, 2009).

Knowledge management investigates the processes of knowledge creation, storage, distribution, and use (Liebowitz, 1999). There are various approaches and methodologies to KM (Liebowitz and Beckman, 1998). This KM methodology includes the following steps: identify, collect, select, store, share, apply, create, and sell knowledge within an organization with the intention of developing a corporate memory to store and distribute information and knowledge relevant for business operations. The KM model proposed in this chapter agrees with the e-learning

Table 5.3   e-Learning Graduate Programs

• Master's in Business Administration
• Master's in Marketing
• Master's in e-Commerce
• Master's in Innovation and Business Development
Information Technologies
• Master's in Administration of Information Technologies
Business
Engineering
• Master's in Science with specialization in Quality Systems and Productivity
Public Management
• Master's in Public Administration
Humanities
• Master's in Humanistic Studies

Table 5.4   e-Learning Graduate Programs in Education

Master's of Education
• Teaching and Learning Processes
• Cognitive Development
• High School Teaching
• Science Teaching
Master's of Education: Administration of Educational Institutions
• Basic Education
• Higher Education
Master's in Educational Technology
• Innovative Media for Learning
• Corporate Training
PhD in Educational Innovation

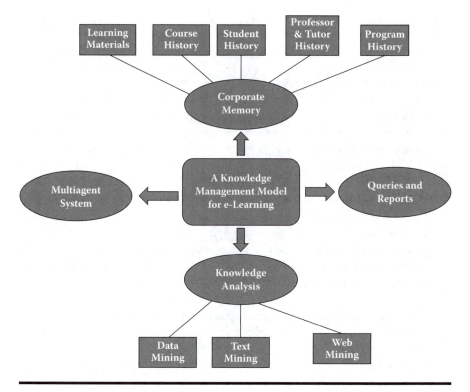

Figure 5.6 Elements of the Knowledge Management Model for e-learning.

model displayed in Figure 5.3 and provides operational support by means of the elements displayed in Figure 5.6.

An E-Learning Corporate Memory

The e-learning corporate memory is a set of entities defined by their attributes, whereby each of the entities is represented by a repository that stores information such as learning materials, courses, students, professors, and tutors. The entities and their repositories are as follows:

Learning materials: This repository stores learning materials for every course offered online each term. The materials are kept online for student consultation during the term. These materials include presentations, videos, case studies, and others.

Courses: This repository stores information about the courses offered each term, including the course syllabi. It also stores interactions and discussions that take place among professors, tutors, and students through discussion forums.

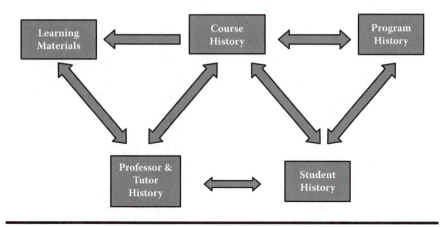

Figure 5.7   Interactions among entities of the e-learning corporate memory.

Students: This repository stores information about students enrolled in every course each term for each program, including scores, homework assignments, projects, and student interactions.

Professors and tutors: This repository stores information about professors and tutors who support each course each term for a given program.

Programs: This repository stores information about the e-learning programs offered at the graduate level or for the continuing education and social programs.

The Blackboard platform provides the means and facilities for storing information from each of these repositories. Interactions among these repositories are shown in Figure 5.7.

Other Elements of the KM Model

The remaining elements of the KM model for e-learning are as follows.

Knowledge Analysis

Knowledge analysis is about the use of either data, text, or Web mining techniques to extract knowledge and useful information from each of the components of the e-learning corporate memory to assist program directors and academic administrators and other decision makers in the design and updating of online academic programs (Cantu et al., 2006). For instance, we can infer the likelihood of student success based on transcript record, SAT scores, university of precedence, and the program of enrollment. We have done student profiling for scholarship allocation as well as text and Web mining for international student exchange and course revalidation (Rios and Cantu, 2006). We can also extend the capabilities of Blackboard's Safe Assign to detect plagiarism in student projects and assignments.

Multiagent System

The use of multiagent system (MAS) technology to automate and provide "intelligence" to the e-Leaning model is another ongoing project that builds upon previous experiences with the MAS technology in knowledge distribution (Aguirre et al., 2001) or managing research assets (Cantu and Ceballos, 2010). E-learning is modeled as an electronic institution in which software agents monitor and execute the transactions that take place around online learning processes (Ceballos and Cantu, 2009). Agents also monitor external events on internet Web pages and, through Web services, update the corporate memory repositories and perform data consistency operations (Ceballos and Cantu, 2007).

Queries and Reports

Finally, queries and report facilities are available at user convenience to obtain information about the various components of the e-learning programs. Data cubes and other visualization techniques are employed to answer queries and obtain views of repository data.

Conclusions

We have presented a description of Tecnológico de Monterrey's Virtual University, its e-learning model for distance education and its online programs, and we have given statistics about student enrolment and social impact. Operations at the Virtual University started in 1989 with satellite transmission and have evolved over the last 20 years with the development of the Internet and with an outreach through the Americas with various kinds of programs that include graduate academic degrees, continuing education, and social programs. The graduate academic degrees are in the areas of business, information technologies, engineering, public management, and the humanities. An ongoing research project for constructing a KM system to administer the operations of the e-learning programs has been outlined, and it will continue under development in the next few years.

Acknowledgment

We acknowledge the leadership and support of Dr. Rafael Rangel Sostmann, President of Tecnológico de Monterrey, Professor Carlos Cruz Limón, Vice President of Institutional Relationships and Development, and former President of the Virtual University, and Professor Patricio López del Puerto, President of the Virtual University. We also recognize Dr. Alberto Bustani Adem, President of the

Monterrey Metropolitan Zone of Tecnológico de Monterrey, for his support for the Knowledge Management and E-Learning research project.

References

Aguirre, J. L., Brena, R., and Cantu, F. J. (2001). Multiagent-based knowledge networks. *Expert Systems with Applications an International Journal*, No. 20, pp. 65–75, Elsevier.

Bates, A. W. (1995). *Technology, Open Learning and Distance Education*. New York: Routledge Publishers.

Cantu, F. J. and Heredia, Y. (2009). A Knowledge Management Approach for On-Line Education. Technical Report, Center for Intelligent Systems, Tecnológico de Monterrey, Mexico.

Cantú, F. J., and Ceballos, H. G. (2010). A multiagent knowledge and information network approach for managing research assets. *Expert Systems with Applications and International Journal*, doi:10.1016/j.eswa.2010.01.

Cantú, F., Garza, L., Robles A., and Morales-Menendez R. (2006). Learning and using Bayesian networks for diagnosis and user profiling. *Proceedings of the Twelfth Americas Conference on Information Systems—AMCIS*. pp. 1402–1409. Acapulco, México.

Ceballos, H. and Cantu, F. J. (2009). Towards a causal framework for intelligent agents development. *Proceedings of the Special Session of the Eight International Conference on Artificial Intelligence (MICAI 2009)*. pp. 67–72. IEEE: Los Alamitos, CA.

Escamilla, J. (2003). Selección y uso de tecnología educativa. México, D. F. Trillas.

Escamilla, J. (2008). Hacia un aprendizaje flexible sin fronteras y limitaciones tradicionales in Tecnología educativa en un modelo de educación a distancia centrado en la persona Lozano A. y Burgos, V. Eds., México, D. F., LIMUSA.

Heydenrych, J. (2000). A comparison of the remote classroom (rc) approach and the guided independent study (gis) approach for the university of South Africa. *Progressio*, 22 (1).

Kerres, M. and De Witt, C. (2003). A didactical framework for the design of blended learning arrangements. *Journal of Education Media*. 28 (2–3): 101–113.

Levenburg, N. and Major, H. (1998). Distance Learning: Implications for Higher Education in the 21st Century. The Technology Source.

Martín, M. (2002). El Modelo Educativo del Tecnológico de Monterrey. ITESM: Monterrey, Mexico.

Moore, M. and Kearsley, G. (1996). *Distance Education: A Systems View*. Belmont, CA: Wadsworth Publishing Company.

Osguthorpe, R. T. and Graham, C. R. (2003). Blended learning environments: Definitions and directions. *The Quarterly Review of Distance Education* 4(3): 227–233.

Rios, M. T. and Cantú, F. J. (2006). Knowledge discovery in academic registrar data bases using source mining: Data and text. *Proceedings of the Twelfth Americas Conference on Information Systems—AMCIS*, pp. 1392–1401. Acapulco, México.

Liebowitz, J. (1999). *Knowledge Management Handbook*. CRC Press, Boca Raton, FL.

Liebowitz, J. and Beckman, T. (1998). *Knowledge Organizations*. Saint Lucie Press Washington, DC.

Chapter 6

A Learning Portfolio Management System for Analyzing Student Web-Based Problem-Solving Behaviors

Gwo-Jen Hwang and Jason C.H. Chen

Contents

Introduction

In order to be competitive and effective, today's educational institution needs to be more knowledge and learning oriented. Therefore, to achieve the ultimate educational goal, it is essential to improve student learning processes such as individual learning, innovation, collective learning, and collaborative problem solving (King, 2007; Liebowitz, 2007).

In the past decades, researchers have paid much attention to applying computer and network technologies to instruction. The development and applications of various learning models, systems, or tools, such as computer Mindtools (Jonassen, 1999), Computer-Supported Collaborative Learning (CSCL, e.g., Harasim, 1999), Computer-Supported Intentional Learning Environments, Computer-Integrated Classroom (CiC, e.g., Eshetet al., 2000), computer-assisted learning diagnosis (Hwang, 2003; Hwang et al. 2008c; Peng et al., 2009), and mobile/ubiquitous learning (Hwang et al., 2008b; Chu et al., 2008) have demonstrated the benefits of such technology-enhanced educational approaches.

Earlier studies on technology-enhanced learning focused on developing computer-assisted instruction (CAI) systems that interacted with students by showing rich instructional information with the multimedia approach (Barrett and Lally, 1999; Gang et al., 1996; Pui and William, 1996; Robert, 1996; Sally, 1996). Later, the popularity of the Internet and the World Wide Web motivated efforts toward integrating Web-based learning activities into the curriculum (Apkarian and Dawer, 2000; Chang, 2001; Tsai et al., 2001; Tsai and Tsai, 2003; Huang and Lu, 2003; Hwang, 1998; Hwang, 2003).

Researchers have indicated that one significant benefit for students to learn in a Web-based learning environment is the participation of learning activities in which they can learn as active and self-directed participants (Bilal, 2000; Hess, 1999; Tsai, 2001; Song and Salvendy, 2003). As the Internet consists of huge number of Web sites that contain rich information, Web-based learning activities are usually relevant to information-searching missions; consequently, many research issues concerning learning with Web information-searching tasks have been raised in recent years, such as the strategies of information seeking and use, the skill of processing Web information, and the development of new environments that enable teachers to observe and analyze the information-seeking behaviors of students in Web-based learning environments.

Researchers found that Internet novice users had difficulty searching information effectively and efficiently on the Web (Dias et al., 1999; Marchionini, 1995). That is, it is important to provide a learning environment to train novice users to use search engines to collect information for problem solving and to observe and analyze their Web information-searching behaviors (Hwang et al., 2008a). Nevertheless, owing to the lack of technical support, most researchers have adopted qualitative methods using interviews about students' perceptions of, and feelings about, their experiences with Web information-searching tasks; therefore, the reliability of these studies are doubtful unless a careful check can be made on the videotapes of Web traversal activities or verbalization during traversal, which is known to be time consuming.

To cope with this problem, researchers have tried to develop Web-search learning environments for recording and analyzing the problem-solving behaviors of students (Hwang et al., 2008a; Tseng et al., 2009). In this study, the learning portfolio management system of a Web-based learning environment, *Meta-Analyzer*, is presented. With this system, teachers and researchers can efficiently and effectively observe and analyze the learning behaviors of students in using search engines to find information for problem solving.

The chapter proceeds as follows. The first section presents some of the background literature. The next section builds the framework of the learning environment for Web-based problem solving. The third section illustrates a learning portfolio management system for analyzing Web-based problem-solving behaviors. The final section summarizes the chapter with contributions on the proposed learning portfolio management system.

Learning Environment for Web-Based Problem Solving

In the past decade, many academic reports have indicated the importance of studying the information about searching behaviors of students on the Internet (Drabenstott, 2003; Ford et al., 2003; Hölscher and Strube, 2000; Hwang et al., 2008a; Tsai, 2004; Tsai and Tsai, 2003). Moreover, researchers also indicated that students who have advanced online searching and evaluating strategies may develop more accurate and in-depth understanding of certain topics; that is, it becomes an important issue to know how students use search strategies for problem solving on the Internet and how to help students in improving their problem-solving ability (Hoffman et al., 2003). Therefore, many studies (e.g., Poindexter and Heck, 1999; Tsai and Tsai, 2003) have been conducted to analyze the learning behaviors of students in using search engines to collect information for problem solving. Furthermore, researchers have tried to develop Web-search learning environments for recording students' problem-solving behaviors when using search engines (Hwang et al., 2008a; Tseng et al., 2009). In this section, Meta-Analyzer, a Web-based learning environment for conducting problem-solving activities, is presented. Meta-Analyzer consists of a Web-based learning system for problem solving that comprises a search engine and a learning portfolio management system, as shown in Figure 6.1.

The learning system includes a "Question and Answer" module that presents questions prepared by the teacher to individual students. Students are asked to use the provided search engine to seek information related to the questions. The "Web Page Analyzing" module will parse the data returned from the search engine and reorganize the data in an intermediate format. The "Presentation Module" then

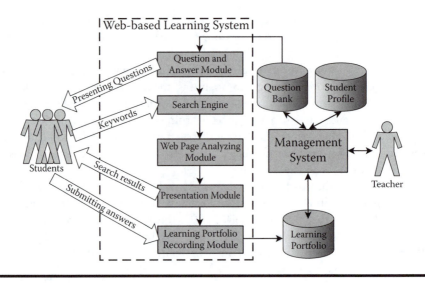

Figure 6.1 A Meta-Analyzer model.

shows the results to the students in a Web-link/abstraction form. The "Learning Portfolio Recording" module will record every detail of the students' behaviors in seeking the information for answering the questions, including the answers students submitted to the learning system. The collection of these modules becomes the knowledge base of the proposed learning portfolio management systems.

Figure 6.2 presents the problem-solving interface for students. It consists of three operation areas: on the left side, a question and answer area is provided; on the upper-right side, the information searching area is located; on the lower-right side, the Web pages found by the search engine are depicted.

After logging into Meta-Analyzer, the students can input keywords to search information, and then browse the Web pages that might be relevant to the questions prepared by the teacher. The entire user portfolio, including the keywords, the browsed Web pages, and the user behaviours on the Web will be recorded in the server for further analysis. Moreover, the control buttons listed on the top of the window provide several useful functions for information searching, such as bookmark management and system demonstration.

Figure 6.3 illustrates an example of presenting the search results. The students can click on the links to browse Web pages found by the search engine. While browsing a Web page, students can copy and paste the text of the Web page to the answer area and make further revisions to the text for answering the question. Once the students submit their answers, with the learning capability of Meta-Analyzer, the next question will be generated by Meta-Analyzer and sent back to the students. The collective learning process will be repeated until all of the questions prepared by the teacher are answered. In addition, the students can insert the Web page to the bookmark list if it is highly relevant to the question to be answered.

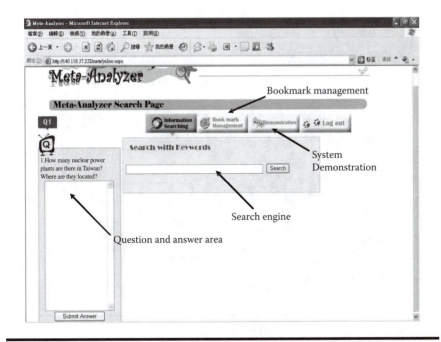

Figure 6.2   Problem-solving interface of Meta-Analyzer.

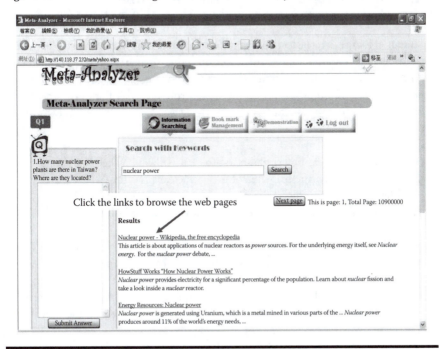

Figure 6.3   Illustrative example of browsing a Web page for problem solving.

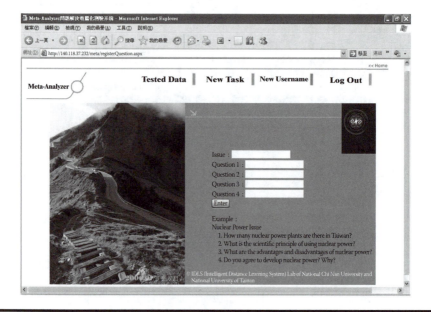

Figure 6.4 Interface for managing the question bank.

Learning Portfolio Management System for Analyzing Web-Based Problem-Solving Behaviors

As shown in Figure 6.1, the learning portfolio management system assists the teacher in maintaining three databases: the question bank, student profiles, and learning portfolios. Figure 6.4 demonstrates the interface for managing the question bank, which keeps a set of questions for each problem-solving issue. For example, the following four questions are included in the "Nuclear electric power in Taiwan" issue (Hwang et al., 2008a):

1. How many nuclear power plants are there in Taiwan? Where are they located?
2. What is the scientific principle of using nuclear power?
3. What are the advantages and disadvantages of nuclear power?
4. Do you agree to develop more nuclear power plants? Why?

Figure 6.5 shows the interface for creating and updating accounts for students. Note that the student accounts are associated with the problem-solving issues created by the same teacher. Only the students whose accounts are created by the teacher are allowed to browse and answer the questions of those issues created by that teacher. Therefore, the teacher has full privileges in managing the Web-based problem-solving activities.

Figures 6.6a, 6.6b, and 6.6c show the teacher interfaces for browsing the information-searching portfolios of individual students. In Figure 6.6a, relevant

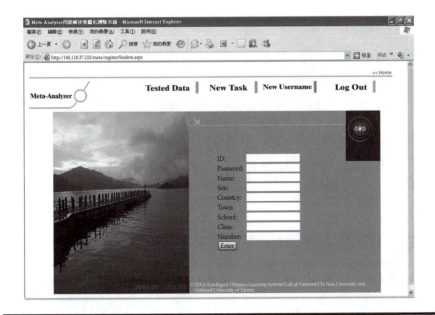

Figure 6.5   Interface for creating and updating accounts for students.

information concerning the answers of students for the corresponding questions is presented, including the question ID, the time of submitting the answers, and the answers. Moreover, a scoring menu is also provided.

Figure 6.6b shows the information-seeking records for individual students. The displayed information includes the answer to each question, the Web pages that have been visited, the browsing time for each Web page, and so forth. The "operation code" represents different behaviours of each learner, where 1 indicates "input keywords"; 2, "browsing Web pages"; 3, "insert Web page to bookmark list"; 4, "remove the Web page from the bookmark list"; 5, "Web page selection"; 6, "revise the submitted answer." With the assistance of these records, the teacher can trace

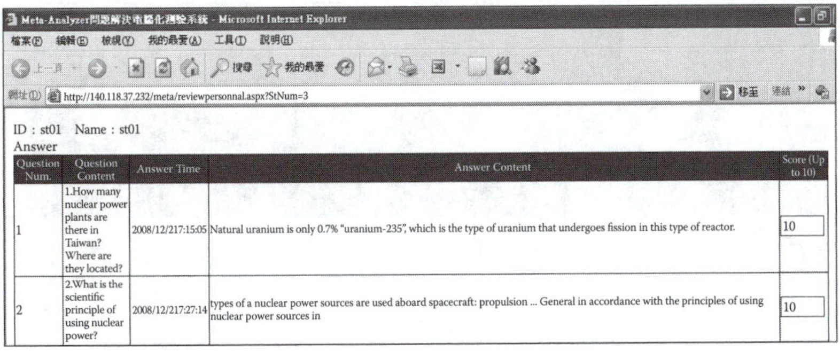

Figure 6.6a   Interface for browsing answers submitted by the students.

Question Num.	Start Time	Second	Operation	Keywords or URL	URL Title
1	2008/12/217:10:09		1	nuclear power	
1	2008/12/217:10:31	00:00:00	2	http://en.wikipedia.org/wiki/Nuclear_power	Nuclear power-Wikipedia, the free encyclopedia
1	2008/12/217:10:40	00:00:09	2	http://www.darvill.clara.net/altenerg/nuclear.htm	Energy Resources: Nuclear power
1	2008/12/217:13:29	00:02:49	2	http://www.darvill.clara.net/altenerg/nuclear.htm	Energy Resources: Nuclear power
1	2008/12/217:13:29		4	http://www.darvill.clara.net/altenerg/nuclear.htm	Energy Resources: Nuclear power
1	2008/12/217:14:23		6	Natural uranium is only 0.7% "uranium-235", which is the type of uranium that undergoes fission in this type of reactor.	
2	2008/12/217:20:39		1	scientific principle	
2	2008/12/217:20:41	00:07:12	2	http://www.aeriagloris.com/HowToLearn/TheScientificPrinciple.htm	The Scientific Principle
2	2008/12/217:20:57		1	the scientific principle of using nuclear power	
2	2008/12/217:21:05	00:00:24	2	http://www.theiet.org/factfiles/energy/nuclear-principles.cfm?type=pdf	Principles of Nuclear Power
2	2008/12/217:22:57	00:01:52	2	http://www.stormsmith.nl/report20050803/Introduction.pdf	Nuclear Power: the Energy Balance Inroduction: General principles ...
2	2008/12/217:25:56		1	the scientific principle of using nuclear power	
2	2008/12/217:26:14	00:03:17	2	http://www.hse.gov.uk/aboutus/meetings/committees/ilgra/pppa.htm	The Precautionary Principle: Policy and Application

Figure 6.6b Interface for browsing the information-seeking behaviors of students.

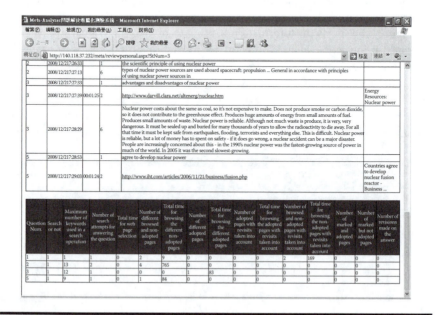

Figure 6.6c   Interface for presenting statistical results from information-seeking records.

the detailed content of each Web page browsed by the students via the corresponding links.

Figure 6.6c presents the statistical results by analyzing the information-seeking records for individual students based on 13 predefined indicators (Hwang et al., 2008). The quantitative indicators are as follows:

- Total time for Web page selection
- Number of different browsed and unadopted pages
- Total time for browsing the different unadopted pages
- Number of browsed and unadopted pages with revisits taken into account
- Number of marked but unadopted pages
- Number of revisions made on the answer
- Number of different adopted pages
- Total time for browsing the different adopted pages for the first time
- Number of times the adopted pages were revisited
- Total time for revisiting the adopted pages
- Number of marked and adopted pages
- Maximum number of keywords used in a search operation
- Number of search attempts for answering the question

Such indicators are very helpful to teachers; they show how students obtain answers and what their barriers in seeking the relevant information are.

Conclusions

Electronic Learning portfolio has been widely known and implemented in the past decade. It provides students and teachers a way to collect evidence for judging the learning status of students (e.g., learning achievements and problems encountered) as well as the effectiveness of the teaching program. Burch (1997) indicated that learning portfolios can reveal and summarize the state of the teaching program; therefore, they can provide valuable insights concerning what students know and how they construct knowledge. As training novice users to use search engines to collect information for problem solving has been recognized as an important objective of modern education, it has become a challenging issue to develop new mechanisms or systems for managing such complex and numerous learning records.

A good management system does not ensure a good organization, but it enables it. However, with a knowledge and learning module embedded in the system, the result shows that the system improves student learning performance in the educational environment. Furthermore, the learning portfolio management system presented in this chapter provides several innovative functions that make it different from the traditional systems. These functions include the recording and tracking functions for the information-seeking behaviors of students and the statistical function based on 13 predefined indicators. Such functions are helpful to teachers in analyzing the learning status of students as well as the effectiveness of the teaching program; therefore, this management system has won acceptance by teachers and researchers in Taiwan.

References

Apkarian, J. and Dawer, A. (2000). Interactive control education with virtual presence on the web. In *Proceedings of American Control Conference*, June 2000, Chicago, 3985–3990.

Barrett, E. and Lally, V. (1999). Gender differences in an on-line learning environment. *Journal of Computer Assisted Learning, 15*(1), 48–60.

Bilal, D. (2000). Children's use of the Yahooligans! Web search engine: I. Cognitive, physical, and affective behaviors on fact-based search tasks. *Journal of the American Society for Information Science, 51*(7), 646–665.

Burch, C. B. (1997). Finding out what's in their heads: Using teaching portfolios to assess English education students and programs. In K. B. Yancey and I. Weiser, (Eds.), *Situating Portfolios: Four Perspectives* (pp. 263–277). Logan: Utah State University Press.

Chang, C. C. (2001). Construction and evaluation of a web-based learning portfolio system: An electronic assessment tool. *Innovations in Education and Teaching International, 38*(2), 144–155.

Chu, H. C., Hwang, G. J., Huang, S. X., and Wu, T. T. (2008). A knowledge engineering approach to developing E-libraries for mobile learning. *Electronic Library, 26*(3), 303–317.

Dias, P., Gomes, M. J., and Correia, A. P. (1999). Disorientation in hypermedia environments: Mechanisms to support navigation. *Journal of Educational Computing Research, 20*(2), 93–117.

Drabenstott, K. M. (2003). Do non-domain experts enlist the strategies of domain experts? *Journal of the American Society for Information Science and Technology, 54*(9), 836–854.

Eshet, Y., Klemes, J., and Henderson, L. (2000). Under the Microscope: factors influencing student outcomes in a computer integrated classroom. *Journal of Computers in Mathematics and Science Teaching, 19*(3), 211–236.

Ford, N., Miller, D., and Moss, N. (2003). Web search strategies and approaches to studying. *Journal of the American Society for Information Science and Technology, 54*(6), 473–489.

Gang, Z., Jason, T. L., and Peter, A. N. (1996). Curriculum knowledge representation and manipulation in knowledge-based tutoring systems. *IEEE Transactions on Knowledge and Data Engineering, 8*(5), 679–689.

Harasim, L. (1999). A framework for online learning: The virtual-U. *Computer, 32*(9), 44–49.

Hess, B. (1999). Graduate student cognition during information retrieval using the World Wide Web: A pilot study. *Computers and Education, 33*(1), 1–13.

Hoffman, J. L., Wu, H.-K., Krajcik, J. S., and Soloway, E. (2003). The nature of learners' science. Content understandings with the use of on-line resources. *Journal of Research in Science Teaching, 40*(3), 323–346.

Hölscher, C., and Strube, G. (2000). Web search behavior of Internet experts and newbies. *Computer Network, 33*(1–6), 337–346.

Huang, H. P., and Lu, C. H. (2003). Java-based distance learning environment for electronic instruments. *IEEE Transactions on Education, 46*(1), 88–94.

Hwang, G. J. (1998). A tutoring strategy supporting system for distance learning on computer networks. *IEEE Transactions on Education,* 41(4), 343–351.

Hwang, G. J. (2003). A concept map model for developing intelligent tutoring systems, *Computers and Education,* 40(3), 217–235.

Hwang, G. J., Tsai, P. S., Tsai, C. C., and Tseng, J. C. R. (2008a). A novel approach for assisting teachers in analyzing student web-searching behaviors. *Computers and Education, 52*(1), 926–938.

Hwang, G. J., Tsai, C. C., and Yang, S. J. H. (2008b). Criteria, Strategies and Research Issues of Context-Aware Ubiquitous Learning. *Educational Technology and Society, 11*(2), 81–91.

Hwang, G. J., Tseng, J. C. R., and Hwang, G. H. (2008c). Diagnosing student learning problems based on historical assessment records. *Innovations in Education and Teaching International, 45*(1), 77–89.

Jonassen, D. H. (1999). *Computers as Mindtools for Schools, Engaging Critical Thinking.* Englewood Cliffs, NJ: Prentice-Hall.

King, W. R. (2007). Keynote paper: knowledge management: a systems perspective. *International Journal of Business and Systems,* 1(1), 5–28.

Liebowitz, J. (2007). Keynote paper: Developing knowledge and learning strategies in mobile organizations, *International Journal of Mobile Learning and Organisation,* 1(1), 5–14.

Marchionini, G. (1995). Information Seeking in Electronic Environments. Cambridge University Press, New York.

Peng, H., Chuang, P. Y., Hwang, G. J., Chu, H. C., Wu, T. T., and Huang, S. X. (2009). Ubiquitous performance-support system as Mindtool: A case study of instructional decision making and learning assistant. *Educational Technology and Society,* 12(1), 107–120.

Poindexter, S. E., and Heck, B. S. (1999). Using the web in your courses: What can you do? What should you do?. *IEEE Control System Magazine, 19*(1), 83–92.

Pui, M. L., and William, G. S. (1996). Developing and implementing interactive multimedia in education. *IEEE Transactions on Education, 39*(3), 430–435.

Robert, O. H. (1996). Teaching in a computer classroom with a hyperlinked, interactive book. *IEEE Transactions on Education, 39*(3), 327–335.

Sally, W. L. (1996). A new approach to interactive tutorial software for engineering education. *IEEE Transactions Education, 39*(3*)*, 399–408.

Song, G. and Salvendy, G. (2003). A framework for reuse of user experience in Web browsing. *Behaviour and Information Technology, 22*(2), 79–90.

Tsai, C.C. (2001). The interpretation construction design model for teaching science and its applications to Internet-based instruction in Taiwan. *International Journal of Educational Development, 21*(5), 401–15.

Tsai, C. C. (2004). Information commitments in Web-based learning environments. *Innovations in Education and Teaching International, 41*(1), 105–112.

Tsai, C. C., Liu, E. Z. F., Lin, S. S. J., and Yuan, S. M. (2001). A networked peer assessment system based on a Vee heuristic. *Innovations in Education and Teaching International, 38*(3), 220–30.

Tsai, M. J., and Tsai, C. C. (2003). Information searching strategies in web-based science learning: The role of Internet self-efficacy. *Innovations in Education and Teaching International*, *40*(1), 3–50.

Tseng, J. C. R., Hwang, G. J., Tsai, P. S., and Tsai, C. C. (2009). Meta-Analyzer: A web-based learning environment for analyzing student information searching behaviors, *International Journal of Innovative Computing, Information and Control*, *5*(3), 1–13.

Chapter 7

The Antecedents and Outcomes of Online Knowledge-Sourcing Behavior: The Influence of Computer Attitudes and Learning Styles

Li-An Ho and Binshan Lin

Contents

Introduction

It is widely acknowledged that developed economies have gradually transformed over the past 50 years. As Grant (1996) points out, organizational resources and capabilities are the principal source of sustainable competitive advantages, and that knowledge is the most important strategic resource of the firm. This increased emphasis on organizational capability and knowledge has led to the development of the knowledge-based view of the firm (Spender, 1996). Numerous researchers and practitioners from various disciplines, such as sociology, economics, and management sciences, generally agree that intangible assets, such as knowledge, have been at the center of further organizational development toward greater performance (Drucker, 1993). In fact, knowledge is posited as a strategic advantage in an organization that helps organizations maintain their competitive ability and is critical for organizational innovation (Jantunen, 2005). Therefore, the success of enterprises in this information-based economy is critically dependent on the adaptation and application of new and existing knowledge assets on key business processes (Ndlela and du Toit, 2001; Teece, 1998).

O'Leary (1998) suggests that the function of knowledge management (KM) is to ensure that organizations are able to access and reuse existing knowledge to improve business operations. However, the results of an effective KM specify that the members of an organization be able to access and apply knowledge in order to improve their business operations (2007). Chae et al. (2005) state that the distribution and coordinated use of knowledge is in itself a complex system within the social network of an organization. Therefore, one of the key issues underlying the knowledge-based view of the firm is to understand how knowledge is integrated in organizations to create organizational capability (Barnett and Hansen, 1996). That is, rather than focusing on a particular factor, such as the IT infrastructure, the successful implementation of KM involves development of the knowledge-sharing culture as well as the coordination of people, technology, and technique within an enterprise (Bhatt, 2001).

The outcome of an individual's KM ability (i.e., his or her effectiveness in accessing and using knowledge) is influenced by the method and extent of knowledge-sourcing activities (Gray and Meister, 2004; Kwok and Gao, 2006). Gray and Meister define a knowledge-sourcing method as "a specific mechanism by which an individual accesses another's knowledge" (p. 821), including those recently proposed in the KM literature, such as knowledge repositories, virtual communities of practice, information seeking, knowledge trading, etc. In fact, individuals learn from personal experience or the experiences of others (Levitt and March, 1988) through the methods of knowledge sourcing, which is sometimes viewed as generically similar (Davenport et al., 1998; Earl, 2001). However, it is evident that different, or combinations of, methods often result in different knowledge utilization dynamics (Choi and Lee, 2003; Hansen et al., 1999; Zairi and Al-Mashari, 2005). Past research demonstrates positive correlations between knowledge-sourcing activities and a number of factors, such as network technology (Fontes, 2005), information technology (IT) investment, individual IT acceptance, IT training (Lin et al., 2007), technological listening archetypes (Gassmann and Gaso, 2004), employees' intellectual property (Ito and Wakasugi, 2007), learning motivation (i.e., job characteristics, sense of achievement, responsibility, professional growth, recognition) (Lin et al., 2007), cognitive style (e.g., learning style), interpersonal trust (Young and Tseng, 2008) and knowledge structure (Korthauer and Koubek, 1994), etc.

Furthermore, Chen and Lin (2004) examine the effect of environment, knowledge attribute, organizational climate, and firm characteristics on knowledge-sourcing decisions. Their study suggests that firms are more likely to develop knowledge internally under four conditions: (1) if the firm is less dynamic and munificent; (2) if the knowledge is more specific to the employees; (3) if the employees possess higher levels of intention, autonomy, and requisite variety; and (4) if the employees have abundant development experience and sufficient capabilities. Thus, the literature indicates that the outcome of KM is the result of employee' knowledge-sourcing activities, which may be influenced by the readiness and preference of the organization (e.g., IT investment, provision of necessary promotion and training, accommodating reward systems, organizational culture, knowledge structure, etc.) as well as the individual employee (motivation, computer literacy, learning style, etc.). However, beyond general assertions that employees' personal preferences for online organizational knowledge will lead to beneficial KM outcomes, KM literature offers no testable theoretical model to explain such connections.

This study addresses this shortfall by presenting a new theoretical model that focuses on the extent to which an individual accesses other employees' expertise, experience, insights, and opinions in an electronic environment. This study elicits the determinants of the KM outcome in technological companies in Taiwan. Specifically, this study investigates the effect of individual employee's computer attitudes and learning style and how they affect knowledge-sourcing activity, and their consequent influence on the outcome of KM capability. A structural equation modeling approach is thus employed to test this model.

Literature Review and Theory Development

The Relationship between Computer Attitude and Knowledge-Sourcing Activity

Lua et al. (2009) found that users' perceived usefulness and perceived enjoyment significantly influence their attitude toward using computers, which in turn impact their behavioral intention. Ranaweera et al. (2008) contend that users' technology perceptions have fundamental relevance to online behaviors. Furthermore, Lin et al. (2007) conclude that technology readiness and acceptance have a significant effect on consumers' adoption of technological innovations. Similar correlations between computer attitudes and online behaviors can also be found in educational settings. For instance, van der Rhee et al. (2007) suggest that learners who are more technology-ready are more likely to participate in a variety of online courses. Song and Shin (2008) propose that users' technological capabilities can influence their motivations to source knowledge.

The Relationship between Computer Attitude and KM Outcome

In recent research, individual attitudes have been recognized as another source of variance for learning outcomes (Dweck, 1986). Gattiker and Hlavka (1992) suggest that the learners' attitudes held before attending a computer course affect their learning outcome. Park and Wentling (2007) discover that learners' computer attitudes influence their perception of the usability of the e-learning courses, and that this perception impacts the degree of their skill development, thus also the transfer of learning. Kim and Davisa (2009) find that negative attitudes toward computer-mediated work, such as low self-esteem or computer anxiety, negatively affect the learning outcome. Existing research indicates that the degree to which a person can effectively apply knowledge and skills gained in a training context in the workplace is dependent on his or her attitudes toward training (Ford and Noe, 1987).

The Relationship between Learning Style and Knowledge-Sourcing Activity

According to Breckler et al. (2009), students' learning may be classified based on the sensory modalities by which they prefer to take in information. In their study, Breckler et al. determine the association between individual learning styles and behavioral intentions. More specifically, various studies have examined personality correlates of modern general knowledge (Chamorro-Premuzic et al., 2006), and it has been suggested that learning style, demographics, and personality trait variables may predict knowledge acquisition behaviors (Furnham et al., 2007). Thus, learning orientations are found to stimulate learners toward constructive, self-directed, or collaborative learning activities (Yew and Schmidt, 2009).

The Relationship between Learning Style and KM Outcome

Most learners have single, strong preferences of learning, whereas others have multiple learning preferences. Knowledge of learner learning preferences is important for reasons of pedagogy, and learning styles may also affect learning outcome and fulfillment of learners' career goals (Breckler et al., 2009). According to Groves (2005), there is a statistically significant association between learning approaches and skill development. In other words, the deep learning approach may be beneficial in the development of clinical reasoning skill through its potential to enhance the development of knowledge representations. In fact, learners' approaches to learning (i.e., learning styles) influence their construction and application of knowledge (Edmunds and Richardson, 2009).

The Relationship between Knowledge Sourcing Activity and KM Outcome

Gray and Meister (2004) as well as Kwok and Gao (2006) have in their researches suggested that employees who actively acquire knowledge are more likely to show increased KM abilities. According to Berkes (2009), bridging organizations and social learning provide a forum for the interaction of different kinds of knowledge generation. The coordination of tasks develops individuals' abilities to access available resources, form work teams, build trust, incorporate new knowledge, and resolve conflicts. In fact, recent research has identified that knowledge-sharing strategies are a crucial factor for enhancing organizational competitive strategic advantages (Chung and Yeaple, 2008). In their research, Lin et al. (2007) also present evidence demonstrating that more knowledge seeking results in improved KM abilities in workers. Based on the literature reviewed earlier, the research structure of the present study is shown in Figure 7.1.

Material and Methods

Research Structure and Hypotheses Development

The relevant hypotheses of the model, the survey questionnaire design, and the research participants are presented in the following subsections.

H1: Employees' computer attitudes significantly influence their knowledge-sourcing activity.

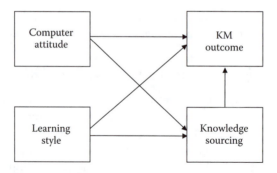

Figure 7.1 Research structure.

H2: Employees' computer attitudes significantly influence their KM outcome.

H3: Knowledge-sourcing activity has a mediating effect on the relationship between employees' computer attitudes and KM outcome.

H4: Employees' learning styles significantly influence their knowledge-sourcing activity.

H5: Employees' learning styles significantly influence their KM outcome.

H6: Knowledge-sourcing activity has a mediating effect on the relationship between employees' learning styles and KM outcome.

H7: Employees' knowledge-sourcing activity significantly influences their KM outcome.

Measures

The questionnaire is composed of five parts, including computer attitudes, learning style, KM outcome, and personal background (i.e., gender, age and position type). The questions were answered using a five-point Likert scale (1 = strongly disagree to 5 = strongly agree). Detailed definitions of the dimensions are described in the following sections.

Computer Attitudes

According to Fishbein and Ajzen's (1975) theory of reasoned action, an individual's beliefs about an object lead to an attitude about it, and this attitude leads to behavioral intentions regarding the object. It has been hypothesized that computer attitudes affect individuals' behavioral intentions, which consequently influence their actual usage of computers (Rainer and Miller, 1996). Computer attitudes can be measured on different dimensions. For example, Gattiker and Hlavka's (1992) five factors of computer attitude, including complexity, productivity, health, increasing work, and consequences of computers; Shashaani (1993, 1994) and Woodrow's (1994) four factor dimension, including interest, confidence, perceived utility, and stereotypical attitudes; Wang, Chen, and Shi's (2007) three-factor model, including sense of benefit, dependence, and harm; as well as Seyal, Rahim, and Rahman's (2002) two-factor measure, namely, perceived usefulness and perceived control. The present study adopts the Computer Attitudes Scale (CAS), which was developed by Loyd and Gressard (1984) and has been adopted in many related studies (e.g., Necessary and Parish, 1996; Parish and Necessary, 1996; Robertson and Stanforth, 1999; Jiao and Onwuegbuzie, 2004). The CAS consists of four scales: (1) anxiety or fear of computers, (2) confidence in the ability to use computers, (3) liking or enjoying working with computers, and (4) computer usefulness.

Learning Style

Learning styles are commonly applied in public education as well as corporate settings as an effective framework for recognizing and accommodating individual differences. The recent literature reviews different classifications of learning style and examines how they relate to curriculum values (Smith, 2002). According to Schaller et al. (2005), there has been little research on the role of individual preferences or learning style in the effectiveness of computer-based informal education. The first challenging task is to choose the most appropriate model that can describe individuals' online cognitive processes, among various learning style models. A popular source of individual differences seems to be the cognitive style construct of field dependent and field independent, generally considered to represent a difference in preference for attending to specific issues or for relying on context (Lin and Davidson, 1994). Another learning style dimension of possible direct relevance to hypermedia use is the passivity/activity of the learner (Lee and Lehman, 1993). In addition, learners can be divided into deeper processors who can relate and structure information actively and surface processor who focus more on memorization and rehearsal of information (Beishuizen et al., 1994). Kolb et al. (1999) identify two major dimensions of learning: perception and processing, which form a four-quadrant field for mapping an individual's learning style: accommodating, diverging, assimilating, and converging. Based on Kolb et al.'s experiential learning theory, Honey and Mumford (1983) have refined and identified four classifications of learning style: activist, reflector, theorist, and pragmatist, which are adopted in the present study.

Knowledge-Sourcing Activity

According to Gray and Meister (2004), the learning outcome of individual workers is strongly influenced by the method and extent of knowledge-sourcing activities. However, the extent to which knowledge is sourced for reuse is dependent on the dissemination mechanisms used by the organization (Yeung and Holden, 2000). Kwok and Gao (2006) point out that knowledge sharing is conducted via channels that serve as connections between the parties of sharing and facilitate the transfer of knowledge from one party to another. Thus, the availability and richness of such channels may influence the success of knowledge sharing. Holtham and Courtney (1998) summarized four types of knowledge transmission channels, namely, informal, formal, personal, or impersonal. Furthermore, Teigland and Wasko (2003) suggest that individual performers may access knowledge from (1) co-located coworkers, (2) coworkers within the same organization but located across intraorganizational boundaries, (3) intraorganizational electronic discussion networks, (4) informal contacts in other organizations, and (5) interorganizational electronic discussion network. Gray and Meister (2006) identify three distinctive forms of knowledge sourcing behaviors, which are adopted in the present study to explore knowledge sourcing as the extent of activity in utilizing various channels of knowledge acquisition. The three forms of knowledge sourcing are (1) dyadic knowledge sourcing (i.e., person-to-person communications, e.g., e-mail), (2) group knowledge sourcing (i.e., knowledge is exchanged among multiple knowledge providers and seekers in an open environment, e.g., online bulletin board), and (3) published sourcing (i.e., online knowledge repository, e.g., data warehouse, ftp server).

KM Outcome

KM is first and foremost about learning: what should be learned, when it should be learned, and who should be learning it. According to Dove (1999), how one achieves these goals depends on management ability, which refers to knowledge identification, acquisition, diffusion, or renewal. Gold et al. (2001) propose that organizations should possess two basic capabilities to manage knowledge, namely, knowledge infrastructure capability and knowledge process capability. The former is concerned with technology, organizational structure, and corporate culture; the latter is concerned with knowledge acquisition, conversion, and application processes. Past research presents various measurements of KM ability in organizations. For example, Tiwana (2002) proposes that organizational KM capabilities include finding, creating, packaging, assembling, reusing, and revalidating knowledge. Tanriverdi (2005) suggests that every kind of KM capability must go through a four-step process, including creation of related knowledge, transfer of related knowledge, integration of related knowledge, and leverage of related knowledge. Gray and Meister (2004) define the outcome of knowledge-sourcing activity as the extent to which an individual's cognitive structures has improved over time. They classify three distinct types of instrumental cognitive changes as the result of knowledge sharing behavior: replication (i.e., an individual is able to gain knowledge from existing cognitive structures for repeating procedures), adaptation (i.e., an individual is able to change in underlying structures of understanding in response to new developments), and innovation (i.e., an individual is able to perform radical changes in knowledge use), which are adopted in the present study to measure the outcome of KM.

Table 7.1 Sample Characteristics

Constructs	Classifications	Number	Percentage (%)
Gender	Male	198	58.9
	Female	138	41.1
Age	<30	53	15.8
	31–40	95	28.3
	41–50	153	45.5
	>50	35	10.4
Position type	Top management	48	14.3
	Middle management	109	32.4
	Professionals	80	23.8
	Clerk	99	29.5

Participants

The data used in this research consists of questionnaire responses from participants in 20 technological companies that are located in Northern Science Parks in Taiwan. The surveys targeted technological companies that have years of experience implementing KM and have the IT infrastructure in place to support the storing, sharing, and utilization of knowledge among employees. Each company received 60 questionnaires to answer; thus, a total of 1200 questionnaires were distributed, among which 397 surveys were returned and 336 were valid for analysis (valid return rate is 28%). Table 7.1 presents the demographic of the sample. Nonresponse analysis was conducted to ensure the absence of nonresponse biases. The results show that there is no difference between respondents and nonrespondents. Table 7.2 shows the description statistics for the dimensions.

Table 7.2 Survey Structure and Descriptive Statistics for Dimension

Dimensions	Number of Items per Dimension	Mean	Std. Dev.	Order	Cronbach's α
Computer attitude	15	3.3046	0.3962	4	0.8079
Learning style	20	3.5122	0.5224	3	0.9470
Knowledge sourcing activity	11	3.5168	0.3539	2	0.9195
KM outcome	13	3.5952	0.3598	1	0.9144

Results

Reliability and Validity Tests

Reliability and validity tests were then conducted for each of the constructs with multivariate measures. Cronbach α reliability estimates were used to measure the internal consistency of these multivariate scales (Nunnally, 1978). In this study, the Cronbach α of each constructs was greater than 0.8079, which indicates a strong reliability for our survey instrument (Cuieford, 1965). In addition, since the item-to-total correlations of each measure were at least 0.5031 (see Table 7.3); the criterion validity of each scale in this study is considered to be satisfactory (Kerlinger, 1999).

Table 7.3 Exploratory Factor Analysis and Internal Consistency Values for the Questionnaire

Dimensions	Factors	% of Variance	Cumulative %	Item-to-Total Correlations	Cronbach's α
Computer attitude	Computer confidence	21.968	78.200	0.5044	0.9269
	Computer liking	20.573		0.5031	0.9012
	Computer usefulness	19.851		0.5195	0.8813
	Computer anxiety	15.807		−0.6094	0.8436
Learning style	Activist	21.211	74.564	0.6135	0.9174
	Reflector	19.222		0.5684	0.9130
	Theorist	18.600		0.5897	0.9065
	Pragmatist	15.531		0.6084	0.9055
Knowledge-sourcing activity	Dyadic knowledge sourcing	29.301	75.633	0.6814	0.9246
	Group knowledge sourcing	24.871		0.6892	0.8502
	Published knowledge sourcing	21.461		0.6161	0.8255
KM outcome	Replication	24.981	70.129	.6473	0.8675
	Adaptation	23.667		.6797	0.9025
	Innovation	21.481		.6039	0.8376

Meanwhile, to ensure that the instrument has reasonable construct validity, confirmatory factor analyses (CFA) were used. Following Campbell and Fiske's (1959) criteria, we tested for construct validity and convergent and discriminant validity. The results reveal that the correlations are all higher than zero and large enough to proceed with discriminant validity. Furthermore, discriminant validity, proposed by Aldawani and Palvai (2002) and Campbell and Fiske (1959), was conducted by counting the number of times an item correlates higher with items in other factors than with items in its own factor. The results confirm adequate discriminant validity. In conclusion, the dimensions used in this study demonstrate both convergent and discriminant validity. Tables 7.4 to 7.11 present the outcome of the second-order CFA, including convergent and discriminant validity for each dimension.

Analysis of the Structural Equation Model

The structural equation modeling approach was applied to test the proposed model and hypotheses. This approach is a multivariate statistical technique for testing structural theory (Tan, 2001). It incorporates both observed and latent variables. The analysis for the present study was conducted using LISREL 8.52 and utilizing the maximum likelihood method. In the proposed model (Figure 7.1), computer attitude and learning style are considered exogenous variables, and KM outcome is considered an endogenous variable. Knowledge-sourcing activity serves as both an endogenous variable (to computer attitude and learning style) and exogenous variable (to KM outcome). The individual questionnaire items were aggregated into specific factor groups. According to Bollen (2002), four rules need to be applied to construct the measurement model and the structure model; they are (1) each observed variable has a nonzero loading on the latent factor within the structure, but has a loading of zero toward other latent factors; (2) no relationship exists among measurement errors for observed variables; (3) no relationship exists among the residuals of latent factors; and (4) no relationship exists among residuals and measurement errors. The measurement model represents the mathematical relationship between one set of observed variables and one set of latent variables (Schumacker and Lomax, 1996); the structure model represents the predicted relationship between one set of independent latent variables and one set of dependent latent variables (Loehlin, 2004).

The reliability results of the factors in each dimension are illustrated in Table 7.12. Additionally, the analytical results of the LISREL model reveal a satisfactory fit for our sample data. Figure 7.2 presents the standardized parameter estimates for the path relations in the adjusted goodness-of-fit model. The absolute fit measures (GFI = 0.95, AGFI = 0.93, and RMSEA = 0.046) indicate that the structural model either meets or exceeds recommended levels, and thus represents a satisfactory fit for the sample data collected. The chi-square statistic divided by the degrees of freedom also indicates a reasonable fit at 1.701. It can be concluded that the proposed model maintains good construct validity (see Table 7.13 for the statistics of the fit test of the model). The results of the effect analysis, including the direct,

Table 7.4 Second-Order Confirmatory Factor Analysis (Convergent Validity) for Computer Attitude

Fit Type		Preliminary Fit			Fit of Internal Structure		
Latent Variables	Item No.	Standardized Factor Loading	Error Variance	Observed Variables Reliability	Composite Reliability	Average Variance Extracted	
First-Order Factor							
Computer confidence	Item 1	0.84***	0.29	0.71	0.93	0.76	
	Item 2	0.88***	0.22	0.78			
	Item 3	0.89***	0.20	0.80			
	Item 4	0.87***	0.25	0.75			
Computer liking	Item 5	0.79***	0.38	0.62	0.91	0.72	
	Item 6	0.88***	0.23	0.77			
	Item 7	0.85***	0.28	0.72			
	Item 8	0.87***	0.24	0.76			

Computer usefulness	Item 9	0.79***	0.38	0.62	0.89	0.67
	Item 10	0.84***	0.29	0.71		
	Item 11	0.87***	0.25	0.75		
	Item 12	0.77***	0.40	0.60		
Computer anxiety	Item 13	0.83***	0.32	0.68	0.85	0.66
	Item 14	0.85***	0.27	0.73		
	Item 15	0.76***	0.43	0.57		
Second-order factor				0.70	0.68	
Computer confidence		0.84***	0.30	0.70		
Computer liking		0.83***	0.31	0.69		
Computer usefulness		0.84***	0.29	0.71		
Computer anxiety		-0.79***	0.38	0.62		

Note: ***$p < 0.001$ (|t| > 3.29).

Table 7.5 Discriminant Validity Analysis for Computer Attitude Using the Chi-Square Test

Models	χ^2	d.f.	$\Delta\chi^2$	Δ d.f.
Unconstrained measuring model (The correlation between paired factors is set to be 1)	138.39	84	—	
Computer confidence/Computer liking	173.63	85	35.24***	1
Computer confidence/Computer usefulness	168.80	85	30.41***	1
Computer confidence/Computer anxiety	285.04	85	146.65***	1
Computer liking/Computer usefulness	169.89	85	31.5***	1
Computer liking/Computer anxiety	287.83	85	149.44***	1
Computer usefulness/Computer anxiety	294.40	85	156.01***	1

Note: ***$p < 0.001$ ($\chi^2 > 10.83$).

indirect, and total effects of the latent variables in the structure model, are shown in Table 7.14. In addition, the relationship between the latent variables and the results of the examination of research hypotheses are demonstrated in Table 7.15. On the basis of Figure 7.2 and Tables 7.14 and 7.15, it can be concluded that H1, H2, H3, H4, H6, and H7 show statistical significance, and thus are accepted.

Discussion

Based on the analysis performed earlier, a number of observations can be made, all positive. It is shown that both computer attitude and learning style have a direct and significant effect on knowledge sourcing; as such, the validity of HYPOTHESIS 1 and HYPOTHESIS 4 is demonstrated. The results thus support the observation that two dimensions, namely (1) computer attitudes of workers toward acquiring online knowledge (Collins et al., 2008; Prinsen et al., 2007; Park and Wentling, 2007; Kwok and Gao, 2006; Shih, 2006) and (2) the type of learning style of the employees within these technological companies positively affects the online knowledge-sourcing behaviors demonstrated by them (Gray and Meister, 2004; Dillon and Gabbard, 1998; Baldwin and Sabry, 2003). The analysis also shows that knowledge sourcing has a direct and significant effect on KM outcomes, establishing HYPOTHESIS 7 as valid. Results show that more knowledge-seeking activities by employees result in improved KM application capability, an observation in partial support of work done by Gray and Meister (2004).

The analysis has shown that while employees' computer attitudes have a direct and statistically significant impact on KM outcome (HYPOTHESIS 2 is accepted),

Table 7.6 Second-Order Confirmatory Factor Analysis (Convergent Validity) for Learning Style

Fit Type		Preliminary Fit			Fit of Internal Structure		
Latent Variables	Item No.	Standardized Factor Loading	Error Variance	Observed Variables Reliability	Composite Reliability	Average Variance Extracted
First-Order Factor							
Activist	Item 1	0.80***	0.36	0.64	0.91	0.67
	Item 2	0.81***	0.34	0.66		
	Item 3	0.90***	0.19	0.81		
	Item 4	0.84***	0.29	0.71		
	Item 5	0.72***	0.48	0.52		
Reflector	Item 6	0.77***	0.41	0.59	0.91	0.68
	Item 7	0.80***	0.36	0.64		
	Item 8	0.86***	0.27	0.73		
	Item 9	0.84***	0.30	0.70		
	Item 10	0.86***	0.26	0.74		
Theorist	Item 11	0.81***	0.35	0.65	0.92	0.65
	Item 12	0.81***	0.34	0.66		

Continued

Table 7.6 (Continued) Second-Order Confirmatory Factor Analysis (Convergent Validity) for Learning Style

Fit Type		Preliminary Fit		Fit of Internal Structure		
Latent Variables	Item No.	Standardized Factor Loading	Error Variance	Observed Variables Reliability	Composite Reliability	Average Variance Extracted
Theorist (continued)	Item 13	0.80***	0.36	0.64		
	Item 14	0.76***	0.43	0.57		
	Item 15	0.83***	0.31	0.69		
	Item 16	0.83***	0.30	0.70		
Pragmatist	Item 17	0.85***	0.28	0.72	0.91	0.71
	Item 18	0.85***	0.27	0.73		
	Item 19	0.83***	0.31	0.69		
	Item 20	0.85***	0.28	0.72		
Second-order factor				0.86	0.61	
Activist		0.76***	0.42	0.58		
Reflector		0.78***	0.40	0.60		
Theorist		0.77***	0.40	0.60		
Pragmatist		0.85***	0.38	0.72		

Note: ***$p < 0.01$ ($|t| > 3.29$).

Table 7.7 Discriminant Validity Analysis for Learning Style Using the Chi-Square Test

Models	χ^2	d.f.	$\Delta\chi^2$	Δ d.f.
Unconstrained measuring model (the correlation between paired factors is set to be 1)	279.74	164	—	
Activist/Reflector	321.99	165	42.25***	1
Activist/Theorist	321.20	165	41.46***	1
Activist/Pragmatist	310.51	165	30.77***	1
Reflector/Theorist	323.95	165	44.21***	1
Reflector/Pragmatist	313.03	165	33.29***	1
Theorist/Pragmatist	311.37	165	31.63***	1

Note: ***$p < 0.001$ ($\chi^2 > 10.83$).

the learning styles of the employees has a direct but not significant effect on KM outcome (HYPOTHESIS 5 is thus rejected). The result of HYPOTHESIS 2 agrees with the argument made by Gattiker and Hlavka (1992), which suggests that employees' attitudes affect their learning outcomes from a computer-based environment. In fact, previous findings show that negative attitudes toward computer-mediated work negatively affect the outcome of online behavior (Ames and Archer, 1988; Dweek, 1986). Furthermore, the failure of HYPOTHESIS 5 supports the observation made by Dillon and Gabbard (1998). They suggest that the interaction of learner style and the use of multimedia content perhaps offer the beginning of an explanation for the generally conflicting results in the literature comparing multimedia-based and nonmultimedia-based learning environments. That is, in most applications of new technologies, learning style has failed to demonstrate much in the way of predictive or explanatory power. Perhaps, future research should focus on identifying learning style dimensions that show greater potential for predicting behavior and performance. Finally, further examination shows that both computer attitudes and learning styles do have an indirect effect on KM outcomes through the mediated dimension of knowledge-sourcing activities (HYPOTHESIS 3 and HYPOTHESIS 6 are valid), a concept that was proposed by Gray and Meister (2004, 2006).

Conclusion

In conclusion, the present study has focused on the discussion and analysis of KM within an organization. Specifically, the study was designed to determine the effect of

Table 7.8 Second-Order Confirmatory Factor Analysis (Convergent Validity) for Knowledge-Sourcing Activity

Fit Type		Preliminary Fit			Fit of Internal Structure	
Latent Variables	Item No.	Standardized Factor Loading	Error Variance	Observed Variables Reliability	Composite Reliability	Average Variance Extracted
First-Order Factor						
Dyadic knowledge sourcing	Item 1	0.85***	0.28	0.72	0.93	0.77
	Item 2	0.87***	0.24	0.76		
	Item 3	0.91***	0.18	0.82		
	Item 4	0.88***	0.23	0.77		
Group knowledge sourcing	Item 5	0.79***	0.37	0.63	0.86	0.60
	Item 6	0.84***	0.29	0.71		
	Item 7	0.76***	0.43	0.57		
	Item 8	0.71***	0.49	0.51		

Published knowledge sourcing	Item 9	0.74***	0.45	0.55	0.83	0.61
	Item 10	0.79***	0.37	0.63		
	Item 11	0.81***	0.34	0.66		
Second-order factor				0.87	0.70	
Dyadic knowledge sourcing		0.85***	0.27	0.73		
Group knowledge sourcing		0.86***	0.26	0.74		
Published knowledge sourcing		0.79***	0.38	0.62		

Note: ***$p < 0.001$ ($|t| > 3.29$).

Table 7.9 Discriminant Validity Analysis for Knowledge Sourcing Activity Using the Chi-Square Test

Models	χ^2	d.f.	$\Delta\chi^2$	Δ d.f.
Unconstrained measuring model (the correlation between paired factors is set to be 1)	65.63	41	—	
Dyadic knowledge sourcing/Group knowledge sourcing	95.14	42	29.51***	1
Dyadic knowledge sourcing/Published knowledge sourcing	101.62	42	35.99***	1
Group knowledge sourcing/Published knowledge sourcing	102.94	42	37.31***	1

Note: ***$p < 0.001$ ($\chi^2 > 10.83$).

employee computer attitude and learning style on knowledge-sourcing activities. In turn, the effect of knowledge-sourcing activities on KM outcome is also examined. An empirical investigation using structural equation modeling shows that both the employees' computer attitudes and learning styles are significant aspects in determining effective application of knowledge within organizations. However, it must be highlighted that (1) employees' learning style does not directly result in greater ability in managing knowledge, and (2) the effect of knowledge sourcing on KM outcome is stronger under the influence of employees' computer attitudes and learning styles. Therefore, both factors may serve as catalysts to facilitate and stimulate knowledge-sourcing activities within the organizations. Increased knowledge-sourcing activities, in turn, serve as the channels for better KM capability within the organization. Employees' computer attitude and learning style can thus be seen as a part of a larger chain, where knowledge-sourcing channels (Gray and Meister, 2004) form the middle ring that links those factors with the KM outcome of workers (Herremans et al., 2005; Liao et al., 2004).

Based on the findings, this study suggests that organizations can improve KM capabilities by facilitating a positive computer attitude (through building employee confidence in using computers, promoting the usefulness of computers, and providing necessary training for online knowledge-sourcing techniques) and a more practical viewpoint of knowledge sharing and utilizations (by underscoring the relationship between knowledge-sharing activities and everyday tasks), and at the same time actively motivating workers to seek new knowledge. Furthermore, organizations are reminded that these factors must be supported by accessibility to various channels of knowledge sourcing, without which effective distribution and application of knowledge cannot occur.

While the empirical data collected have largely supported the proposed model, it is necessary to point out the limitations of this research. Even though the

Table 7.10 Second-Order Confirmatory Factor Analysis (Convergent Validity) for KM Outcome

Fit Type		Preliminary Fit		Fit of Internal Structure		
Latent Variables	Item No.	Standardized Factor Loading	Error Variance	Observed Variables Reliability	Composite Reliability	Average Variance Extracted
First-Order Factor						
Replication	Item 1	0.73***	0.47	0.53	0.57	0.57
	Item 2	0.78***	0.39	0.61		
	Item 3	0.75***	0.43	0.57		
	Item 4	0.77***	0.41	0.59		
	Item 5	0.73***	0.47	0.53		
Adaptation	Item 6	0.87***	0.24	0.76	0.90	0.70
	Item 7	0.85***	0.27	0.73		
	Item 8	0.87***	0.25	0.75		
	Item 9	0.75***	0.43	0.57		

Continued

Table 7.10 (Continued) Second-Order Confirmatory Factor Analysis (Convergent Validity) for KM Outcome

Fit Type		Preliminary Fit			Fit of Internal Structure		
Latent Variables	Item No.	Standardized Factor Loading	Error Variance	Observed Variables Reliability	Composite Reliability	Average Variance Extracted
Published knowledge sourcing	Item 10	0.80***	0.37	0.63	0.84	0.57
	Item 11	0.72***	0.48	0.52		
	Item 12	0.72***	0.48	0.52		
	Item 13	0.77***	0.40	0.60		
Second-order factor					0.85	0.65
Replication		0.84***	0.29	0.71		
Adaptation		0.74***	0.46	0.54		
Innovation		0.83***	0.31	0.69		

Note: ***$p < .001$ ($|t| > 3.29$).

Table 7.11 Discriminant Validity Analysis for KM Outcome Using the Chi-Square Test

Models	χ^2	d.f.	$\Delta\chi^2$	Δ d.f.
Unconstrained measuring model (the correlation between paired factors is set to be 1)	104.88	62	—	
Replication/Adaptation	142.22	63	37.34***	1
Replication/Innovation	140.77	63	35.89***	1
Adaptation/Innovation	139.90	63	35.02***	1

Note: ***$p < 0.001$ ($\chi^2 > 10.83$).

Table 7.12 Observed Indicator Reliability of Factors

Dimensions	Factors	Observed Indicator Reliability
Computer attitude	Computer confidence	0.62
	Computer liking	0.62
	Computer usefulness	0.62
	Computer anxiety	0.57
Learning style	Activist	0.57
	Reflector	0.53
	Theorist	0.56
	Pragmatist	0.64
Knowledge sourcing activity	Dyadic knowledge sourcing	0.65
	Group knowledge sourcing	0.64
	Published knowledge sourcing	0.53
KM outcome	Replication	0.57
	Adaptation	0.59
	Innovation	0.51

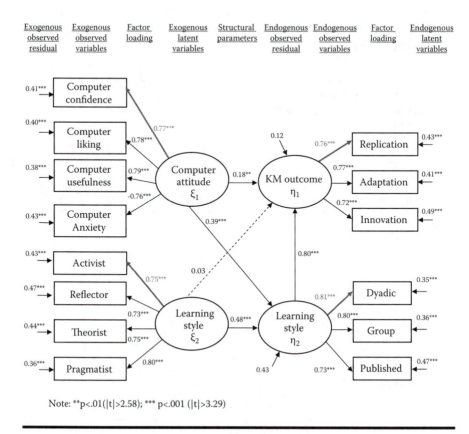

Figure 7.2 Standardized parameter estimates for the path relations in the adjusted goodness-of-fit model.

responding individuals consisted of well-informed and active members of these participating organizations, the existence of possible biases cannot be discounted. Furthermore, it is evident that KM approaches can differ among organizations in different countries, industries, or even those in the same industry working on dissimilar business models (Echeverri-Carroll, 1999; Hansen et al., 1999). Therefore, the current data collected from these particular organizations in Taiwan may not be fully representative of other scenarios. However, the findings and recommendations provided by the present study may present useful insights for companies in similar industrial contexts.

Table 7.13   Fit Test of the Model

Measures	Indicators
Absolute Fit Measures	Chi-Square with 71 Degrees of Freedom=120.31 (P>0.0001)
	Goodness of Fit Index (GFI) = 0.95
	Root Mean Square Error of Approximation (RMSEA) = 0.046
	P-Value for Test of Close Fit (RMSEA < 0.05) = 0.68
	Expected Cross-Validation Index (ECVI) = 0.56
	90 Percent Confidence Interval for ECVI =(0.48; 0.67)
	ECVI for Saturated Model = 0.63
	ECVI for Independence Model = 17.08
	Adjusted Goodness of Fit Index (AGFI) = 0.93
Incremental Fit Measures	Normed Fit Index (NFI) = 0.98
	Non-Normed Fit Index (NNFI) = 0.99
	Comparative Fit Index (CFI) = 0.99
	Incremental Fit Index (IFI) = 0.99
	Relative Fit Index (RFI) = 0.97
Parsimonious Fit Measures	Parsimony Normed Fit Index (PNFI) = 0.76
	Parsimony Goodness of Fit Index (PGFI) = 0.64
	Critical N (CN) = 277.08
	Normed chi-square 120.80/71 = 1.701

Table 7.14   The Effect Analysis for the Latent Variables in the Structure Model

Independent Variables		Dependent Variable (Endogenous Latent Variables)			
		η_2		η_2	
		Knowledge Sourcing Activity		KM Outcome	
		Standardized Effect	t Value	Standardized Effect	t Value
Exogenous Latent Variable					
ξ_1	Computer attitude				
	Direct effect	0.39	6.25***	0.18	2.88**
	Indirect effect			0.31	5.29***
	Total effect	0.39	6.25***	0.49	7.32***
ξ_2	Learning style				
	Direct effect	0.48	7.30***	0.03	0.41
	Indirect effect			0.38	5.73***
	Total effect	0.48	7.30***	0.41	6.25***
Endogenous Latent Variables					
η_2	Knowledge sourcing activity				
	Direct effect			0.80	8.62***
	Indirect effect				
	Total effect			0.80	8.62***

Note: **$p < 0.01$ ($|t| > 2.58$; ***$p < 0.001$ ($|t| > 3.29$).

Table 7.15   The Relationship between Latent Variables and the Examination of Hypotheses

Path Relationships	Direct Effect	Indirect Effect	Total Effect	Hypothesis	Results
Computer attitude → Knowledge-sourcing activity	0.39***	—	0.39***	H1	Accepted
Computer attitude → KM outcome	0.18**	—	0.18**	H2	Accepted
Computer attitude → KM outcome (through Knowledge sourcing activity)	—	0.31***	0.49***	H3	Accepted
Learning style → Knowledge sourcing activity	0.48***	—	0.48***	H4	Accepted
Learning style → KM outcome	0.03	—	0.03	H5	Rejected
Learning style → KM outcome (through Knowledge sourcing activity)	—	0.38***	0.41***	H6	Accepted
Knowledge sourcing activity → KM outcome	0.80***	—	0.80***	H7	Accepted

Note: **$p < 0.01$ ($|t| > 2.58$); ***$p < 0.001$ ($|t| > 3.29$).

References

Aldawani, A.M., and Palvai, P.C., 2002, Developing and validating an instrument for measuring user-perceived web quality. *Information and Management, 39,* 467–76.

Ames, C., and Archer, J., 1988, Achievement goals in the classroom: Students strategies and motivation processes. *Journal of Educational Psychology, 80,* 260–267.

Baldwin, L., and Sabry, K., 2003, Learning styles for interactive learning systems. *Innovations in Education and Teaching International, 40*(4), 325–340.

Barnett, W.P., and Hansen, M.T., 1996, The red queen in organizational evolution. *Strategic Management Journal, 17,* 139–158.

Beishuizen, J., Stoutjesdijk, E., and van Putten, K., 1994, Studying textbooks: Effects of learning styles, study task, and instruction. *Learning and Instruction, 4,* 151–174.

Berkes, F., 2009, Evolution of co-management: Role of knowledge generation, bridging organizations and social learning. *Journal of Environmental Management, 90,* 1692–1702.

Bhatt, G.D., 2001, Knowledge management in organizations: Examining the interaction between technologies, techniques, and people. *Journal of Knowledge Management, 5,* 68–75.

Bollen, K.A., 2002, Latent variables in psychology and the social sciences. *Annual Review of Psychology, 53,* 605–634.

Breckler, J., Joun, D., and Ngo, H., 2009, Learning styles of physiology students interested in the health professions. *Advances in Physiology Education, 33,* 30–36.

Campbell, D.T., and Fiske, D.W., 1959, Convergent and discriminant validation by the multitrait-multimethod matrix. *Psychology Bulletin, 53,* 81–105.

Chae, B., Koch, H., Paradice, D., and Huy, V.V., 2005, Exploring knowledge management using network theories: Questions, paradoxes and prospects. *The Journal of Computer Information Systems, 45,* 62–74.

Chamorro-Premuzic, T., Furnham, A., and Ackerman, P., 2006, Ability and personality correlates of general knowledge. *Personality and Individual Differences, 41,* 419–429.

Chen, C.-J., and Lin, B.-W., 2004, The effects of environment, knowledge attribute, organizational climate, and firm characteristics on knowledge sourcing decisions. *R & D Management, 34,* 137–146.

Choi, B., and Lee, H., 2003, An empirical investigation of km styles and their effect on corporate performance. *Information and Management, 40,* 403–417.

Chung, W., and Yeaple, S., 2008, International knowledge sourcing: Evidence from U.S. firms expanding abroad. *Strategic Management Journal, 29*(11), 1207–1224.

Collins, K.M.T., Onwuegbuzie, A.J., and Jiao, Q.G., 2008, Reading ability and computer-related attitudes among African American graduate students. *CyberPsychology and Behavior, 11,* 347–350.

Cuieford, J.P., 1965, *Fundamental Statistics in Psychology and Education.* New York: McGraw-Hill.

Damodaran, L. and Olphert, W., 2000, Barriers and facilitators to the use of knowledge management systems. *Behaviour and Information Technology, 19*(6), 405–413.

Davenport, T.H., De Long, D.W., and Beers, M.C., 1998, Successful knowledge management projects. *Sloan Management Review, 39,* 43–57.

Dillon, A., and Gabbard, R., 1998, Hypermedia as an educational technology: A review of the quantitative research literature on learner comprehension, control and style. *Review of Educational Research, 68,* 322–349.

Dove, R., 1999, Knowledge management, response ability, and the agile enterprise. *Journal of Knowledge Management, 3*, 18–35.

Drucker, P., 1993, *Post-Capitalist Society*. New York: Harper Collins.

Dweck, C.S., 1986, Motivational processes affecting learning. *American Psychologist, 41*, 1040–1048.

Earl, M.J., 2001, Knowledge management strategies: Towards a taxonomy. *Journal of Management Information Systems, 18*, 215–233.

Echeverri-Carroll, E.L., 1999, Knowledge flows in innovation networks: A comparative analysis of Japanese and us high-technology firms. *Journal of Knowledge Management, 3*, 296–303.

Edmunds, R., and Richardson, J. T. E., 2009, Conceptions of learning, approaches to studying and personal development in UK higher education. *British Journal of Educational Technology, 79*, 295–309.

Fishbein, M. and Ajzen, I., 1975, *Belief, attitude, intention and behavior*. Reading, MT: Addison-Wesley.

Fontes, M., 2005, Distant networking: The knowledge acquisition strategies of "out-cluster" biotechnology firms. *European Planning Studies, 13*, 899–920.

Ford, K. J., and Noe, R.A., 1987, Self-assessed training needs: The effects of attitudes toward training, managerial level, and function. *Personnel Psychology, 40*, 39–53.

Furnham, A., Christopher, A., N., Garwood, J., and Martin, G. N., 2007, Approaches to learning and the acquisition of general knowledge. *Personality and Individual Differences, 43*, 1563–1571.

Gassmann, O., and Gaso, B., 2004, Insourcing creativity with listening posts in decentralized firms. *Creativity and Innovation Management, 13*, 3–14.

Gattiker, U.E., and Hlavka, A., 1992, Computer attitudes and learning performance: Issues for management education and training- Summary. *Journal of Organizational Behavior, 13*, 89–101.

Gold, A.H., Malhotra, A., and Segars, A.H., 2001, Knowledge management: An organizational capabilities perspective. *Journal of Management Information Systems, 18*, 185–214.

Grant, R., 1996, Prospering in dynamically competitive environments: Organizational capability as knowledge integration. *Organization Science, 7*, 375–387.

Gray, P., and Meister, D., 2004, Knowledge sourcing effectiveness. *Management Science, 50*, 821–834.

Gray, P., and Meister, D., 2006, Knowledge sourcing methods. *Information and Management, 43*, 142–156.

Groves, M., 2005, Problem-based learning and learning approach: Is there a relationship? *Advances in Health Sciences Education, 10*, 315–326.

Hansen, M.T., Nohria, N., and Tierney, T., 1999, What's your strategy for managing knowledge? *Harvard Business Review, 77*, 106–116.

Herremans, I.M., Reid, R.E., and Wilson, L.K., 2005, Environmental management systems (EMS) of tour operators: Learning from each other. *Journal of Sustainable Tourism, 13*, 311–338.

Holtham, C., and Courtney, N., 1998, The executive learning ladder: A knowledge creation process grounded in the strategic information systems domain. *Proceedings of the Fourth Americas Conference on Information Systems* (pp. 594–597), Baltimore, MD.

Honey, P., and Mumford, B., 1983, *Using Your Learning Styles*, Maidenhead: Honey.

Ito, B., and Wakasugi, R., 2007, What factors determine the mode of overseas R&D by multinationals? Empirical evidence. *Research Policy, 36*, 1275–1287.

Jantunen, A., 2005, Knowledge-processing capabilities and innovative performance: An empirical study. *European Journal of Innovation Management, 8*, 336–349.

Jiao, Q.G., and Onwuegbuzie, A.J., 2004, The impact of information technology on library anxiety: The role of computer attitudes. *Information Technology and Libraries, 23*, 138–144.

Kerlinger, F.N., 1999, *Foundations of Behavior Research.* Fort Worth, TX: A Harcourt College Publishing.

Kim, H.-K., and Davisa, K.E., 2009, Toward a comprehensive theory of problematic Internet use: Evaluating the role of self-esteem, anxiety, flow, and the self-rated importance of Internet activities. *Computers in Human Behavior, 25*(2), 490–500.

Kolb, D.A., Boyatzis, R.E., and Mainemelis, C., 1999, Experiential learning theory: Previous research and new directions. In R.J. Sternberg and L.F. Zhang (Eds.), *Perspectives on Cognitive, Learning, and Thinking Style* (pp. 227–248). NJ: Lawrence Erlbaum.

Korthauer, R.D., and Koubek, R.J., 1994, An empirical evaluation of knowledge, cognitive style, and structure upon the performance of hypertext task. *International Journal of Human-Computer Interaction, 6*, 373–390.

Kwok, S.H., and Gao, S., 2006, Attitude towards knowledge sharing behavior. *The Journal of Computer Information Systems, 46*, 45–51.

Lee, Y., and Lehman, J., 1993, Instructional cueing in hypermedia: A study with active and passive learners. *Journal of Educational Multimedia and Hypermedia, 2*, 25–37.

Levitt, B., and March, J.G., 1988, Organizational learning. *Annual Review of Sociology, 14*, 319–340.

Liao, S.-H., Chang, J.-C., Cheng, S.-C., and Kuo, C.-M., 2004, Employee relationship and knowledge sharing: A case study of a Taiwanese finance and securities firm. *Knowledge Management Research and Practice, 2*, 24–34.

Lin, C., and Davidson, G., 1994, Effects of Linking Structure and Cognitive Style on Students' Performance and Attitude in a Computer-Based Hypertext Environment. Paper presented at the annual convention of the Association for Educational Communication and Technology, Nashville, TN.

Lin, C.-Y., Kuo, T.-H., Kuo, Y.-K., Ho, L.-A., and Kuo, Y.-L., 2007, The KM chain- empirical study of the vital knowledge sourcing links. *The Journal of Computer Information Systems, 48*, 91–99.

Lin, C.-H., Shih, H.-Y., and Sher, P. J., 2007, Integrating technology readiness into technology acceptance: The TRAM model. *Psychology and Marketing, 24*(7), 641–657.

Loehlin, J. C., 2004, *Latent Variable Models: An Introduction to Factor, Path, and Structural Analysis* (4th ed.). Mahwah, NJ: Lawrence Erlbaum Associates.

Loyd, B., and Gressard, G., 1984, Reliability and factorial validity of the computer attitude scale. *Educational and Psychological Measurement, 44*, 501–505.

Lua, Y., Zhoub, T., and Wangc, B., 2009, Exploring Chinese users' acceptance of instant messaging using the theory of planned behavior, the technology acceptance model, and the flow theory. *Computers in Human Behavior, 25*(1), 29–39.

Ndlela, L.T., and du Toit, A.S.A., 2001, Establishing a knowledge management programme for competitive advantage in an enterprise. *International Journal of Information Management, 21*, 151–165.

Necessary, J.R., and Parish, T.S., 1996, The relationships between computer usage and computer-related attitudes and behaviors. *Education, 116*, 384–388.

Nunnally, J.C., 1978, *Psychometric Theory.* New York: McGraw-Hill.

O'Leary, D.E., 1998, Enterprise knowledge management. *Computer, 31*, 54–61.

Parish, T.S., and Necessary, J.R., 1996, An examination of cognitive dissonance and computer attitudes. *Education, 116*, 565–566.

Park, J.-H., and Wentling, T., 2007, Factors associated with transfer of training in workplace e-learning. *Journal of Workplace Learning, 19*(5), 311–329.

Prinsen, F., Volman, M.L.L., and Terwel, J., 2007, The influence of learner characteristics on degree and type of participation in a CSCL environment. *British Journal of Educational Technology, 38*(6), 1037–1055.

Rainer, R.K., and Miller, M.D., 1996, An assessment of the psychometric properties of the computer attitude scale. *Computers in Human Behavior, 12*, 93–105

Ranaweera, C., Bansal, H., and McDougall, G., 2008, Web site satisfaction and purchase intentions: Impact of personality characteristics during initial web site visit. *Managing Service Quality, 18*(4), 329–348.

Robertson, L.J., Stanforth, N., 1999, College students' computer attitudes and interest in Web based distance education. *Journal of Family and Consumer Sciences, 91*, 60–64.

Schaller, D.T., Allison-Bunnell, S., and Borun, M., 2005, Learning Styles and Online Interactive. Retrieved August 28, 2008, from http://www.archimuse.com/mw2005/papers/schaller/schaller.html.

Schumacker, R, E. and Lomax, R, G., 1996, *A Beginner's Guide to Structural Equation Modeling*. Hillsdale, NJ: Lawrence Erlbaum Associates.

Seyal, A.H., Rahim, M.M., and Rahman, M.N.A., 2002, A study of computer attitudes of non-computing students of technical colleges in Brunei Darussalam. *Journal of End User Computing, 14*, 40–47.

Shashaani, L., 1993, Gender-based differences in attitudes toward computers. *Computers and Education, 20*, 169–181.

Shashaani, L., 1994, Gender-differences in computer experience and its influence on computer attitudes. *Journal of Educational Computing Research, 11*, 347–367.

Shih, Y.-Y., 2006, The effect of computer self-efficacy on enterprise resource planning usage. *Behaviour and Information Technology, 25*(5), 407–411.

Smith, J., 2002, Learning styles: Fashion fad or lever for change? The application of learning style theory to inclusive curriculum delivery. *Innovations in Education and Teaching International, 39*(1), 63–70.

Song, J., and Shin, J., 2008, The paradox of technological capabilities: a study of knowledge sourcing from host countries of overseas R&D operations. *Journal of International Business Studies, 39*(2), 291–303.

Spender, J., 1996, Making knowledge the basis of a dynamic theory of the firm. *Strategic Management Journal, 17*, 45–62.

Tan, K.C., 2001, A structure equation model of new product design and development. *Decision Science, 32*, 195–226.

Tanriverdi, H., 2005, Information technology relatedness, knowledge management capability, and performance of multibusiness firms. *MIS Quarterly, 29*, 311–334.

Teece, D.J., 1998, Capturing value from knowledge assets: The new economy, markets for know-how, and intangible assets. *California Management Review, 40*, 55–79.

Teigland, R., and Wasko, M.M., 2003, Integrating knowledge through information trading: Examining the relationship between boundary spanning communication and individual performance. *Decision Science, 34*, 261–286.

Tiwana, A., 2002, *The Knowledge Management Toolkit: Practical Techniques for Building a Knowledge Management*. Upper Saddle River, NJ: Prentice Hall.

van der Rhee, B., Verma, R., Plaschka, G.R., and Kickul, J.R., 2007, Technology readiness, learning goals, and eLearning: Searching for synergy. *Decision Sciences Journal of Innovative Education, 5*(1), 127–149.

Wang, L., Chen, Y., and Shi, J., 2007, Attitudes toward computers: A new attitudinal dimension. *CyperPsychology and Behavior, 10,* 700–704.

Woodrow, J.E.J., 1994, The development of computer-related attitudes of secondary students. *Journal of Educational Computing Research, 11,* 307–338.

Yeung, C., and Holden, T., 2000, *Knowledge Re-Use as Engineering Re-Use: Extracting Values from Knowledge Management.* Practical Applications of KM (PAKM2000), Switzerland.

Yew, E. H., J., and Schmidt, H. G., 2009, Evidence for constructive, self-regulatory, and collaborative processes in problem-based learning. *Advances in Health Sciences Education, 14,* 251–273.

Young, M.-L., Tseng, F.-C., 2008, Interplay between physical and virtual settings for online interpersonal trust formation in knowledge-sharing practice. *CyberPsychology and Behavior, 11,* 55–64.

Zairi, M., and Al-Mashari, M., 2005, The role of benchmarking in best practice management and knowledge sharing. *The Journal of Computer Information Systems, 45,* 14–31.

Chapter 8

From Self-Service to Room Service: Changing the Way We Search, Sift, and Synthesize Information

Charles S. (Steve) Knode and Jon-David W. Knode

Contents

Introduction

Obtaining, organizing, and incorporating the necessary information for actions or decision-making has, until now, been solely left to the individual efforts of the user. Usually the user searched a finite information source (a library or database), found and extracted the needed information, and then synthesized it into the proper format (e.g., white paper, term paper, report, action paper, etc.). This approach, primarily one of "self-service," has been the norm. Within this self-service model, the user has the burden of finding the proper information, filtering it into the proper format, fusing it into a credible document relevant to the need, and distributing that document to the appropriate parties. In an era where information was relatively limited and access to that information mainly local (e.g., the local library or a database within the organization), this model worked well for many. The user simply found whatever information he or she required and synthesized it into the necessary form.

Now, with an information hyper-abundance, the tasks of searching, sifting, and synthesizing information may no longer be manageable by human effort alone. Indeed, the "self-service" model of information retrieval and digestion might necessarily have to change to more of a "room service" model, wherein alternate approaches to dealing with information have to be explored and, where useful, adopted. In the room service model, the user orders what information (contextually based) he or she needs, in what format the information is needed, the time when the information is needed, and the way in which the information should be delivered. Then, in an effective room service approach, the information would arrive at the proper time, in just the right amount, in the proper format, and contextually relevant to the problem or request at hand. In essence, the user is ordering information to be prepared in advance, not unlike room service in a hotel. If the room service is successful, the user will be provided with the right goods, in the right format, at the proper time. Room service, properly implemented, relieves the user of some of the burden of finding, filtering, and fusing the information.

The Information Overload Situation

There is a unique confluence of events contributing to the situation in which obtaining and digesting the needed information is practically unmanageable by human effort alone. Those events include

- *The amount of information already available has reached epic proportions.* In one of the earliest attempts to measure the amount of information available, researchers at the School of Information Management and Systems at the University of California at Berkeley estimated that by the year 1999, mankind had accumulated a total of 12 exabytes of information over the previous 300,000 years (Woodman, 2000). At that time, further estimates were that it would only take about 3 years to accumulate another 12 exabytes (Woodman, 2000). However, more recent estimates of the size of the digital universe calculate that by 2007 there were already 281,000,000,000 gigabytes (281 exabytes) of information available, or about 45 gigabytes for every man and woman on the planet (Gantz et. al, 2008, p. 7). Even more disturbing is the claim by some that the "invisible Web" (i.e., that portion of the World Wide Web not accessible by normal search engines) may actually be 500 times larger than the visible Web (Boswell, n.d.)! Included in this "invisible or hidden" Web would be private Web sources, Web sites that can only be accessed by forms, scripted pages, unlinked pages, databases, etc. Clearly, the information warehouse now contains much more information than at any time in history and certainly much more than can be digested. Indeed, there is even an organization dedicated to dealing with the information overload, the Information Overload Research Group (IORG).

■ *There is an increase in the rate of information growth.* As though the amount of information already available were not enough, the pace at which information is created is continuing to increase. According to one recent report by Gantz et al. (2009), the amount of information (paper and digital combined) created in organizations has been growing faster than 65% per year (p. 2). Recent estimates now put the total amount of information created in just one year (2008) at the phenomenal number of 487 billion gigabytes (Gantz and Rentzel, 2009, p. 1). Additionally, in 2007, for the first time, the amount of information created was more than could be stored (Gantz and Rentzel, 2009, p. 2). Further estimates are that in 2012 the amount of information created and added to the information universe will be five times that of 2008 (Gantz and Rentzel, p. 1). Compounding the problem, this information now comes in many forms, not just words. Much of the information being created is in the form of audio and video, requiring more diverse methods of cataloging and analyzing these different forms of information. Increasingly, there is a lot of wasted energy dealing with this information. Workers, for example, consumed more than $1.5 trillion in salaries just doing nonproductive information work, such as reentering documents into databases and reformatting documents for use (Gantz et al., 2009). Significantly, workers rate the use of technology to help manage the information overload as a positive (Gantz et al., 2009).

■ *Access to information has been greatly expanded.* Not only is the amount of information being generated growing at an amazing rate, but coincidentally the ability to access this information is also growing. Indeed, the development of the Internet, with the bulk of the generated information now available to many with a computer equipped with a browser and access to the internet, means that no longer is there a need to even visit a library to find information. Although the actual number of persons with Internet access remains relatively low on a global basis—25.6%, (according to Internet World Stats)—penetration in the industrialized countries of the world is much higher. Further, the growth over the past decade has been phenomenal, with access growth up over 380% (Internet World Stats, n.d.). Broadband penetration alone has increased over 300% between 2002 and 2008 (The need for Internet speed, 2008). Library databases are online for many, access is getting close to ubiquitous in the developed world, and the ease with which information can be accessed continues to improve.

■ *There is an increased amount of information generated by things (e.g., sensors, RFID chips, etc.) rather than people, that is, the "Internet of things"* (Perez, 2009). Adding to the information overload created by humans is an ever-increasing amount of information created by "things". Embedded sensors, radio frequency identification (RFID) chips, etc., are proliferating, thereby contributing large amounts of data (and "noise") to the information ware-house. HP, for example, plans to build a planetwide network of billions of sensors, capable of interacting in various manners including recognizing, interacting, and adapting to humans (Wylie, 2009). Likewise, in a recent speech, Samuel J. Palmisano, IBM Chairman of the Board, outlined IBM's effort to develop a "smarter planet," one equipped with sensors and other intelligent systems to provide and act on information (*Welcome to the Decade of Smart*, 2010). Other estimates are that by 2010 there could be as many as 14 billion devices connected to the Web as compared to the estimated 100 million devices connected to the Web in 2000 (Swanson and Gilder, 2008, p. 18). With so many devices "talking", there would seem to be little pos-sibility for humans to listen and digest the vast amount of information cre-ated by these sensors and other devices. Yet the talking could be of extreme relevance to the situation. Imagine an overheated toaster trying to commu-nicate to the nearby curtain that a fire is imminent; or, a sensor in a broken water pipe calling for help; a lost wallet trying to "phone home." Listening to all this noise will require the use of advanced, automated agent technology capable not only of listening to but interpreting (and, in many cases, acting upon) the information.

■ *There is a growing need for real-time information.* Compounding the informa-tion overload problem is the need for real-time information to accommodate the reduction in decision times available for modern organizations, especially those decisions at the operational level. With the pace of business so rapid and the need to make and implement key decisions on an almost real-time basis, there is a tremendous compression of time available to find, digest, and act on information. Delays in obtaining the needed information can result in missed opportunities. In a recent article, Bernard Moon summarized con-cisely the key trends in the growth of the need for real-time information (Moon, n.d.). First, collaboration is ripening and companies that can keep immediately abreast of key information and adjust accordingly in real-time have an advantage. Changes to products, response to customers, adjustments to strategies can all be made quickly. Second, real-time analytics has become more important. Shopping information, point-of-sale data, customer reviews, etc., all need to be quickly analyzed and acted upon. Third, the expansion of real-time search is growing. As life-streaming activities continue to expand, the need to be able to search (and act upon) these activities will increase. The fourth trend is that of real-time ecommerce, necessitating keeping instantly informed about changes to inventories, adjustments in the pricing of commodities, even maintaining watch over the organization's supply chain management function.

With the developing information tsunami now clearly evident, the "what" of the information overload situation is also fairly obvious—too much information to digest. However, the "so what" aspects are more difficult to quantify, namely, exactly what happens in an era where information is too plentiful to digest? There seem to be several subtle negative effects that become noticeable. First, analysis becomes almost impossible due to the sheer amount of information to be processed and the rapid pace at which new information is created. Second, shallow knowledge becomes the norm as users move quickly from information item to information item in a vain attempt to keep up. Third, there is an increase in stress levels as users realize they are falling further and further behind—causing more instances of burnout or information fatigue.

Taken together these factors are combining to create a situation where, in order to effectively manage information overload, the use of advanced information technology is becoming a must rather than a nice-to-have. Fortunately, there are concurrent developments in the arena of information technology approaches which can assist in managing this new information rich environment—things such as the semantic Web, Web 2.0 technologies, intelligent sensors, learning agents, etc. The task for the user is how to adapt and leverage these technologies to accommodate this new overwhelmingly information rich environment.

Moving Toward a Room Service Model

One of the most important aspects of dealing with information is the ability to synthesize various pieces of information together into a coherent final product. Prior to the information hyperabundance, the synthesis problem often meant taking a few pieces of information and filling in the missing parts. Now, given the information overload, the problem is one of filtering out unnecessary, unneeded, or irrelevant information. Too much information, not too little, is available.

Fortunately, as the information overload situation has worsened, opportunities for utilizing information technology and other methods designed to help mitigate the situation have begun to emerge. Even now, there are possibilities for using information technology combined with alternate approaches to assist in automating how information is searched, sifted, and synthesized. Using these methods can help move information management from the self-service paradigm to the room service paradigm. By using some of these emerging technologies, users can leverage their ability to navigate the information hyperabundance and move closer toward the "room service" model of information interaction.

Dealing with the information overload will require adapting to new approaches and experimenting with new ideas as well as new technologies. Early adopters will, no doubt, find roadblocks and encounter difficulties as they blaze the trail for others. Many of the new approaches for interacting with information are only in their formative stages, so adjustments will be required as these approaches evolve and mature. However, trying to maintain the "self-service" model in an era of information overload would seem to be destined for failure. Thus, the approach of trying newer methodologies has merit, including some of the following ideas:

- *Employ a myriad of search engines and search methods.* Certainly, finding the proper and needed information starts with the search function. Although there are many avenues to pursue when searching for information, most people simply choose to use the large search engine services. Large search engines, which are extensive in their coverage and easy to use, operate mostly in the self-service mode, meaning the user has to do much of the work (i.e., put in the search terms of relevance, sift through the many hits, try to avoid duplicate and dead links, etc.). However, there are other search engines that contain features more closely approximating the room service model. One example, Copernic Agent, offers a search engine which differs in many ways from the larger, more popular search engines. The Copernic search engine, for example, requires that a search term be entered only once. After that, the search term is remembered by the engine for future searches that are conducted automatically, according to a predetermined schedule. Additionally, any changes to the found links are automatically sent to the user (if desired). Further, Copernic will automatically remove dead and duplicate links, search social media, and even search much of the invisible Web. In this sense, Copernic functions much more like an automated service (e.g., room service), understanding (to a degree) what it is you are seeking and bringing it to you. Moreover, there are many other nontraditional search engines that attempt to improve or differentiate the searching process. Some examples include
  - Wolfram alpha—a long-term project designed to give everyone access to expert knowledge, with results computed to make more sense than traditional searches. Includes methodology for how information was obtained (Lardinois, 2009). *Note*: Wolfram|Alpha is especially effective at questions with a mathematical basis, for example, any type of calculus or algebra problem can be solved with the methodology shown in detail.
  - Lecture Browser—a specialized search engine, developed and released by MIT, which solves an annoying problem, namely how to search through video lectures for the appropriate material. This tool can pinpoint keywords in audio and video lectures (Greene).
  - Cha-Cha—a no-cost search engine that combines machine intelligence with humans to provide answers to almost any type of question, including very mundane ones such as: (1) who plays Allison in the Payton Manning

VISA commercial? (2) What percentage of Americans have more than $10,000 in credit card debt? (3) How do I get a book published? (4) What are the requirements for welfare? (ChaCha).
- Collecta—one of the first search engines to specialize in "real-time" data, collected from blogs, tweets, social networks (e.g., facebook, myspace). (Morgan)
- Goggles—no words needed, just take a picture with your intelligent phone, feed it into the Google database, and the gap is bridged between the physical world and the Web. Information will be automatically returned relevant to the picture (Helft, 2009).
- Hakia—one of the first search engines to employ semantic concepts. Hakia's search results, for example, must (1) come only from credible Web sites recommended by librarians; (2) represent the most recent information available; (3) remain absolutely relevant to the query (Hakia).

In each case, these search engines, although still mainly in early releases, are changing the way in which information is found. Depending on what type of information is needed, the format in which it is needed, and the time frame in which it is needed, these different modes of searching are becoming more and more useful in finding information more suitable to the request. They provide, in many cases, more *context relevant* methods for searching.

■ *Utilize methods that "push" information rather than "pull" information.* Many still employ the self-service model by doing their own searching for information. However, a room service model is often a preferable approach. When users look for their own information, they must remember to redo searches as information changes or is updated. The chances of missing valuable information are heightened as users forget or run out of time to keep redoing searches. Instead, why not rely on "room service" to bring information on demand to the user? There are currently several ways to insure that changed information is automatically brought to the user. The use of really simple syndication (RSS), for example, allows for information from Web sites to be automatically and continuously "pushed" to the user. Many sites now offer RSS links, allowing for information to be relayed to the user when it changes. Other sites (e.g., Accenture, Educause, ReadWriteWeb, Google, among others) offer their own notification service and send updates when key information changes. In fact, some of these sites are now offering more selective updates, providing information more focused on the exact need of the user. An example of this evolving approach would be the ReadWriteWeb notifier widget (Perez, 2010). With this widget, users can specify a more focused notification, only receiving updates related to a particular interest. Finally, yet another way to receive automatic updates is to subscribe to "twitter" feeds from those who are providing information of interest. Persons using twitter send "tweets" about subjects at any time. Upon finding a person tweeting on a subject of interest, the user can follow the tweets and remain continuously updated.

■ *Find ways to make information more contextually relevant.* A point has been reached where *content* is no longer the problem, but *context* is. Unlike a decade ago, when content was lacking, the current information rich environment contains a plethora of content. What is needed now is the ability to put that information into proper *context.* Gathering lots of information, even automatically, is not of significant value if much of the information is not relevant to the need. Improving the context of information found and synthesized adds measurably to the overall process. Already there exist nascent methods that can be employed in an attempt to make information more relevant contextually to the situation, that is, provide information that is more appropriate and useful for the particular situation. Some of the emerging approaches that appear to provide assistance in adding context include

1. *Location awareness:* providing information contextually relevant to the location of the user. Knowing where sources, especially human ones, of key information are located can help make information more contextually relevant. In some instances, the location of the source of the information is relevant (e.g., directions, location of stores, location of friends, location of meeting places, etc.) Twinkle, for example, can provide location awareness for tweeters, thus help users locate those nearby who might be able to provide context relevant tweets, or instant information. In a similar manner, the Firefox browser can tell Websites your location so that information provided is more contextually relevant. According to an article in Wired (Honan, 2009), WhosHere is an iPhone app that can provide relevant information, based on location, for shopping, social events, dating, providing pictures, etc.

2. *Semantic Web:* establishing relationships among online pieces of information to make the information more "context" relevant. Now, several years into development, initial aspects of the semantic Web are starting to emerge. Early efforts to develop a common semantic approach seem promising (Greenemeier, 2009). If successful, the semantic Web would add a measure of 'understanding' to concepts being searched, thereby enhancing the relevance of returned items. No longer would search words be misunderstood (e.g., does a search for 'chips' mean California Highway Patrol, computer chips, or potato chips?). Rather, the term would be understood much more appropriately based on other search relevant aspects. As the Greenemeier article points out, "You ask your question at very high level, and it takes care of filling in the details for you." One illustrative example of technology making use of the semantic Web concept is Twine. Twine discovers information that matters to the user automatically once primed. By building on the technologies of the semantic Web, notably the Rich Description Framework (RDF) language, Twine is able to distill

additional knowledge from links and recommend additional links with similar or complimentary information (Twine homepage, n.d.). Other examples of how the semantic Web is already making information more context relevant at the corporate level include using the semantic Web to improve back-end operations (Vodaphone), leveraging the semantic Web to help vendors develop joint products (British Telecom), employing semantic Web technologies to help the U.S. military interpret rules of engagement for convoy movements (MITRE), providing annotated timelines of current events (Harper's) and managing the schedules and program guides for television viewers (Joost)(Feigenbaum, et. al, 2007).

3. *Crowdsourcing:* making use of the collective wisdom of crowds to improve on the information provided. Part of the popularity of this approach, undoubtedly, is due to the successful book by James Surowiecki, *The Wisdom of Crowds.* In his book, Surowiecki provides numerous examples wherein crowds of persons dealing with a problem were able to provide better answers than experts. Key aspects to successful use of the wisdom of crowds include (1) groups have rules governing behavior, (2) groups talk to each other, but only in a limited manner and not always, (3) groups have an optimal size, neither too large nor too small, (4) diversity and independence are present in the group, (5) the groups are informed (Surowiecki (2005) pp. 33–50). Leveraging the wisdom of crowds, either through collaborative documents or a wiki approach could assist in sifting and sorting data.

4. *Real-time information:* capturing information almost as it happens. Information, in some instances, has more value when it is obtained in real-time. Latency in information can be destructive to its value. Real-time information, properly acted upon or incorporated into the decision process, can often result in better outcomes. Marshall Kirkpatrick has outlined three models of value for real-time information (Kirkpatrick, 2009), including ambiance, automation, and emergence. In his article, Kirkpatrick points out that each of these can add significant value to the information provided. The use of ambiance, for example, provides additional links to search results, thereby giving more depth (and significance) to the found results. Automation encompasses the concept of continuously monitoring information and 'pushing' relevant real-time information to the user. Emergence is an approach to real-time information that focuses on "hot topics" that become important quickly (i.e., emergent), so that users can have the latest information on these hot topics. In each instance, ambiance, automation, or emergence, the value of the information is increased because it is discovered in real time.

5. *Intelligent agents:* software programs (agents) that can autonomously help find, filter, and fuse information. Imbued with elements of natural language processing, virtual personas, clever programming, and fuzzy

logic, intelligent agents are yet another technology being developed to assist in searching, sorting, and synthesizing information. The *Knowledge Navigator* video vignette (circa 1988), produced by Apple Computer, has long exemplified one version of this room service model. In this vignette, information is supplied and interpreted by intelligent assistants—assistants capable of finding, filtering and fusing information. These agents work in conjunction with the user to provide information of the proper kind in the proper format. Not only do the agents have the capability to find information for the user, but they have enough understanding of what the user actually wants to automatically filter information into the proper context. We are not yet at the knowledge navigator level with the tools that currently are available, but we are approaching such rapidly. Bainbridge argues, for example, that the next stage of the integration of information technology with human thought and perception is on the near horizon, featuring agents which are beginning to take over cognitive tasks from humans (Bainbridge, 2008, p. 8). Indeed, several tools or programs that feature an intelligent agent approach to dealing with information already exist, including: (1) Copernic Summarizer (Copernic summarizer, n.d.), an agent which can summarize virtually any document, maintaining the relative importance of terms and concepts within the document; (2) virtual experts, several of which are available for demonstration at http://www.nextit.com/, including a virtual expert on Alaskan Airlines and an expert on the U.S. Army; (3) Maria, a statistics agent possessing over 118,000 rules of logical inference, capable of conversing about statistics (Artificial intelligence is alive and well, n.d.); (4) Virtual Eve, a virtual teacher that can pick up body language and facial expressions like a real teacher and, thus, maintain interaction with students (Massey university, 2007), and; (5) Siri, an agent capable of finding movie theaters, booking flight reservations, answering questions, etc. (Ackerman, 2009). Siri, an offshoot from the Cognitive Assistant that Learns and Organizes (CALO) DARPA project, is not yet ready to perform at the level postulated in the Knowledge Navigator, but, equipped with speech recognition, a measure of fuzzy logic, and built-in clever programming, it does exemplify the latest in where intelligent agent technology is headed (Spivack, 2009). Siri has the potential to markedly shift the emphasis on search to an emphasis on assistance, thereby providing 'room service'. With Siri, the focus is on performing a task rather than just providing information. As demonstrated at the SemTech2009 Conference, Siri is amazingly capable, even in her first release. Virtual personal agents such as Siri are beginning to take on serious tasks, tasks heretofore only performed by humans (Hamm, 2009).

6. *CYC project:* Unique among efforts to provide context to information was the CYC project. More than twenty-five years in development, the goal

of CYC is to embody enough "common sense" that deeper knowledge can be obtained (CYC Website, n.d.). Over time, CYC has developed an extensive knowledge base on many subjects from which it can reason to find more information (Lenat, 2006). By combining this knowledge base with the many hundreds of thousands of assertions or rules contained in CYC, the ability of CYC to understand not just store information is being developed (Lenat, 2006).

Challenges and Obstacles

The path towards a more "room service" mode of dealing with information will certainly not be without interruptions and challenges. Technology advances do not occur in an extremely predictable manner, nor does the adoption of new methods to incorporate advances occur all at once. The early adopters (even the early major-ity) who go first run the risk of spending time and effort (not to mention money and other resources) investigating approaches that may not have the desired out-comes. Many potential roadblocks will need to be navigated during the transition from self-service to "room service." Some key likely occurrences include

- *Finding time to learn new technologies:* Learning to interact and leverage new technologies, especially those still early in the development cycle, requires "play" time—time to experiment and make mistakes, to try out different strategies, to move up the learning curve. Today's users are so overwhelmed with the information overload situation that it becomes almost impossible to find such experimental time. Just keeping slightly abreast of new information requires more time than available. Finding additional play time is impossible for many. To understand new information of any kind, a certain process must take place according to Richard Saul Wurman (Wurman, 1989, p. 53). First, the information has to have some interest for the user. Next, the information must be relatable to ideas already understood. However, the most essential prerequisite is to admit when you don't understand some-thing. Admitting you don't know leads to questions enabling you to learn (Wurman, p. 54).
- *Adopting a new information interaction paradigm:* Switching to a new infor-mation paradigm (i.e., "room service" vice "self-service") will not be easy or smooth. Innovative development in all areas, including information technol-ogy, tends to be uneven. Often innovations are "disruptive" in nature, not just "sustaining" modest improvements in the current technology. As Clayton Christensen outlined in his work on disruptive innovation, established orga-nizations and individuals have trouble embracing disruptive innovations that radically change the current method of operation (Prewitt, 2001). Doing what one has always done is difficult to change. The added complexity and

rapid pace of change in information technology only makes the adjustments more difficult.

■ *Adjusting to new privacy and security concerns:* There are two sides to the "room service" paradigm. Once implemented, room service can be extremely functional, especially as technologies such as the semantic Web and intelligent agents begin to learn and know more about those they are assisting. However, knowing more about someone could also mean knowing about their financial situation, their medical condition, their ethical standards, their political views, etc. Until now, many have zealously guarded these private areas. However, to be effective, the room-service savants will need to have extensive information about those they are assisting in order to provide information more focused on their needs. This loss of privacy, combined with the inevitable security concerns, will mean that exposure to the room service paradigm will not come without risk. A vignette illustrating the extensive nature to which information could be known in the near future about a person is available at: The Big Brother Pizza Shop.

■ *Changing the culture of information interaction:* Cultural resistance is yet another barrier to be overcome in changing the information paradigm. Just as disruptive innovation causes angst among those set in comfortable ways of doing something, organizational cultures will resist change. Established ways, unless they are clearly failing, are often slow to lose their following. Things rarely break entirely, they just become less efficient. Shocking an organizational culture into a new paradigm for dealing with information will require more than minor adjustments. The current culture is primarily a by-product of a generation which did not grow up comfortable with computers. Today's leaders, those in their 50s and 60s, have not experienced the constant hum of information noise until now, and the methods for dealing with that noise will not be quickly adopted by many.

Summary and Conclusion

An information tidal wave is upon us. The vast amount of information already existent is enormous and quickly becoming unmanageable by current methods. Further, other trends, including the increasing pace of information creation, development of the "internet of things," proliferation of real-time information and the shrinking decision cycle are making the situation even more overwhelming. The current "self-service" mode for dealing with information is likely to be less than sufficient to deal with this overload.

A new model, based on the concept of room service and featuring the leveraging of emerging information technology approaches offers a possible way to improve the searching, sifting, and synthesizing of information. Ideas such as employing a variety of search methods and engines, "pushing" rather than "pulling" information, and employing methods which make information more context relevant offer promise in assisting with the information navigation needed. Although still mostly in the developmental stage, technologies associated with the room service approach are already making a mark with the early adopters.

There will, however, be challenges and obstacles moving from the current method of information searching, sifting, and synthesizing information. Changing the corporate culture, finding time to experiment with new approaches without penalty, and adjusting to a new information paradigm, while at the same time accommodating the need for security and privacy, will not be easy. Those failing to change, however, seem destined only to watch the problem worsen as the information tsunami crashes to shore.

References

Ackerman, E. (2009, May 28). Siri lifts veil on intelligent assistant. Retrieved October 1, 2009, from http://www.physorg.com/news162754631.html.

Artificial Intelligence Is Alive and Well. (n.d.). Retrieved October 1, 2009, from http://www.scoop.co.nz/stories/SC0501/S00029.htm.

Bainbridge, W. (2008). Cognitive Expansion Technologies. *Journal of Evolution and Technology*, 19(1), 8–16.

Boswell, W. (n.d.). The Invisible Web. Retrieved December 10, 2009, from http://websearch.about.com/od/invisibleweb/a/invisible_web.htm.

ChaCha: Your mobile BFF (n.d.). Retrieved December 10, 2009, from http://www.chacha.com/.

Copernic Agent—More Than a Simple Web Search Engine. (n.d.). Retrieved October 1, 2009, from http://www.copernic.com/en/products/agent/features.html.

Copernic Summarizer—Free Yourself from Information Overload. (n.d.). Retrieved October 1, 2009, from http://www.copernic.com/en/products/summarizer/features.html.

CYC Website (n.d.). Retrieved October 1, 2009, from http://www.cyc.com/.

Feigenbaum, L., Herman, I., Hongsermeier, T., and Stephens, S. (2007, December). Retrieved October 1, 2009 from http://www.thefigtrees.net/lee/sw/sciam/semantic-web-in-action#to-how-it-works.

Gantz, J., Chute, C., Manfrediz, A., Minton, S., Reinsel, D., Schlichting, W., and Toncheva, A. (2008, March). An Updated Forecast of Worldwide Information Growth through 2011. Retrieved October 1, 2009, from http://www.emc.com/collateral/analyst-reports/diverse-exploding-digital-universe.pdf.

Gantz, J., Boyd, A., and Dowling, S. (2009, March). Tackling Information Overload at the Source. Retrieved October 1, 2009, from http://www.xerox.com/downloads/usa/en/n/nr_IDC_White_Paper_on_Information_Overload.pdf.

Gantz, J., and Rentzel, D. (2009, May). As the Economy Contracts, the Digital Universe Expands. Retrieved October 1, 2009, from http://www.scribd.com/doc/15748837/IDC-Multimedia-White-Paper-As-the-Economy-Contracts-the-Digital-Universe-Expands.

Greenemeier, L. (2009, November 9). It's All Semantics: Searching for an Intuitive Internet that Knows What is Said—and Meant. Retrieved December 19, 2009, from http://www.scientificamerican.com/article.cfm?id=semantics-searching-intuitive-internet.

Hakia Website (n.d.) Retrieved October 1, 2009, from http://company.hakia.com/about.html.

Hamm, S. (2009, June 4). How Cloud Computing will Change Business. Retrieved October 1, 2009, from http://www.businessweek.com/magazine/content/09_24/b4135042942270.htm.

Helft, M. (2009, December 19). Snap and Search (no words needed). Retrieved December 19, 2009 from http://www.nytimes.com/2009/12/20/business/20ping.html?_r=1.

Honan, M. (2009, January 19). I Am Here: One man's experiment with the Location-Aware Lifestyle. Retrieved October 1, 2009, from http://www.wired.com/gadgets/wireless/magazine/17-02/lp_guineapig?currentPage=all.

Information Overload Research Group (IORG) (n.d.). Retrieved October 1, 2009, from http://www.iorgforum.org/.

Internet World Stats. (n.d.) Retrieved December 12, 2009, from http://www.internetworld-stats.com/stats.htm.

Kirkpatrick, M. (2009, May 8). 3 Models of Value in the Real Time Web. Retrieved December 12, 2009, from http://www.readwriteweb.com/archives/three_models_of_value_in_the_real_time_web.php.

Knowledge Navigator [video] (n.d.) Retrieved October 1, 2009, from http://video.google.com/videoplay?docid=-5144094928842683632#.

Lenat, D. (2006, December 6). Computers vs. Common Sense [Presentation]. Retrieved October 1, 2009, from http://content.digitalwell.washington.edu/msr/external_release_talks_12_05_2005/14019/lecture.htm.

Lardinois, F. (2009, April 25). Wolfram|Alpha: Our First Impressions. Retrieved October 1, 2009, from http://www.readwriteweb.com/archives/wolframalpha_our_first_impressions.php.

Massey University (2007, November 19). Virtual Eve: First in Human Computer Interaction. Retrieved October 1, 2009, from http://www.physorg.com/news114704050.html.

Moon, B. (n.d.). 4 Emerging Trends of the Real-Time Web. Retrieved December 12, 2009, from http://mashable.com/2009/10/29/real-time-web-trends/.

Morgan, K. (2010, January 10). Collecta: Real-Time Search. Retrieved January 12, 2010 from http://www.seochat.com/c/a/Search-Engine-News/Collecta-Real-Time-Search/.

Perez, S. (2009, February 13). 5 Companies Building the Internet of Things. Retrieved October 1, 2009, from http://www.readwriteweb.com/archives/5_companies_building_the_internet_of_things.php.

Perez, S. (2010, January 27). Get the ReadWriteWeb Chrome Extension. Retrieved January 27, 2010 from http://www.readwriteweb.com/archives/get_the_readwriteweb_chrome_extension.php.

Prewitt, E. (2001, April 1). Interview: Clayton Christenson on Disruption. Retrieved October 1, 2009, from http://www.cio.com/article/30099/Interview_Clayton_Christenson_on_Disruption.

Pioneers in Harvesting the Deep Web. (n.d.) Retrieved October 1, 2009, from http://web-search.about.com/gi/o.htm?zi=1/XJ&zTi=1&sdn=websearch&cdn=compute&tm=7&f=00&su=p284.9.336.ip_p504.1.336.ip_&tt=2&bt=0&bts=0&zu=http://bright-planet.com/.

Spivack, N. (2009, May 27). Siri: A Powerful Virtual Assistant for the iPhone. Retrieved October 1, 2009, from http://www.techcrunch.com/2009/05/27/siri-the-virtual-assistant-that-will-make-everyone-love-the-iphone-even-more/.

Surowiecki, J. (2005). *The Wisdom of Crowds*. New York: Anchor Books.

Swanson, B., and Gilder, G. (2008, January). Estimating the Exaflood. Retrieved October 1, 1009, from http://www.discovery.org/scripts/viewDB/filesDB-download.php?command=download&id=1475.

The Need for Internet Speed: Broadband Penetration Increased more than 300% Since 2002. (2008, April 15). Retrieved October 1, 2009, from http://www.scarborough.com/press_releases/Broadband%20FINAL%204.15.08.pdf.

Twine homepage. (n.d.). Retrieved October 1, 2009, from http://www.twine.com/.

"Welcome to the Decade of the Smart." (n.d.). Retrieved January 12, 2010, from http://www.ibm.com/smarterplanet/us/en/events/sustainable_development/12jan2010/.

Woodman, E. (2000, October 19). Information Generation. Retrieved October 1, 2009, from http://www.cni.org/tfms/2000b.fall/handout/How-KSwearingen2000Ftf.pdf.

Wurman, R.S. (1989). *Information Anxiety*. New York: Doubleday.

Wylie, M. (2009, November). Earth Calling: Turn Off the Lights!. Retrieved December 12, 2009 from http://www.hpl.hp.com/news/2009/oct-dec/cense.html.

KM AND E-LEARNING: CASE STUDIES

Chapter 9

Performance-Based Learning and Knowledge Management in the Workplace

Minhong Wang, Jürgen Moormann, and Stephen J.H. Yang

Contents

Introduction

Fierce competition, globalization, and a dynamic economy have forced organizations to search for new ways to improve their competitive advantages. In pursuance of this, *knowledge* is seen as the core resource and *learning* is viewed as the important process. It is crucial for organizations to enhance their capabilities for effective learning and knowledge management, especially by using information and communication technologies (ICTs) in the digital economy.

Recent studies have motivated the integration of learning and knowledge management for organizational strategic development (Wang and Yang, 2009). While formal learning or training programs deliver explicit knowledge and skills, everyday work practice and activities generate implicit or tacit knowledge. Learning is seen as a knowledge creation and transfer process where explicit and tacit knowledge embedded in organizations meet each other via social interaction (Nonaka and Takeuchi, 1995). It requires a range of approaches and technologies to create, retain, and distribute knowledge for awareness, learning, and reuse.

This chapter investigates performance-based approaches to improve learning and knowledge management in workplace settings. Learning in the workplace is built on practical tasks and work situations. It takes place in the context of use, and thus the result often remains implicit and embedded in work practice. Performance-based approaches represent a set of strategies for the acquisition and application of knowledge, skills, and work habits through the performance of tasks that are meaningful and engaging to learners or knowledge workers (Hibbard, 1996; Berman, 2008). They make learning become more "real" and more significant to learners and knowledge workers.

In addition to the focus on meaningful tasks for learning and knowledge acquisition, performance-based approaches also pay high attention to learning targets and outcomes. In workplace settings, learning and knowledge management should not only concentrate on the ways individuals learn but also on the ways organizations achieve their goals (Rosenberg, 2006; Wang, 2010). More attention is needed on organizational policies, structures, and systems that link individual practice and organizational success. Performance-based approaches in the workplace are devoted to (1) ensuring that learning or knowledge management solutions are driven by business requirements and result in targeted performance, (2) supporting learners and managers with consistent and accurate administration, and (3) facilitating summative and formative evaluation of training or knowledge management programs for continuous improvement.

With respect to performance-based approaches, a variety of issues—such as business alignment planning, performance gap analysis, curriculum design, blended learning, performance support, coaching, and measurement and analysis—have been explored. In this chapter, two case studies are presented to investigate relevant issues.

The first case shows the use of role-play simulation as a coaching method to support performance-based learning in the banking sector. It is focused on the acquisition and application of tacit knowledge embedded in business practice. This case demonstrates how the training program actively involved employees and made them aware and participating in business process improvement. A process is a type of knowledge that is more tacit and embedded in practice or experiences. In order to help employees and senior managers acquire and apply such tacit knowledge, a role-play simulation program called KreditSim has been developed in Germany at the Frankfurt School of Finance and Management (Börner et al., 2009). In addition, software was applied to simulate and manage the process by automation.

The second case presents the development of a performance-oriented e-learning system for a software company. It aims to drive learning and knowledge management practice towards the goal of improving work performance by linking individual learning targets and organizational goals. This study used Key Performance Indicators (KPIs) to make organizational goals accomplishable by showing a clear picture to each individual as to what is important and what each one needs to learn. The KPI model was also used to identify each individual's work context, expertise, and proficiency, as well as to organize knowledge assets, with a view to facilitating knowledge sharing and social networking in the learning community (Wang, 2010). Using this approach, a prototype system has been developed with empirical evaluations to demonstrate the effectiveness of the approach.

Case I—Role-Play Simulation-Based Training for Business Process Improvement in Banking

Business processes has become a major topic in management. In fact, turning a company into a process-oriented organization is seen as a competitive advantage and fundamental to its success (Harmon, 2008). On one hand, radical approaches to business process management such as *Business Reengineering* are suggested (Hammer and Champy, 1993). They are implemented top-down by a company's management. On the other hand, there are evolutionary approaches offered, often referred to as *Business Process Improvement* (Harrington, 1991). They follow a bottom-up procedure that stresses explicitly the importance of employee involvement.

Six Sigma is a methodology belonging to the latter category and accentuating the importance of employee commitment. Within Six Sigma projects, data and statistical analyses of business processes are used to measure and improve the output of production- and service-oriented processes (Harry and Schroeder, 2006; Magnusson et al., Kroslid and Bergman, 2004). The methodology was named Six Sigma because it has been derived from the definition of a normal distribution. The standard deviation (σ) shows the deviation (rate of defects) from the statistical mean. A standard deviation of 6σ represents a 99.99966% quality level which means 3.4 defects per 1 million opportunities (Pande et al., 2000). The objective of Six Sigma initiatives is not only to eliminate any kind of defects but also to implement a culture of customer-orientation, process-awareness, and quality in the respective organization.

The success of such projects does not depend solely on the methodology itself but on the motivation and the commitment of employees. Service providers in particular face the challenge that some factors, such as human behavior (e.g., friendliness and willingness to help the customers), are difficult to control and have a decisive impact on the quality of the final product or the service delivery (Antony, 2004). Although banks are increasingly committed to the idea of business processes management, employees often struggle to transfer the process improvement concepts to their own industry since many of the concepts are derived from manufacturing. Hence, well-trained and motivated employees play an even more crucial role in the execution of service providers' processes. In a recent study conducted in the financial services industry, more than 70% of the respondents indicate that extensive and qualitatively excellent training courses are required to increase the chances of success for Six Sigma projects (Heckl et al., 2010). The role of people to the success and failure of business improvement initiatives is evidenced by many critical success factor studies (e.g., Amoroso, 1998).

The following case demonstrates how employees can be actively involved in the awareness of and participation in sustainable process improvement. In particular, it shows the use of role-plays as a training method and how performance-based learning can be supported. The case is illustrated with the example of the banking industry. Employee training plays a crucial part in the banking sector (e.g., Pollitt, 2008; Rohmetra and Easter-by Smith, 2004; Sappey and Sappey, 1999).

In addition to training, knowledge management plays an important role in this case. A process is a type of knowledge more tacit and embedded in practice or experience than other knowledge. In this training program, business process knowledge is predescribed in standardized materials, and is then applied in a role-play simulation program with relevant guidance and instructions. After performing the first round simulation in groups, learners are led by the facilitators to analyze and discuss their performance using the Six Sigma method. After identifying deficiencies in the current process, the learners optimize their process in a new simulation. In this way, the tacit knowledge of process improvement is externalized, delivered, refined, and reused via the performance-based learning approach. Social learning is also supported for knowledge creation and sharing.

The case is organized as follows. First, we provide an introduction as to how role-plays can support the training of employees. Second, the underlying idea and the procedural implementation of the bank-related role-play KreditSim are explained. Third, we consolidate our observations and point out the potential for enhancements.

Role-Play Simulation as Employee Training Instrument

Whenever companies send employees to training courses or seminars, they are interested in having their employees learn something valuable. The exact nature of what is actually learned depends on the particular context. Moreover, one specific training activity may actually aim at meeting multiple objectives. The training initiators may not have explicitly articulated these objectives and may not even be fully aware of them. For example, in order to convey information about and know-how of new legislation, the head of a loan department could easily provide each employee with a book outlining regulatory changes in the banking industry. But why would the manager send the employees to a training seminar instead? This question can be best answered by looking at the different types of learning. According to Klippert (2007) learning is generally divided into four categories:

- *Content and factual learning:* The acquisition of knowledge and facts, understanding explanations and phenomena, recognizing relationships and evaluating hypotheses provide together the basis for all other types of learning.
- *Methodological and strategic learning:* The focus is on structuring, organizing, and arranging the acquired knowledge. This entails the ability to independently apply, reflect, or further develop learnt lines of reasoning, working techniques, problem-solving or learning strategies within a subject-matter or cross-functional context (Hechenleitner and Schwarzkopf, 2006).
- *Social and communicative learning:* Utilizing the learned facts and knowledge as a basis for argumentation and discussion with other members in society, social competence can be developed. Central to this type of learning is a rational and responsible discourse, as such "behavior fosters teamwork," which in turn serves to enhance social-communicative abilities.
- *Affective learning:* The so-called self-competence encompasses the development of self-confidence, commitment, and motivation. Affective learning enables the individual to recognize and bring out his or her own talents and abilities and to develop reasoned ethical values and moral concepts (Hechenleitner and Schwarzkopf, 2006).

Referring to the example above, handing a book to each employee would certainly be sufficient to enable content and factual learning. However, the other three types of learning usually occur automatically during any training seminar, and thus positively influence employees' willingness and ability to perform. Moreover, these four types of learning are typically highly interrelated.

A role-play simulation-based training seminar KreditSim is introduced in this case. Simulation-based training offers certain advantages like learning histories as Parush et al. (2002) state. The authors show that a better performance was obtained via a simulation teaching tool that made the learning history available to the users during the learning process itself. Role-plays, being a specific type of simulation, support a number of different training objectives. They are also one of the widely used methods for training employees (Furunes, 2005). In role-plays participants assume particular responsibilities, i.e., a "role." Typically, role-plays are used as one of various different teaching methods within the course of a training seminar.

In particular, role-plays support the three latter types of learning. Commonly articulated objectives of role-plays contain the ability to deal with difficult situations, developing self-assurance, improving auto-perceptive and self-reflection skills, increasing motivation, and raising communicative effectiveness (Bliesener, 1994). But, it is important not to pursue too many objectives with a role-play. An overload of differing objectives may unsettle participant groups with little previous role-play experience, and thus inadvertently result in a defensive attitude towards the role-play (Broich, 1994).

Idea and Steps of KreditSim

Since Six Sigma originated in the production sector, Six Sigma training often focuses on examples from manufacture or the logistics sector. Subsequently, employees in the banking industry often find it difficult to cope with those processes. They also find it elusive to apply Six Sigma to the highly individualized (from their perspective) processes within the banking world (e.g., Snee and Hoerl 2009).

In order to sensitize employees and senior managers of banks to process problems and corresponding process improvement opportunities, the role-play simulation KreditSim has been developed at Frankfurt School of Finance and Management (Börner, Heckl & Hilgert, 2009). Since its introduction KreditSim has been conducted in many cases ranging from practitioners training to academic classes. The following description is based on Börner and Uremovic (2010).

KreditSim, a paper-based role-play, simulates the processing of a loan application from a new customer, i.e., the loan approval process, a core activity in bank business. The participants assume the roles of loan processing specialists, department head, controller, and management director of the fictitious Home Loan Bank Ltd., and they have to process loan applications in accordance with their given job descriptions. Each participant is responsible for handling only a small part of the entire process; when each participant fulfils his or her process tasks at their best, the entire process nevertheless yields an unsatisfactory result. Eliminating errors on the loan applications as well as reducing the long overall processing time can only be accomplished through a holistic, cross-functional analysis.

In this role-play, participants actively utilize Six Sigma tools to analyze and improve the process. Six Sigma offers the methodological support for conducting such process analysis. The starting point and the subsequent phases of the role-play KreditSim are illustrated in the following sections.

Initial Situation in the Role-Play

The role-play KreditSim is typically conducted as part of a one-day or multiple-day training seminar. At the beginning, the facilitator introduces the current situation that serves as a starting point for the role-play, providing the following overview: Home Loan Bank Ltd. is a regional bank that specializes in real estate financing. The bank maintains four branch offices. In these branch offices, sales specialists for real estate loans and financing services advise potential customers. The decision whether or not to approve a loan application is made at headquarters. The core of the loan approval process is intended to ensure time and quality in processing loan applications. The requirements for the processing of loan applications are represented by the following quality criteria:

■ Processing of the loan application with an approval or rejection decision within 4 days (in the role-play this equates to 4 minutes)
■ Determination of the correct credit rating
■ Consideration of customer requirements (e.g., interest rates, payment terms)

However, in most cases, the decision of a loan application will take 9 or 10 days (i.e., minutes). In addition, a number of errors will occur in the credit rating, which may result in wrong decisions about the approval of loan applications. Finally, specific customer requirements often will not have been sufficiently addressed during the processing of the loan application. Therefore, the facilitator can easily convince participants of the necessity to analyze and optimize the loan approval process.

To support the first-hand experience of the loan approval process and the subsequent optimization, facilitators often divide the seminar into three phases. The first phase consists of conducting the simulation of the predescribed loan approval process of Home Loan Bank Ltd., i.e., the current process. This phase is standardized and predetermined through the use of the game materials and adherence to the role-play instructions. The second phase focuses on optimizing the existing process. The facilitator guides the participants in the use of the tools within the DMAIC (Define, Measure, Analyze, Improve, Control) cycle, which is the main procedural method of Six Sigma (Pande et al., 2000). This model serves as the foundation for developing a new and improved loan approval process. In Phase III, participants simulate the optimized process design. Results from the new process are captured and compared with the results from the original process.

Simulation of Loan Approval Process (Phase I)

In Phase I, the loan approval process of the Home Loan Bank is simulated. Prior to Phase I, the facilitator has to prepare the simulation room. He arranges the

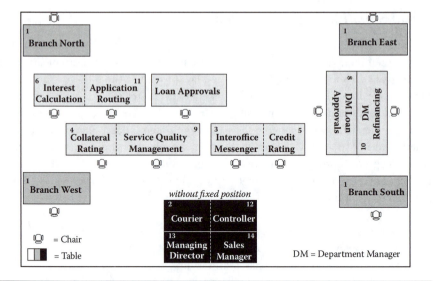

Figure 9.1 Outline of the floor plan.

work stations in the predefined floor layout (Figure 9.1) and distributes the job descriptions. Each participant chooses one of the prepared work stations randomly. The job descriptions help the participants become familiar with their working tasks.

In order to address potential kick-off problems and to avoid any misunderstanding, a trial run of the simulation is conducted first. The actual simulation of the loan approval process then begins. The objective is to process as many error-free loan applications as possible within 20 minutes. All quality criteria, namely time (a maximum of 4 minutes per application), correct credit rating, and consideration of additional customer requirements have to be met. Each minute the branch offices submit loan applications via a branch courier to headquarters. After a short time, it becomes apparent that the given process results in significant problems.

After the first simulation round, the facilitator leads participants in collecting data for the further analysis of the process. In a first step, incorrect loan applications are analyzed and documented according to quantity and types of errors. Generally, most applications will contain a time error, i.e., their processing required more than the allotted four minutes. An incorrect credit rating occurs frequently as well. An analysis of "Work-in-Process" provides an indication of how many incomplete loan applications have accumulated at each step of the process, highlighting bottlenecks within the process. An analysis of the processing times provides insights regarding the individual processing times of each function within the overall loan approval process (e.g., Collateral Rating). An optional analysis can be conducted for total processing time for each loan application since such data has been captured on each loan document.

In accordance with the facilitator's expectations, seminar participants easily recognize the need for process optimization when looking at the large number of processing errors and the long processing time. The facilitator can then move on to Phase II, the optimization of the loan approval process.

Optimization of Loan Approval Process (Phase II)

The facilitator can freely decide how to conduct the optimization of the loan approval process. In principle, the optimization can utilize the entire spectrum of available Six Sigma tools. Especially those tools that are most frequently applied in the financial services industry (Heckl and Moormann, 2008) can be illustrated through KreditSim completely. If seminar participants are familiar with Six Sigma, they should be free to select the tools of their choice.

In most instances, participants use the Project Charter and SIPOC (Supplier, Input, Process, Output, and Customer) from the Six Sigma toolbox to define the framework of the project. These two tools have proven to be especially useful during the Define–Phase. Process measurement and analysis can be conducted on the basis of the data which were collected during the first phase of the simulation (quantity and types of error analysis, Work-in-Process analysis, processing time analysis). Additional suitable tools are the Ishikawa Diagram and the Value Stream Map (Lunau et al., 2007). After the analysis, participants should be given sufficient time for the Improve Phase to optimize the loan approval process. There is no single "correct" solution for the redesigned process. Instead, the participants learn to identify causes for process deficiencies, such as duplicate tasks, redundant tasks, or unnecessary transportation and idle time.

Simulation of Optimized Loan Approval Process (Phase III)

The newly developed loan approval process is validated by a new simulation. Now, the participants prepare the simulation room, arrange the floor layout of working places, and distribute the new job descriptions. The new simulation only needs to take 10 minutes this time. The participants are able to measure the process by counting the amount of correct loan approvals within the given time frame and comparing the results to the previous simulation.

The experience with KreditSim shows that a significant improvement in process performance has been made in each case. Participants are usually very pleased with the outcome of their efforts. Often, additional ideas for further optimization are generated during or after the second simulation run, resulting in lively and fruitful discussions among participants. Generally, such additional ideas could be implemented after a further optimization phase followed by an additional simulation run.

Observations and Potential for Enhancements

Observations indicate that participants are highly receptive to the role-play simulation because the elements of active participation and first-hand experience serve to highlight the relevance and applicability of the Six Sigma tools to their day-to-day responsibilities. As one participant mentioned, "Now I really understand the problems we face in our headquarters; it is because of the interfaces between the departments."

Role-plays are widely accepted to support methodological and strategic learning. Hence, they are well-suited for Six Sigma training and the application of its tools. Since role-plays also encompass social and communicative learning as well as affective learning, they foster involvement and motivation of employees participating in trainings. Feedback such as "It was fun to participate in this role-play and to learn at the same time" demonstrates the motivational and learning effects. Thus, the role-play simulation not only helps boost awareness but also helps engage the staff members of banks in process improvement efforts.

One of the most commonly heard statements is, "It is important that all involved colleagues know the whole process. To achieve this, we have to talk *with* each other instead of *about* each other." This again highlights that social and communicative learning is an important part of role-plays in general and KreditSim in particular. Employees engaged in a process for many years often do not know the required input for following process steps. Consequently, they are not able to deliver satisfactory results in terms of quality no matter how hard they try. This is simply because of lack of communication and holistic process view. By participating in the role-play, the participants experience that many problems and annoyances can be mitigated or even resolved by better communication. Particularly, where a cross-functional process spans multiple divisions, exchange of information is insufficient in many cases.

Comments from participants, such as "I learned that it is important to raise awareness for business processes among employees," showed that the simulation is far more than factual or methodological learning. Although applying Six Sigma tools in practice is one of the main goals of the training, KreditSim is not limited to conveying certain techniques but is also useful for enhancing social and affective learning.

After successfully applying KreditSim in multiple scenarios of employee training, participants and facilitators proposed to enhance the simulation by software. Subsequently, a tool has been developed that simulates the process and manages workflows electronically instead of paper-based (Börner and Uremovic, 2010). The software supports the loan approval process described in the above section. Application of the software impressively shows how automation of routing work items (which is only one possibility of process improvement) and providing work lists for the respective roles can radically improve processes.

The simulation KreditSim can be used to target management and staff members alike. For a successful implementation of Six Sigma, it is indispensable to gain both management's support and employees' commitment. Usually, the former one is easier to achieve than the latter one. Most staff members overcome an early scepticism and feel enthusiastic about the improvements in time, cost, and quality of the optimized process. However, some are afraid of falling victim to another cost-cutting initiative. They are anxious of losing their job once the process is optimized. The simulation tackles this problem in prohibiting any layoffs so that all participants gain a (new) role in the improved process. Nevertheless, the facilitator should be well-prepared to argue that process improvement does not lead to layoffs. A failure to convey this message convincingly could lead to a loss of employees' support and commitment to a Six Sigma project or a process improvement initiative in general.

As organizations are becoming more business–process-oriented, the need for process management expertise and experience is increasing. Skills are considered a key factor of any process improvement initiative. The case of KreditSim shows that a role-play-based simulation can substantially support educational goals in this field (like teaching Six Sigma tools) and thus improve performance-based learning in the workplace.

Case II—KPI-Oriented E-Learning in the Workplace

With the rapid development of ICTs, e-learning is increasingly being used by organizations to explore new ways of learning and training for developing required workforce competence (Welsh et al., 2003) and enhancing human resource management professionals (Hussain et al., 2007). However, most e-learning applications have been developed for school learning programs; ignored the special feature of workplace learning that is based on practical tasks and work situations (Tynjälä, 2008). In most applications, the complexities of the interactions between e-learning and organizations have been underestimated. As a result, current e-learning applications are perceived as being less goal-effective due to a lack of alignment of learning with work performance.

To solve this problem, this study proposes conceptualization, development, and evaluation of a performance-oriented e-learning environment for the workplace. We use performance measurement to clarify organizational goals and individual learning needs, and link them in e-learning applications. The key idea lies in a Key Performance Indicator (KPI) model, where the organizational mission and vision are translated into a set of key performance targets for driving learning towards the goal of improving work performance. The KPI model helps an employee identify key performance indicators for his/her position, capabilities to be developed to improve the performance, knowledge topics relevant to the capability, and learning resources under the knowledge topic. This conceptualization makes organizational goals accomplishable by showing a clear picture to each individual as to what is important and what he/she needs to learn.

Further, this approach supports social learning and knowledge management in the workplace. The KPI model can be used to identify each individual's work context, expertise, and proficiency, as well as to organize knowledge assets, with a view to facilitating knowledge sharing and social networking in the learning community (Wang, 2010).

To implement the approach, ontology (Gruber, 1993) is utilized for a formal and explicit representation of the KPI model, so as to facilitate semantic reasoning of performance-oriented learning process. A set of adaptive functionalities has been developed to assist learners in performing customized learning activities according to their performance gap and learning progress.

The case study is organized as follows: First, we introduce the background knowledge of the KPI-based approach with its relation to learning in the workplace. Second, we elaborate the design of a KPI-oriented workplace e-learning system for a selected medium-size company in China. Third, the implementation of the approach in a prototype is demonstrated. Fourth, we present the empirical evaluations of the developed system to illustrate the effectiveness of the approach.

Key Performance Indicator (KPI)-Based Approach

While there is no doubt that the goal of e-learning in the workplace is to enhance individual and organizational performance (Rosenberg, 2006), there is a lack of concrete strategy or approach for achieving this goal in e-learning development. In this study, a KPI-based approach is proposed. Performance measurement is used by organizations as a procedure to improve performance by setting performance objectives, assessing performance, collecting and analyzing performance data, and utilizing performance results to drive further development. KPIs are financial and nonfinancial metrics used to help an organization define and measure progress towards organizational goals. A set of KPIs can be established to represent a set of measures focusing on different aspects of organizational and individual performance that are critical for the success of the organization (Parmenter, 2007). The KPI framework has a special meaning in workplace learning. KPI bridges the gap between an organization's mission and its employees' targets, making organizational goals accomplishable. KPI can be used to help employees set up rational learning objectives according to the knowledge gap. It can be used as a systemic scheme to organize and manage learning resources and activities in line with work context and performance requirement.

A KPI framework is designed based on an organization's structure and job system. It consists of three levels: organizational level, business unit level, and position level. In this study, we focus on KPIs at the position level, which have a closer relationship with e-learning development in the workplace. The KPI at the position level consists of three components: KPI item, rating criterion, and KPI value. *KPI items* are a set of performance indicators specified for a job position. For each KPI item, a *rating criterion* is set up to assess the performance of that KPI item. For each KPI item, the proficiency level achieved by an employee is called a *KPI value*. An employee's performance measure is a set of KPI values of his/her job position.

KPI-Oriented System Design

Based on the proposed KPI-based approach, we have developed a workplace e-learning system in this study. The system was developed for the Testing Unit of PEANUT software, a medium-size company. Testing is an important and mandatory part of software development, essential for evaluating the quality of software products by identifying their defects and problems.

In this study, a KPI framework is constructed to identify the KPI items of each position in an organization. KPI is used as a systemic scheme to direct learning targets and activities, and organize and manage learning resources in line with work context. To improve work performance, relevant capabilities need to be developed; the e-learning system is to help employees develop the capabilities by learning relevant knowledge. To design the KPI-oriented learning environment, ontology is used to conceptualize the KPI framework into a machine-readable format. The main concepts in this framework include position, key performance indicator (KPI), capability, and knowledge component (KC). This conceptualization helps an employee identify *key performance indicators* specified by the organization for his/her *position*. To improve the performance, the employee needs to develop relevant *capabilities*. To develop the capabilities, the employee needs to learn relevant knowledge, which can be represented as a number of *knowledge components* (KCs). In sum, one position is linked with one or more performance indicators; one performance indicator is linked with one or more capabilities; and one capability is linked with one or more KCs. In addition, relations between different KCs are also specified. For example, one KC can be linked to another KC based on relations such as prerequisite, composition, and relevance. Based on these concepts and their relations, a learning ontology can be defined for guiding individual learning processes.

To develop the prototype system, a KPI framework is constructed via intensive collaboration with the system designers, training managers, and experts of the company. The design of the framework is according to the company's organizational structure, job system, performance indicators (organizational level, business unit level, and position level), as well as the IEEE standards for software testing (Bertolino, 2001). Based on the designed KPI framework that can be implemented using ontology, performance-oriented learning can be facilitated by setting up rational learning objectives, accessing relevant knowledge artifacts, and directing individual learning processes through appropriate reasoning mechanism. In addition, relevant learning instructions should be specified to support effective navigation in the learning environment. For example, a capability can be acquired after its prerequisite is achieved. The details of how the performance-oriented learning process can be facilitated by the system are described as follows:

■ An employee's job performance is evaluated and recorded as a set of KPI values. If one or more KPI values of the employee do not meet the required level, an improvement is suggested.

- Based on the learning ontology, a set of KCs that are relevant for the KPI items to be improved are identified, and a customized assessment package to test the employee's knowledge is generated.
- The employee's learning profile is created and updated based on the outcome of the assessment.
- A personalized learning syllabus (a set of KCs and their relations) is generated to guide the learning process of the employee. The employee may consult a domain expert if the assessment results are not consistent with the KPI values.
- According to the learning syllabus or process guideline, a number of learning objects related to the KCs are recommended to the employee. During the learning process, the employee may take quizzes to assess his/her level of understanding of the subject matter.
- If the employee is not able to pass the quiz within a reasonable time frame, additional learning objects or suggestions will be provided, such as supplement materials relevant to the KCs, prerequisite knowledge that should be obtained before promotion to the current position, etc.
- The employee may continue to learn until he/she quits the learning process.

In addition to individual learning, social networking and knowledge management are also facilitated in the KPI-oriented learning environment. Learners are able to share and evaluate learning resources, discuss their learning problems or experiences at forums, and conduct peer evaluation of work performance. Each employee is provided with a KPI-based identification, that is, a set of KPI values that indicates his/her expertise and proficiency level, stored in the learner's profile. Learners, including domain experts, are able to get familiar with each other based on their KPI identifications and contribution to the learning community. In this way, self-directed and socially constructed learning activities in the workplace are effectively directed via integration of organizational interests, individual needs, work performance, and social context (Wang, 2010).

Implementation

To demonstrate the effectiveness of the approach, a prototype of the KPI-oriented workplace e-learning system has been developed. A set of screenshots from the prototype is shown in Figure 9.2. In this prototype, we used computational languages and tools to implement the ontology in the e-learning system. OWL-DL (Description Language) was used to define the KPI-based learning ontology. To support the reasoning services, instruction rules were bound with the ontology using DL safe SWRL (Semantic Web Rule Language). To implement both OWL ontology and SWRL rules, we used OWL-API to access Pellet (Sirin et al., 2007) as the semantic reasoning tool.

Moreover, to enable domain experts and training managers to construct and maintain the ontology, tools for ontology editing and visualization are necessary.

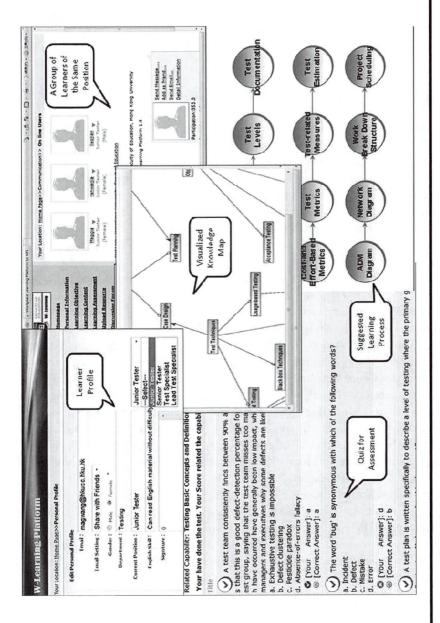

Figure 9.2   Screenshots of the prototype.

In this study, Protégé together with "SWRL tab" and "Jambalaya tab" plug-in were employed. Protégé is a free open-source ontology editor developed by Stanford Medical Informatics (SMI) at Stanford University (Noy et al., 2000). Protégé holds a library of plug-ins that adds more functionality to the environment. "SWRL tab" is a plug-in for protégé, which provides a SWRL Editor that supports the editing of SWRL rules. "Jambalaya tab" is another plug-in for Protégé to visualize the OWL ontology.

Evaluation

Twenty-four employees who were currently working or previously worked with the Testing Unit of the company participated in the experiments. Two parallel prototypes were used for evaluation—the prototype system developed using the KPI-oriented approach, and another traditional system without KPI support. The participants were divided into two groups of 14: the treatment group that used the KPI-based system and the control group that used the traditional system. There was no significant difference between the treatment group and the control group in the software industry work experience and the number of e-learning systems used before.

The data collected include learning-outcome related data obtained through pretests and post tests, and participants' perception data obtained through questionnaires and interviews. The evaluation was conducted based on Donald Kirkpatrick's model (Kirkpatrick, D.L. and Kirkpatrick, J.D., 2006), which includes four levels: reaction (how participants react to the learning system), learning (knowledge learning or skill development by using the application), behavior (transfer of learning into change of behavior by using the system), and result (organizational and individual outcome as a result of the training program). Questionnaire items were developed based mainly on Kirkpatrick, D.L. and Kirkpatrick, J.D. (2006) and Sun et al. (2008) with respect to evaluation of workplace learning and e-learning systems. Pretest and post test questions were designed based on certification examinations in the software testing profession and adjusted by subject experts.

The data collection process can be roughly divided into four stages. First, the participants finished the pretest. Second, after using the system for 4 weeks, participants completed the post-test and the first questionnaire for evaluation of the system. Third, the two groups were asked to swap and use the prototypes for two weeks; the participants were asked about their preference towards the two prototypes. Fourth, interviews were conducted for qualitative feedback from the participants.

Findings from the Surveys

There were 20 out of 24 participants who finished both first and second questionnaires and the interview: 9 (including 5 learners, 3 experts, and 1 training manager) from the treatment group and 11 (including 7 learners, 3 experts, and 1 training manager) from the control group. All learners completed the pretest and posttest. The initial findings show the following: The KPI-oriented system is perceived to be more effective in terms of meeting individual learning requirement and functional support for learning; the KPI-oriented system is more helpful for learners to obtain knowledge and skill; and the KPI-oriented system is more helpful in enabling learners to integrate learning into practice and transform individual learning into collaborative learning. On the other hand, the results of the pretest and posttest scores indicate that there is no significant difference between the two groups in the pretest or posttest score. The results are understandable since the time (4 weeks) of the experiment is not quite sufficient for evaluation and other factors of the learners (e.g., learning capability and efforts) and learning environment (e.g., Internet accessibility, speed and cost) may affect the results.

As a supplement of the first-round evaluation, the second-round evaluation was conducted by swapping the learning systems between the two groups. It was found that a majority of the participants preferred the KPI-oriented learning system in terms of user reaction, knowledge or skill learning, behavioral change, and learning outcomes. The number of participants who preferred the prototype with the KPI framework is significantly larger than that of participants who preferred the prototype without the KPI framework.

Findings from the Interviews

The 20 participants who finished the experiment and two rounds of questionnaires were interviewed for their feedback on the prototypes. The findings from the interviews are organized in terms of the role of the interviewee—employee, expert, and training manager.

Most of the employees felt that the KPI-oriented prototype was more helpful because it provided a broad scope of learning materials and helped learners become familiar with the domain knowledge of software testing in a systemic way. They also gave positive comments to the KPI-oriented system on its facilities for communications, knowledge sharing, and discussion. Further, some employees reported that a clear and flexible classification scheme of learning materials is very important and could be improved in the prototype.

The experts were more concerned about how an e-learning system can guide employees to learn. They gave more positive comments on the KPI-based learning system than the employees. Moreover, the experts stressed the importance of providing convenient and instant help for learners to solve their learning problems.

Positive comments were also received from the training managers. They felt that the KPI-based system provided flexible and useful ways of learning assessment. Moreover, they showed great concern about cost, which directly links to the benefit of the organization from using the e-learning system. They preferred to adopt e-learning systems than traditional ways of training in classrooms.

Conclusion

This chapter has presented two case studies that use performance-based approaches to improve learning and knowledge management in organizations. The first case describes a role-play simulation-based training program for business process improvement in banking. The results show that the role-play simulation substantially supports the training goals in terms of active participation and first-hand experience. Meanwhile, the role-play simulation is found to enhance social and affective learning. By participating in the role-play, many problems and annoyances can be mitigated or even resolved via better communication, which is particularly useful for cross-functional processes that span multiple divisions. Further, the simulation has been enhanced by the application of software to automate and manage the process. Knowledge embedded in process management practices is captured and specified in the software to enhance the delivery, sharing, and reuse of knowledge for business process management. It is also noted that while using the role-play simulation, it is important not to pursue too many objectives with a role-play, as an overload of differing objectives may unsettle participants and result in a defensive attitude towards the role-play.

The second case has addressed the problem to align learners' needs and organizations' quest for success in e-learning applications. It presents the development of a performance-oriented e-learning environment. The key idea lies in a KPI model, where the organizational mission and vision are translated into a set of key performance targets for driving learning towards the goal of improving work performance. In this approach, self-directed and socially constructed learning and knowledge management activities in the workplace are effectively managed via integration of organizational interests, individual needs, work performance, and social context. The results of the study have shown positive feedback and comments from the learners, experts, and training managers. It is also noted that this work has focused on e-learning development in view of short term learning needs to improve job performance. In the workplace settings, learning needs should be extended to enhance personal and career development in the long term. The future work will look into long term needs of workplace learning by integrating economic, social, and personal dimensions, and adopting human resource management and organizational learning perspectives.

Acknowledgments

This research is partially supported by a UGC GRF Grant (No. 717708) from the Hong Kong SAR Government and a Seeding Funding for Basic Research (200911159142) from the University of Hong Kong.

References

Amoroso, D.L. (1998). Developing a model to understand reengineering project success. In *Proceedings of the Thirty-First Annual Hawaii International Conference on System Sciences*, Vol. 6, 500–509.

Antony, J. (2004). Six Sigma in the UK service organizations: Results from a pilot survey. In *Managerial Auditing Journal*, Vol. 19, No. 8, 1006–1013.

Berman, S. (2008). *Performance-Based Learning: Aligning Experiential Tasks and Assessment to Increase Learning.* Thousand Oaks, CA: Corwin Press.

Bertolino, A. (2001). Chapter 5—Software testing. In Abran, A. and Moore, J.W. (Eds), *Swebok: Guide to the Software Engineering Body of Knowledge.* Trial Version 1.00, IEEE.

Bliesener, T. (1994). Authentizität in der simulation. In Bliesener, T., Brons-Albert, R (Eds), *Rollenspiele in Kommunikations-und Verhaltenstrainings.* Opladen: Westdeutscher Verlag, 13–32.

Börner, R., Heckl, D., and Hilgert, M. (2009). Erfahrungen mit dem Schulungsinstrument KreditSim. In Moormann, J., Heckl, D., Lamberti, H.-J. (Eds.): *Six Sigma in der Finanzbranche,* 3rd ed., Frankfurt: Frankfurt School Verlag.

Börner, R. and Uremovic, A. (2010). Sparking employees' interest in Six Sigma: Transferring a paper-based simulation to a workflow management application. In *Proceedings of the International Conference on Computer Supported Education (CSEDU 2010)* Vol. 2, 203–210.

Broich, J. (1994). *Rollenspiele mit Erwachsenen,* 5th ed., Köln: Maternus.

Furunes, T. (2005). Training paradox in the hotel industry. *Scandinavian Journal of Hospitality and Tourism,* Vol. 5, No. 3, 231–248.

Gruber, T. (1993). A translation approach to portable ontology specifications. *Knowledge Acquisition,* 5, 199–220.

Hammer, M. and Champy, J. (1993). *Reengineering the Corporation—A Manifesto for Business Revolution.* New York: Harper Business.

Harmon, P. (2008). *Business Process Change: A Guide for Business Managers and BPM and Six Sigma Professionals,* 2nd ed., Amsterdam: Morgan Kaufmann.

Harrington, H.J. (1991). *Business Process Improvement: The Breakthrough Strategy for Total Quality, Productivity, and Competitiveness.* New York: McGraw-Hill.

Harry, M. and Schroeder, R. (2000), *Six Sigma: The Breakthrough Management Strategy Revolutionizing the World's Top Corporations.* New York: Currency.

Hechenleitner, A. and Schwarzkopf, K. (2006). Kompetenz—ein zentraler Begriff im Bildungsbereich, In *Schulmanagement,* No. 1, 34–35.

Heckl, D., Moormann, J., and Rosemann, M. (2010). Uptake and success factors of six sigma in the financial services industry. In *Business Process Management Journal* Vol. 16, No. 3, 436–472.

Heckl, D. and Moormann, J. (2008). *Six Sigma in der Finanzbranche,* Process Lab Survey, Frankfurt: Frankfurt School Verlag.

Hibbard, K.M. (1996). *A Teacher's Guide to Performance-Based Learning and Assessment.* Alexandria VA.: Association for Supervision and Curriculum Development.

Hussain, Z., Wallace, J., and Cornelius, N.E. (2007). The use and impact of human resource information systems on human resource management professionals. *Information and Management,* Vol. 44, No. 1, 74–89.

Kirkpatrick, D.L. and Kirkpatrick, J.D. (2006). *Evaluating Training Programs,* 3rd ed. San Francisco, CA: Berrett-Koehler Publishers.

Klippert, H. (2007). *Methoden-Training*, 17th ed. Berlin: Beltz.

Lunau, S., Mollenhauer, J.-P., Staudter, C., Meran, R., Hamalides, A., Roenpage, O., and von Hugo, C. (2007). *Design for Six Sigma+Lean Toolset*. Berlin: Springer.

Magnusson, K., Kroslid, D., and Bergman, B. (2004). *Six Sigma. The Pragmatic Approach*, 2nd ed. Studentliterature, Lund.

Nonaka, I. and Takeuchi, H. (1995). *The Knowledge-Creating Company: How Japanese Companies Create the Dynamics of Innovation*. New York: Oxford University Press.

Noy, N.F., Fergerson, R.W., and Musen, M.A. (2000). The knowledge model of Protege-2000: Combining interoperability and flexibility. *2nd International Conference on Knowledge Engineering and Knowledge Management (EKAW'2000)*, France.

Parmenter, D. (2007). *Key Performance Indicators (KPI): Developing, Implementing, and Using Winning KPIs*. Hoboken, NJ: John Wiley & Sons.

Parush, A., Hamm, H., and Shtub, A. (2002). Learning histories in simulation-based teaching: The effects on self-learning and transfer. *Computers and Education*, Vol. 39, 319–332.

Pande, P., Neuman, R., and Cavanagh, R. (2000). *The Six Sigma Way: How GE, Motorola and Other Top Companies Are Honing Their Performance*. New York: McGraw-Hill.

Pollitt, D. (2008). Training accounts for big improvements at Fairbairn Private Bank. *Human Resource Management International Digest*, Vol. 16, No. 1, 32–34.

Rohmetra, N. and Easter-by Smith, M. (2004). Training and development in the changing technological environment. The case of Barclays, UK. *Journal of Management Research*, Vol. 4, No. 2, 67–76.

Rosenberg, M.J. (2006). *Beyond E-Learning: Approaches and Technologies to Enhance Organizational Knowledge, Learning, and Performance*. San Francisco: Pfeiffer.

Sappey, R.B. and Sappey, J. (1999). Different skills and knowledge for different times: training in an Australian retail bank. *Employee Relations*, Vol. 21, No. 6, 577–589.

Sirin, E., Parsia, B., and Grau, B.C. (2007). Pellet: A practical OWL-DL reasoner. *Web Semantics*, Vol. 5, No. 2, 51–53.

Snee, R.D. and Hoerl, R.W. (2009). Turning to service sectors. *Industrial Engineer*, No. 10, 37–40.

Sun, P.C., Tsai, R.J., Finger, G., Chen, Y.Y., and Yeh, D. (2008). What drives a successful e-Learning? An empirical investigation of the critical factors influencing learner satisfaction. *Computers and Education*, Vol. 50, No. 4, 1183–1202.

Tynjälä, P. (2008). Perspectives into learning at the workplace. *Educational Research Review*, Vol. 3, 130–154.

Wang, M. and Yang, S.J.H. (2009). Editorial: Knowledge management and e-learning. *Knowledge Management and E-Learning: An International Journal (KM&EL)*, Vol. 1, No. 1, 1–5.

Wang, M. (2010). Integrating organizational, social, and individual perspectives in Web 2.0-based workplace e-learning. *Information Systems Frontiers*, in press.

Welsh, E.T., Wanberg, C.R., Brown, K.G., and Simmering, M.J. (2003). E-learning: Emerging uses, empirical results and future directions. *International Journal of Training and Development*, Vol. 7, No. 4, 245–258.

Chapter 10

Knowledge Management in Agricultural Research: The CGIAR Experience

Enrica Porcari

Contents

Introduction

The use of technology in agricultural research is rapidly changing the way in which knowledge is created, stored, and distributed. Online training/learning is now considered the way of the future, with knowledge being distributed across time and distance. Knowledge management/sharing (KM/S) techniques can capture, organize and deliver this knowledge, while management systems can cater for specific needs by zoning in on relevant information. In this chapter, KM/S and learning in the Consultative Group on International Agricultural Research (CGIAR) is highlighted.

> Learning is an HR/training department responsibility. Its focus is primarily on supporting formal learning and linking it to performance. Knowledge management addresses learning as part of the knowledge sharing processes and pays more attention to specific forms of informal learning (e.g., learning in a community of practice) or to providing access to learning resources or experts (e.g., yellow pages or knowledge bases).
>
> **—Efimova and Swaak (2002)**

For this chapter, this interpretation of learning as an essential element of KM/S prevails.

The Consultative Group on International Agricultural Research

The Consultative Group on International Agricultural Research (CGIAR http://cgiar.org/) is a strategic partnership whose members support 15 international research centers, working in collaboration with government and civil society organizations, as well as private businesses around the world. Today, approximately 8,000 CGIAR scientists and staff are active in over 100 countries throughout the world. This global organization generates cutting-edge science to foster sustainable agricultural growth that benefits the poor through stronger food security, better human nutrition and health, higher incomes, and improved management of natural resources. The new crop varieties, knowledge, and other products resulting from the CGIAR's collaborative research are made widely available to individuals and organizations working for sustainable agricultural development throughout the world.

The ICT-KM Program

If the CGIAR is to sustain its mission, it must continue to generate, safeguard, and share knowledge in new ways, and this is where the organization's ICT-KM Program (http://ictkm.cgiar.org/) plays a large role. The ICT-KM Program promotes and supports the use of information and communications technology (ICT) and knowledge management (KM) to improve the effectiveness of the CGIAR System's work on behalf of the poor in developing countries.

Scientific practices are becoming more and more information intensive and multidisciplinary, requiring up-to-date communications infrastructure and knowledge-sharing practices. The ICT-KM Program helps the CGIAR develop and sustain a culture of active information and knowledge sharing. This involves timely yet cost-effective multidirectional communications, the know-how to collaborate, and the tools to support multidisciplinary and multicultural teams. The program also supports champions of these changes throughout the system, explores and encourages incentives for change, and sponsors projects that show demonstrable value and impact.

Why Knowledge Management/Sharing?

The CGIAR is a fascinating consortium of research organizations, donors, and developing countries interested in advancing agricultural research for improved livelihoods. While being a consortium, the 15 CGIAR research centers are also unique organizations competing for resources and individual success. When the center directors general were considering the possibility of creating a cross-cutting program to support ICT development and uptake to advance the performance of the CGIAR in 2002/03, they recognized that support for connectivity and tools would be insufficient. They recognized that the work culture required attention; as a result, they decided to create the ICT-KM Program.

Since its inception, the ICT-KM Program has striven to embed a culture of knowledge-sharing in CGIAR events and has successfully mainstreamed knowledge-sharing principles and tools in CGIAR centers and programs. In the early days of the program, there was much debate about just what KM meant; as a result of these debates, the term *knowledge sharing* was deemed to better capture the essence of what was meant by KM, and, as a result, the program tends to use this term (KM or KM/S) in its language.

In 2004, the program kicked off with an investment plan that was built around three thrusts that supported 14 interrelated projects that were designed to improve connectivity in the CGIAR and enable staff located in even the remotest of regions to access a wide range of online tools and services. The goal was to give staff the necessary connectivity, tools, and know-how that would equip them to collaborate and share information in a way that would be beneficial to all participants.

KM/S Project Phase I

As one of the 14 Phase I projects, the Knowledge Management/Sharing (KM/S) Project was established to create and strengthen a knowledge-sharing culture through workshops and knowledge fairs; institutionalize KM/S through participatory KM/S strategy development for individual centers, programs, and challenge programs; provide access to KM/S tools and techniques through training courses, practical guides, and best practices; and support communities of practice by facilitation training and demonstration projects.

Four CGIAR centers were actively involved in testing KS approaches and tools in the CGIAR. Under pilot initiatives supported by the project, each center successfully incorporated KS principles and approaches into high-profile events, which served as entry points for promoting change in the centers' institutional culture. Specifically, the events demonstrated how centers can plan, conduct, and evaluate their work with greater efficiency by drawing more fully on the collective knowledge of their staff.

KM/KS Project Phase II

To build on the interest and gains generated by this first phase, the second phase of the KS Project was launched in early 2007 to offer CGIAR centers new opportunities to develop, apply, evaluate, and share innovative approaches for making their work more effective. The project initiative comprised two main components: Institutional Knowledge Sharing (IKS) and Knowledge Sharing in Research (KSinR). This second phase sought to scale activities up across the 15 research centers, as well as begin to scale out to partners beyond the centers.

IKS

The IKS project demonstrated how KS methods and principles can open up meaningful spaces for face-to-face dialogues. Pilot initiatives at two centers resulted in the centers' organizing and conducting their annual staff meetings differently. Another center's pilot led to the formation of an integrated team of scientists who share knowledge and information, and work towards common goals, while yet another pilot helped another center launch its own pilot project to embed knowledge-sharing principles in the research cycle.

At the end of 2008, the program helped facilitate the third CGIAR Annual General Meeting held in Maputo, Mozambique, that saw active, strategic participation from the program. The following are just some of the other ICT-KM-supported events that incorporated knowledge-sharing methodologies: CIAT's (www.ciat. cgiar.org) Annual Knowledge Sharing Week held in Cali, Columbia; CGIAR Strategic Communications Workshop, held in Penang, Malaysia; Web2forDev (www.web2fordev.net) Conference, held in Rome; KS Pilot Project Inception Workshop, held at IRRI (www.irri.org); Knowledge Management for Development (KM4Dev: www.km4dev.org) Meeting 06, held in Zeist, Netherlands; Knowledge Fair held during CIFOR's (www.cifor.cgiar.org) Annual Meeting; Research plan week in WorldAgroforestry Center (www.worldagroforestry.org) in Nairobi; and the Knowledge ShareFair in Rome, January 2009.

IKS Pilot Projects

The project also supported three pilot projects at three centers to experiment with innovative KS techniques:

Good Practices for Managing Research Data

> There is still little experience in using wiki technology within CGIAR Centers to support communities of practice or institutional change processes. The openness and visibility of a wiki is often seen as a risk, rather than an opportunity for increased participation and collaboration in communities of practice.
>
> **—Thomas Metz, Project Leader**

Effective and efficient research data management requires special skills and experience, but there is seldom a systematic approach to teaching and training new staff to manage research data, or to update existing staff on new methodologies and technologies. Good practices are often not recorded in the form of institutional guidelines and training materials of practical relevance for day-to-day research data management work or the induction of new staff members. This project developed, collected, recorded, and applied good practices in research data management, and initiated a community of practice for research data managers. As a result, it is enabling scientists to produce better quality research and release their primary data as global public goods that will be available and usable for future secondary use. This effort will add value to current CGIAR research for future generations.

Using KS Approaches to Facilitate Organizational Learning and Change

CIFOR, one of the 15 CGIAR research centers, was among the first small group of centers to experiment with novel KS techniques. "This early experience," says Fiona Chandler, former leader of the Center's KS pilot project, "paved the way for using new KS techniques in the strategic planning exercise."

Due to the decentralized nature of CIFOR, understanding and participation in the center's new strategy development was uneven. With greater understanding and use of KS approaches, it was felt that staff would feel that their input is solicited, valued, and put to good use. This project used KS approaches to (1) increase staff and board of trustee participation in the CIFOR strategy development process to identify and address common issues and concerns, (2) ensure open and participatory discussions on CIFOR's core values by all staff, (3) facilitate internal communication and build trust while addressing potentially sensitive strategic issues; and (4) capture and document lessons from the overall strategy process and from specific activities to facilitate communication, share lessons learned, and design a framework for monitoring and evaluating strategy implementation.

Storymercials: Attracting People to Our Knowledge and Keeping Their Attention

"At the heart of the storymercial is the story, the oldest, best-proven way humans learn and remember information," says Helen Leitch, who led this pilot project that examined the role punchy videos (storymercials) of 3 minutes' duration or less can play in attracting investors, partners, and media to support research and apply its outputs. The project also shared this innovative knowledge sharing approach across the CGIAR, so that others could learn and benefit from its success.

All three pilots led to concrete outcomes and/or products that can be replicated in other centers or partner organizations. In another area, the use of social media helped raise the profile of both the project and the program in the research and development arena.

KS Toolkit

In terms of tools, one of the most popular online knowledge-sharing resources developed by the KS Project is the KS Toolkit (http://www.kstoolkit.org). Developed in collaboration with the United Nations Food and Agriculture Organization (FAO) and other partners, the toolkit contains more than 70 tools and methods for sharing knowledge and receives more than 20,000 visits per month. This living knowledge repository about knowledge sharing was created to be both a resource for KS workshops and an ongoing place to learn about, improve upon and generally share knowledge-sharing practices. While anyone may use the toolkit, it targets professionals working in international development, with a special emphasis on those engaged in agriculture and agricultural research. There are other KS toolkits out there, but most of them are static, not updated.

The toolkit has three main sections: two "libraries," one for KS methods and one for tools that can be used for knowledge sharing, as well as a set of perspectives and guidance that can help visitors choose tools and methods for their individual needs and contexts. Tools are Web-based software and offline physical tools that can be used with a variety of methods. Methods are group processes that people can use to interact with each other, online or offline. The toolkit focuses on online tools and offline methods, but the plan over time is to include a wide range that will work in both or either environment. Tools are identified through "contexts." It is felt that that just having access to tools without knowing what they can be used for, what the context for their use would be, what the experiences are, etc., diminishes their value.

The origins of the toolkit speak to the power of the network that created it: the KM4Dev wiki as source of inspiration to CARE (www.care.org), which agreed to let the CGIAR use its content as the base of the CGIAR KS Toolkit, and FAO, which added its support. This cross-organizational cooperation reduces the individual organizational costs, while adding the diversity that each organization brings and mitigating the risks of the content becoming stagnant.

KM4Dev

The KS Project personnel plugged into a wider community of practice, as it is impossible for a single person or organization to know everything about knowledge sharing. As such, it is important to belong to professional communities of like-minded people, fuelled by the enthusiasm of individual members. Knowledge Management for Development (KM4Dev) is a community of international development practitioners interested in knowledge management issues and approaches. The community runs a journal, listserv, and Web site, and organizes face-to-face workshops to allow development practitioners to share their ideas and experiences.

The following are just some examples of tangible results and mutual benefits arising from this continuous collaboration: Over the last two years, the KS Project sponsored CGIAR staff working on knowledge sharing to attend the annual KM4Dev community workshop. The KS Project leader is a member of the core group of the KM4Dev community; the project contributed to and guest-edited one issue of the KM4Dev Journal, in which various CGIAR staff had already published articles; and the KM4Dev community helped create a pool of coworkers and consultants that the ICT-KM Program can call upon when needed. Being a member of the community has helped project personnel to gain a greater understanding of knowledge management in the context of a development-oriented organization such as the CGIAR, and has offered insights into tools and techniques to promote knowledge management and sharing.

Additional IKS Work

Since the end of the formal IKS project, follow-on work by the KS Project leader, Simone Staiger-Rivas, continues. Here's what she has to say about it (http://ictkm. cgiar.org/2009/11/20/ict-km-knowledge-sharing-scales-up-and-out-up-and-out-up-and-out/):

> Some of the ICT-KM-originated KS action took place behind the scenes or on the platforms of partner organizations, which basically means that we are currently still up- and out-scaling our KS work. I have been mainly collaborating with the CGIAR Secretariat (http://www.cgiar.

org/who/structure/system/secretariat.html) and the Global Forum on Agricultural Research (GFAR: http://www.egfar.org/). In both cases, most of the support involved technological stewardship, and the very exciting and rewarding coordination/facilitation of virtual consultation processes that had to do with the CGIAR change process (http://www.cgiar.org/changemanagement/index.html).

The following are some insights gained from the different activities in which Simone was involved:

CGIAR Change E-Consultations

Two e-consultations with the CGIAR secretariat were organized, one of which was related to some key issues around the Fund Framework (http://www.cgiar.org/fund/index.html) and was conducted over Skype chat. The short after-action review with the secretariat staff revealed that the process was quick and efficient, and worked well for the small group. In a second consultation in October 2009, the objective was to enroll CGIAR members, Science Council, center board chairs, and center directors general in a 3-day e-consultation on the critical elements of the CGIAR Reform.

Observations:
- It was encouraging to see the openness of the CGIAR Secretariat toward the principles of consultation processes, as well as their interest in trying out innovative solutions for virtual dialogues.
- The ease of use and the zero cost of both tools were big advantages compared to the minor difficulties that were encountered. The team is now able to undertake further exercises on their own without external support, because a capacity-strengthening component was included in the exercise.
- An interesting discussion arose when Simone was defining mutual roles with the various groups. Together they distinguished between content and process facilitators, with Simone suggesting the medium and the respective timeline for each exercise and setting up the platforms. The secretariat staff clarified the objectives and ensured that the background documents were ready and available on time.

GCARD E-Consultation Process

The consultation process of the Global Conference on Agricultural Research for Development (GCARD: http://www.egfar.org/egfar/website/gcard) saw Simone I am involved in the process as a coordinator of the six regional e-consultations. In addition, she facilitated the Asia Pacific e-consultation. The GCARD process consists of a step-by-step stakeholder involvement approach in each region, each coordinated by one of the six regional forums through which the stakeholders were represented within GFAR. The GCARD process is an integral part of the new CGIAR and serves as its stakeholder platform.

"The enthusiasm created around the e-consultation is evident. 500 members from 65 countries signed up for the event," says FARA's (www.fara-africa.org) Myra Wopereis-Pura, during one of the consultations. "Up to the moment, the GCARD-Africa group is still very active. We don't know how to stop people!"

Observations: Obtaining broad representation and trust ultimately depends on the capacity of the research community to listen actively to those with whom it is trying to engage. Active listening is a key skill and challenge. It indicates a willingness to take the participant's wisdom into account, beyond the usual too-narrow economic evidence-based science approach.

KSinR

The KSinR project focused on knowledge-sharing good practices that can be used within research projects/programs to improve the effectiveness and impact of CGIAR work. One of the primary avenues for learning in the project was through its six pilot projects, which integrated various KS approaches into the different stages of the research process.

The impact of research can be limited by the lack of inclusion of priorities, needs, and realities from the ground; inadequate use of other sources of knowledge; poor collaboration with stakeholders during the research; limited understanding of how research results can most effectively be made use of; ineffective ways of getting knowledge to target groups; or limited opportunities for learning within the research process. Knowledge sharing can help address these problems and improve the way research is carried out by improving the collaboration, learning, and knowledge flows in research, which can help to improve impact.

The components of the research process (as shown in Figure 10.1, where M&E means "monitoring and evaluation") all offer an entry point in which knowledge sharing (approaches, methods, tools) can be integrated and used to improve those stages and the process as a whole. The KSinR pilot projects were developed with this approach in mind. Highlights of several examples of these pilots are presented in the text following.

Stage 1: Identifying Research (Questions) to Undertake

The Shared Learning to Enhance Research Priority Assessment Practices pilot project was implemented to help improve innovation, documentation, and communication of collaborative priority assessment approaches involving the CGIAR System and its partners and resulted in a book, *Prioritizing agricultural Research for Development: Experiences and Lessons.* The most important influence thus far, in part as a result of this project, is the rise of priority assessment and ex ante impact

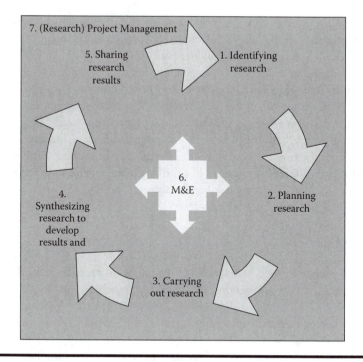

Figure 10.1   Stages of the research process.

assessment in visibility in the CGIAR system. It is now being increasingly recognized that good practice in research planning means that the selection of research topics should be based on systematic analysis of impact potential, and that investment and dedicated effort is needed to do so.

Stage 2: Planning Research (Activities/Projects/Programs)

The ICARDA International Farmers Conference (http://www.icarda.org/FarmersConference/Home.html) was organized in part to better understand existing knowledge, needs and situations on the ground when planning research activities to make them more inclusive and relevant. A few days after the conference took place, Nadia Manning and Alessandra Galie (conference organizers), performed an informal evaluation of the conference with the women farmers and gathered several interesting stories. In their words:

Story 1. I was particularly interested in assessing the empowerment effects of the conference in the framework of my research on participatory plant breeding and the empowerment of women farmers. Some women talked about the initial difficulties they experienced when talking to male strangers. Ruqeia, a young farmer, told us how she slowly grew confident in addressing male farmers and scientists, even older than her, after she received comments of appreciation for her knowledge.

This helped her present her story from the microphone—and also approach an FAO representative who organizes integrated pest management courses—to find out about possible collaborations. Before leaving her house, Ruqeia showed us the stretch of garden where she had just planted the seeds she had picked up during the Seed and Food Fair.

The experience of Ruqeia showed the organizers how the exchange with other farmers and scientists motivated her in continuing her agricultural work, supplied her with new knowledge and seeds, stimulated her curiosity and, finally, constituted an empowering experience by increasing her self-esteem and self-confidence. Ruqeia's contribution to the conference, together with that of other female farmers, showed both the actual involvement of women farmers in agriculture and their knowledge in agronomic management that are often overlooked in Syria. This appeared to show the need to include both men and women among the stakeholders of agricultural research.

Story 2. The Seed and Food Fair proved to be a very energizing event that transformed the discussions into visible and tangible products—mainly seeds, breads, and sweets—to show off and exchange together with the related preparation or cultivation knowledge. A highlight was a beautiful thyme bag brought by a Syrian farmer, Ahmed, that related to the story he had told on old agricultural practices. The story was about his grandfather, who used to spread thyme on the ground while ploughing the fields and never explained to his nephew the reason for doing so. A few days later, Ahmed was excited to announce that while talking to another participant he found out that in Canada thyme was used to repel some insects that damage the crops; he had finally discovered a possible explanation to his grandfather's practice. For the organizers this event summed up the main aims of the conference. The story Ahmed told revived lost traditional practices and triggered the exchange of more stories, revealing at the same time the tacit knowledge of farmers and some of the problems they used to deal with. Also, it showed the emerging network of direct relationships between farmers within and across countries and the potential benefits of farmers collaborating and sharing knowledge across the world.

Stage 3: Undertaking Research (Activities Like Fieldwork, Data Collection, etc.)

To better collaborate with and involve stakeholders in research activities, researchers in the Learning Alliance for 'Wastewater, Agriculture and Sanitation for Poverty Alleviation' (WASPA: http://www.lk.iwmi.org/WASPA/) project used and built into their research activities knowledge-sharing methodologies for the interaction with the end and next users of their research results. Farmers and caterers were involved in the process of developing the key messages for health-risk-reducing good practices. The Ministry of Food and Agriculture and its agricultural extension agents were involved in the development of media materials to distribute the messages. The project started off with having "World Cafes" in the three cities for farmers and caterers to discuss and evaluate the first set of good practices. The project collaborated with the World Health Organization (WHO) to develop a version for West Africa for the "Five Keys" to safer food in local languages (Dagbani and Twi). The messages were for agricultural extension agents packaged as flip charts with training instructions for their use in the field. There was also a radio program on a local radio station, Justice FM, using the local language, Dagbani. The discussion brought together the key players in urban vegetable production (i.e., farmers, vegetable traders, fast food vendors, caterers and researchers from UDS).

Stage 5: Sharing Research Results/Messages with Relevant Stakeholders

The Knowledge Management Harmonizing Research Output pilot project explored how knowledge generated from the research project can be shared with target groups in ways which are appropriate and effective. The project used workshops and in-house traineeship to develop local capacity and share knowledge, exchange visits for farmers, knowledge fairs, and developed fact sheets (in local languages). The most significant change brought about by the project was the change in attitudes and mind sets of the major actors in the project. Attitudinal changes involved issues about working together and confidence in each other's competencies. The project made it possible for actors to work together on a functional basis. The project helped identify a common deficiency that hindered the actors from achieving their mandated work—the lack of a reliable, up-to-date source of knowledge (information, tested and validated technologies, etc.) that can be disseminated and used by the actors on their target audiences and clients. More importantly, the project empowered actors by providing the means to do something concrete together.

Stage 7: Research Project Management

The Knowledge Sharing Approach to Safe Food pilot project was designed to explore how a research project can be managed in a more collaborative way with colleagues, partners, and stakeholders, as well as with those who are geographically dispersed. The project used a World Cafe approach to discuss research results with stakeholders. To develop appropriate messages, trained extension agents used flip charts, DVDs, and "roadshows" to take stakeholders along the contamination pathway. An interview with Phillip Amoah and Tonya Schuetz from the International Water Management Institute (IWMI: www.iwmi.cgiar.org/) adds color to this project: "Lack of knowledge in Ghana can get you thrown in jail or even killed. Such are the stakes when dealing with the food that people eat.

Progress has been swift. *With this KSinR pilot project, I really felt like a lot went very well,"* says Tonya.

Before beginning a concerted campaign of knowledge sharing in research, Philip says he sometimes had difficulty communicating even simple messages like the need for farmers to water crops at the root so as not to splash soil on to the leaves, causing a potential health hazard:

> One time I was chased out of a vegetable growing site in Accra when I went to take water samples, because at that time the farmers were not involved in the project. They said that people had come before and taken water samples, after which some of the farmers had been arrested and people wouldn't buy their vegetables. But now that we've got them involved, we better understand their situation and find better ways to communicate the results of the research to them to help them make changes and improvements. I'm free to go there at any time, to take samples and to do whatever research I want to do. And that has really helped a lot. So knowledge sharing is something I really want in my future research. I've even joined the farmers association now, attend meeting and pay dues and they now recognize me as one of them.

Tonya says it was not only farmers, but researchers, too, who changed their attitudes.

> We started off working with researchers who were open to it but did not really believe in it. They felt that knowledge sharing was something they had already been doing for a long time. But when they saw how we used various knowledge sharing methodologies even at a very early stage in our project and the results we got, they realized that it was slightly different to what they'd been doing before. It's a lot more about continuous interaction with stakeholders, rather than just going there once, talking to your partners and then just going and doing your research. Knowledge sharing has changed the way they work.

Gateway to Global Agricultural Knowledge

As quoted from Efimova and Swaak at the beginning of this chapter, access to learning resources, expertise, and knowledge bases is an important part of knowledge management.

The CGIAR Virtual Library (http://vlibrary.cgiar.org/), sometimes called "CGVlibrary," provides instant access to research results (information and knowledge) on agriculture, hunger, poverty, and the environment. From just one search engine, users can tap into leading agricultural information databases, including the online libraries of all 15 CGIAR Centers. These shared integrated services have removed barriers to information and made publicly available information more accessible to researchers in the CGIAR and partners in developing countries.

The CGVlibrary has continued to grow in usage while expanding resources and improving services since its launch in June 2006. There are now more than 180 electronic databases available for conducting federated searches through the CGVlibrary site. Besides the databases of the centers and the CGIAR Secretariat, users can also access image repositories for several centers. Many of these databases are organized into topic-specific QuickSets for federated searching; at the last count, there were 21 QuickSets preselected by CGIAR information specialists. The CGVlibrary also offers integrated access to more than 8,000 electronic journal titles.

The CGVlibrary can be accessed by anyone, anywhere, at anytime.

ICT-KM Program Blog

On the ICT-KM Program blog the program posts its latest news, upcoming events, articles on the latest ICT-KM tools, and methodologies and interviews. Visitors can also find all the background information about the program's work, what it has done, its strategy, who the people behind the scenes are, etc.

The blog was started in the summer of 2007 as an initiative of the two knowledge-sharing project coordinators, who initiated it as a way of "walking the talk." They advocated improved, more effective sharing of information, the involvement of partners, and transparency. While these are all tenets of the work the research centers carry out, they also wanted to apply these principles to their team's work.

The blog was kicked off mainly as a way to document program meetings, initiatives, and pilot projects spread over different locations. Later, the content was extended with "live blogging" from events, opinion pieces, tutorials, and guides. The tutorials and guides proved to be very successful, especially a 13-part series on social media tools, which garnered quite a following from audiences both within and beyond the CGIAR.

The Way Ahead

At publishing time, the CGIAR is engaged in a change management initiative designed to introduce reforms to enhance the CGIAR's effectiveness and efficiency. The ICT-KM Program has been looking at ways in which it can support the new CGIAR, and asks the question: How do information, knowledge, ICTs, and related areas fare in the proposals under consideration?

The CGIAR Reform recognizes the importance of knowledge and information as well as ICT applications and tools within both CGIAR research processes and the agricultural innovation systems where organizations doing research and development interact. Hopefully, It will boost scattered efforts to increase research uptake, interaction, and collaboration using ICTs and other innovative approaches to knowledge sharing in research.

Many of the program's KS projects and activities have chartered new waters in the CGIAR. It has taken on new ideas, adopted and adapted new technologies, and attempted to change mindsets—all without being 100% sure that they would succeed. In that regard, there are similarities between the program's work and that of a venture capitalist: it is willing to take a calculated risk or two in the hope that some activities will turn out well. And some of the KS activities that turned out well, turned out really well. Some of the outputs and outcomes are also changing the way things are done in the CGIAR, and that's both gratifying and motivational, because there is still so much more that the program can do in a large organization like the CGIAR.

References

Efimova and Swaak, 2002: http://www.jucs.org/jucs_9_6/converging_knowledge_management_training/Efimova_L.html.

CGIAR ICT-KM Program. ICT-KM Program. http://ictkm.cgiar.org/index.php.

CGIAR ICT-KM Program. The Knowledge Sharing Project of ICT-KM. http://www.ks-cgiar.org/.

Chapter 11

Experiences and Recommendations on Required Student Knowledge and E-Skills

Frederik Truyen, Jan Vanthienen,
and Stephan Poelmans

Contents

Introduction

It needs no argument that the information society and the reality of ubiquitous computing have had a considerable impact on professional labor in general and on the way we do science in particular. The growing need for specific computer-related skills is being felt throughout the many disciplines of higher education. However, in many cases, today's academic specialization means more generic skills often do not find their way into the different study curricula. This has been the case with computer initiation. On the one hand, it has been advanced to high school education and even basic education in an attempt to learn the skills early on; on the other hand, it has been stripped from many higher education programs on the presupposition that these skills should already have been mastered or that they have no intrinsic academic merit.

In our research, we wanted to take a closer look at both these premises: Do higher education students indeed have the necessary computer skills? And is there really no academic merit in those skills? The Leuven University's Association for Higher Education provided the ideal testing ground for this research, being a multicampus organization with about 75.000 students in disciplines ranging from professional bachelors in arts to advanced masters in biomedical sciences. A large survey was held aiming, in a first research phase, to examine personal computing proficiency perception within the student population. This research will be complemented with a survey of academic staff perception of relevant student skills and an actual test environment to measure skill level. The research described here was presented at the ICERI, MICTE, and ICDE international conferences during 2009 (Poelmans et al., 2009; Cannaerts et al., 2009; Truyen et al., 2009). In order to address the perceived deficiencies in computer proficiency, we argue that there is some academic merit to a continued learning path for computing skills at the higher education level.

Required Student Competencies and E-Skills

Offering students the right level of computer competences and designing appropriate computer-related courses require more insight into the actual degree of computer literacy or knowledge of (under)graduate students. Within the literature, computer literacy has been defined in multiple ways, using synonyms such as computer competences, computer knowledge, computer experience, information literacy, and information (or computer) fluency (see, for example, Arndt et al., 1999; Baron et al., 1986; Shih, 2006; Smith et al., 2000). Although "computer literacy" sometimes connotes only the ability to use several specific applications (such as word processing, database knowledge, or the use of a spreadsheet), the term is frequently used in a broader perspective, including competences to use ICT to satisfy personal needs or to maximize performance of specific (job-related) tasks (Baron et al., 1986; Shih, 2006).

In our perspective, computer literacy is to be seen as a collection of skills pertaining to the use of basic information and communication technology in an Internet-oriented environment, as well as the knowledge that relates to the legal and ethical issues and risks of ICT usage. In the following, the terms "computer literacy" and "computer knowledge" will be used interchangeably.

We include the following items in a broad perspective on computer literacy:

- *Computer experience:* Basic computer usage, Internet usage, social networks usage
- *Computer skills:* Basic productivity tools, for example, word processing, spreadsheets, databases
- *Legal knowledge:* Author rights, copyright
- *Security:* Viruses, firewalls, backups
- *Internet risk awareness:* Tracing, profiling, Facebook
- *Information retrieval*
- *Multimedia storage*

Within the related educational literature, computer literacy has been measured and assessed using both students' self-assessments and more objective tests (for instance, Anderson et al., 2008; McCourt et al., 2003; Van Braak, 2004). Most investigations show that students' essential computing competences—including issues such as application knowledge, operating systems skills, and Web skills—are frequently overestimated, not in the least by computer experienced study.

In the first phase of our research, a survey was administered to all students of the K.U. Leuven Association, measuring their perceived computer skills and competences. The survey was administered in 2008 and resulted in 7896 responses. The results and its implications will be analyzed and discussed in the rest of this chapter. We start with a concise presentation of the educational project in the next section.

A Survey on Perceived Computer Literacy

Perceived computer literacy (and its related constructs) has been appraised in various ways. Whereas computer competences were measured as being able to master a limited number of applications and programming languages in the 1980s and 1990s, the focus has shifted to measuring the ability to handle a range of Web-related applications as well as more general competences with respect to the management of information. Bunz et al. (2007), for instance, include general operating system skills (tasks related to saving, storing, and retrieving files), and e-mail and

Web skills (activities related to the use of e-mail and Internet applications), asking respondents how much thought the listed activities would require. In the enquiry of van Braak (2004), word processing skills were measured, alongside operating system and Web skills. Ballantine et al. (2007) and McCourt et al. (2003) measured computer literacy using several subdimensions such as "knowledge of general computing," spreadsheets, word processing, databases, e-mail/Internet, and presentation software, both as perceptions and in an objective way. In a survey of Hakkarainen et al. (2000), a broader concept is measured, including attitudes towards ICT, networking, and the collaborative use of ICT, next to typical "technical ICT skills" (including text processing, programming, authoring tools, and file management).

Survey Design

We developed the survey based on typical experiences of the members of the project group. As such, the questionnaire did not focus in particular on the ability of students to interact with a number of well-known types of ICT applications (such as word processing, databases, or presentation software). Instead, questions were more related to the student's awareness of the possible consequences, risks, and legal issues of using the Internet, as well as (electronic) information in general. Following this, questions that are related to the storage and retrieval of information were added. In order to facilitate the interpretation of the results, we grouped the questions into five primary categories or "factors": security, legal issues, Internet risk awareness, information retrieval, and multimedia information storage. Each was measured using multiple formative items (varying between 2 and 4 items per category).

> *Security*: Evaluation of a student's awareness of firewalls, virus scans, and the risks of using a laptop as the main storage device
> *Legal issues*: Measuring a student's knowledge concerning the implications of copyrights, author rights, public property, and creative commons
> *Internet risk awareness*: evaluation of students' awareness of the Internet trail they might leave on the Web
> *Information retrieval*: Measuring skills related to the retrieval and recovery of historical data
> *Multimedia information storage*: Questions related to the storage and usage of data on CDs and DVDs.

We also calculated one secondary-order factor, using all 15 items.

In the related literature, a number of determinants of students' computer literacy or competences have been identified and investigated, including computer experience and access to personal computers (both at home and at school), computer anxiety and age (see, for example, Link and Marz [2006]). The studies report different and sometimes contrary findings. Van Braak (2004), studying perceived computer literacy among 137 freshman students, found that computer confidence, computer experience, intensity of computer use, and home access are four significant determinants. Link and Marz (2006) reported that in their sample of first-year medical students, age, computer use, and previous exposure to computers are significant determinants. In Bunz et al. (2007) computer anxiety was tested as a determinant, but it did not have a significant impact on their fluency measures.

Another possible determinant is gender. In general, there seems to be no consensus on the gender-effect on (educational) IT usage and attitudes (Milis et al., 2008). While some studies report existing gender differences regarding measures such as computer self-efficacy, computer experience, or computer-related attitudes, others report a declining gender gap (Durndell et al., 2002; Schumacher et al., 2001). In Bunz et al. (2007) gender had a significant impact on perceived computer e-mail and Web fluency, but not on an actual computer fluency test.

In our investigation, we also added gender as a possible significant determinant of perceived computer literacy. Because of the potential effect of computer experience, we asked respondents to indicate their level of computer usage and the extent of their interactions with the Internet. In particular, we asked them whether they use computers frequently, to what degree they post messages on the Internet, to what extent they are an active member of social networks (like Facebook, LinkedIn, etc.) and to what degree they deploy several online identities. Due to the vast number of study subjects, and corresponding to the classification used in the Association, we grouped them into three main study branches: exact sciences, medical sciences, and humanities. The humanities branch comprises several faculties and programs, such as business economics, psychology, philosophy, linguistics, and law. The branch of the exact sciences includes subjects related to engineering, mathematics, and IT.

The survey was administered online to enrolled students of every institution (and every grade) of the Association K.U. Leuven. No less than 7896 students completed the survey. In the following section we will first give a more detailed overview of the sample. Next, we present the descriptive statistics of the degree of computer literacy, and finally we investigate and analyze the impact of gender, computer experience, educational type, and study branch on perceived computer literacy.

Distribution of Respondents

In Table 11.1 the sample size is presented according to gender, type of education, and study branch. Globally, 54.4% of the sample are female respondents. 55.7% stem from the humanities (being the biggest study branch in the Association), and 44.6% are studying an academic bachelor's degree. The distribution of Table 11.1 reflects the structure of the Leuven Association. The huge sample size guarantees a reliable analysis and enables testing differences between different types of students.

Table 11.1   Sample Composition

Type of Education	Both Genders		Females		Males	
	No.	%	No.	%	No.	%
Antecedents						
Professional Bachelor's	2573	33.6	1514	19.2	1059	13.4
Academic Bachelor's	3521	44.6	1829	23.2	1692	21.4
Master's	1492	18.9	771	9.8	721	9.1
Other	308	3.9	183	2.3	125	1.6
Total	**7894**	**100**	4297	54.4	3597	45.6
Study Branch						
Medical sciences	1602	20.3	1068	13.5	534	6.8
Exact sciences	1888	23.9	385	0.5	1503	19.1
Humanities	4396	55.7	2837	36.0	1559	19.8
Total	**7886**	**100**	4290	54.4	3596	45.6

General Survey Results

In Table 11.2 the means of the different scales of computer literacy are displayed. In Figure 11.1 the distribution of computer literacy is shown. In general, we observe that students are positive about their knowledge, yet the scores indicate no extreme self-appraisal. The means vary between 3.45 and 4.07 on a 6-point scale. On 4 of the 5 subscales, more than 40% of the respondents assess their literacy as being at

Table 11.2   Degree of Computer Literacy

Subject	Mean	S.D.	No. >4	No. <3
General Computer Literacy (2nd order factor)	3.94	0.60	3300 (42%)	333 (4%)
Internet Risk Awareness	4.01	0.82	3372 (43%)	618 (8%)
Security	4.07	0.94	3692 (47%)	728 (9%)
Multimedia Storage	3.95	1.05	3565 (45%)	1131 (14%)
Information Retrieval	4.60	0.90	5356 (68%)	244 (3%)
Legal Knowledge	3.45	0.79	1432 (18%)	1860 (24%)

Note: Scale: 1 to 6; N = 7896.

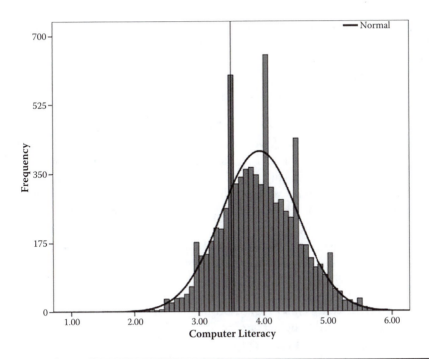

Figure 11.1 Distribution of computer literacy.

least "rather good" (>4). In particular, students seem to lack legal knowledge; while their "information retrieval" skills receive the highest mean rate (4.6).

The Impact of Gender, Study Branch, and Type of Education

A one-way ANOVA between-groups analysis of variance was conducted to explore the impact of gender, study branch, and type of education (academic bachelor, professional bachelor, master, and "others") on computer literacy (seen as one second-order factor, but also considering the five primary factors). In a final subsection (D), the relative importance of these factors will be analyzed with multiple regression.

As a part of this project, we explored in this chapter the level of perceived computer literacy and the disparities in the perceptions of different cohorts of (under) graduate students of the Association. Perceived computer literacy was measured as a multidimensional second-order factor, consisting of five primary factors (security, information retrieval, legal issues, Internet risk awareness, and multimedia storage).

A strong feature of our research was the large sample size composed of different cohorts, which allowed us to make reliable measurements. In the literature we often find more limited samples directed toward one particular study program or faculty, with sometimes a focus on application-based knowledge. We did not, however, involve application-based skills in our inquiry on computer literacy, focusing instead on risk management, security, Internet risk awareness, and information management.

When we looked into the five primary factors that we used to determine computer literacy, the following conclusions emerged:

Gender difference: Male correspondents have significantly higher perceived computer literacy. We have argued that this seems more related to technical prowess than to more functional perceived differences in general information management. In particular, gender differences are the highest when considering technical topics such as multimedia storage and security. The more ICT is ripped off from technical issues, the more these gender differences can be expected to diminish. Next, interaction analyses indicate that gender differences decline with an increase in computer experience. Finally, we note that, as we focused on students' self-reports, the revealed gender differences might reflect differences in gender self-awareness, rather than differences in actual competences.

Differences in study branch: Unsurprisingly, students of exact sciences have a higher perceived computer literacy. This relationship can be interpreted in two ways. On the one hand, it is plausible that students of exact sciences are more confronted with technical and ICT topics; on the other hand, it is also possible that technically-oriented students more likely choose an exact sciences' program, thus reversing the relationship. Another, more remarkable finding is that humanities students generally perform better than those of medical sciences. Both findings deserve special attention in follow-on studies.

Differences in educational type: the differentiating results for bachelor's and master's students confirm the initial expectations that led to the project funding. It clearly shows that there is room in higher education to work on Internet risk awareness, in particular at the bachelor's level. For the K.U. Leuven Association, our recommendations will be that basic skills of information management belong to students' essential competences. We will provide them with self-evaluation and remediation tools; learning how to take responsibility for information, however, is something that needs to be actively addressed in the study curricula of bachelor's degrees. Working on a virtual personal and professional identity and Web presence is something that can be supported in more advanced studies.

Impact of computer experience: The more a student interacts with the Internet—using several identities, posting items on the internet, or using social internet networks (such as Facebook)—the higher the degree of perceived computer literacy will be but, strange and counter-intuitive as it may seem, this does not relate to (file-oriented) information retrieval skills. This means that a presupposition of university curriculum designers that basic computer skills education isn't needed, now that everyone uses the Internet, is not valid.

Our recommendation would be to keep it the responsibility of the learner to address this, but to provide self-assessment and remediation tools.

Relative importance of factors: Comparing the strength of the three effects simultaneously, it is clear that the gender effects are equally strong as impacts of computer (and Internet) experience. The effect of study branch is less but remains significant.

Knowledge Management Solution: The Information Companion Project

At the K.U. Leuven Association level we have initiated a multidisciplinary effort to develop tools for the students to acquire the essential skills to improve their personal information management. This implies not only a wide range of practical competences, but also more conceptual skills and, more important, a consistent attitude, which are necessary in their educational careers and later in their professional life (see Figure 11.2).

It is a common misunderstanding that these computer-related skills are only relevant at a basic level. Quite to the contrary, our research aims to show how deeply skills and attitude relate to the development of a professional profile and identity. These proficiencies are something that can only be learned during the whole path

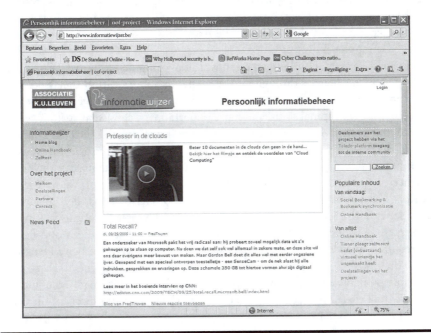

Figure 11.2 The Information Companion environment (in Dutch).

of higher education, where students will, hopefully, gather a structured amount of knowledge in particular domains and externalize this on their computers, other devices, and the Internet.

The main goal of our project is to make the students more aware of the need for adequate information skills, and to teach them that it is their own responsibility to upscale their competences where and when required.

In order to achieve this goal, we are working towards the implementation of a community where existing information, projects, and experience from teachers and institutes throughout our association can be consolidated. Toward this goal we are providing a single point of contact for the student about information skills: http://www.informatiewijzer.be. Additionally, we wish to develop tools such as tests, information leaflets, learning objects, and news articles, which may help the students train in these competences.

Project Context

The Leuven University Association involves 13 institutions for higher education, geographically dispersed throughout the Flanders region. Some of them provide academic education; quite a few offer professional education. The Association wants to stimulate students to go from one institution to another during their study. One visible tool to achieve a common feeling is the common digital learning platform or CDLP, a common learning space for all students—however, allowing institutional "branding" at the front-end level. This common platform, used by students from the first day they start their study at the Association, enforces a common level of required computer skills.

The project aims at building upon those initial computer skills to develop a consistent computer literacy throughout the many disciplines within the association, The competence aimed at not only implies a wide range of practical competences, but also more conceptual skills, and more importantly, a consistent attitude, which is necessary in their educational careers and later in their professional life. The strategic goal of the project is to make the students more aware of the need for adequate information skills, and learn that it is their own responsibility to upscale their competences where and when required. In order to achieve this goal, we have developed a Web portal, www.informatiewijzer.be, also referred to as the Information Companion. The Web portal (written in Dutch at the moment of this writing), is constructed around three methods: an online manual that gives an overview of all required knowledge, a blog where the project members post news items that grasp the student's attention, and a self test that enables the students to check their information management skills. The purpose of this Web site is to give the students a handy tool that will enable them to deal with the numerous aspects of their personal information management.

The project group consists of more than 25 members, representing different divisions, faculties, or participating educational institutions. They are either ICT lecturers, educational coordinators, or directors of various graduate or undergraduate programs. The Information Companion is perceived as a work-in-progress project that will be extended and appropriated in the future. The objective is not only to inform students about this "companion," but also to encourage educators and lecturers to integrate all or parts of the content of the Web portal into their ICT-related courses.

In order to be able to develop and further enhance the information companion, it was useful to collect different experiences from lecturers and administer a survey that can shed a light on how students ascertain their own competences. Therefore, a survey was developed to measure the perceived computer literacy of different cohorts of students of the association.

The Layers of the Information Companion

While developing the Information Companion for the K. U. Leuven Association for Higher Education, we opted for a layered approach. First and foremost, at the entry point in the higher education study path, students should be tested to see if they actually do have the basic computing skills presupposed, as our research clearly shows these competencies are not evenly distributed amongst the student population.

Level 1: The Basics

To this end, we offer a self-test and extra-curricular remediating study materials for all new students in the Association. Each year, a large awareness campaign will provide the right mental context and attitudes so that students have the opportunity to become aware of and understand the importance of having the basics right from the start of their study career.

The basics involve file management, information retrieval, and computer and Internet security.

Level 2: Trust and Responsibility

However, on a second level—and this is a radical departure from the set of skills that are already taught in primary and secondary education—the students learn to take responsibility for digital information. They learn the basic social ethics involved in working with computers and managing information others rely on. These are the kind of competencies that do not immediately translate into a set of well-defined skills, but involve a growing attitude adopted throughout study in a particular field, in social interaction with others. To hit home with these competencies, we try to embed specific course materials into curricular courses, in dialogue with academic staff in the different disciplines. These involve issues like information privacy, integrity, and authenticity, attitudes toward plagiarism, and fostering an awareness of the value of information.

Trust and responsibility are important notions in professional activity. Being able to trust someone else's competences is one of the reasons the scholarly system leads to degrees and certificates. A degree shows you that a person has reached a certified minimal required level of competence in a certain field, so that you can entrust him or her with tasks others will depend on. Formal learning strongly focuses on this requirement. Of course, degrees are not the only element of proof taken into consideration when assessing whether someone is "fit for the job." The personal pedigree and the social network that someone has built can be valuable indicators. A lot of valid, socially accepted knowledge is obtained through informal learning, in social contacts or on the job. More and more, people tend to professionalize their hobbies into added competences that can be of value for their professional career. The trail of past activities one carries along is kept increasingly in digital form: papers, articles, blog posts a candidate has written, his or her presence on social Web sites, maybe even in the more formal context of a true electronic portfolio; it all helps to add credentials to someone as employable for a certain set of tasks. Besides the intricate relationship between knowledge and professional activity—and as a consequence of continuous learning—it is reasonable to claim that the expertise that someone builds within his social network is an inextricable part of his personal development. In the same way, the virtual personality that emerges from the multitude of online activities someone deploys can be an important part of his or her personality as a whole. It is difficult to separate personal and professional development, whether in real life or online, and it is our feeling that institutions devoted to learning should take that issue with due attention and care.

Level 3: The Information Professional

On a third level, we consider something we hope students will acquire by the end of their study career, when they will become ready to take up professional responsibilities. We will focus on higher-level information management skills, like managing one's personal portfolio and trail on the Web. It also involves teaching the student how the digital media can be an extension of one's professional knowledge when transformed into a usable, accessible, and controlled memory environment. Even these higher-level competencies will involve rather practical skills like managing bibliographies and bookmarks, or keeping up personal databases. Looked at in the right way, these computing skills do have substantial academic merit, and are without any doubt part of the rucksack filled with competencies that our students should have when they graduate.

Conclusions

Although students in higher education are increasingly required to work with electronic information and informational processes, studies have shown that students' essential computing skills and knowledge are frequently overestimated. In order to improve ICT-related education and create more awareness towards computing capabilities and risks, a project was started at the Association of the Katholieke Universiteit of Leuven (Belgium) to develop an information compendium, called the Information Companion. The "companion" is comprised of a manual, a self-test, and a blog, explaining and testing several ICT-related competences that are often not taught explicitly in a higher educational curriculum.

In future research, these effects will be further scrutinized using extended and finer-grained computer literacy measures and also adding objective indicators to the research design. Likewise, the success and consequences of the information companion will be evaluated in order to improve its scope, contents, and usability over time.

Acknowledgments

The support of the OOF (Onderwijs Ontwikkelings Fonds) of the Association K. U. Leuven is gratefully acknowledged.

References and Bibliography

Anderson, N., Lankshear, C., Timmsa, C., and Courtney, L. (2008), Because it's boring, irrelevant and I don't like computers: Why high school girls avoid professionally-oriented ICT subjects. *Computers and Education, 50*(4), pp. 1304–1318.

Arndt, S., Turvey, C., and Andreasen, N. (1999). Correlating and predicting psychiatric symptom ratings: Spearman's r versus Kendall's tau correlation. *Journal of Psychiatric Research*, Vol. 33, pp. 97–104.

Ballantine, J.A., McCourt Larres, P., and P. Oyelere (2007). Computer usage and the validity of self-assessed computer competence among first-year business students. *Computers and Education*, 49, pp. 976–990.

Baron, R.M. and Kenny, D.A. (1986). The moderator-mediator variable distinction in social psychological research: Conceptual, strategic, and statistical considerations. *Journal of Personality and Social Psychology*, 61(6), pp. 1173–1182.

Bunz, U., Curry, C., and Voon, W. (2007). Perceived versus actual computer-email-web fluency. *Computers in Human Behavior*, 23, pp. 2321–2344.

Cannaerts, M., Deslé, R., and Truyen, F. (2009). Personal information management. In *Research, Reflections and Innovations in Integrating ICT in Education*, 1. 5 International Conference on Multimedia and Information and Communication Technologies in Education. Lisbon, 2009 (pp. 102–107). Badajoz: Formatex.

Durndell, A. and Haag, Z. (2002). Computer self efficacy, computer anxiety, attitudes towards the internet and reported experience with the internet, by gender, in an East European sample. *Computers in Human Behavior*, 18, pp. 521–535.

Frand, J. (2000). The information-age mindset: Changes in students and implications for higher education. *EDUCAUSE Review*, vol. 35, no. 5, pp. 15–24.

Hair, J.F., Anderson, R., Tatham, R.L., and Black, W.C. (2006). *Multivariate Data Analysis.* Prentice Hall: Upper Saddle River, NJ.

Hakkarainen, K., Ilomäki L., Lipponen, L. , Muukkonen, H., Rahikainen, M. Tuominen, T., Lakkala, M., and Lehtinen, E. (2000). Students' skills and practices of using ICT: Results of a national assessment in Finland. *Computers and Education*, 34, pp. 103–117.

Howe, N. and Strauss, W. (2000), *Millennials Rising.* New York: Vintage Books.

Jones, W. (2007). *Keeping Found Things Found: The Study and Practice of Personal Information Management.* San Francisco, CA, Morgan Kaufmann Publishers.

Kirkwood, A. (2006). Getting networked learning in context: Are On-line students' technical and information literacy skills adequate and appropriate? *Learning, Media and Technology*, *31*(2), pp. 117–131.

Kisla, T., Arikan, Y.D., and Sarsar, F. (2009). The investigation of the usage of ICT in university lecturers' courses. In *Procedia Social and Behavioral Sciences* 1, pp. 502–507.

Link, T.M. and Marz, R. (2006). Computer Literacy and attitudes towards e-learning among first year medical students. In *BMC Medical Education*, 6:34, pp. 8.

McCourt Larres, P., Ballantine, J.A., and Whittington, M. (2003). Evaluating the validity of self-assessment: Measuring computer literacy among entry-level undergraduates within accounting degree programmes at two UK universities. In *Accounting Education*, 12(2), pp. 97–112.

Milis, K., Wessa, P., and Poelmans, S. (2008). The impact of gender on the acceptance of virtual learning environments. In *Proceedings of the International Conference of Education, Research and Innovation*, Madrid, Spain, November 2008.

Oblinger, D. (2003). Boomers, Gen-Xers, and Millennials: Understanding the "new students." *EDUCAUSE Review*, vol. 38, no. 4.

Oblinger, J.L. (Eds.) (2005), Educating the Net Generation. An EduCause e-book, http://www.educause.edu/books/educatingthenetgen.

Pletka, B. (2007), *Educating the Net Generation: How to Engage Students in the 21st Century.* Santa Monica. 168 pp.

Poelmans, S., Truyen, F., and Deslé, R. (2009). Perceived computer literacy among different types of (under)graduate students: Findings of a survey. In *ICERI 2009 Proceedings of ICERI 2009 Conference.* Madrid, November 16–18, 2009 (pp. 4910–4921).

Poynton, T.A. (2005). Computer Literacy across the lifespan: A review with implications for educators. *Computers in Human Behavior*, 21, pp. 861–872.

Prinsen, F., Volman, M.L.L., and Terwel, J. (2007), The influence of learner characteristics on degree and type of participation in a CSCL environment. *British Journal of Educational Technology*, *38*(6), pp. 1037–1055.

Schiltz, M., Truyen, F., and Coppens, H. (2007). *Cutting the Trees of Knowledge: Social Software, Information Architecture and Their Epistemic Consequences.* Thesis Eleven 89. pp. 94–114.

Schumacher, P. and Morahan-Martin, J. (2001). Gender, internet and computer attitudes and experiences. *Computers in Human Behavior*, 17, pp. 95–110.

Seago, B.L., Schlesinger, J.B.B., and Hampton, C.L. (2002). Using a decade of data on medical student computer literacy for strategic planning. *Journal of the Medical Library Association*, 90, pp. 2202–2209.

Selwyn, N. (2008). An investigation of differences in undergraduates' academic use of the internet. *Active Learning in Higher Education*, *9*(1), pp. 11–22.

Shih, H.-P. (2006). Assessing the effects of self-efficacy and competence on individual satisfaction with computer use: An IT student perspective. *Computers in Human Behavior*, 22, pp. 1012–1026.

Smith, B.L., Caputi, P., and Rawstorne, P. (2000). Differentiating computer experience and attitudes toward computers: An empirical investigation. *Computers in Human Behavior*, 16, pp. 59–81.

Stensaker, B., Maassen, P., Borgan, M., Oftebro, M., and Karseth, B. (2007). Use, updating and integration of ICT in higher education: Linking purpose, people and pedagogy. *Higher Education: The International Journal of Higher Education and Educational Planning*, 54(3), pp. 417–433.

Stefani, L.A.J. (1994). Peer, self and tutor assessment: Relative reliabilities. *Studies in Higher Education*, 19(1), pp. 69–75.

Tisaun, J., Buelens, H., and Vanthienen, J., 2004. Organizing decentralized support for a virtual learning environment, *Proceedings of IADIS International Conference on Cognition and Exploratory Learning in the Digital Age (CELDA 2004)*, ISBN 972-98947-7-9, Lisbon (Portugal), December 15–17, pp. 504–507.

Truyen, F., Deslé, R., and Cannaerts, M. (2009). The information companion. *23 ICDE World Conference*. Maastricht, June 7–10, 2009.

Truyen, F. and Van Rentergem, L. (2005). Preparing the university information architecture for net-centric e-learning and research: A case-study, in *4th European Conference on E-Learning: Amsterdam*, The Netherlands, November 10–11, 2005. Ed. by Dan Remenyi. Reading: ACL, 2005. pp. 479–492.

van Braak, J.P. (2004). Domains and determinants of university students' self-perceived computer competence. *Computers and Education*, 43, pp. 299–312.

Young, B.J. (2000). Gender differences in student attitudes toward computers. *Journal of Research on Computing in Education*, 33(2), p. 204.

Chapter 12

Harnessing the Web: Social and Personal Learning

Stella Porto and Allison Kipta

Contents

Introduction

We start this chapter with a living example of social software "in the works." Two authors using social software tools created this chapter collaboratively. In our initial step in writing this chapter, we created a wiki (See section titled "Essential Web Learning Tools: Wikis" for a full description). The wiki is organized in sections accessible by links in such a way that we can edit it at anytime and anywhere a computer with a Web browser and Internet connection are available. We kept the wiki private, not visible to the outside world and not accessible by others, thus protecting it from any sort of cyber vandalism. At any point in time, we can find the latest version of our work and update our individual collection of notes and links to resources outside of the wiki. In addition, we are able to review the history of our revisions, sorted by time and date. We communicate and provide comments on each other's contributions as our wiki content grows and matures. We also upload and share content from other sources as we work together.

In addition to the wiki, we also shared bookmarks through a social bookmarking service (see section titled "Essential Web Learning Tools: Social Bookmarking" for a full description), creating lists of links to our sources on the Web. Like the wiki, all our Web references can be accessed anytime, anywhere. We can check what the other has found, contribute to the list, and continue to build what has become our "living" bibliography.

In this instance, the book chapter wiki is a two-person endeavor, but think of the possibilities if it involved a larger group of people, collaborating on a larger project with a more complex structure. A wiki can serve not only as a repository for documents being edited, but also can serve as a coordinating tool, with schedules and ongoing discussions about issues that have yet to be resolved—all in one place. Project collaborators can also share their bookmarks, their Web resources of information, without having to e-mail information back and forth, and have difficulty keeping up with whatever the rest of the group is doing. This is an example, a real-world example, and it showcases an important aspect of social software: at its heart, it is about facilitating interaction, collaboration, and diffusion of information.

Now imagine the difference if this entire book were "alive," not in print or on any static electronic form in front of you. Let's say the book as a whole was provided as a wiki with a link to a list of ever growing bookmarks of Web resources. You might receive a license to access this book, and the many authors involved would add and revise its content regularly. It has continuously new content and a growing Web bibliography. If we were to take a weekly snapshot of this wiki-book, we could see it evolving. This situation is not at all futuristic. In a way, the most well known wiki, Wikipedia (http://www.wikipedia.org/), is in fact an encyclopedia "in the works," in a continuous process of being edited, being changed and enhanced by thousands of collaborators and reviewers. Who are these collaborators? They can be anyone, even you. However, in the particular case of Wikipedia there are supervisory roles to keep things somewhat in order. We will discuss the issue of "order," supervisory roles, and so forth later in this chapter. For now, we would like you to visualize what this "living book" could be like if it were developed and presented through social media tools (social software). There is potential for feedback from users, for increasing the number of collaborators, for updating information with advances in the field, and more. The possibilities become endless. This is definitely the same promise of social media to learning.

With this concrete example in hand as motivator, we want to discuss in this chapter many of the developments in the recent wave of change taking place on Web. These new developments, which for the most part have been labeled as "Web 2.0" or can be referred to as "social software," have been the catalysts of a dramatic change in the role of users of the Web. We will discuss what these changes are, their impact on e-learning, and how we can we these novel and accessible tools to generate creative and effective e-learning experiences, be it as an educator or on a personal basis.

The Web presents a dynamic environment for learning, allowing participants to interact with others within an entirely new social construct. The ecosystem in which education operates has changed dramatically. There is a shift in the concept of the control of information (November, 2008), and "perceptions of time, space, and relationships are expanded. The audience moves from teacher and class to the world" (p. 81).

Drucker (2003) writes "Since school learning and school diplomas increasingly control access to jobs, livelihoods, and careers in the knowledge society, all members of society need to be literate—and not only in "reading, writing, and arithmetic." Literacy now includes elementary computer skills" (pp. 224–225). Bleed (2006) suggests that change in the form of a new literacy is required, using today's information technology tools. The reasons, Bleed says, are that we have "twenty-first-century students" and have reached a "tipping point." Where technology developed our left-brain abilities, a new "Conceptual Age" of right-brained "pattern recognizers" and "meaning-makers" with highly developed visual literacy skills is emerging. "Thus, the preservation of traditional literacy formats and their use ... will work to the detriment of an increasingly large number of students" (Bleed, 2006, p. 36).

We live in an increasingly connected world, and the Web makes it easier to collect, create, contribute, and collaborate. "Not only that," writes Harold Jarche (2009), "it may be our social responsibility to be contributors to our common knowledge. How else will we be recognized as professionals in our fields unless we actively contribute to them?" (para. 15).

To better understand these positions, it is best, perhaps, to explore how our connectedness evolved and how we reached the tipping point, the moment in time when the unique Web became the ubiquitous Web. In the next section, we provide a brief history and the circumstances that set Web 2.0 in motion.

Historical Perspective and Context

On April 30, 1993, the European Organization for Nuclear Research (CERN), home to the birth and development of Tim Berners-Lee's World Wide Web (WWW) project, declared the WWW protocol and its code free for all to use (World Wide Web Consortium, 2008). This was the start of several years of extraordinarily rapid development beginning in 1994 with the growing commercialization of the Web and the sudden appearance of countless Internet service providers and other information technology services. These were known as the "dot-coms" for the .com denoting "commercial" in their top-level domain names. This time, also known as the "dot-com bubble," reached its peak prosperity in the spring of 2001 and then collapsed six months later.

Tim O'Reilly (2005), credited with coining the term "Web 2.0," noted that the companies surviving the "bursting of the dot-com bubble" in 2001 seemed to have characteristics unlike their predecessors. This second generation Web was "more important than ever, with exciting new applications and sites popping up with surprising regularity" (para. 2). Drawing from software code versioning conventions, it was playfully dubbed "Web 2.0."

According to learning technology researcher Sam Adkins (2007), in the education arena, there are three distinct waves of innovation in learning software: commercial/proprietary, open source, and open learning (or Web 2.0). The value propositions associated with each of these waves, respectively, are product, services, and community. The forecast is a shift from the paradigm of the one-size-fits-all learning management system model, first wave, to the widely distributed learning communities, second wave. The third wave (Adkins, 2007) is dominated by Web 2.0 technology. "The learning paradigm is personalization. Suppliers define their core value as providing technology that supports communities of individual contributors" (para. 8).

The definition of Web 2.0 changes with time as more products, services, and communities are introduced. Some have tried other names, but the label, which has been criticized for not capturing the essence of what it should represent, remains in use as a main identifier of all things "dynamic and user-generated" on the Web. Mike Elgan (2006) presents this basic definition: "Web 2.0 is all the Web sites out there that get their value from the actions of users" (para. 3). This is pretty simple indeed! The problem is that it doesn't help much to assimilate this concept if you are not one of those users. However, as you will see, this definition does encompass all the traits that define Web 2.0.

Tim O'Reilly, chief executive officer of O'Reilly Media, calls it an "architecture of participation" (O'Reilly, 2004). "The Web," O'Reilly says, "... took the idea of participation to a new level, because it opened that participation not just to software developers but to all users of the system" (para. 6). The result, writes Yochai Benkler (2006) in *The Wealth of Networks: How Social Production Transforms Markets* is

> ... a flourishing nonmarket sector of information, knowledge, and cultural production, based in the networked environment, and applied to anything that the many individuals connected to it can imagine. Its outputs, in turn, are not treated as exclusive property. They are instead subject to an increasingly robust ethic of open sharing, open for all others to build on, extend, and make their own. (p. 23)

Web 2.0 represents a set of read–write Web applications that become more valuable the more that people contribute to them. They encourage participation, collaboration, and sharing.

Today's Online Environment

In a series of studies focused on the state of online learning in higher education in the United States, Allen and Seaman (2007) present statistics revealing that the number of online students had more than doubled in 4 years and that nearly 70% of academic leaders believe that demand for online learning is still growing. There are growing numbers on the corporate side as well. A survey (Ellis, 2004) of attitudes toward e-learning in a corporate setting indicates that 50.6% of employees and 69 of managers are interested in using e-learning to train employees.

We often hear that we live in a knowledge economy today. "The capacity to form connections between sources of information, and thereby create useful information patterns, is what is needed in a knowledge economy" (Mason and Rennie, 2008, p. 10). With the advent of new "social software" networking technologies, folksonomies, and protocols, the "read-write Web," or "Web 2.0" (O'Reilly, 2005) facilitates an environment that encourages collaboration, creativity, and sharing among participants. A philosophy of sharing and "rip, mix, burn" (Apple, 2001) of digital content is now the norm. This is true even to the extent that many have adopted new "2.0" terms for their own genre, such as "E-Learning 2.0" (Downes, 2005, 2007, 2008; Karrer, 2007b; Mayoud, n.d.), "Library 2.0" (Birdsall, 2007; Casey and Savastinuk, 2006; Jayasuriya and Brillantine, 2008; Maness, 2006; Miller, 2006), and even "Law 2.0" (Kennedy and Mighell, 2006). Everything is "2.0."

The thing to remember is that "Web 2.0 is all about harnessing collective intelligence. Collective intelligence applications depend on managing, understanding, and responding to massive amounts of user-generated data in real time" (O'Reilly and Battelle, 2009, p. 1). This is why the power of Web 2.0 resides on capturing, storing, and using content effectively; it also depends on getting people to interact with the Web and through the Web in order to generate new content. With emerging technologies such as Web-enabled mobile gadgets, more real-time content is being produced. Technology is making it easier for people to create, organize, share, and collaborate.

Learning with the Web

In *Grown Up Digital*, Dan Tapscott (2009) discusses the differences concerning the change in habits of learning, working and playing of the so-called NetGeners:

> The Net Generation has come of age. In 2008, the eldest of the generation turned 31. The youngest turned 11. Around the world the generation is flooding into the workplace, marketplace, and every niche society. They are bringing their demographic muscle, media smarts, purchasing power, new models of collaborating and parenting, entrepreneurship, and political power into the world. (p. 3)

It is true, nonetheless, that the changes in the last 20 years, almost in totality, are due to the "rise of the computer, the Internet, and other digital technologies" (Tapscott, 2009, p. 17) that have affected many more than just those from the Net Generation. It is conceivable that such changes are more ingrained in NetGeners, because they were born into this digital life, and therefore all such technologies are part of their first contact with the world, "the first generation to be bathed in bits" (p. 17).

Even more recently, the change brought by the Web 2.0 wave is having an increasing impact on NetGeners and is pushing its way through previous generations as well. The number of users of the social networking site, Facebook (Table 12.1), is currently composed of almost 40% of those in the age group above

Table 12.1   United States Facebook Users Over 34 Years Old (November 2009)

Percent of U.S. Facebook Population	Facebook Age Distribution
17.8%	35–44
12.0%	45–54
6.7%	55–64
3%	>65
Sum 39.5%	

Source: Gonzalez, N. (2009). *Facebook Marketing Statistics, Demographics, Reports, and News—CheckFacebook.* Retrieved December 13, 2009, from http://www.checkfacebook.com/

Note: Almost 40% of the U.S. Facebook users are above the age of 34 and are not NetGeners.

34 years old, not the NetGeners. This means that adult learners are also embracing the new Web-based technologies.

This is key for those professionals involved in providing training and education to a growing adult population that will have technology as an intrinsic part of their jobs in one way or another. Computers have moved from a computing-exclusive role to a major communication role. Virtual interaction among people across the globe as well as those working in the same building is commonplace for many corporations. The culture that "face time" is a measure of productivity is slowly changing, and as work and leisure activities move to the online environment, so does learning.

Jarche (2009) describes personal knowledge management in terms of "looking inward" and "looking outward." Inwardly, we categorize, make explicit, share publicly, and retrieve information valuable to us. Outwardly, we make connections, exchange information, and contribute information valuable to others. On using his digital tools for personal knowledge management, Jarche writes

> I have been creating a powerful resource. My annotated bookmarks and my blog are the first places I search when I have an article or report to write. My [personal knowledge management] process has given me a digital library brimming with my own sticky notes that I can easily find. (Jarche, 2009)

The same "looking inward" and "looking outward" concepts Jarche (2009) applies to his personal knowledge management can also be adapted for and applied to personal learning.

The essential aspect of all social software discussed here, and others, is that the users generate content. "This has potentially profound implications for education" (Mason and Rennie, 2008, p. 4). As Mason and Rennie (2008) note "the benefits of user generated content in education is fairly obvious" (p. 4): (1) through social software, the tools are available for user to "actively engage in the construction of their experience" (p. 4); (2) content is continually renewed by users; (3) most of the tools support collaboration, which supports the development of skills associated to team work; and (4) young people are more engaged and motivated to learn when there are "shared community spaces and intergroup communications" (p. 5). Nonetheless, critics will say that the transition between the use of such tools for entertainment to their use in education is not always straightforward or natural. For that matter, Mason and Rennie (2008) suggest that Tim O'Reilly might have the key when he states "One of the key lessons of the Web 2.0 era is this: Users add value" (in Mason and Rennie, 2008, p. 5). Mason and Rennie claim "Through appropriate course design, we can help learners to pursue their 'selfish interests' of passing the course, while at the same time adding value to the learning of other students" (p. 5). In what follows, we don't discuss specifically course design issues, but we consider a few major social software tools and how they can be used in learning. Such discussion has the potential of being directly integrated into course design or morphed into further more complex learning activities within different settings.

Essential Web Learning Tools: Blogs

In 1977, Jorn Barger, editor of *Robot Wisdom,* used the term "Weblog" to describe a Web page containing news, opinion, and links to other Web sites. On his FAQ (Frequently Asked Questions) page, Barger (1999) writes

> A Weblog (sometimes called a blog or a newspage or a filter) is a Webpage where a Weblogger (sometimes called a blogger, or a pre-surfer) "logs" all the other Web pages she finds interesting. The format is normally to add the newest entry at the top of the page, so that repeat visitors can catch up by simply reading down the page until they reach a link they saw on their last visit. (paras. 1–2)

This term evolved into "blogging" (Leadbeater, 2008) when Peter Merholz used the phrase "wee blog" (as in "we blog") in 1999. The term was then shortened to "blog." According to Lee Rainie (2005), director of the Pew Internet and American Life Project, in November of 2004

> Eight million American adults say they have created blogs; blog reader-ship jumped 58% in 2004 and now stands at 27% of Internet users; 5% of Internet users say they use RSS aggregators or XML readers to get the news and other information delivered from blogs and content-rich Web sites as it is posted online; and 12% of Internet users have posted comments or other material on blogs. Still, 62% of Internet users do not know what a blog is. (p. 1)

In its basic form, a blog works as an online journal or personal diary. Current blog "engines" (the Web-based software for authoring, editing, and organizing blog posts) provide several other functionalities such as a button for subscribing, archives of older postings, and links to other blogs. Every blog has a theme, or a "reason for existence." The theme is a topic of interest, such as a blog about cats, a blog about learning with technology, travel adventures, or a blog that represents a personal commentary on current events.

In fact, the world of news and information diffusion has been greatly changed with the increasing use of blogs for journalistic information, commen-tary, and editorials. Most print, radio, and television news media are now repre-sented online and provide blog spaces for their writers. Blogs can be maintained by an individual, a group of individuals, or an organization. Bloggers often form social networks by creating "blogroll," a list of links to other bloggers.

The "blogosphere" is the community of blogs and bloggers. Blogs can have a focus on a specific medium, such as photographs (photoblog), audio recordings (audioblog), or motion pictures (videoblog or vlog). Paul Snow's photoblog (http://paulsnow.shutterchance.com/) and Howard Rheingold's vlog (http://vlog.rheingold.com/) are good examples of these types of blogs. Microblogs are blogs with short messages, usually sent from cell phones or other messaging systems like Twitter (http://www.twitter.com/).

Learning with Blogs

Although blogs facilitate two-way communication as a basic purpose (Efimova, 2009), it doesn't have to be the singular focus or the reason for blogging. Bloggers often share their writings with others, but they don't have to. Using her blog as a "filing cabinet" (Pollard, 2003) for collecting and storing ideas she wanted to discuss in her PhD dissertation, Lilia Efimova (2009) explains that in her case, "blogging grew out of a need for a place to organize my professional thinking and exploration; the readers, as well as writing for them, came later" (p. 289).

Sharing ideas publicly in a blog invites feedback, and commenting offers a "venue for rebuttal and engagement with the reader" writes Anderson (2006), and the "feedback and immediacy demonstrates very high relative advantage for blogs (para. 10)." On her experience with reader feedback, Efimova (2009) says "Over time I have learnt not to count on it, as it is difficult to predict whether anyone will comment and what exactly might catch their attention. However, I have also learnt to appreciate unexpected turns in my own thinking triggered by the feedback of others" (p. 294).

Sharing your writings online and creating conversations with readers by inviting comments can be considered "inward-looking" benefits of blogging. Reading other people's blogs and engaging in conversations is "outward looking" and equally rewarding to personal learning. Downes (2004) shares this idea: "The process of reading online, engaging a community, and reflecting it online is a process of bringing life into learning" (p. 26). With regard to teaching and learning, Will Richardson writes (Downes, 2004)

> Could blogging be the needle that sews together what is now a lot of learning in isolation with no real connection among the disciplines? I mean, ultimately, aren't we trying to teach our kids how to learn, and isn't that [what] blogging is all about? (p. 26)

Blogging is about creating, collecting, categorizing, analyzing, reflecting, connecting, collaborating, and contributing. Bloggers write, reflect, and clarify thoughts for themselves, and if the writing is made public, for others as well. Receiving feedback, blog authors can start meaningful exchanges with readers that help clarify their own thoughts. Reading other people's blogs provides a different perspective and another opportunity for dialog. Farmer, Yue, and Brooks (2008) offer four pedagogic benefits of blogging for learners: (1) Blogging encourages learners to become subject matter experts "through a process of regular scouring, filtering and posting"; (2) blogging fosters ownership in learning; (3) it cultivates communities of practice; and (4) offers opportunity for "diverse perspectives" (p. 124).

Wordpress (http://www.wordpress.com), Blogger (http://www.blogger.com), and TypePad (http://www.typepad.com) are three highly popular blogging platforms today. While registration may take only a few seconds, there are scores of personalization options involved in setting up a blog. General blog options such as the title, language, time zone, and time and date format are relatively easy choices to make. Personalization in visual themes (color schemes, fonts, and icons) writing and posting templates, navigation features, commenting permissions, and privacy settings will take a bit more consideration. However, once you have personalized your blog, posting is as easy as sending an e-mail message. Links (Richardson, 2009) are a key characteristic of blogs. Links within a blog post can point to other posts within the blog, or to outside resources such as other blogs or Websites. Many blog hosts have a mail-to feature that allows a blogger to send posts to the blog via e-mail or mobile phone by using a special e-mail address generated by the blog. Taking advantage of the multimedia-rich environment of the Web, bloggers can also embed audio, video, and photographs to provide a centerpiece for their writing or to enhance their postings. While blogging software offers a powerful publishing technology, O'Donnell (2005, citing Wrede) reminds us that it isn't the technology that sets blogs apart, it's the "practice and authorship they shape. And it is a practice that will require a Weblog author to be connected to processes, discourses, and communities" (p. 5). To get started blogging, see the list of resources at the end of this chapter.

Essential Web Learning Tools: Wikis

The term "wiki" is Hawaiian for "fast," and wikis earned this name by being quick and easy. The first wiki software, developed by Ward Cunningham, was called WikiWikiWeb. Cunningham (Leuf and Cunningham, 2002) describes the wiki as "The simplest online database that could possibly work" (What Is Wiki? para. 1).

Wikis are Web pages, usually tabbed or with links, and are a popular place to disseminate information and share in the creation of new content. Users can read a wiki as content-consumer, use a wiki as a personal content organizer, or join a multiuser wiki and become part of a community of collaborators, content creators, reviewers, and editors. Again, we remind our readers that this book chapter was authored and organized in a wiki.

The most notable wiki, perhaps of all time, is Wikipedia (http://www.wikipedia.org/), the "Free Encyclopedia," which at the time of this writing has amassed 3,171,134 articles in English (Wikipedia, 2010c. Main Page). While anyone can create an account and start writing, to prevent it from becoming a free-for-all mess, articles must meet Wikipedia's editing policies and standards. Some pages have public editing privileges removed to prevent vandalism. Such pages, especially articles related to highly controversial topics, are maintained by a staff of administrators. Like blogs, wikis also have a theme, or "reason for existing." There are wikis with teaching and learning themes, such as Wikiversity, "a project devoted to learning resources, learning projects, and research," and WikiEducator, "turning the digital divide into digital dividends using free content and open networks." *Note*: During the time it took to write this section, 35 new articles were added to Wikipedia.

Learning with Wikis

The fact that anyone can edit wiki pages is often cited as a reason for not using them in learning activities. However, this is actually a good reason to use them. A wiki fosters collaboration and "deliberately encourages participation in the joint creation of content" (Mason and Rennie, 2008, p. 65). However, the fear of vandalism persists. "A way to manage vandalism," recommends Wikiversity (2009a), "is to assume good faith and not create vandals. Newcomers often try a few tests as they try to get familiar with the Wiki interface, format, syntax, etc. Please do not bite the newcomers ..." (Managing vandalism, para. 6). Another solution is to set up the wiki for registered members only. Should problems continue, vandals can be blocked from further participation by the wiki administrator. However, through constant editing and revising of information, the wiki, write Mason and Rennie (2008), can be "effectively self-policed to reduce misinformation through inaccuracy or malicious intent" (p. 65). Although the debate over accuracy of the content of wikis will likely continue, "educators have argued the importance of using the opportunities of this medium to educate learners to make their own judgments regarding the accuracy of information" (Mason and Rennie, 2008, p. 67).

Like blogs, a wiki can be maintained by an individual, a group of individuals, or an organization. The content of a wiki, like a blog, is usually focused on a theme. Will Richardson (2009) provides several examples of model wikis used to support learning, including Welker's Wikinomics (http://welkerswikinomics.wetpaint.com/) with resources organized to support AP Economics courses, and PlanetMath (http://planetmath.org/), a collaborative effort to collect mathematical knowledge. Others examples of how wikis are used to collect and organize resources surrounding a certain theme include CR 2.0 (http://wiki.classroom20.com/), Web 2.0 resources for learning; MobileRead Wiki (http://wiki.mobileread.com/), featuring lists of e-book repositories, file formats, reading devices; The Comic Book Wiki (http://comicbooks.wikidot.com/), everything related to comic books; the "Twitter Fan Wiki" (http://twitter.pbworks.com/), providing links to applications, add-ons, books, and other resources of interest related to Twitter; and Project Gutenberg (http://www.gutenberg.org/), the "first producer of free electronic books," founded in 1971, and now home to over 30,000 electronic documents in the public domain (Project Gutenberg, 2009, Main Page, para. 1). Wikis in a corporate enterprise are used for customer support, such as Dell Computer's, inviting users to "add your input" (Dell Computer, 2010); and Cisco Systems (https://supportforums.cisco.com/index.jspa).

As you can see, as a database, a wiki can collect and organize just about any information. As a personal learning tool, a wiki can be used to collect and organize articles and notes for writing a book chapter (like this one), for keeping a reflective journal, or creating an online e-portfolio like Dr. Helen Barrett (http://eportfolios.wikispaces.com/). Like blogs, wiki editors can also embed audio, video, and other multimedia to wiki pages to support and enhance its content. A wiki as a group or personal knowledgebase has seemingly endless uses.

Essential Web Learning Tools: Social Bookmarking

Bookmarking is a method for saving links to Web pages for revisiting later. In Microsoft's Internet Explorer, a bookmark is called a "Favorite." Bookmarks are stored locally, inside the user's browser.

Social bookmarking services allow users to store their bookmarks on the Web instead of locally on their computer. The advantages to social bookmarks are that they can be retrieved from anywhere and shared with other people. If tags are used, bookmarks can be categorized for searches. The social nature involves sharing them publicly, so other people can view and save them, facilitating knowledge building. The sharing capability also allows the creation of sets of bookmarks ("lists") that are a result of collaboration of several people. "Lists" have names that might identify the topic, the purpose, or the group responsible for the bookmarking. This aspect is one that enables the use of social bookmarking for learning in creative ways as discussed below.

On many social bookmarking sites, when more than one user saves the same bookmark, it is then given a rank. The more users with the same bookmark, the higher the rank the bookmark receives. On the social bookmarking home page, the top five to ten bookmarks are often displayed, higher ranking bookmarks displayed at the top of the page, usually with a number indicating the number of times the bookmark has been saved. "Tagging," the use of single keyword descriptors that users assign to a bookmark to assist in organizing and searching, is an important aspect in exploring social bookmarking. According to Hammond, Hannay, Lund, and Scott (2005), the annotation of links with tags is "very much a 'bottom-up' (or personal) approach compared with the traditional 'top-down' (or organizational) structured means of classification" (Hammond et al., 2005, para. 14). This form of classification without a predefined, structured, or any kind of underlying ruling is commonly referred to as a "folksonomy," and several other similar terms are used interchangeably. The scheme works well because it is based on the principle of the "architecture of participation" defined previously by Tim O'Reilly (in Hammond et. al, 2005), where a group establishes a self-regulating system within a network of collaboration. Such systems evolve as more users participate. In the context of social bookmarking, the more users participate in the bookmarking process, the richer the system becomes. Tags become meaningful in describing the listed resources and can be further used to showcase the relevance of certain descriptors ("tags") within a certain field or simply for that particular group (Hammond et al., 2005). The advantage of this system is that resources are labeled in a natural way that makes sense to the users themselves. Once more, as you have seen in other social software tools, social bookmarking reaffirms the power of "crowdsourcing." Crowdsourcing has gained widespread acceptance as the numbers of people connected through the Internet and mobile service increased (Hewlett-Packard Development Company, 2010). In principle, it is a mechanism through which tasks are accomplished by large numbers of people, instead of being assigned to a particular person or selected group. The final solution, or solutions, rise up as more people provide input, ranking, and support to some solutions offered by the "crowd." Companies are also learning how they can "harness new technology to mine the collective wisdom of the crowd—tapping into new levels of ideation and innovation, intelligent prediction, and solution-finding schemas" (Hewlett-Packard Development Company, 2010; Surowiecki, 2010).

Delicious (http://www.delicious.com) is perhaps the best-known and most popular social bookmarking service on the Web. Launched in 2004, the site popularized the process of "tagging," so important to social bookmarking as discussed above. On September 25, 2006, founder Joshua Schachter (2006) reported on the Delicious blog that the service registered its one millionth user, more than triple the number of users it had nine months prior, shortly after its acquisition by Web giant Yahoo!

Diigo (http://www.diigo.com), another popular bookmark-sharing site, offers a browser toolbar from which users can search, bookmark, and even highlight and comment on a Web page with a "sticky note" that other users can read when they visit the site. Diigo also offers groups, communities of like-minded bookmarkers, the ability to share sites, notes, and information with each other. Highlighting text on Web pages is a special effect achieved when using the Diigo browser toolbar highlighting and sticky note tools. Note that sticky notes can be kept private, shared with all Diigo users, or specific groups.

Social citation services cater to users with more scholarly bookmarking tasks. The user interfaces on these sites recognize bibliographic reference fields from site-preferred journals and will automatically populate the bookmarking submission form for easy formatting. Academic-themed social bookmarking services like CiteULike (http://www.citeulike.org/) and Mendeley (http://www.mendeley.com/) also offer interest groups in specific academic disciplines that users can join.

Learning with Social Bookmarking

Social bookmarking can be extremely useful for group projects, collaborative research, or in keeping a database of resources for a specific community of practice.

Group projects, especially for students working at a distance, can rely on social bookmarking to collect resources that are to be used in the project. In the same line of thought, a collaborative research done with different researchers from the same or different institutions can gain from the exchange of one anothers' Web-based bookmarks while working on a paper or other long term project. The annotations that can be made by the participants enable a dialogue about the relevance of each of the resources, without having to engage in side conversations via other technology means. Communities of practice have emerged in many fields of study. Besides the professional networking among its members, such communities now can share user-generated content, which is at the core of all Web 2.0 developments. Social marking enables such a community to create and maintain a common set of resources, which can be enriched by the entire group with relevant information to their field of study and interest. Tagging enables the sorting of such resources, and annotations support the exchange of knowledge among participants. The fall out of such potential is that social bookmarking tools themselves have integrated functionalities that allow groups to be formed around specific topics, and users can share lists of bookmarks (user-generated subsets of bookmarks) with specific groups they might have who use the referred social marking tools. This, in fact, is the evolution of a social bookmarking tool into a social networking with specific purposes. This kind of evolution, where functionalities are added to social software tools is inherent in the Web 2.0 wave. As an example, within Diigo one will find special interest groups that they might want to join. The topics vary tremendously from, as for "example," techies interested in Mac developments all the way to people discussing matters involving newborns. Tagging is at the heart of finding groups, since a group's resources will have tags that are relevant to that group's interests.

Essential Web Learning Tools: Social Networking Services

The term "social networks" outside of the realm of the Web 2.0 wave, refers to a group of individuals (or organizations) drawn together by some common interest, be it in favor or against a political candidate or idea, a love for animals, a celebrity, a common ideology, a shared professional practice, financial or commerce exchanges, a field of study, religious belief, family ties, etc. In the Web world, the term *social networking* in fact is used to represent the real concept of Web-based "social network services." A social network service is one that will provide the tools to build social networks as defined above. These services on the Web are then the so-called social networking sites, such as Facebook, Ning, MySpace, LinkedIn, etc. The social networking sites provides users the necessary tools to interact with other members through various Web-based means, as well as to create, find, and connect with common interest subgroups within the larger social networking site membership group. Wikipedia currently keeps a list of most known active social networking Websites (Wikipedia, 2010a). The list includes the main purpose of each of the Websites and the average number of users registered in each of them (when available). Some of these Websites are specific in their purpose or focused on specific groups (e.g., Blackplanet and Cafemom); other are general sites, where subgroups are formed within the networking site (e.g., Facebook and MySpace). Others yet, like Ning, serve as portals for the creation of special focus social networks, and do not offer wide-open interconnectivity among its members.

According to Wikipedia (2010b), "Social networking began to flourish as a component of business Internet strategy at around March 2005 when Yahoo launched Yahoo! 360°. In July 2005 News Corporation bought MySpace, followed by ITV (UK) buying Friends Reunited in December 2005 History, para 3." This is an area that evolves quickly as technologies become available and new functionalities are created. One clear trend is the integration of specific functionalities amongst different social networking services, such as updating your status on Facebook and having your status in LinkedIn change accordingly. This results from the recognition that many people will be part of different social networking sites, and will use them for various purposes, but are willing to have their Web persona or Web identity kept throughout the several different cyber environments. Another example of the rapid change in the landscape can be attested by the surge of Twitter, which was only launched in 2006, but by 2009 had "eclipsed many other social network services and—although lacking in some of what were considered the essential aspects of a SNS—has allowed add-on services to connect and supply these services via its public API" (Wikipedia, 2010b, History, para 3). For the most part, social network services offer the ability to create a profile and to connect to "friends," also members of the network. However, in the last 2 years many more services have been slowly added, especially in cases such as with Facebook, where third party developers can now offer applications to be connected to and through Facebook. In many of these networks, you can upload pictures, comment on pictures from friends, share links, create groups (private or public), create virtual events, play interactive games, and a myriad of other functions provided by other networks that might have been connected to the one you belong.

Social network Web sites have also gained more serious acceptance among institutions, professional associations, and corporations, instead of being seen as a platform exclusively dedicated to leisure among youngsters. This tendency can also be observed within the formal education environment:

> Social networks are also being used by teachers and students as a communication tool. Because many students are already using a wide-range of social networking sites, teachers have begun to familiarize themselves with this trend and are now using it to their advantage. Teachers and professors are doing everything from creating chat-room forums and groups to extend classroom discussion to posting assignments, tests, and quizzes to assisting with homework outside of the classroom setting. Social networks are also being used to foster teacher–parent communication. These sites make it possible and more convenient for parents to

ask questions and voice concerns without having to meet face-to-face (Wikipedia, 2010b, Emerging trends in social networks, para. 5).

The list of the more tailored social networking sites include LinkedIn (http://www.linkedin.com), which is focused on creating networks of professionals, helping employers find and hire quality professionals, posting jobs to niche groups, providing professionals in distinct areas with customized business advice and expertise, and helping professionals promote their professional services. LinkedIn has had enormous growth, currently holding more than 55 million members (LinkedIn, 2010), and has increased the number of tools available to its users as well as connecting to other social networking sites such as Facebook and Twitter. In fact, the interconnectivity of different social network services among themselves, as well as with other Websites, including media outlets and virtual stores, has become a major asset for users. While reading news on the Web, one can easily share an article with one's friends on a social network service. This is much easier than, for example, to copy and paste the article or link to the article into the Learning Management System (LMS) used in one's virtual classroom. Right there, advantages of using social network services for learning are bluntly apparent: they are and are increasingly becoming more easily connected to the information out on the Web, and thus sharing is made easy and accessible.

Given its recent unprecedented growth, Twitter is definitely worth mentioning:

> Twitter is an online application that is part blog, part social networking site, part cell phone/IM tool, designed to let users answer the question "What are you doing?" Users have 140 characters for each posting (or "tweet") to say whatever they care to (EDUCAUSE Learning Initiative, 2005, p. 1).

Twitter, like Facebook, also "lets users create formal friendships, which collectively establish numerous and interconnected networks of users" (EDUCAUSE Learning Initiative p. 1). Its pervasiveness is linked to its availability through mobile devices. Twitter creates the concept of "followers," people who sign-up to be updated every time another member posts a new "tweet." Twitter is being used not only by individuals but by organizations and corporations to share information with clients, sometimes through many different channels, tailored to niche groups.

Learning with Social Networks

General social networking sites such as Facebook and MySpace are frequently already part of students' lives. This can be taken as input when considering the value of social networking in learning. Mason and Rennie (2008) suggest that teachers should recognize the already existing familiarity of students with such environments and focus on teaching them how to more appropriately use them and avoid many of their pitfalls related to ethical and privacy issues. They list several key points for effective practice, which include several learning opportunities for students, such as: (1) "to discriminate content on social network sites" (p. 79); (2) "not to accept profiles at face value" (p. 79); (3) "to realize that in addition to one's peers, others—marketers, university authorities, law enforcement personnel—can and do access profiles" (p. 79); and (4) "provide opportunities for discussion about profiles—how to construct them and what it means to present "oneself" online" (p. 79).

With the advent of environments such as Ning, the creation of social networking sites is also now available to users for customized use. The basic premise for using such environments is that they allow the creation of online communities that extend the learning beyond the classroom or the regular setting. However, when it comes to real learning, "the motivation created by these kinds of networks must be maximized by the instructor to benefit the students in their growth and development as learning community participants" (Reynard, 2009, p. 4). Reynard reinforces that "It is important to move students beyond social interaction to the kind of learning communities that are dynamic, rich, and very much reflective of the students who are participating" (p. 4). Ning has been extensively used by educators to share information on how to effectively use new technologies in education. Classroom 2.0 (http://www.classroom20.com/) and Ning in Education (http://education.ning.com/) are social networking sites created using the Ning social software tool. Ning has also been used frequently as a place for online workshops as Work Literacy: Web 2.0 for Learning Professionals (http://workliteracy.ning.com/), which took place online during six weeks between September and November 2008. There are also credible reports of Facebook being used as an online classroom platform (Karrer, 2007a), in this particular case an experiment done by a Stanford professor, who challenged students to in fact develop Facebook applications as part of their activities in the course. Creative ways of learning are also being promoted via social networks. Jane Hart recently created what she calls "140 University" (http://www.c4lpt.co.uk/140university/) "to demonstrate the power of Twitter and Facebook as tools to enable formal approaches to learning" (Hart, 2010, para. 2). Jane wants to promote the use of such tools for formal learning, beyond the personal learning aspect for which these tools have been known for thus far. Jane explains:

> The way the 140 University works is that you receive "classes" in the form of daily knowledge nuggets with links to supporting Web resources (pages, videos, etc.) that provide further explanation and clarification—in tweets of less than 140 characters. You can comment on the "classes," and also share your own "classes," too. (Hart, 2010)

Such initiatives open the window to many possibilities. It goes without saying that for those already teaching online, Twitter can actually serve very well as short, immediate communication among class members that carry reminders or just links to news and Web sites with more information on a certain topic being studied in a virtual classroom. With the increase of applications available through mobile devices, it is clear that such supporting tools have a place associated to online learning. It is worth noting that in the discussion of the future of LMSs such as Blackboard, these experiments encourage the development of more open learning platforms, which would allow the integration of personal tools for collaboration and communication. This has taken an entire field of discussion within the e-learning community, under the umbrella of Personal Learning Environments (PLEs). "A PLE is a single user's e-learning system that provides access to a variety of learning resources, and that may provide access to learners and teachers" (Van Harmelen, 2006, p. 1) using different virtual learning environments, including their own PLE. Attwell (2007) makes a strong case for PLEs as being the future of e-learning, since the motivation for considering PLEs lies on "the idea that learning will take place in different contexts and situations and will not be provided by a single learning provider" (p. 2). The use of PLEs is also a clear "recognition of the importance of informal learning" (p. 2). These trends only shed greater light on the importance of the new technologies in learning in years to come.

Final Remarks

In this chapter, we attempted to capture the attention to the impact of the new wave of Web tools, still named Web 2.0, on learning in general, but with some special attention to their potential in e-learning.

As we finalize the chapter, we could not go without mentioning the dark side associated with many of these new technologies, and thus refer to the challenges and some of the defying critiques. For the most part, the questioning arises from issues related to privacy and security, which directly connect with aspects of copyright and intellectual property. These are definitely aspects that need to be dealt with and were not the focus of this chapter. Nonetheless, it is worth sharing some thoughts concerning this aspect, which is and will continue to be a hot topic. McDonald (2006) summarizes the issue and its origins well:

> Documents are no longer static and unchanging. As the creation and distribution of information become more collaborative, dynamic, and social, and as application software evolves to support "mashups" that combine both content and functionality from various sources, traditional definitions of "documents," their authorship, and their ownership are becoming obsolete. (p. 1)

Meanwhile, there are many solutions and mechanisms being created to tackle such situations. And some aspects of the technology itself support greater transparency than before, as noted by McDonald (2006):

One thing I do find encouraging is the increased availability of tools such as wikis and other collaborative authoring systems. These systems cannot operate without sophisticated internal change tracking systems, and they are increasingly being made available as remotely hosted services. [...], collaborative authoring systems can be developed as "heavy duty" utilities that can offer more and better authoring, tracking, and security features than are possible with applications designed for the desktop. (p. 2)

Another common critique is the so-called "white bread for the mind" heightened in the book *The Google University* by professor Tara Brabazon. She discusses that new technologies symbolized in many ways by the thrusting power of Internet search by Google will in fact produce an entire generation of noncritical thinkers (Porto, 2008). Brabazon's assertions have been quickly (as everything else in the blogsphere) refuted, in many cases with lots of supporting statistics. We should not blind ourselves from the fact that "the phenomenon of 'harnessing collective intelligence' might represent, however, reaching the 'lowest common denominator'" (Porto, 2008, p. 2). On the other hand, the democratization of information has generated self-correcting systems never seen before, which in most cases produce more accurate and recent data than that available in many other conservative venues. "The Web has the power to transform the work of a student shared with an audience of one teacher into a publication for all classmates, friends, peers, and the rest of the entire world" (Stanton, 2008, para. 2).

Surfacing back to the bright side, we reconnect with the grand promise of PLEs. We see PLEs as an iconic development, since it embodies in a concrete form the potential for transforming learning through the integration of the new technologies. "The PLE approach is based on a learner-centered view of learning and differs fundamentally from the alternative Learning Management Systems or Virtual Learning Environments approach, both of which are based on an institution- or course-centered view of learning" (Attwell, 2008, p. 119). The PLEs are not strictly Web 2.0, but are a result of the existence of such tools and applications. It "allows a learner (or anyone) to engage in a distributed environment consisting of a network of people, services, and resources" (Downes in Attwell, 2008, p. 120). PLEs rely on the assumption that learning is "as much social as cognitive, as much concrete as abstract, and becomes intertwined with judgment and exploration" (Seely Brown in Atwell, 2008, p. 120). Thus, the pedagogical approach of PLEs is the perfect match for the learner-centered approach sought by distance educators and the new technologies discussed here. It empowers learners to manage their own learning space, it promotes intense exchange with other learners through networks, and it integrates formal and information learning.

At the heart of all these tools, there is a very peculiar and transformative dimension: the power of users to generate content. This power has elevated collaboration and sharing to the forefront of the "Web experience." Since constructivist principles of learning are intrinsically based on collaboration and sharing, in moving the learner from a passive to an active role in the learning process, these tools have then taken prominence in their abilities to implement constructivist learning activities:

> As we begin to focus more on the learning process, it becomes evident that various skills are developed as a result of using specific tools or applying ideas to a specific context. For example, the skills of discussion and dialog can be enhanced through in-class or online discussion groups, and collaboration can be developed through ideas sharing and concept building. (Reynard, 2009, p. 3)

After all the excitement that technology buffs might have when exposed to the new tools that become available everyday, it is essential to balance such state of elation with the grounding reality that technology does not contain the holy grail of learning challenges. The new technologies, like all technologies before them, are not bound to the realization of such pedagogical goals and the expected learning. At the end of the day, it all depends on learning design, and that requires solid understanding of pedagogy and instructional design. Nonetheless, it is imperative that educators quit hiding their heads in the sand, thinking that these technologies are either fads, or have not in fact caused changes in the ways we learn. We could obviously continue to take ships across the Atlantic in the age of airplanes, and one might say that the final outcome is the same. But, as we all know it is impossible to avoid changes in education when societal behaviors have moved elsewhere. These technologies are and will have serious impact in education, because they intrinsically changed the way we deal with, share, and diffuse information. The building blocks of new knowledge production have been altered.

Resources

Here we provide lists of popular blog, wiki, social bookmarking, and social networking resources on the Web today.

Blog Software Used in E-Learning

Examples:

- Wordpress: http://www.wordpress.com
- TypePad: http://www.typepad.com
- Tumblr: http://www.tumblr.com
- Tabulas: http://www.tabulas.com
- Blogger: http://www.blogger.com
- Edublogs: http://www.edublogs.org
- Posterous: http://www.posterous.com
- LiveJournal: http://www.livejournal.com

Wiki Software Used in E-Learning

Examples:

- PBWiki: http://pbworks.com
- Wetpaint: http://www.wetpaint.com
- Wikidot: http://www.wikidot.com
- Wikispaces: http://www.wikispaces.com
- Zoho Wiki: http://wiki.zoho.com

Social Bookmarking Sites Used in E-Learning

Examples:

- Delicious: http://del.icio.us
- CiteULike: http://www.citeulike.com
- iCyte: http://www.icyte.com
- Diigo: http://www.diigo.com
- Conotea: http://www.conotea.com
- StumbleUpon: http://www.stumbleupon.com

Social Networking Sites Used in E-Learning

Examples:

- Facebook: http://www.facebook.com
- MySpace: http://www.myspace.com
- Twitter: http://www.twitter.com
- LinkedIn: http://www.linkedin.com
- Ning: http://www.ning.com

References

Adkins, S. S. (2007, July 7). Waves of Innovation: From Open Source to Open Learning. Learning Circuits. Retrieved February 5, 2008, from http://www.learningcircuits. org/2007/0707adkins.html.

Allen, I. E., and Seaman, J. (2007). Online Nation: Five Years of Growth in Online Learning. Needham, MA: Sloan Consortium (Sloan-C). Retrieved May 13, 2008, from http://www.sloan-c.org/publications/survey/pdf/online_nation.pdf.

Anderson, T. (2006). Blogging as Academic Publication. Virtual Canuck: Teaching and Learning in a Net-Centric World (Vol. 2010). Retrieved, from http://terrya.edublogs. org/2006/03/09/blogging-as-academic-publication/.

Apple. (2001). Apple Unveils New iMacs With CD-RW Drives and iTunes Software: Rip, Mix, Burn Your Own Custom Music CDs. Retrieved February 12, 2008, from http://www.apple.com/pr/library/2001/feb/22imac.html.

Attwell, G. (2007). Personal Learning Environments—The Future of eLearning? *eLearning Papers*, *2*(1), from http://www.elearningpapers.eu/index. php?page=doc&doc_id=8553&doclng=6.

Attwell, G. (2008). The social impact of personal learning environments. In S. Wheeler (Ed.), Connected minds, emerging cultures: Cybercultures in online learning (pp. 119–137). Charlotte, NC: Information Age Publishing.

Barger, J. (1999). FAQ: Weblog Resources. Retrieved June 6, 2008, from http://www.robot-wisdom.com/Weblogs/index.html.

Benkler, Y. (2006). *The Wealth of Networks: How Social Production Transforms Markets and Freedom*. New Haven, Connecticut: Yale University Press.

Birdsall, W. F. (2007). Web 2.0 as a Social Movement. *Webology, 4*(2). Retrieved March 12, 2008, from http://www.Webology.ir/2007/v4n2/a40.html.

Bleed, R. (2006). The IT Leader as Alchemist: Finding the True Gold. *EDUCAUSE Review, 41*(1), 32–43. Retrieved May 13, 2008, from http://www.educause.edu/apps/er/erm06/erm0611.asp.

Casey, M. E., and Savastinuk, L. C. (2006). Library 2.0: Service for the Next-Generation Library. *Library Journal, 131*(14), 40–42. Retrieved February 22, 2008, from http://ezproxy.umuc.edu/login?url=http://search.ebscohost.com/login.aspx?direct=true&db=aph&AN=22171693&site=ehost-live&scope=site.

Dell Computer. (2010). *Dell Wiki*. Retrieved December 28, 2009, from http://en.community.dell.com/wikis/.

Downes, S. (2004). Educational Blogging. *EDUCAUSE Review, 39*(5), 14–26. Retrieved May 13, 2008, from http://www.educause.edu/ir/library/pdf/ERM0450.pdf.

Downes, S. (2005). E-Learning 2.0. *eLearn Magazine*. Retrieved October 15, 2007, from http://elearnmag.org/subpage.cfm?section=articles&article=29-1.

Downes, S. (2007). E-Learning 2.0 in Development. (slide presentation). Retrieved January 28, 2008, from http://www.slideshare.net/Downes/elearning-20-in-development.

Downes, S. (2008). Web 2.0, E-learning 2.0 and the New Learning (slide presentation). Retrieved February 17, 2008, from http://www.slideshare.net/Downes/Web-20-elearning-20-and-the-new-learning.

Drucker, P. F. (2003). *The New Realities*. New Brunswick, NJ: Transaction Publishers. From http://books.google.com/books?id=WmAsWS9-fFsC&printsec=frontcover&source=gbs_v2_summary_r&cad=0#v=onepage&q=&f=false.

EDUCAUSE Learning Initiative (2005). 7 things you should know about Twitter. (Electronic document). Retrieved from http://educause.edu/ir/library/pdf/ELI7027.pdf.

Efimova, L. (2009). Weblog as a Personal Thinking Space. 289–298. Paper presented at the 20th ACM conference on Hypertext and hypermedia. Retrieved from http://blog.mathemagenic.com/download/WeblogAsPersonalThinkingSpace.pdf.

Elgan, M. (2006). Here's the Skinny on Web 2.0: Get the Lowdown on Today's Hottest Tech Buzzword. *Information Week*. from http://www.informationweek.com/news/software/open_source/showArticle.jhtml?articleID=193000630.

Ellis, R. (2004, November). E-learning trends 2004. *Learning Circuits*. Retrieved June 17, 2006, from http://www.learningcircuits.org/2004/nov2004/LC_Trends_2004.htm.

Farmer, B., Yue, A., and Brooks, C. (2008). Using blogging for higher order learning in large cohort university teaching: A case study. *Australasian Journal of Educational Technology, 24*(2), 123–136. Retrieved March 23, 2008, from http://www.ascilite.org.au/ajet/ajet24/farmer.html.

Gonzalez, N. (2009). Facebook Marketing Statistics, Demographics, Reports, and News—CheckFacebook. Retrieved December 13, 2009, from http://www.checkfacebook.com/.

Hammond, T., Hannay, T., Lund, B., and Scott, J. (2005). Social Bookmarking Tools I. *D-Lib Magazine, 11*(4). Retrieved February 23, 2006, from http://www.dlib.org/dlib/april05/hammond/04hammond.html.

Hart, J. (2010). 140 University—Extend your Education via Twitter or Facebook! In J. Hart (Ed.), *Jane's E-Learning Pick of the Day*. Retrieved January 21, 2010, from http://janeknight.typepad.com/pick/2010/01/140-university.html.

Hewlett-Packard Development Company. (2010). Powering Crowdsourcing: Technology's Role in the New Way of Working. *Business Week*. (Webcast). Retrieved January 3, from http://bx.businessweek.com/crowdsourcing/view?url=http%3A%2F%2Fwww.hp.com%2Flarge%2Fcampaign%2Finput%2Findex. html%3Fjumpid%3Dex_r11400_us%2Fen%2Flarge%2FIPG%2Fico_twtr_.

Jarche, H. (2009). Sense-making with PKM, Learning and Working on the Web (Vol. 2009). Retrieved, from http://www.jarche.com/2009/03/sense-making-with-pkm/.

Jayasuriya, K. and Brillantine, F. M. (2008). Student Services in the 21st Century: Evolution and Innovation in Discovering Student Needs, Teaching Information Literacy, and Designing Library 2.0-Based Services: Social Science Research Network (SSRN). Retrieved March 24, 2008, from http://ssrn.com/abstract=1103090.

Karrer, T. (2007a). Facebook as Learning Platform, *eLearning Technology*. Retrieved January 21, 2010, from http://elearningtech.blogspot.com/2007/10/facebook-as-learning-platform.html.

Karrer, T. (2007b, July). Understanding E-Learning 2.0. *Learning Circuits*. Retrieved April 15, 2008, from http://www.astd.org/LC/2007/0707_karrer.htm.

Kennedy, D. M., and Mighell, T. (2006). Web 2.0: The Strongest Links. *Law Practice Today* (January). Retrieved March 28, 2008, from http://www.abanet.org/lpm/lpt/articles/slc01061.html.

Leadbeater, C. (2008). *We-Think*. London: Profile Books, Ltd.

Leuf, B., and Cunningham, W. (2002). What Is Wiki. The Wiki Way. Retrieved April 22, 2008, from http://wiki.org/wiki.cgi?WhatIsWiki

LinkedIn. (2010). Relationships Matter (Vol. 2010). Retrieved from http://www.linkedin.com/.

Maness, J. M. (2006). Library 2.0 Theory: Web 2.0 and Its Implications for Libraries. *Webology, 3*(2). Retrieved March 31, 2008, from http://www.Webology.ir/2006/v3n2/a25.html.

Mason, R., and Rennie, F. (2008). *E-Learning and Social Networking Handbook: Resources for Higher Education*. New York: Routledge.

Mayoud, C. (n.d.). ELEARNING 2.0. All Things Web 2.0. Retrieved January 23, 2008, from http://www.allthingsWeb2.com/mtree/ELEARNING_2.0/.

McDonald, D. (2006). Web 2.0 and Maintaining the Integrity of Online Intellectual Property: Is "Meta-Information" the Answer? *Web 2.0 Journal* (March 3). Retrieved January 12, 2010, from http://Web2.sys-con.com/node/190346.

Miller, P. (2006). Coming together around Library 2.0. *D-Lib Magazine, 12*(4). Retrieved March 29, 2008, from http://www.dlib.org/dlib/april06/miller/04miller.html.

November, A. (2008). *Web Literacy for Educators*. Thousand Oaks, CA: Corwin Press.

O'Donnell, M. (2005). Blogging as Pedagogic Practice: Artefact and Ecology. Paper presented at the Blogtalk Downunder. Retrieved from http://incsub.org/blogtalk/images/Odonnell.doc.

O'Reilly, T. (2004). The Architecture of Participation. Retrieved April 24, 2008, from http://www.oreillynet.com/pub/a/oreilly/tim/articles/architecture_of_participation.html.

O'Reilly, T. (2005). What is Web 2.0: Design Patterns and Business Models for the Next Generation of Software. Retrieved January 31, 2008, from http://www.oreillynet.com/pub/a/oreilly/tim/news/2005/09/30/what-is-Web-20.html.

O'Reilly, T., and Battelle, J. (2009). Web Squared: Web 2.0 Five Years on. Paper presented at the Web 2.0 Summit. from http://assets.en.oreilly.com/1/event/28/Web2009_Websquared-whitepaper.pdf.

Petrushyna, Z. (2008). Personal Learning Environment (PLE)—A New Learning Concept or a New Learning System, *PROLEARN Academy Portal.* Retrieved, from http://www.prolearn-academy.org/Events/summer-school-2008/workshops/personal-learning-environment-ple-2013-a-new-learning-concept-or-a-new-learning-system/.

Pollard, D. (2003). Blogs in Business: Weblog as Filing Cabinet, *How to Save the World.* Retrieved January 10, 2010, from http://blogs.salon.com/0002007/2003/03/03.html#a101.

Porto, S. (2008). Disrupting the Technological Culture: A Faculty Perspective on the Impact of Web 2.0 in Online Education Practices. Paper presented at the EDEN Annual Conference, 2008: How Do We Learn? Where Do We Learn?.

Project Gutenberg. (2009). The Project Gutenberg Wiki. Retrieved December 12, 2009, from http://www.gutenberg.org/wiki/Main_Page.

Rainie, L. (2005). The State of Blogging. Washington, DC: Pew Research Center's Interent and American Life Project, from http://www.pewinternet.org/Reports/2005/The-State-of-Blogging.aspx.

Reynard, R. (2009). Beyond Social Networking: Building toward Learning Communities. *Campus Technology.* Retrieved January 21, 2010, From http://campustechnology.com/Articles/2009/07/22/Beyond-Social-Networking-Building-Toward-Learning-Communities.aspx.

Richardson, W. (2009). *Blogs, Wikis, Podcasts, and Other Powerful Web Tools for Classrooms* (2nd ed.). Thousand Oaks, CA: Corwin Press.

Schachter, J. (2006). Now Serving 1,000,000 (Vol. 2006). Retrieved, from http://blog.delicious.com/blog/2006/09/million.html.

Stanton, M. (2008). Observations from the bottom up, *Edumorphy* (January 31 ed.). Retrieved February 1, 2008, from http://www.edumorphology.com/2008/01/observations-from-the-bottom-up/.

Surowiecki, J. (2010, January 3). Powering Crowdsourcing: Technology's Role in the New Way of Working. *Business Week.* Retrieved January 21, 2010, from http://bx.businessweek.com/crowdsourcing/view?url=http%3A%2F%2Fwww.hp.com%2Flarge%2Fcampaign%2Finput%2Findex.html%3Fjumpid%3Dex_r11400_us%2Fen%2Flarge%2FIPG%2Fico_twtr_.

Tapscott, D. (2009). *Grown Up Digital: How the Net Generation is Changing Your World.* New York: McGraw-Hill.

Van Harmelen, M. (2006). Personal Learning Environments. 815–816. Paper presented at the Sixth IEEE International Conference on Advanced Learning Technologies (ICALT'06). from http://doi.ieeecomputersociety.org/10.1109/ICALT.2006.263.

WikiEducator. (2009). Main Page—WikiEducator. Retrieved February 17, 2008, from http://wikieducator.org/.

Wikipedia (Ed.) (2010a). From http://en.wikipedia.org/wiki/List_of_social_networking_Websites.

Wikipedia (Ed.) (2010b). From http://en.wikipedia.org/wiki/Social_network_service.

Wikipedia. (2010c). Wikipedia. Retrieved December 28, 2009, from http://www.wikipedia.com/.

Wikiversity. (2009a). Managing Vandalism. Retrieved January 21, 2010, from http://en.wikiversity.org/wiki/Managing_vandalism

Wikiversity. (2009b). Wikiversity: Main Page. Retrieved February 17, 2008, from http://en.wikiversity.org/wiki/Wikiversity:Main_Page.

World Wide Web Consortium. (2008). About W3C: History. Retrieved March 24, 2008, from http://www.w3.org/Consortium/history.

Chapter 13

Lifelong Learning Links in the ePortfolio

Stella Porto and Christine Walti

Contents

Introduction

Taking a Master of Distance Education degree as the backdrop for this chapter, we intend to demonstrate that the ePortfolio can be an important milestone and tool in lifelong learning and the continuing professional education of adult learners. The ePortfolio lays the foundation for an ongoing process of multifaceted uses and is, as Lakin (2005) states, the "catalyst for lifelong learning ownership" (para. 1). The

219

authors discuss ePortfolio development in the MDE program as an illustrative case study, the historical context of lifelong learning/education, foundational information on and various aspects concerning ePortfolios, how ePortfolios tie in with and are an important feature of lifelong learning and continuing professional education, and how it can help connect the links in an individual's lifetime of learning.

As in many different programs, the Master of Distance Education (MDE) at the University of Maryland University College (UMUC) has adopted since its inception the use of an ePortfolio as a way to capture students' journeys and growth in the distance education field (Walti, 2004). The idea was that the ePortfolio would gather, organize, and present evidence of students' qualifications for practice in the field of distance education. It would demonstrate their knowledge and skills in a variety of distance-education contexts. Thus, the MDE student ePortfolio contains both required and optional artifacts. The more formal required elements are substantive assignments selected from each of the previous MDE courses completed. The optional artifacts include any documents or components that display other activities and accomplishments the student has achieved throughout their journey in MDE program. These optional components can either be related directly to distance education activities or can be part of other facets of the students as a professional, which portray each student in his/her full spectrum of abilities, skills, and knowledge. In addition, the ePortfolio contains the student's resume or biodata, and perhaps a photo or other appropriate graphics or visual. The ePortfolio is a requirement for completion of the entire MDE program and should exhibit the student's best work. It should effectively reveal a progression of increasing professionalism in the field. In this regard, a critical component of the ePortfolio is a reflective summative statement, in which students should attempt to convey how they have developed personally and professionally. MDE students show how the MDE curriculum has affected their evolution as learners and practitioners in the field, what future goals are, and how they intend to pursue them.

This activity has proven throughout the years to be one that, although planned to be presented at the end of the program, needs constant attention and work from the student throughout the entire program. It challenges students to understand the nature of this activity, its purpose, importance, and usefulness as a lifelong learning tool, and to focus their attention on the artifacts they have created throughout the program. To promote success in this new area, the authors of this chapter studied the general topic of ePortfolios, analyzed students' needs, and strategized simple ways to engage students in the process of ePortfolio building and development in a continuous fashion. This corresponds with Thorpe's (2003) understanding of the "... new generation of student support services [where] the role of the tutor or mentor must be seen as central to facilitation of the process ... of mediating and managing the process of creating the ePortfolio" (as cited in Ó Súilleabháin and Coughlan, n.d., para. 17).

The nature of the graduate program and of UMUC as the home institution put the MDE in the forefront to adopt student ePortfolios as a showcasing and potentially lifelong learning tool. Stefani et al. (2007) discuss extensively the existing requirements for institutions in order to be successful in implementing ePortfolio initiatives, whatever these might be. They refer to these cumulatively as constituting an institution's "e-learning maturity level," which determines how much e-learning practice has been in fact adopted, integrated, and employed within the institution. This maturity measures how comfortable faculty and students have become with the use of e-learning tools and online collaboration.

> [There] is a challenge in both e-learning and "traditional" classroom teaching and learning environments. Do our students understand the concept of collaborative learning? Are they attuned to the ideas of information exchange and knowledge construction? Would they be able to participate in online conferencing and Internet searching with fellow students? [p. 8]

UMUC has a long history of using distance education, and today is, for the most part, identified as a virtual university. All its programs are offered online, and the MDE in particular is exclusively offered over the Internet. Moreover, the main theme of the program is distance education. Thus, it would not make any sense to have it delivered as a traditional program. The MDE is the signature program at UMUC; it covers all topics that are at the heart of the operations of UMUC as an online institution. These aspects thus suggest that the institution and, even more so, the program have the necessary infrastructure, experience, and practice deemed required for an expected and acceptable e-learning maturity level for a successful ePortfolio undertaking.

However, despite the maturity of e-learning at an institutional level and an ingrained constructivist (McPherson and Nunes, 2004) approach in the teaching and learning process, ePortfolios are not adopted throughout the institution, and thus the MDE ePortfolio activity has faced a few barriers of its own in order to succeed. The process of providing support to students at the program level has stimulated a more critical reflection about the goals, benefits, and constraints of using ePortfolios as an integrated part of learning. It has brought the ePortfolio building process to the heart of the program, and has helped students feel more empowered during this process. This is an ongoing initiative and, as it evolves, we have learned about the potentials and the limitations of ePortfolios as a learning tool. On the other hand, institutional involvement can be controversial when it comes to student ownership and the use of the ePortfolio as a life-long learning tool, so it has actually been to the program's and students' advantage that the institution has not been at the forefront of decision making about how ePortfolios should be implemented within the program. There is definitely a conundrum between student ownership, interoperability, and the continuous use of ePortfolios beyond the program. Faced with this peculiar context, the MDE—based on its core content—is in a prime position to research, analyze, further develop, and adapt ePortfolios. Porto and

Walti (2008) have worked through an action research framework in a series of consecutive iterative steps to identify and enhance the support to students developing their ePortfolios. The latest snapshot of this process reveals a composition of elements that provide the supporting nest for the activity, including

- Tutorials available on the Web
- Initial experience with a learning journal during the first course in the program
- A 1-week orientation offered free of charge to all students every semester
- An always-open wiki for consulting, as well as the base for orientation and a capstone course

This experience has demonstrated the power of the existing technology in allowing students to easily document their achievements and reflect on their personal learning. It has also shown how essential it is to continuously promote lifelong learning to adult students, exemplifying how ePortfolios can help them throughout their professional lives. Finally, the ePortfolio activity has definitely been an integrated part of the community-building initiative also taking place in the program. This synergy of community building and ePortfolio development stands as concrete and tangible proof of the strength of the principles behind ePortfolios. Mason and Rennie (2008) make the connection between ePortfolios and the dialogue within an online community when they state, "Communication through the learning environment is a key feature of constructivist design, especially where the students are geographically isolated" (p.17). The self-expression through ePortfolios is an important ingredient for students in their process of becoming members of this learning community.

The Larger Context of Lifelong Learning

Lifelong learning is a term and a concept that is used in a variety of contexts and is strongly related to historical and societal practices and processes that may vary considerably and have evolved over the course of time. Lifelong learning is generally associated with adults and is often referenced in terms of its political and societal developmental perspective that supports empowerment (Gvaramadze, 2007). Lifelong learning is a multidisciplinary field that can include professional development, personal enrichment, continuing education, community education and outreach, and vocational. It includes a wide variety of methodological approaches, can be accomplished formally and informally, and in many instances some type of recognition is bestowed on the learner.

We purport that, if it is accepted that lifelong learning is the broad spectrum of learning from "cradle to grave" for the purposes of personal enrichment and meeting economic and employment imperatives, the ePortfolio is an ideal basis with which to capture one's formal and informal learning experiences, gains, and insights, despite a still-existing tendency (in western-oriented educational systems) to value the acquisition of formal qualifications (as conveyed with certificates, diplomas, and degrees), whereas "… learning to learn, problem solving, critical understanding and anticipatory learning … are only a few of the core skills and competencies needed for all" (Medel-Añonuevo et al., 2001, p. 4) that are somewhat neglected. Lifelong learning (education) covers "… formal, non-formal and informal patterns of learning throughout the life cycle of an individual for the conscious and continuous enhancement of the quality of life, his own and that of society" (Dave, 1976 as cited in ILO, 2000).

The Growth in Use of ePortfolios

There are multiple definitions of ePortfolios available in the literature. One simple definition is used on McDaniel's College Web site: "A portfolio is an organized, goal-driven collection of documentation that presents a student's growth and achievement over time" (http://www2.mcdaniel.edu/its/digital_portfolios.htm).

More commonly than not, these definitions include the following ePortfolio traits, which also constitute the basis of the ePortfolio concept embraced within the MDE (Stefani, 2003; Walti, 2006):

- ePortfolios are electronic versions of portfolios and as such they are collections of artifacts in different digital media
- ePortfolios serve the purpose of assessment of competencies, skills, and knowledge
- ePortfolios showcase and evidence abilities and achievements in specific areas
- ePortfolios promote reflection of one's development and learning

Independent of the type or format of the ePortfolio, the literature states that it should "encourage learners to develop the skills to continue building their own personal portfolio as a life-long learning tool" (Siemens, 2004, p. 1). This aspect will be further explored in this report.

Pedagogically, it is understood that ePortfolios have enormous educational potential. They promote the integration of students' works in such a way that students are encouraged to reflect on their achievements and competencies. It serves the purpose of not only looking back and showcasing abilities and skills, but also planning future professional development steps. As Barrett (2002) states "An online portfolio system needs to support a culture of evidence," which is exemplified by the collection of artifacts created by students, reflections of the learner on development and learning that has taken place, and some kind of validation or external feedback from other stakeholders, in this case peers or instructors.

Considering technological aspects, the development of ePortfolios has a lot to gain from advances in digital technologies. The advent of the Web has made ePortfolios portable and eliminates the need for replication or transportation of documents and artifacts. The more recent changes under the Web 2.0 umbrella have reduced the developmental efforts of such Web-based ePortfolios significantly, allowing users to publish content on the Web without any special skills in Web-publishing software or Web page design. Institutions still have the possibility of providing students with in-house systems, which facilitate the collection, reflection, feedback, and view of their academic work, but the need is no longer as crucial as it was several years ago.

EPortfolios are inherently personal and focus on an individualized management of one's collection of documents and artifacts. However, when they are implemented in an academic setting with goals associated to assessment, institutions will need to carefully consider implementation aspects. Issues such as permanence, storage space, security, and stakeholders' involvement will be part of planning an ePortfolio initiative for students.

Challenges and Issues

The institutional involvement can be controversial when it comes to student ownership and the use of the ePortfolio as a lifelong learning tool.

> At the moment, the development of ePortfolios is caught in a dilemma: the imaginary scenario or even mundane scenario of students having a portfolio throughout their college or university career, needs the user to feel ownership of the portfolio in order to have any chance of success. [...] However, for a portfolio to be useful it needs to integrate with many other systems and institutions so that vital information can be transferred [...] and the software can be interoperable and "future-proof." Current practices [...] pay lip-service to student ownership, but remain largely teacher- and institution-led. The technology is still immature; the uses are still fluctuating, and even the definitions, the concept of what an ePortfolio is, are hugely varied." [Stefani et al., 2007, p. 8]

Other challenges and issues the authors encounter in the MDE experience of students' development of their portfolios are the lack of time they have to devote to this activity throughout the duration of the program and an ongoing disconnect or disintegration in the courses that lie between the foundational and the capstone course. It can be assumed that if the ePortfolio activity were consistently reinforced in each course, either in the form of frequent reminders to collect and reflect on one's work or through the integration of course activities and/or assessments that directly support meta-reflection, the time factor mentioned previously would most likely be less of a factor. The insufficient preliminary knowledge of the basic concepts of ePortfolios and the available tools (Porto and Walti, 2008) was addressed by implementing a one-week portfolio orientation each term. The feedback from students thus far has been overwhelmingly positive and the authors expect that results of this support activity will show pronounced advances in terms of preparedness when learners reach the capstone course in the future. These challenges are certainly not restricted to the MDE experience. Mason and Rennie (2008) list "key points for effective practices" (p. 75) in the development of ePortfolios, including: "Use formative iterative assignments with comments from the teacher and peers" (p. 75), and "Integrate the ePortfolio with the users' online workspace in order to encourage regular updating and seamless moving from course to portfolio" (p. 75). These suggest the difficulty in keeping up a continuous practice of the ePortfolio as the students progress throughout the program.

On a broader level, there are other barriers to the implementation/use of ePortfolios, including "funding patterns that reward student contact hours and credit, but not learning outcomes and students success" (Flynn, 2004, p. 5). In addition, on the community college level, Flynn (2004) notes that union contracts; slow adaptation of new initiatives by campus constituencies; part time faculty issues and overall reluctance; lack of agreement on best practices; workload issues; tech support constraints; training needs; and liability issues and (software) integrations issues, as well as college internal processes were the major barriers at higher ed institutions at the community college level. "Aligning curriculum with the needs of the community, market forces and demographic and student changes" (p. 6) is increasingly difficult when employers want information on the "abilities" (i.e., "assessment-driven outcomes attainment, conveyed in an informative manner, [that] would erode ... longstanding commitment to recording letter grades..." (p. 6)) of a potential employee.

The authors feel strongly that the ePortfolio experience in the MDE should and can empower and encourage learners to continue documenting their learning even after they have graduated from the MDE program. This provides the opportunity to demonstrate sustained professional development, which continues to require "... reflection, careful needs assessment and planning" (Commission on Dietetic Registration (CDR), 1999. p. 612). The CDR noted that the use of portfolios impacts performance more than, for example, attending conferences without additional reinforcement practices because effective continuing professional education, too, requires the following steps: "professional self-direction; learning needs assessment; learning plan development; implementation of the learning plan and evaluation of the learning plan outcomes" (p. 612). However, the ePortfolio also allows the validation of other formal and informal learning experiences such as independent learning, leadership, mentorships, reading, publication, and presentation contributions, while allowing the learner to establish areas for further growth and development. Mason and Rennie (2008) alert, "It is hard to imagine that ePortfolios can really be a lifelong learning tool either at a technical or personal level, given the speed of technical advance" (p.75). However, they and the authors agree "this is how their full potential will eventually be reached" (p. 75).

A Brief Historical Perspective of Lifelong Learning

Lifelong learning is closely tied to the challenge of openness and change the modern individual must face in a lifetime (Medel-Añonuevo et al., 2001, p. 6).

Lifelong learning can be traced back to the 1920s, where Yeaxlee and Lindeman from England understood (lifelong) "education" "… as an ongoing process, affecting mainly adults, and certainly not restricted to formal school" (WSCF, n.d., para. 1). Farris, 2004 (as cited in WSCF, n.d., para. 1) reports that they also introduced the concepts of "life-as-education" and the valuing of individuals' experiences as much as formal education.

Until the 1970s lifelong learning (education) was linked to adult or popular learning and was also closely associated with the worker's education movement with its focus on training workers and linking their achievements to formal education. Lifelong (continuous) learning received a major thrust when UNESCO, in the face of literacy campaigns in developing countries of the early 70s, promoted "… the concept of lifelong learning as a cultural policy which promoted social change … [and] as encompassing the whole life span, being inclusive of different social sectors, occurring across different formal and informal settings (home, communities, workplaces), and addressing a broad range of social, cultural, and economic purposes" (Kearns, 2005 as cited in WSCF, n.d., para. 2). This changed as the OECD focused on the four pillars "learning to live together"; "learning to be," which address social goals; and "learning to know" and "learning to do" that stress economic factors and currently seem to be the more widely applied goals, while later "… explicitly linking learning and work, assessing and recognizing skills and competencies, developing new Lifelong Learning opportunities, and rethinking the roles and responsibilities of unions, employer organizations, civil society and governments (Kearnes, McDonald, Candy, Knights, and Papadopoulos, 1999 as cited in WSCF, n.d., para. 7). The OECD notes that lifelong learning is based on three objectives: personal development, social cohesion, and economic growth (Ryan, 1999).

This highlights the recognition of formal, nonformal, and informal learning, the importance of self-motivated learning, and the universal participation in lifelong learning. Nonetheless, there are different concepts and emphases with respect to lifelong learning, reflecting the influence of people such as Freire, Dewey, Montessori, Knowles, Rogers, and Schultz that form the ends of the spectrum of lifelong learning: personal fulfillment and social well-being, paired with personal and community empowerment to human capital theory that links learning to economic advancement through employment. Cornerstones are education and skills acquisition (International Labor Organization, 2000).

We purport that, if it is accepted that lifelong learning is the broad spectrum of learning from "cradle to grave" for the purposes of personal enrichment and meeting economic and employment imperatives, the ePortfolio is an ideal basis with which to capture one's formal and informal learning experiences, gains, and insights, despite a still-existing tendency (in western-oriented educational systems) to value the acquisition of formal qualifications (as conveyed with certificates, diplomas, and degrees). Conversely, "… learning to learn, problem solving, critical understanding, and anticipatory learning … are only a few of the core skills and competencies needed for all" (Medel-Añonuevo et al., 2001, p.4) that are somewhat neglected. Lifelong learning (education) covers "… formal, nonformal, and informal patterns of learning throughout the life cycle of an individual for the conscious and continuous enhancement of the quality of life, his own and that of society" (Dave, 1976 as cited in Medel-Añonuevo et al., 2001, p, 2). Lifelong education in the early '70s was associated with the more comprehensive and integrated goal of developing more humane individuals and communities in the face of rapid social change. On the other hand, the more dominant interpretation of lifelong learning in the '90s was linked to retraining and learning new skills that would enable individuals to cope with the demands of the rapidly changing workplace" (Medel-Añonuevo et al., 2001).

Using ePortfolios allows a wide audience to look into learners' past experiences, self-image, personal and societal attitudes and values, as well as current life circumstances that encompass time and diversity. Lifelong learning should also address existential themes such as the meaning of life, self, growing-up, friendship, love, courtship, sexuality, loneliness, violence, hate, death—the positive and negative aspects of life—and encompass a holistic view of "education" as progress towards human growth and maturity.

Siemens (2004) noted that we must

> … recognize the significance of learning that happens in communities, on the job, and from personal knowledge networks. Learning is now a process of living. Formal education is only a stage of learning. Learning continues in virtually all aspects of life. Schools assign grades to demonstrate competency. Learning through life experiences creates artifacts instead. The ability to include these is an important motivation for ePortfolio development. [para. 8]

To begin this process we advocate that the implementation of ePortfolios should begin in the formative years. Alas, it does not and, consequently, based on our experiences in the MDE program, we will demonstrate that it takes much advocacy, guidance, and support from educators and institutions, while at the same time it takes motivation, tenacity, and reflection on the part of the learner. As reinforced by Mason and Rennie (2008), a key point in the effective practice of developing ePortfolios includes the provision of "scaffolding, advice, and resources on what constitutes evidence of learning" (p. 75). But perhaps as important, it takes the understanding and appreciation from society and employers after completion of the graduate program to bring the process to fruition and to increase acceptance of informal and nonformal learning. Making this visible in an ePortfolio can be one step to increase acceptance and recognition.

For the purposes of this chapter we rely on a brief OECD (1996) definition of the following terms:

- *Formal learning* is always organized and structured, and has learning objectives. From the learner's standpoint, it is always intentional, that is, the learner's explicit objective is to gain knowledge, skills, and/or competences. Typical examples are learning that takes place within the initial education and training system or workplace training arranged by the employer. One can also speak about formal education and/or training or, more accurately speaking, education and/or training in a formal setting.
- *Informal learning* is never organized, has no set objective in terms of learning outcomes, and is never intentional from the learner's standpoint. Often it is referred to as "learning by experience" or just as "experience." The idea is that the simple fact of existing constantly exposes the individual to learning situations, at work, at home, or during leisure time, for instance.
- *Nonformal learning* is the concept about which there is the least consensus, which is not to say that there is consensus on the other two, but simply that the wide variety of approaches in this case makes consensus even more difficult. Nevertheless, for the majority of authors, it seems clear that nonformal learning is rather organized and can have learning objectives. The advantage of the intermediate concept lies in the fact that such learning may occur at the initiative of the individual but also happens as a by-product of more organized activities, whether or not the activities themselves have learning objectives (para. 4).

Learning can be defined in terms of outcomes, competencies, and processes (ILO, 2000). Our educational systems are (most often) vested in the transcript and grade, which is a "… unidimensional system symbol into which multidimensional phenomena have been incorporated" (Milton, Pollio, and Eison as cited in Flynn, 2004, p. 3). However, in the area of workforce development (in the United States), an increasingly important area in the noncredit, continuing education, and lifelong learning field, there is increased pressure for competency-based certifications with additional credentials that inform on a learner's abilities that are not necessarily represented by diplomas or degrees (Carew, 2003). Adult workers are now able to access more formal education in order to adapt to new challenges that arise with economic and work pressures.

Statistics from the U.S. Department of Education (2008) state

> In the 2006–07 academic year, 66 percent of the 4,160 2-year and 4-year Title IV degree-granting postsecondary institutions in the nation offered college-level distance education courses. The overall percentage includes 97 percent of public 2-year institutions, 18 percent of private for-profit 2-year institutions, 89 percent of public 4-year institutions,

53 percent of private not-for-profit institutions, and 70 percent of private for-profit 4-year institutions.

Sixty-five percent of the institutions reported college-level credit-granting distance education courses, and 23 percent reported noncredit distance education courses. There was a total of an estimated 12.2 million enrollments (or registrations) in college-level credit-granting distance education courses in 2006–07. Of these enrollments, 77 percent were reported in online courses, 12 percent were reported in hybrid/blended online courses, and 10 percent were reported in other types of distance education courses.

In 2006–07, there were approximately 11,200 college-level programs that were designed to be completed totally through distance education; 66 percent of these programs were reported as degree programs and the remaining 34 percent were reported as certificate programs. [para. 2–4]

Adult learning and continuing education programs are growing at 2-year and 4-year institutions that now accommodate work, childcare schedules, and the commitments of adult students. The American Association of Community Colleges (AACC) (as cited in Carew, 2003, p. 9) reports

- 49% of their 10.4 million students are noncredit students.
- 28% of community college credit students already have their bachelor's degree.
- The average age of a community college student in the United States is 29.

A fundamental change in the last decade of higher education has been the integration of technology to support instruction. For example,

- 70% of college classes use e-mail versus 20% in 1995.
- 50% of college courses use Internet-based resources versus 11% in 1995.
- 35% of college courses have a Web page versus 9% in 1996. (Carew, 2003, p. 8)

Technology has been a contributor to the rise of the nontraditional adult learner, providing access and flexibility for those who are most interested in self-improvement, personal enrichment, and professional development and who look to institutions for this as opposed to credit in their second or third educational "careers." As Flynn (2004) notes "… the just-in-time, noncredit learning that adults achieve is rarely documented or recorded in an official transcript" (p. 5). In some instances (community) colleges offer a certificate of completion, but often there is no documentation of accomplishment. To meet adult learners' needs and contend with institutional circumstances and barriers (funding, institutional resources, employer demands) learning must be offered in a variety of formats, with various media, in diverse modes, often "… heavily mediated and automated" (p. 5), "chunked" and in collaboration with vendors. The ePortfolio can alleviate this circumstance by serving as a hub for a holistic view of a learner's lifelong learning and achievements. In addition, concerns regarding FERPA and confidentiality can be addressed if the learner/student is the owner of the ePortfolio as s/he will control content and access, while having institutions and/or agencies validate those parts of what is traditionally referred to as "directory information."* Flynn (2004) stated that widespread implementation of ePortfolios is "… hampered by a lack of funding and institutional will, not because the technology does not exist to implement such a system" (p. 6). The circumstances described at UMUC earlier seem to support this supposition. ePortfolios can be useful in answering questions such as "What did I learn?," "How can I apply it?" and "How can I demonstrate this?," and thus demonstrate competency and the use and application of knowledge—often across disciplines and/or contexts. It seems that there is not a lack of standards for what is sought in the educational, lifelong learning arena, but ways and processes that convey accurate (validated), updated knowledge, skills, and abilities as the basis.

Foundations of ePortfolios

In this section we take a closer look at some foundational pillars within the ePortfolio field discussed in the literature, including definitions, pedagogy, technology, and implementation issues.

Purpose and Definitions

As we have experienced in previous sections, ePortfolios have multiple purposes—"as a showcase, development tool, assessment approach, or resource for reflection" (Stefani et al., 2007, p. 1). These purposes may be combined, depending on the context and the scope of the implementation.

Lorenzo and Ittelson (2005a) define ePortfolios as

> … a digitized collection of artifacts, including demonstrations, resources, and accomplishments that represent an individual, group, community, organization, or institution. This collection can be comprised of text-based, graphic, or multimedia elements archived on a Web site or on other electronic media such as CD-ROM or DVD. [p. 1]

Acker (2005) states simply that an ePortfolio is "a digital representation of self on characteristics of interest to a community" (p. 1). Treuer and Jenson (2003)

---

* "Directory information" is part of a larger education record and includes degrees and awards, major fields of study, dates of attendance, and enrollment status.

define electronic portfolios "as an organized collection of digital and/or analog artifacts and reflective statements that demonstrate growth over time" (p. 34). They shed light on the potential of ePortfolios going beyond the paper-based portfolio counterparts.

Siemens (2004) highlights that "ePortfolios can best be viewed as a reactionary response to fundamental shifts in learning, teaching, technology, and learner needs in a climate where learning is no longer perceived as confined to formal education" (p. 1). The term "webfolios" has also been used in order to be clear about the Web-based implementation of such portfolios. In those cases, the term *ePortfolio* was used to refer to portfolios residing on CD-ROMs or other physical media. With the widespread adoption of Web-based tools and storage, this distinction has been lost, and the more common term in use is ePortfolio "as an umbrella concept that includes Webfolios" (p. 1).

The growing interest in ePortfolios is "fuelled by three broad factors: the dynamics of functioning in a knowledge economy, the changing nature of learning, and the changing needs of the learner" (Siemens, 2004, p. 1). In the knowledge economy, knowledge is of primary value and represents "opportunities for employment and access to education" (p. 2). The ePortfolio allows the learner to display and evidence such knowledge through multiple media. The change in learning approaches is also a current trend. Learner-centered approaches are the focus of those promoting a higher quality of learning experience. Learning is not restricted to formal education, but is seen as a process that endures throughout life. ePortfolios are tools that support the concept of lifelong learning and learner-centered approaches of learning. Since learners have become more technically proficient information technology plays a social role that affects learning and the workplace. Thus, the use of ePortfolios is supported by the widespread use of Internet-based tools in everyday life.

Considering the myriad of definitions found in the literature, electronic portfolios—"whether produced by a student, a faculty member, or an institution—is for collection, reflection, and assessment" (Greenberg, 2004, p. 34). As mentioned by Barrett (1999), "A portfolio without standards, goals, and/or reflection is just a fancy resume, not an electronic portfolio" (p. 56). Ravet (2007) adds an important twist to some of the given definitions by questioning if ePortfolios should be considered a "product" or a "process." He has, thus, used the definition from NLII 2003 as a base and rewritten it to say that an ePortfolio is "a collection of authentic and diverse evidence, drawn from a larger archive, representing capital developed by a reflective learning individual or organization designed to exploit/valorize their assets in a particular context." (p. 3). Thus, the conclusion of his questioning is that "an ePortfolio is not a product and a process, but is a product created as the result of a process, this process being managed by digital means" (p. 3).

Gibson and Barrett (2002) shed light on an earlier conception of ePortfolio by Mary Diez, which evokes almost poetic metaphors, namely the portfolio as mirror, map, and sonnet:

The mirror concerns the portfolio's reflective nature that allows us to see our own growth over time. The map includes concerns of the portfolio's ability to aid us in planning, setting goals, and navigating the artifacts we create and collect. And the sonnet points to the portfolio's role as framework for creative expression, encouraging diversity within the template or structure for thinking about work and presenting it to others." [Gibson and Barrett, 2002, p. 1]

This perspective is inherently present in the ePortfolio approach used within programs such as the MDE, where Collection, Reflection, Assessment, and Showcasing are, in fact, the main goals, with a lifelong-learning perspective.

Three main stakeholders are involved in the ePortfolio development process: learners, instructors, and institutions. "The end-users of ePortfolios are prospective employers, instructors (for assessment), parents, and award-granting agencies" (Siemens, 2004, p. 1). The benefits of ePortfolios are distinct to each of the stakeholders. As learners "seek to create and reflect on life experiences" (p. 2), ePortfolios serve students as "personal knowledge management" (p. 2), recorded "history of development and growth" (p. 2), and a "planning/goal setting tool" (p. 2). Faculty are able to "share content with other faculty" (p. 2), employ "more authentic assessment" (p. 2) practices in their teaching and promote life-long learning among students. Institutions are able to provide "value to learners by allowing personal control" (p. 2) of the learning process and have the potential of playing "a more permanent role in the lives of learners" (p. 2).

The process of ePortfolio creation can be seen as composed of four major tasks, as discussed in the ePortfolio portal (2004): Collection of artifacts for the ePortfolio; selection of artifacts that will demonstrate the aimed competencies; reflection on the artifacts that were selected as well as on the learning/self-development process; and finally connection to others, who will see, assess, and possibly provide feedback to the posted materials. In the case of the MDE, the first three tasks are of major focus since they are the ones that should be ongoing throughout the program. In some cases, and for some components of the ePortfolio, the students might have the opportunity to practice their Connection. Within the MDE, the final moment of Connection is, in fact, during the capstone course. However, given that we foresee this ePortfolio as a lifelong learning tool, students are encouraged to continue this process after they have graduated.

Types of ePortfolios

The literature is rich in taxonomies to classify ePortfolios. The different types are labeled according to a distinct set of criteria.

ePortfolios can be used by individuals, by groups or by institutions. Thus, this criterion is based on who manages the ePortfolio and its main use. Lorenzo and Ittelson (2005a) classify ePortfolios in three main categories, namely student ePortfolios, teaching ePortfolios, and institutional ePortfolios. Student ePortfolios are the evolution of print-based portfolios commonly used during the 80s, especially in the art-related programs. These portfolios gained acceptance, and use spread during the 90s. The focus has been on showcasing students' work, as well as reflecting on the learning process. With the diffusion of electronic media, the natural enhancement for the print version was to move into electronic storage, which thus allowed for better dissemination and maintenance. The success of student ePortfolios arises from their potential for

- "Helping students become critical thinkers" (p. 3)
- "Aiding in the development of their writing and multimedia communication skills" (p. 3)
- "Helping students learn information and technology literacy skills and how to use digital media" (p. 3)
- "Creating a digitized showcase of their work and skills that can be presented to prospective employees" (p. 3)
- Connect "students to their alma mater after graduation" (p. 3)

Teaching ePortfolios are those developed by faculty members and are used frequently to "introduce themselves and showcase their accomplishments to students, as well as to share ideas inside a class or other community" (p. 4). On the other hand, institutional ePortfolios "incorporate student and teaching ePortfolios as well as ePortfolios from a wide range of programs and departments" (p. 5). It is mainly used for institutional accountability and serves as a "vehicle for institution-wide reflection, learning, and improvement" (p. 5).

Greenberg (2004) lists three main types, based "on when the work was organized relative to when the work is created" (p. 31):

- For showcase ePortfolios, the "organization occurs after the work has been created" (p. 31).
- In structured ePortfolios, there is a predefined organization for the work that will be created later on.
- Learning ePortfolios have their organization evolving as the work is created.

Stefani et al. (2007) provide different classifications. One such classification refers to the scope of application of ePortfolios:

- Course ePortfolios refer to ePortfolios "assembled by students for one course" (p. 11) that are usually used for assessment.
- Program ePortfolios are those "that students develop to document the work they have completed, the skills they have learned, and the outcomes they have met in an academic department or program" (p. 11).

- Institutional ePortfolios (different from the category similarly named by Lorenzo and Ittelson [2005a]) refer to ePortfolios that function as a "personal development tool, in which employees record achievements, future plans, and extracurricular activities (Stefani et al., 2007; p. 11).

According to Stefani et al. (2007), another distinction can be made based on the European Initiatives Coordination Committee concerning the purpose of the ePortfolio in different learning contexts:

- Assessment ePortfolios "would generally be used in situations where students are not tested or examined in conventional ways, but rather are expected to provide evidence of their competence in particular subject areas" (p. 41).
- Showcase ePortfolios here are seen as the closest to the conventional view of portfolios used by artists, where students display their best pieces of work and could also include revisions and feedback.
- Development ePortfolios are a work in progress and are to promote discussion between students and tutors.
- Reflective ePortfolios are a personal portfolio where students are able to reflect on their achievements and self-assess their growth over time.

In the ePortfolio portal (2004) one more type is cited as a combination of the others discussed above, the so-called "Hybrids." "Rarely will you find an ePortfolio that is strictly used for assessment, development, or showcase purposes" (ePortfolio Portal, n.d., p. 1).

Although in many cases there is an underlying premise of assessment, it is not the main focus of this ePortfolio discussion. Our focus is one where students will be developing a program tool that will serve the longer-term purpose of portraying the students as competent professionals and continuous learners in their field. In the case of the MDE, for example, this would mean to portray competencies of a distance educator. When created and developed formally within a program such as the MDE, it is not under the program's control whether students will keep this tool after they leave, but there is certainly the clear intent to encourage graduates' future use of this tool.

It should be remembered that ePortfolios could certainly be used for formative and summative assessment. Stefani et al. (2007) shed light on the pedagogical potential of ePortfolios in this area, though the more recent trends and approaches to assessment are more through constructivism, authentic assessment, and peer assessment. Constructivism deals with knowledge that students are able to create based on their learning experiences: "In the constructivist theory the emphasis is placed on the learner or the student rather than on the teacher or the instructor" (p. 11). Authentic assessment is closely related to constructivist principles because it deals with assessment through activities that resemble real-world situations, scenarios, and problem solving that require students' active involvement and critical thinking. ePortfolios promote the depiction of such learning processes, which are student-centric and related to students' personal development as more autonomous learners (Moore and Kearsley, 2004). It is also commonly accepted that most Web-based courses are designed on principles that promote student autonomy.

However, in order to use ePortfolios in formal assessment associated with grades and students' records it would be necessary to "create matrices with grading rubrics that measure the degree to which students have met specific learning outcomes or competencies" (Lorenzo and Ittelson, 2005b, p. 2). As discussed by Acker (2005), faculty workload is one of the obstacles and critical issues when implementing ePortfolios within a program or institution. In many cases, such as in the MDE, the decision to not use the ePortfolio as an assessment tool throughout the program is based on this reasoning, as well as the limitations regarding institutional support.

Technologies Supporting ePortfolios

The evolution of ePortfolios has occurred primarily in the area of ePortfolio editing tools (Ravet, 2007). However, "The most obvious gap today is the inability of ePortfolio systems to extract automatically meaningful information collected in an ePortfolio repository" (p. 1). As discussed in this and the next sections, the diversity of systems and technologies at both infrastructure and functionality levels characterizes the field of ePortfolio development today. With the growth of Web applications that support users in content creation, the landscape of technologies is changing quickly. Moreover, not-for-profit organizations, educational institutions, and corporate companies have stepped into this market with different goals, but also shared interests. In many cases, such projects have crossed the borders of the initial categories: off-the-shelf tools have been incorporated into fully-fledged systems; generic software applications have been backed-up by consortiums creating customizable features; and diverse groups have joined forces towards the definition of standards and common functionalities. Nonetheless, in what follows we attempt to describe the software supporting ePortfolios as part of large categories according to the nature of its developers and its consequent reach to stakeholders, with close resemblance to the taxonomy adopted by Stefani et al. (2007).

Commercial software for ePortfolios is currently provided by a myriad of companies with and without hosting capabilities. In many cases, such systems are focused on delivering services exclusively to organizations, and individuals cannot create or maintain personal ePortfolios within such systems if they are not associated with an institution that has purchased the particular system. The dependency on outside parties and their financial health and commercial interests are the major drawback of such approaches. However, the reduction of complexity in dealing with technical support and updates could be a reason to adopt such solutions. eFolioMN (Campus Technology, 2006) is an example of a system that has adopted a commercial solution, in this case from the company Avenet.

More recently, commercial endeavors supported by consortiums and groups of institutions have increasingly stood out as feasible ePortfolio system solutions for individuals and organizations. Epsilen ePortfolio is one good example of such a product. Epsilen today is a full-blown learning environment "combining fully integrated Web 2.0 social networking with the best practices of eLearning course delivery" (Epsilen), one of the modules being responsible for ePortfolio functions. This module "lets educators and students store a wide array of materials to showcase performance and progress—an ever-changing collection of multimedia artifacts, course-created materials, blogs, discussions, and wikis" (Epsilen ePortfolio).

The history of Epsilen is summarized as one of more than "six years of research and development activities at the CyberLab Purdue School of Engineering and Technology at IUPUI" (Epsilen, n.d. p. 2). It was initially proposed as the Jafari model discussed in more detail in the following section of this document.

Proprietary systems are those often designed by individual institutions or groups of institutions. For the most part, such initiatives originate because of the existence of legacy systems, such as a proprietary learning management system (like WebTycho at UMUC). The fact that such LMSs are being maintained at high costs is offset by the gains perceived from the institution such as control, independence from commercial development cycles, and a possible competitive advantage. The clear disadvantage is the need to provide the entire chain of development and support for such systems, which can translate into prohibitive costs or dated technology. This is the case of Pennsylvania State University's ePortfolio system, a collaborative effort of Penn State's Information Technology Services, the Division of Student Affairs, and the EMS e-Education Institute (Pennsylvania State University, n.d., p. 1).

The open-source approach "is steadily gaining adherents" (Stefani et al., 2007, p. 119). The underlying conceptual platforms vary, some focusing on providing frameworks and tools that can be adopted by different institutions while others simply define the standards for building such environments with a focus on interoperability and transportability. One such group is the Open Source Portfolio Initiative (OSPI). "Open Source Portfolio (OSP) is a robust, non-proprietary, open-source electronic portfolio application, developed by a community of individuals and organizations from around the world" (OSPortfolio, n.d., p. 1), associated with the Sakai project, which is a robust collaboration and learning environment. OSP is a suite of Sakai tools whose main components are the Matrix and the Portfolio, the first representing the institutional perspective, while the latter represents the students' perspective. Elgg is another initiative that can be categorized under this same umbrella:

> Elgg is an open-source social networking platform. It offers blogging, networking, community, collecting of news using feeds aggregation and file-sharing features. Everything can be shared among users with access controls and everything can be cataloged by tags as well. [Elgg, 2008, para. 1]

Although the definition refers to social networking, by nature such applications include most features desirable for maintaining a personal ePortfolio through its profile features and the functionalities of attaching and hyperlinking to anything stored on the Web. "Elgg works with the two most popular virtual learning environments, Blackboard and WebCT" (Elgg, 2008, para. 2), which lends itself to the activities of collecting students' work in a transparent way.

One important European initiative in this field is the Europortfolio consortium, led by EIfEL (European Institute for E-learning),

> [...] an independent, not-for-profit European professional association whose mission is to support organizations, communities and individuals in building a knowledge economy and learning society through innovative and reflective practice, continuing professional development and the use of knowledge, information, and learning technologies. [EIfEL, n.d., p. 1]

The Europortfolio is an "orchestrated effort involving both educational and corporate institutions to define, design, and develop digital portfolio systems that meet the needs of all stakeholders" (Europortfolio, n.d., p. 1). The mission of the Europortfolio includes diffusion of the use of ePortfolios as a foundation "of a learning economy and society" (p. 1); definition of standards that ensure interoperability among ePortfolio systems; promotion of the development of standards of competence "in the fields of education, training, human resource, and development" (p. 2); and support and coordination of European initiatives in the field of ePortfolios.

Helen Barrett is a commonly encountered name in the literature on ePortfolios, and many of her contributions relate to the availability and use of technologies for the development of ePortfolios by individuals, with a special focus on teachers. Gibson and Barrett (2002), based on the status of technologies available at the time, compare two major categories of technological approaches in the development of ePortfolios, namely generic tools (GT) and customized systems (CS). The difference between these two groups has become blurred with the rapid change in Web-based tools, but the general conclusion is still valid: "Either approach can stand alone, but they may be weaker for doing so. A CS approach by itself soon loses touch with the individuality of inquiry and expression of learners. A GT approach by itself limits its contribution to a program's validity as well as accountability" (p. 10).

Early on in the study of ePortfolio technologies, it was clear that the choice of tools and/or systems depends directly "upon the purpose and audience for the information within and connected to learner's portfolios" (Gibson and Barrett, 2002, p. 10). Although the benefits of bringing together both GT and CS approaches are numerous, contextual constraints need to be taken into consideration. As discussed previously, the MDE initiative at the moment is just that: a program initiative within an institution that does not provide adequate support for the adoption of a more complex and comprehensive ePortfolio system solution. Thus, the understanding of the overarching possibilities is essential to plan for the long-term future, while near-term decisions will need to be based on "low-hanging fruits" through the use of generic tools.

Until recently, generic tools (proprietary, commercial, or open-source) relied on the development of Web pages, which required technical skills, more or less complex depending on the learner's creativity. These included "word processing, HTML editors, multimedia authoring tools, portable documents format (PDF), and other commonly used productivity tool software" (Gibson and Barrett, 2002, p. 1). This landscape has experienced a significant breakthrough with the advent of Web 2.0 technologies.

The term *Web 2.0* was coined by O'Reilly when referring to practices and technologies emerging on the Web after the fall 2001 dot.com shake-up (O'Reilly, 2005). Although some would say the term is still being debated and there seems little rigor in its use, the last few years have demonstrated that there is an essentially new way of capitalizing on the use of Web-technologies. The original meaning of the term has been diffused, resulting from a growing community-based "intuitive recognition" that it is a useful label for a trend and a set of new paradigms for this Web usage. Users in growing numbers have found in the expanding services a resonance with their personal needs and expectations.

The principle of "the Web as a platform" sheds light on the fact that the value-added moved from Web-applications (such as browsers, which have become mere commodities) to "services" over the Web platform. As stated by Roush (2005), the Internet has moved from "collection of static pages into a vehicle for software services." The database is where the power of the tools resides, but the tools allow the data to be managed and produce usable information: "The value of the software is proportional to the scale and dynamism of the data it helps to manage" (O'Reilly, 2005, p. 3).

The inherent nature of Web-based hyperlinking generates a continuous organic growth of the "collective activity of all Web users" (O'Reilly, 2005, p. 4). Most of the organizations, including many start-up companies (e.g., eBay and Amazon), have capitalized on this principle, reaching out to all sorts of groups, including smaller niches—reaching out to the entire Web, not just the majorities in the center (i.e., "The Long Tail"). The collective intelligence has also been embraced through innovative approaches such as Wikipedia, del.ici.ous, Flickr, Technorati, etc. Although there may be resistance based on the fact that these initiatives are rooted primarily in new business models, and lack of control and lingering security issues, they are definitely becoming part of everyday practice of all those with access to computers and mobile devices, and in search of cheap or free products and services.

Barrett (2006, 2007) explores "the potential for allowing students to incorporate a variety of Web 2.0 services in their portfolios" (Barrett, 2006, p. 1). Such tools have changed the way we interact with the Web, and thus it is natural to see a change in the use and perspectives on ePortfolios as well. According to Barrett, ePortfolio 2.0 (as opposed to ePortfolio 1.0) is networked, emergent, and learner-driven, focuses on individuality, is composed of small pieces loosely joined, uses blogs and/wikis as its architectural base, tends to follow open standards, and is stored in a distributed fashion across the network. As stated by Jong, Specht and Koper (2007) "blogs recently have become a popular way of collecting personal information and learning experiences related to formal education" (p. 1). With the functionalities of comments and thus interaction "blogs offer learners a great degree of autonomy to structure information while also embed reflection in a peer community" (p. 1). It is interesting to notice that although unaware of the conceptual notions of ePortfolios, "a healthy culture of sharing and documenting learning is already occurring in the field of 'bloggers'" (Siemens, 2004, p. 5). The critique in the use of such tools could also flourish from those with a strict focus on full-blown systems and universally accepted standards. However, "to assume that a standardized portfolio is required for interoperability ignores the successful growth of simple social technologies like blogs, wikis, Rich Site Summary (RSS), and social networking tools" (p. 5).

In many situations Siemens' (2004) suggestion plays out as wise advice: "In situations, where full-scale implementation of ePortfolios is not possible, instructors can begin to foster a culture of digital documentation by encouraging learners to practice blogging, developing simple Web sites, or storing their content online" (p. 6). Moreover, we also need to consider the aspect of "beta" development of all Web 2.0 technologies and aspire to more capabilities than those we have had the chance to experience thus far. Ravet (2007) translates such a vision well when he states

> … What about more sophisticated processes such as reflection and connection? Such processes could greatly benefit from technologies issued from semantic networks such as semantic annotation, topic maps, and mind mapping. One has to recognize that current ePortfolio editing systems have not really moved much beyond the very first paperless portfolios in their ability to support reflective activities effectively. [p. 2]

ePortfolio Systems and Standards

In Siemens (2004), the requirements of an ideal ePortfolio system are thoroughly discussed. Basically, it should allow flexible input, organization, retrieval, and display. The content displayed through ePortfolios is varied, including personal information, educational history, reflective comments, feedback from instructors and peers, awards and certificates, presentations, papers, pieces of written work, professional history, etc.

The approach considered within the University of Minnesota system (Treuer and Jenson, 2003) is one where students, faculty, and staff members at the institution should have "lifelong ownership and control of his or her individual electronic portfolio [to] selectively share information in that portfolio with anyone, anywhere, at any time" (p. 34). However, what happens when the student leaves the institution to move on to further studies at other institutions or simply into their professional life? Would the institution of origin be able to or wish to maintain such ePortfolios and who should have control over them? Treuer and Jenson (2003) provide a long and detailed set of standards that should serve all organizations wanting to define and implement an ePortfolio system. This set of standards would allow for full interoperability. Minnesota's initiative has evolved immensely since Treuer and Jenson's 2003 publication. The current version—Efolio Minnesota (Campus Technology, 2006)—is a result of the effort of Minnesota State College and Universities system (MnSCU). It was created to serve faculty, students, alumni, and staff. The idea of supporting alumni is critical in this initiative because it provides the continuity of ePortfolios beyond the lifetime of the student within the institution and as mentioned before, reinforces education institution's goals to encourage and promote lifelong learning and to "retain" lifelong learners. An ePortfolio hosted at a home institution could have the positive effect that alumni would look to the institution first to continue their studies and/ or pursue their professional development. Efolio Minnesota has grown "beyond the higher ed community, expanding to provide services for all students (K-20) and residents statewide" (p. 2). The system is based on a solution provided by Avenet and was selected after a request for a proposals (RFP) process. The goals of the project included "supporting Minnesota students and residents at no cost to the individual user"; "deployment of Web-based multimedia tools to support the needs of the individual learner"; and "adoption of eFolioMN by other colleges and universities—even those that compete with MnSCU" (p. 2). Although the achievements of eFolioMN are extraordinary in terms of expansion of the system and becoming available for adoption by any other institution, the issues of standards and their adoption "worldwide" remains an open question and far from being resolved.

Cohn and Hibbitts (2004) go beyond the concept of a lifelong learning tool and present the concept of the "lifetime personal Web space" (LPWS)—a "beehive configured Web space that possesses sufficient organizational plasticity to accommodate the user's developmental capacities and needs across a lifetime" (p. 8). Such a space would start at birth and accompany individuals in all their learning throughout life. "The LPWS construct will enable users to preserve more knowledge over time and to forge richer connection between their academic and work endeavors" (p. 9). Although such a concept might sound somewhat futuristic, it brings to light the nature of the digital identify—an idea cultivated by many others in the literature:

> In this electronic age, wouldn't it make more sense for a student's multiple records of academic performance to reside not in a separate

registrar's offices, but in a professional academic reservoir? Such a universal academic electronic-identify (e-identity) clearinghouse might look much like a credit bureau, though clearly it would have to be easier to use by individuals and institutions needing information from it. [Ittelson, 2001, p. 44]

In the literature (Aalderink and Veugelers, 2006; Gathercoal, 2002; Greenberg, 2004; Jafari, 2004; Jafari, McGee, and Carmean, 2006; Johnson and DiBiase, 2004; Love, 2004; and Suter, 2003), there is a clear and sharp push for the evolution of ePortfolios through the doors of "standardization": The holy grail of an electronic portfolio that can be managed as a lifelong work in progress is found through "standardization, interoperability, a universally agreed-upon set of definitions, and adoption of policies that will help guide both behavior and expectations when it comes to copyright law and easy access to digital information" (Suter, 2003, p. 1).

Other ongoing projects also translate to the same ambition as eFolioMN—to define standards and become a default system to be adopted by a growing number of institutions. Under this umbrella we can cite ePortfolio.org platform, which is a "student-centered platform … augmented by Project Builder and an Assessment module" (ePortfolio.org, n.d., p. 1). This platform is being used by more than 20 institutions and is under the leadership and development efforts of the Connecticut Distance Learning Consortium. Representatives of all these institutions sit on the advisory board and help shape the final product. Portfolios can be created and maintained by students, while sharing and receiving feedback from faculty, advisors, and other institutional staff members. Assessment reports can be generated based on specified rubrics. "ePortfolio is a centrally hosted application" (p. 1), which reduces the costs and complexity for campuses involved in this initiative. The platform is also integrated to both Blackboard and WebCT Vista "allowing for single Sign-On" (p. 1); thus, transferring work from the respective LMS to the ePortfolio is made easy. Since the platform serves many institutions, "new users select the institution in which they are enrolled as part of their profile. The ePortfolio is then branded with the institution's logo and name" (p. 1).

In the area of consortiums, a different initiative—ePortConsortium—has grown to prominence, where the focus resides on collaborating "to define, design, and develop electronic portfolio software environment and management systems" (ePortconsortium, n.d., p. 1). Participants of this endeavor include higher education institutions and IT organizations. The focus is "to define and adopt interoperability and transportability measures and standards when building prototypes to test potential scenarios and conceptual environments" (p. 1). The goal is that ePortfolios developed by educational institutions and commercial enterprises will all be compatible. The main mediator towards the research efforts in the design of such a system is Dr. Ali Jafari, whose discussion is thoroughly addressed in the end of this section, given its currency and timeliness.

Meanwhile, many other institutions have promoted their systems, limited to their constituent body, such as Penn State (Johnson and DiBiase, 2004) and the University of Denver (Gilbert, 2005):

> The University of Denver Portfolio Community (DUPC) is a fully developed Web-based application that supports the academic community with a searchable database of electronic portfolios for students, faculty, staff and alumni, community discussion, academic program assessment based on student work, and an assessment rubric library. [p. 1]

Although in several cases alumni are considered to be stakeholders, issues of interoperability and lifelong use of ePortfolios are not directly addressed.

The broader perspective of a lifelong ePortfolio connects to the concept of virtual identity, which should be managed by each individual and used in a customized way, depending on the context and an individual's goal at a certain moment in time. Longer-term views of ePortfolios bring an enormous set of challenges with respect to its implementation, namely institutional support, technological change, interoperability, and ownership. eFolioMN's approach rests on the premise that it is possible to define a set of standards to be discussed and agreed upon by all organizations adopting ePortfolios. Based on other technological advances that are much more diffused and have a far greater reach than ePortfolios, such attempts seem destined to fail. Siemens (2004) notes

> Standardization of ePortfolios is a potential challenge. Heavily regulated efforts may stifle creativity and innovation. ... The field of learning objects, as an example, seems to be hindered in development due to the proliferation of complex standards. The flaw in learning objects standardization appears to be the attempt to create the system on the assumptions that interoperability is what end users need. ... EPortfolios will be successful if the urge to excessively standardize is resisted. Simple technologies like RSS and SOAP reveal that content can be shared when interoperability is built into the sharing structure, not the content itself. [p. 4]

This debate between highly structured and regulated institutional approaches and other more open trends is an important one within the MDE ePortfolio project. It impacts the decisions related to requesting and pushing for institutional involvement and support. Siemens (2004) highlights the basis for making ePortfolios a "personal life–learning tool": "One of the most critical aspects of successful ePortfolio use is the creation of neutral ePortfolio providers. The institution should not be in control of the portfolio. As a personal life-learning tool, there is no place for organizational control" (p. 4).

Such beliefs lead to projects involving open-source (discussed elsewhere in this chapter) or ePortfolio providers approved by the institution, which allow the user to remain in control of their own ePortfolios. Ravet (2007) from the Eifel project provides a deeper understanding of this debate:

> The common misconception about the relation between ePortfolios (eP) and ePortfolio Management Systems (ePMS) is that the function of an ePMS is to host ePortfolios. The main function of an ePMS is not to host ePortfolios but to manage a process during which an ePortfolio can be consumed or produced. [p. 2]

From this differentiation Ravet arrives at a more formal definition of an ePortfolio Management System:

> A system used to manage (produce, consume, and exploit elements) of individual ePortfolios for a specific purpose—scaffolding learning, assessment, employment, competency management, organizational learning, knowledge management, etc. [p. 4]

Looking at some of the systems discussed thus far, it is clear that most systems have been built to "fit the needs of an organization" (Ravet, 2007, p. 4). At this point the individual learner is not at the center of the decisions about tools to create and manage artifacts or archived materials. Thus, learners are not and would not be in control of their own digital identity. Individual ePortfolio management systems would be the answer to this issue. Ravet calls such tools the ePortfolio "organizer," which "belongs to individuals and provides them with the ability to create and control their digital identity" (p. 5), and suggests that Eifel was founded to fill this void in the arena of ePortfolio systems. "While an ePortfolio provides a snapshot of the learning state, an ePortfolio organizer should be able to provide a deeper view and understanding of the learning process" (p. 5). However, it is exactly in the area of tools that support such "deeper understanding" that one finds a gap in the technologies used within ePortfolio organizers:

> [...] There is no tool providing the kind of instant feedback a mirror would. In order to play the role of a mirror it is important to develop technologies that provide dynamic analysis of ePortfolios through data mining and spatial representation. [p. 5]

Against most of the trends in ePortfolio systems discussed, Ravet concludes that it is not realistic to plan to have one single provider for the hosting of an ePortfolio: "It goes against the nature of the World Wide Web" (p. 5). On the other hand, it seems feasible and desirable to provide one single point of control from which multiple services of managing one's identity through the ePortfolio are available. Ravet's discussion is extremely timely given the spread of our identity imprint through blogs, social networks, wikis, etc. Ravet's point is that these are all components of the ePortfolio organizer "as they hold some of the assets of an individual" (p. 6). This is true for "all services contributing to the construction and expression of one's digital identity" (p. 6). Using IT standards developed by several groups, one current important trend in the field of ePortfolio systems is to move "from [the] organization-centered IS [information system], where individuals were offered a space, to [a] people-centered IS, where [an] organization's IS behaves as an aggregator of individual or departmental IS" (p. 9). Thus, ePortfolio systems for organizations and individuals will take on distinct lives. There are currently many providers of organizational ePortfolio systems, such as Nuventive with its iWebfolio solution that encompasses "documentation, management and display of competencies and professional accomplishments from the individual through the institution" (Nuventive, n.d., p. 1). As part of the ePortfolio organizer (ePortfolio individual management system) set of requirements, one needs to consider elements such as "single sign on, to control who has access, to what and when" (p. 9), as well as "data mining, aggregation, and spatial representation" (p. 9) of an individual's personal assets distributed across multiple systems.

In Jafari, McGee, and Carmean (2006) the discussion of new e-learning environments encompasses similar goals. "The next-generation e-learning environment includes Google, IM, SMS, Web 2.0 social knowledge and software, intelligent systems with memory and personalization of the learner's needs, mobile learning, wireless learning" (p. 62). The so-called "Jafari model" integrates five design requirements, namely: lifelong, outsourced, global, comprehensive, and smart. The lifelong aspect allows each learner to automatically have a permanent URL forming "a lifelong repository, lifelong contact information, and a cyber-identity" (p. 66). An outsourced model is represented by "a strategic outside hosting solution that offers full-scale services to students" (p. 66) independent of the location where the learner is studying and/or working. The "global" reach is characterized by a system that offers "networking and collaboration among the global communities" (p. 66) beyond specific campuses or workplace. Being "comprehensive" entails providing an extensive toolbox containing "all the necessary tools for day-to-day learning and teaching tasks" (p. 67). This toolbox includes tools for specifically managing one's ePortfolio, as well as social and professional networking and various communication and collaboration tools. Finally, being smart means to include "personal intelligent agent software" (p. 70), which can support the learner performing many of the activities and functionalities available in this system.

Despite the fact that current contextual factors are definite obstacles for pursuing solutions of this caliber, for many higher-ed programs such as the MDE ePortfolio initiative, it is nonetheless essential to have a vision for an ideal implementation. Ravet and Jafari offer such a vision while providing proposals where the organizational support and the individual ownership and control are kept in balance.

ePortfolios and Lifelong Learning

As noted earlier, in 2001 the Commission on Dietetic Registration decided that recertification of their professionals was to be accomplished through the use of a portfolio model. This approach was novel for the periodic assessment of competence and placed professional accountability for continuing competence at the center of this approach. In preparation for this, the documentation of "sustained performance changes" (p. 612) was central in documenting the value of CPE. The commission recognizes that CPE is an integral part of the portfolio process—and vise versa—and that an ePortfolio can play a critical part in the overall process.

Gvaramazde (2007) notes that while barriers regarding access to lifelong learning may hinder participation, increasing more and better opportunities alone may not necessarily increase participation, and refers to recognition, validation, and certification of increased competencies and "added value to prior learning" (p. 130) as important societal mechanisms. The ePortfolio could be one such mechanism.

Flynn (2004) makes the case that employers seek potential employees that have a specific range of skills and competencies (along with general knowledge), and they are interested in demonstrations and application of skills and abilities. While these authors do not support overarching standardization (see previous discussions), they do support the notion that these discussions must be carried forth by all stakeholders to allow current academic transcript to be expanded with ePortfolios that can provide complementary alternatives and "… convey a great deal more about the abilities of a student than what colleges currently provide" (p. 9).

The authors have always encouraged learners in the MDE program to include non-MDE-related accomplishments and experiences in their ePortfolios. This is an opportunity "to document both formal and informal learning … without academic credits attached" (Lakin, 2005, para. 6). In addition it "credentials prior learning" (para. 5) that is of particular importance in the distance education and adult learning arena that could include "early school leavers, immigrants, … prisoners and job-seekers …" (para. 5). In today's increasingly "global" environment the documentation of a variety of educational and work experiences along with "softer skills" (para. 7) is an important aspect in terms of transferability and employment, and the constant interchange between learning and working and learning and making sense of and bundling "experience from dissimilar environments" (para. 7).

Beyond the collegiate career, ePortfolios lend themselves as tools for "… authentic documentation and assessment, providing evidence of outcomes attainment, competency and readiness for work … [and] can include papers, presentations, projects, or research, much of it in multimedia format, enabling users to share their accomplishments with faculty, peers, and family as well as potential employers and education providers" (p. 9).

The Waukesha County Technical College (2009) established a list of 23 critical life skills, which are integrated into all campus activities to ensure that "… students become proficient in four broad areas:"

- Communication skills
- Analytical skills
- Group effectiveness skills
- Personal management skills (para. 1–5)

The assessment rubric provides a list of indicators that serve as examples of elements that contribute to the documentation of the 23 critical life skills. This approach, which relies on the integration and assessment of these skills throughout courses, programs, and activities, as well as many other learning opportunities, serves not only the demonstration of learning, performance, and development, but generates a wide array of artifacts that can easily be stored in an ePortfolio, while at the same time building a foundation for links in an individual's lifelong learning journey. The American Association of Community Colleges (Flynn, 2004) suggested that a " … national task force involving all stakeholders to identify the essential components and consensus-based guidelines and standards [were] needed to document noncredit learning, and work with national organizations …" (p. 11) with select colleges serving as regional centers of excellence and training for new transcription techniques.

Cooperation with the IT industry, where issues surrounding selected criteria, ownership, security, and FERPA compliance and standards are examined; with employer groups to identify the skills identified as missing and discuss adequate documentation methods; with the education community, public policy organizations, and other national organizations to heighten awareness, provide advocacy, identify best practices in transcription, and promote acceptance of the ePortfolio as a documentation of formal degree and nondegree and informal learning (Flynn, 2004, p.12).

As Flynn (2004) notes, a number of issues need to be addressed in order to value and validate all learning:

> … Why is learning acquired outside the academic credit format not accorded the same documentation via the transcript? Why is the transcript viewed by many in business and industry as … uninformative and unhelpful in the hiring process? With the available and affordable [software] … what is preventing colleges from adopting and supporting the electronic portfolio as a valuable asset to the students and the institution? Why is the college transcript limited to letter grades and length of attendance? [p. 13]

Yancy et al. (2009) state that international experiences in issues and challenges with the implementation of ePortfolios are quite similar: motivation (faculty and learners), integration in programs, balance between learning and assessment, working across disciplines and professions, and support and evaluation of reflection (p. 5).

One interesting example illustrates the power of ePortfolios to connect students' formal learning to a larger community, including professionals in specific fields. A professor from Washington State University used an ePortfolio approach to engage "students and industry professional colleagues, as well as faculty in her department, in a transformative and authentic (real life) project in an upper division apparel merchandizing class" (Brown et al., 2009). From these groups, a community of practice was formed, and was able to provide ample feedback to students based on "engaged professional community standards."

All stakeholders should consider the value of including assignments, work samples, surveys, awards, honors, continuing education (conferences, seminars, workshops, certifications, licenses, language skills), volunteer and extracurricular activities (music, sports, arts), references, letters of recommendation, testimonials, military records, awards, and anything else that can document and pinpoint links to lifelong learning. By keeping such a record and "… making links among occasions and products of learning, and building on past experiences …" (Yancey et al., 2009, p. 7), we learn how we learn. This is also consistent with the concept of learning as an ongoing lifelong activity and is comprised of mandatory and voluntary participation and "… is considered to contribute not only to competitiveness and employability, but is necessary condition also for social inclusion, active citizenship, and personal development" (Council of the European Union, 2006 as cited in Gvaramadze, 2007, p. 130). Yancy et al. (2009) discuss the ePortfolio as an "outgrowth" of the nationally mandated personal development plans (p. 6).

Conclusions

In this chapter, we have seen the growing importance of ePortfolios at an institutional level as a way to assess students more holistically, as well as their inherent trait of showcasing students' achievements and helping learners better plan and strategize their continuous professional and personal development. Without trying to give ePortfolios a "jack-of-all-trades" role or trying to push them as the solution for all maladies in education, it is worth mentioning that much is still to be explored in terms of the potential of ePortfolios. These considerations should include learning in the wake of the drastic changes taking place in the way we access information in the digital age and changes all stakeholders experience in terms of meeting lifelong learning and employability demands. As we have discussed throughout this chapter, there are yet many questions unanswered when it comes to fulfilling the real mandate of lifelong learning. Schaffhauser (2009) briefly summarizes the current debate on ePortfolios when she lists a few essentials such as "How are they evolving with the growth of Web 2.0? What are the right tools to create them? And do they have a role beyond the academic setting as part of a person's lifelong learning endeavors?" (p.1). The ultimate idea of a meaningful Web space from cradle to grave is obviously still utopist. However, the authors conclude that the principles that support ePortfolios matter when considering their effective use and in understanding the diverse approaches to their development. Their major foundations are a solid route to reflect on and implement any initiatives that might consider the adoption of ePortfolios for lifelong learning and bring together the links in a central space.

While we have a way to go in terms of working out how to deal with the (institutional) challenges and barriers, we can contribute to raising awareness at the level of students and faculty at our respective institutions by sharing lessons learned and some of the best practice from our experience in the MDE. The authors believe this will help to educate interested parties and stakeholders, and will support their own continuous collaboration and research with peers and learners. The number of individuals, institutions, associations, and other bodies are increasing when it comes to looking at and reflecting on the use of ePortfolios, the associated issues and challenges, and trying to find ways to develop processes that take the concerns of all stakeholders into account. As in other higher education programs, the graduates and others involved in the MDE are at the forefront to bear the torch of the ePortfolio based not only on their own experience in the program, but in their future roles as distance education professionals, who work in diverse settings and fields. As authors we value being a part of and contributing to the community in a national and international context.

References

Aalderink, W., and Veugelers, M. (2005). EPortfolios in the Netherlands: Stimulus for Educational Change and Life Long Learning. *EDEN Conference*. Helsinki, June 2005. Retrieved on February 8, 2008, from http://e-learning.surf.nl/docs/portfolio/helsinki_eden_-_wijnand_aalderinkmarij_veugelers.pdf.

Acker, S. (March 14, 2005). Overcoming Obstacles to Authentic ePortfolio Assessment. *Campus Technology*. Retrieved February 8, 2008, from http://campustechnology.com/articles/40147/.

Barrett, H.C. (1999, October 14). Student Electronic Portfolios. Paper presented at *ESSDACK*, Hutchinson, Kansas. Retrieved February 8, 2008, from http://electronic-portfolios.com/portfolios/ESSDACKStudent2.pdf.

Barrett, H. (2002). Pedagogical Issues in Electronic Portfolio Implementation. Electronicportfolios.org. Retrieved January 20, 2010, from http://electronicportfolios.com/EPpedissues.pdf.

Barrett, H. (2006). Authentic Assessment with Electronic Portfolios Using Common Software and Web 2.0 Tools. Electronicportfolios.org. Retrieved January 25, 2008, from http://electronicportfolios.org/web20.html.

Barrett, H. (2007). My "Online Portfolio Adventure." Electronicportfolios.org. Retrieved January 25, 2008, from http://electronicportfolios.org/myportfolio/versions.html.

Brown, G., Peterson, N., Chida, M., and Desrosier, T. (2009). EPortfolios, The Harvesting Gradebook, Accountability, and Community. *Campus Technology*. Retrieved on January 20, 2010, from http://campustechnology.com/articles/2009/02/04/ePortfolios-and-communities-of-practice.aspx.

Campus Technology. (2006). 2006 Campus Technology Innovators: ePortfolios. *Campus Technology.* July 7, 2006. Retrieved April 21, 2008, from http://campustechnology. com/articles/41070/.

Carew, D. (2003). Educating the 21st Century Citizen. Microsoft White Paper. Retrieved December 12, 2009, from http://www.nccet.org/resource/resmgr/Publications/ Educating_the_21st_Century_C.pdf.

Cohn, E., and Hibbitts, B. (November, 2004). Beyond the Electronic Portfolio: A Lifetime Personal Web Space. *Educause Quarterly, (4),* 7–10. Retrieved February 8, 2008, from http://www.educause.edu/ir/library/pdf/EQM0441.pdf.

Commission on Dietetic Registration. (1999). The professional development 2001 portfolio. *Journal of the American Dietetic Association, 99*(5), pp. 612–614. Retrieved December 2, 2009, from Science Direct database.

EifEL. (nd). About EifEL. EifEL homepage. Retrieved on April 21, 2008, from http://www. eife-l.org/about.

Elgg Org. (2008). About Elgg. Elgg Homepage. Retrieved on April 6, 2008, from http:// elgg.org/mod/mediawiki/wiki/index.php/About_Elgg.

ePortconsortium. (n.d). About Us. ePortconsortium webpage. Retrieved April 21, 2008, from http://www.eportconsortium.org/Content/Root/aboutUs.aspx.

ePortfolio Portal. (n.d). Types of ePortfolios. ePortfolio Portal Homepage. Retrieved on February 8, 2008, from http://www.danwilton.com/ePortfolios/types.php.

ePortfolio.org. (n.d). ePortfolio Platform: Overview of the ePortfolio Platform. ePortfolio. org homepage. Retrieved April 20, 2008, from http://ePortfolio.org/about.htm.

Epsilen. (n.d.). About Us. Retrieved January 20, 2010, from http://www.epsilen.com/ LandingSite/ContentPage.aspx?ContentSysName=drcsvssiWzCWElNWKEBHaA== &tab=3.

Epsilen ePortfolio (n.d.). Collect Your Lifelong Work History. Retrieved January 20, 2010, from http://www.epsilen.com/LandingSite/ContentPage.aspx?ContentSysName=drcs vssiWzAEbN5mKkIrw7dqgONyvyOMg6wxmi94yU4qrH235tARRA==&tab=2.

Europortfolio. (n.d.). Europortfolio. EIfEL homepage. Retrieved on April 21, 2008, from http://www.eife-l.org/about/europortfolio.

Flynn, W. (2004). Why Not Tell It Like It is? The Case for Revitalizing the Traditional Academic Transcript. NCCET Report retrieved December 13, 2009, from http://efo-liomn.com/vertical/Sites/%7B54359267-AFF1-4313-A9D7-7271C0ACAFB7%7D/ uploads/%7B45E28EB7-0E29-48C2-9C5F-9B166C870AB7%7D.PDF.

Gathercoal, P. (2002). On Implementing Web-Based Electronic Portfolios. *Educause Quarterly (2),* 29–37. Retrieved February 8, 2008, from http://www.educause.edu/ir/ library/pdf/eqm0224.pdf

Gilbert, J. (2005). University of Denver Portfolio Community. Center for Teaching and Learning. Retrieved on April 21, 2008, from http://www.google.com/url?sa=t&ct=res&cd =3&url=http%3A%2F%2Fctl.du.edu%2FModuleSupport%2Fdocuments%2FDUP Cdescription.doc&ei=JFQPSN6_Cp6ezQS_mYGqqCA&usg=AFQjCNF37fVsKyX_ CnlNVgPjo1JSO8xbrQ&sig2=uRdocynki21BhHOZ7Wvu-w.

Gibson, D., and Barrett, H. (2002). Directions in Electronic Portfolio Development. ITForum 2002. Retrieved on April 21, 2008, from http://itech1.coe.uga.edu/itforum/ paper66/paper66.htm

Greenberg, G. (2004). The Digital Convergence: Extending the Portfolio Model. *Educause Review,* (July/August 2004), 28-36. Retrieved January 25, 2008, from http://www. educause.edu/ir/library/pdf/ERM0441.pdf.

Gvaramadze, I. (2007). Adult participation in lifelong learning. *The International Journal of Learning 14*(5), pp. 123–130. Retrieved November 20, 2009, from Ebcohost.

International Labor Organization. (2000). *Lifelong Learning in the Twenty-First Century: The Changing Roles of Educational Personnel.* Geneva: Publications Bureau International Labor Organization.

Ittelson, J. (2001). Building and E-Dentity for Each Student. *Educause Quarterly, (4),* 43–45. Retrieved February 8, 2008, from http://www.educause.edu/ir/library/pdf/EQM0147.pdf.

Jafari, A. (2004). The "Sticky" ePortfolio System—Tackling Challenges and Identifying Attributes. *Educause Review,* (July/August 2004), 38-48. Retrieved January 30, 2008, from http://connect.educause.edu/Library/EDUCAUSE+Review/TheStickyePortfolioSystem/40485.

Jafari, A., McGee, P., and Carmean, C. (2006). Managing Courses, Defining Learning: What Faculty, Students, and Administrators Want. *Educause Review* (July/August 2006), 50–70. Retrieved on April 22, 2008, from http://www.educause.edu/ir/library/pdf/ERM0643.pdf.

Johnson, G., and DiBiase, D. (2004). Keeping the Horse before the Cart: Penn State's ePortfolio Initiative. *Educause Quarterly, (4),* 18–26. Retrieved February 8, 2008, from http://www.educause.edu/ir/library/pdf/EQM0443.pdf.

Jong, T., Specht, M., and Koper, R. (2007). Contextblogger: Learning by Blogging in the Real World. ePortfolio Conference 2007. Retrieved January 25, 2008, from http://www.eife-l.org/publications/ePortfolio/proceedings/ep2007/papers/ePortfolio/contextblogger-learning-by-blogging-in-the-real-world/view.

Lakin, M.B. (2005, December 3). Multipurpose ePortfolios: Catalysts for Lifelong Learning Ownership. American Council on Education. Retrieved December 7, 2009, from http://www.acenet.edu/AM/Template.cfm?Section=Search&template=/CM/HTMLDisplay.cfm&ContentID=13108.

Lorenzo, G., and Ittelson, J. (2005a). An overview of ePortfolios. *Educause Connect.* Retrieved January 28, 2008, from http://www.educause.edu/ir/library/pdf/ELI3001.pdf.

Lorenzo, G., and Ittelson, J. (2005b) Demonstrating and Assessing Student Learning with ePortfolios. *Educause Connect.* Retrieved January 25, 2008, from http://www.educause.edu/ir/library/pdf/ELI3003.pdf.

Love, D. (2004). Portfolios to Webfolios and Beyond: Levels of Maturation. *Educause Quarterly (2),* 24–37. Retrieved February 8, 2008, from http://www.educause.edu/ir/library/pdf/EQM0423.pdf.

Mason, R., and Rennie, F. (2008). *E-Learning and Social Networking Handbook.* New York: Routledge.

McPherson, M.A., and Nunes, J.M. (2004). *Developing Innovation in Online Learning: An Action Research Framework.* London: RoutledgeFalmer.

MDE Outcomes Assessment Plan. (2007). Retrieved on February 8, 2008, from http://www.umuc.edu/outcomes/gsmtplans/MDE.pdf.

MDE/UMUC. (2008). EPortfolios Guidelines: OMDE 670. Retrieved April 5, 2008, from http://tychousa7.umuc.edu/OMDE670/0802/9040/class.nsf/20562a5b592bbae1852573c9003e1466/0d4bfa2fe906164b852573c9004060fd?OpenDocument.

Medel-Añonuevo, C., Ohsako T., and Mauch, W. (2001). Revisiting Lifelong Learning for the 21st Century. Hamburg: UNESCO Institute for Education. Retrieved December 10, 2009, from http://www.unesco.org/education/uie/pdf/revisitingLLL.pdf

Moore, M., and Kearsley, G. (2005). *Distance Education: A Systems View* (2nd ed.). Belmont, CA: Thompson Wadsworth.

Nuventive. (nd). About Nuventive. Retrieved on April 22, 2008, from http://www.nuventive.com/about.html.

OECD. (2006). Recognition of Non-Formal and Informal Learning. Retrieved January 15, 2010, from http://www.oecd.org/document/25/0,3343,en_2649_39263238_371369 21_1_1_1_37455,00.html.

Office of Outcomes Assessment. (2005). UMUC Core Learning Areas. Retrieved February 4, 2008, from http://www.umuc.edu/outcomes/areas.shtml.

O'Reilly, T. (2005). What is web 2.0: Design Patterns and Business Models for the Next Generation of Software. Retrieved January 31, 2007, from http://www.oreillynet.com/lpt/a/6228.

Ó Súilleabháin, G., and Coughlan, R. (n.d.). Portfolio Student Support Services for E-Learning: Collaborative Tutoring and Authentic Assessment. Retrieved January 10, 2010, from http://www.changetraining.com/docs/eden/OSuilleabhain.pdf.

OSPortfolio. (n.d.). What is OSP? Retrieved on April 21, 2008, from http://osportfolio.org.

PennState. (n.d.). About ePortfolios/ePortfolios at Penn State. Retrieved on April 21, 2008, from http://portfolio.psu.edu/about.

Porto. S., and Walti, C. (2008). Expanding Possibilities of Student ePortfolios: The MDE Experience. Presentation at the 5th EDEN Research Workshop, October 20–22, 2008, Paris, France.

Ravet, S. (2007). For an ePortfolio Enabled Architecture: ePortfolios, ePortfolio Management Systems and Organisers. ePortfolio Conference 2007. Retrieved January 25, 2008, from http://www.eife-l.org/publications/ePortfolio/proceedings/ep2007/papers/ePortfolio/ePortfolio-architecture-ePortfolios-ePortfolio-management-systems-and-organisers/view.

Roush, W. (2005). "Web 2.0" Has Arrived. Technology Review—MIT. Retrieved on January 10, 2008, from http://www.techreview.com/Infotech/14869/?a=f.

Ryan, R.J. (1999). From Recurrent Education To Lifelong Learning. Invitational Seminar on the Delors Report: Learning—The Treasure Within. Flinders University Institute of International Education; Flinders University, Adelaide. 1999. Retrieved December 10, 2009, from http://ehlt.flinders.edu.au/education/publications/REPORTS/fuiie99a/RYAN.DOC.

Schaffhauser, D. (2009). Here, there, and everywhere. *Campus Technology* (11/01/09). Retrieved on January 21, 2010, from http://campustechnology.com/Articles/2009/11/01/ePortfolios.aspx.

Siemens, G. (2004, December 16). ePortfolios. elearnspace. Retrieved December 10, 2009, from http://www.elearnspace.org/Articles/ePortfolios.htm.

Stefani, L., Mason, R., and Pegler, C. (2007). *The Educational Potential of EPortfolios*. Oxon, U.K.: Routledge.

Suter, V. (2003). The Digital Me—Standards, Interoperability, and Common Vocabulary Spell Progress for ePortfolios. NLII 2002–2003 Annual Review, July 2003. Retrieved April 5, 2008, from http://connect.educause.edu/Library/ELI/TheDigitalMeStandardsInte/42537?time=1208871497.

Treuer, P., and Jenson, J. D. (2003). Electronic portfolios need standards to thrive. *Educause Quarterly, 2*, 34-42. Retrieved February 8, 2008, from http://www.educause.edu/ir/library/pdf/eqm0324.pdf.

U.S. Department of Education, National Center for Education Statistics. (2008). Distance Education at Degree-Granting Postsecondary Institutions: 2006–07. Retrieved December 12, 2009, from http://nces.ed.gov/fastfacts/display.asp?id=80.

Walti, C. (2004). Implementing web-based portfolios and learning journals as learner support tools: An illustration. In J. E. Brindley, C. Walti, and O. Zawacki-Richter (Eds.), *Learner Support in Open, Distance and Online Learning Environments* (pp. 157–168). Oldenburg: Bibliotheks- und Informationssystem der Universität Oldenburg.

Walti, C. (2006). Net-Based Portfolios and Learning Journals: The Journey of Learning. Tutorial for the MDE ePortfolio. Retrieved on January 25th, 2008 from http://www.uni-oldenburg.de/zef/christinewalti/tutorial/index.htm.

Waukesha County Technical College (WCTC). (2009). Critical Life Skills. Retrieved January 8, 2010, from http://www.wctc.edu/programs_&_courses/general_education/critical_life_skills/index.php.

Webtycho. (2008). What is WebTycho? Retrieved on April 5, 2008, from http://www.ed.umuc.edu/de/webtycho.html.

Western Sydney Community Forum (WSCF). (n.d.) Lifelong Learning: History. Retrieved December 10, 2009, from http://www.wscf.org.au/uploads/File/Lifelong%20Learning%20(History).pdf.

Yancey, K., Cambridge, B., and Cambridge, D. (2009). Making common cause: Electronic portfolios, learning and the power of community. *Academic Commons*, 2009. Retrieved November 27, 2009, from http://www.academiccommons.org/files/Yancey.pdf.

Chapter 14

Knowledge Management as Professional Development: The Case of the MDE

Thomas Hülsmann and Ulrich Bernath

Contents

Knowledge Management and Professional Development

The purpose of this chapter is to discuss knowledge management (KM) with respect to the Master of Distance Education (MDE) degree, a postgraduate program jointly offered by the University of Maryland University College (UMUC) and the Carl von Ossietzky University Oldenburg (Germany).*

A discussion of the nature of knowledge or, in particular, the difference between knowledge and information is beyond the scope of this chapter.† We tend to use the words "information" (or "data") when we talk about encoded messages flowing in digital networks, and "knowledge" when people are concerned with interpreting these data. Information, says Peters, can be disseminated today with the speed of light, while the spreading of knowledge is still slow and cumbersome (Peters, 2003). While information management is a necessary ingredient of knowledge management, it is by no means exhaustive. Knowledge management (KM) is about managing people as well as information.

In this chapter, we will largely ignore the aspect of information management. Not because we underrate the importance of digital technologies (as this chapter will amply demonstrate), but because, as far as our case study is concerned, the technical aspects of information management are of secondary importance. We want to focus on KM as far as people are concerned, this is, on KM as professional development. Hence, we define KM in an organization as "capturing the knowledge distributed within the organization, eliciting/generating new knowledge, and leveraging it for improving the organization's performance."

Applying this definition to education, one cannot help noticing that the MDE program was launched at a specific historic juncture in the development of distance education as a discipline, that is, at a time when the information and communication technologies (ICT) led to deep transformational changes thoroughly affecting the practice and theory of distance education and training. As a consequence, the MDE was faced with a major aporia: It embarked on teaching distance education as a subject of a graduate degree program at a time when the subject itself was in flux. Moreover, the aporia was hard to ignore since the innovative delivery format of online teaching and learning sat uncomfortably with the classical body of theories informing the program's curricular content.

---

* Cf. UMUC MDE Web site: http://www.umuc.edu/programs/grad/mde/; or the respective Oldenburg Web site: http://www.mde.uni-oldenburg.de/.

† However, the issue is thoroughly treated in Volume 5 of the ASF Series under the title "'Information' and 'Knowledge'—On the Semantic Transformation of Two Central Terms" by Otto Peters (Peters, 2003).

The Tectonic Shift: From Distance Education to Online Learning

As a consequence of the ICT revolution in the late 1990s and in the first years of the new millennium, distance education as a discipline was undergoing a tectonic shift. For a better understanding of what happened, one needs to revisit traditional distance education and mark precisely the point of impact of the digital technologies leading to new teaching and learning formats—for example, online learning—in order to be able to appreciate the tensions induced.

Traditional (pre-Internet/Web-based) distance education practice was built around one major deficit: Responsive interaction at a distance was technically not feasible at the time. By "responsive," we mean a turn-around time of messages short enough to justify speaking about dialog or discussion, rather than of receiving feedback to an assignment.*

How much the whole structure of distance education was developed around this deficit can be seen by analyzing three critical aspects: (1) instructional design, (2) systems, and (3) cost.

1. *Instructional design:* Distance education had to disentangle presentation and interaction and, indeed, shift the onus of teaching toward presentation. In turn, it developed a specific instructional design approach aiming at embedding dialog into the course material itself. The respective theoretical underpinnings can be found in Holmberg's concept of "guided didactic conversation" and "tutorial in print," both elements of his "theory of the empathetic teaching–learning conversation" (Holmberg, 1960; 2007) or, though from a slightly different point of view, in Moore's "theory of transactional distance" (Moore, 1973, 2007).

2. *Systems:* The inherent shift towards the presentational aspect of teaching allowed an "industrialized" approach to distance education, leading to a specific configuration of distance education as a system (Moore and Kearsley, 2005). At its heart, there was a course development unit (including academic specialists) and a course production unit (including mass media production specialists), and at the periphery,† tutors, with the very restricted teaching remit to help students to understand the course material. The most prominent theoretical underpinning of this is certainly Peters' "theory of distance education as most industrialized form of education" (Peters, 1973, 2010).

---

* The only technology supporting responsive interaction at the time was the telephone, which was not useful as a main platform or teaching aid because it was essentially a one-on-one technology and because it could not convey written messages.

† This refers both to geographical distance to the center as well as employment status.

3. *Cost*: Systems approaches in distance education allowed a specific cost structure characterized by possibly high but fixed (!) development and production costs and comparatively low variable cost per student (due to limited interaction and use of comparatively low-cost personnel). It is on this potential for *economies of scale* and the acknowledged high quality course material that the claim of distance education as being more cost-effective does rest. (Hülsmann, 2008)

The ICT revolution in the digital era did change all this because, for the first time in history, Web-base teaching and learning arrangements allowed responsive interaction at a distance. While this spurred much enthusiasm since it seemed to address the Achilles' heel of distance education, it soon became clear that it did challenge traditional distance education arrangements. There was no rationale anymore for shifting the focus of teaching to course development. In the new virtual seminar mode of online learning, the question came up, "Why design interaction into the course material when one could take off-the-shelf material and wrap dialogue around it?" Once you take away one of the dominos, the rest of the configuration falls. In online distance education there is no longer a need for costly prefabricated course development, which in turn pushes over the scale-economies argument and with it the claim for cost-efficiency (Hülsmann, 2009).

This reading of the impact of the ICT revolution admittedly focuses on the *communicative* capabilities of ICT rather than the *information processing* capabilities. It is true that the digital technologies also afford opportunities more in line with the traditional distance education systems configuration than is suggested by the above usage of digital technologies focusing on communicative capabilities. In fact, the information processing capabilities allow all sorts of new and interesting options, ranging from simple automated multiple choice questions to interactive spreadsheets, simulations, or all sorts of software agents. Exploiting ICT along these lines would be more in line with the traditional distance education arrangements*.

However, this second way of using the affordances of the new technologies would not address the Achilles' heel of distance education, that is, its lack of responsive interaction at a distance. But fully exploiting the capabilities of digital technologies for interaction turns them into disruptive technologies. Online learning, especially in its format as "virtual seminar," is a disruptive technology as far as traditional distance education is concerned.

---

* Hülsmann (following Rumble, 2004, p. 165) distinguished the two modes of ICT usage as type-i, exploiting the information processing capabilities the ICT revolution affords, and type-c, where ICT is used to sustain a communicative bridge between real people (Hülsmann, 2004, p. 244). Type-i is in terms of cost-structure and instructional approach much in line with traditional distance education, while type-c comes with an unavoidable trade-off in terms of scale economies.

The MDE: Managing a Community of Reflective Practitioners

This above described context, especially the fascination with the new interactive responsiveness of distance education, allows us to fully appreciate the particular situation of the program at the time it was launched: The MDE is about DE and DE was in flux, as visibly epitomized by its own online delivery format.

In terms of professional development this meant professional development as development of the profession. It could not just be read as implementing a set of professional standards; these had, at least to some extent, to be invented.

In this situation, where even experienced distance educators had to explore new modes of practice, two concepts are helpful for framing our analysis of (1) the *reflective practitioner* and (2) the *community of practice*. Given that the MDE was embarking on uncharted waters and the theoretical maps available were incomplete or even misleading, the special abilities of the reflective practitioner were called for. Following Dewey, the concept of the reflective practitioner embraces the dynamic relation of reflective thinking to the educative process that continuously generates new experiences and leads its reorganize and reconstruction (Dewey, 1910, 1933).

At the same time, launching a fully fledged Master's program is not an individual endeavor for each faculty involved. It requires a group effort. Managing a group of internationally distributed faculty in this context of a tectonic shift required developing the group into a "community of practice" (Wenger, 1998) sharing new insights and experiences in a common enterprise and transforming them into a collective knowledge base that is continually negotiated and applied to teaching, as well as to administering the MDE program as a whole.

Two things were necessary for this to happen: providing a forum for articulating (making explicit) reflections on the experience of this innovative learning format (induced by the described tectonic shift) and bundling them into self-energizing feedback through the participation of a community of practice. The forum was provided by the various platforms for publication, most important among which was the ASF Series. The community of practice was first and foremost the MDE-faculty and, more widely, the community of practice of online teachers, especially those convened at the EDEN Research Workshops.

Elaborating on this background, the following three sections will describe (1) MDE faculty development, (2) EDEN Research Workshops, and (3) the ASF Series as a means for knowledge management and professional development. These three ongoing threads are intertwined, and their description makes some redundancies unavoidable: Some faculty development meetings happened in conjunction with the EDEN Research Workshops, and some articles published in the ASF Series are based on papers presented at these workshops. The EDEN Research Workshops served as a hub, allowing the MDE faculty to present their practitioner–research findings to a wider community as well as capturing some relevant ideas from the wider community of practice and feeding it back to the MDE.

MDE Faculty Development

Following the above assessment of the historical juncture at which the program was launched, there was an urgent need to involve faculty, not only in course but also in curriculum development, and in various other aspects of program quality management. There was no off-the-shelf standard curriculum for a Master's program in distance education and even less so for delivering it fully online. In fact, one of the affordances of the new communicative capabilities was blurring the roles of course development and academic tutoring. All these decisions, formative for the curriculum and shaping the process could—and better should not—be decided *par ordre de mufti*. It can be argued that ownership and motivation is considerably enhanced when faculty are involved in these program management decisions.*

Meeting face-to-face played an important role in this process. Face-to-face meetings may not be a necessary ingredient to forge a community of practice of geographically dispersed faculty but during the initial development of the MDE program, extraordinary efforts were taken to allow a few of such most helpful opportunities. Face-to-face meetings for program planning, curriculum design, collaboration, and professional development took place in 2000, 2001 (this time in conjunction with the 20th ICDE World Conference in Germany), and two more meetings in 2002 (one of those in conjunction with the 8th Sloan-C Conference in Orlando, Florida). Since 2004, the faculty meetings regularly are taking place on occasion and in connection with the bi-annual EDEN Research Workshops.

To support faculty, development with respect to teaching has to be read against the described background of deep transformation in distance education. Many faculty members, while being old hands in distance education, were new to online learning. In fact, given the thin layer of experience to draw from (due to the very novelty of the technology), all of us entered waters largely uncharted by the classical theories. This applied to handling the technical features of the learning management system (which was learned fairly quickly†) and to exploiting the additional affordances of *responsive interaction* pedagogically. For lead faculty, a mandatory 5-week WebTycho course provided the required navigational skills, together with the first very useful pedagogical advice. Beyond that, and especially for visiting experts and guest lecturers, additional help and/or peer teaching opportunities were offered (Brindley et al., 2003).

---

* There is, however, another side to the coin. Ownership contradicts depersonalization policies. Emphasizing ownership produces an uncomfortable dependency on key personnel. Preferring depersonalization may mean having to run the program with only superficially interested "mercenaries."

† It has to be said that, at the beginning, the LMS used (WebTycho) was not as convenient as what was available later. At the time, to present messages using styles (e.g., italics, colors, numbering) or including pictures, one had to edit HTML code and handle FT Protocol. All not difficult—if appropriate faculty support is available.

While the focus of faculty development has initially been to capture/elicit knowledge from within the MDE, there were increasingly good reasons to open up to a wider community of practice in order that personal experiences could be shared and one could draw on the experience of others. In this context conferences played a major role: Here the focus shifted from the world conferences of the International Council for Open and Distance Education (ICDE; 1997, 1999, and 2001) to the bi-annual research workshops of the European Distance and E-learning Network (EDEN), beginning in 2002.

The European Distance Education and E-Learning Network (EDEN)

The Second EDEN Research Workshop on Research and Policy in Open and Distance Learning in 2002 was a starting point for paying particular attention to this forum. The authors of this chapter presented at this workshop on "Asynchronous Learning Networks—May This Work?" (Bernath and Hülsmann, 2002).

The Third EDEN Research Workshop in Oldenburg in 2004 let to a flurry of preparatory activities. Incentives were given to MDE faculty, alumni, and students for submitting papers to the conference. The turn out was impressive: 17 papers of a total of 84 accepted conference papers have been originated by MDE faculty and students (11 from faculty members and six from students). One of the 18 workshop sessions was sponsored by the Volkswagen AutoUni exclusively for MDE students.* It is worth noting that all six students became distance education professionals: Two joined the MDE faculty, three became administrators at institutions in higher education, and one made a career as a manager and trainer in the private sector.

Of the 17 papers, seven reflected on the MDE, nine were related to the MDE in various contexts, and only one was not related to the MDE at all. The impressive presence of the MDE at the conference even served as a "recruitment drive": In the wake of the conference, five presenters became members of the MDE faculty team.†

The Fourth EDEN Research Workshop on Research into Online Distance Education and E-Learning: Making the Difference was organized by EDEN in cooperation with the Open University of Catalonia (UOC). This workshop took place October 25–28, 2006 in Barcelona/Castelldefels, Spain.

At this conference event, MDE faculty contributed to one of the highlights of the conference: the panel discussion between Peters, Holmberg, and Moore, three of the major theoretical contributors to the field. The panel discussion has been summarized by Bernath and Vidal and published in *Distance and Savoirs*, the leading French journal on distance education (Bernath and Vidal, 2007). Together

---

* Workshop 15: Creating Global Proximity in a Corporate University: Collaborative Learning at Volkswagen AutoUni.
† Recalculating MDE presence with hindsight (i.e., including these members as part of the MDE), the percentage of papers contributed by MDE associates would rise up to 26%.

with a comment on the session by Hülsmann, was also published in *Distance and Savoir* (Hülsmann, 2008), these papers feed back into the Foundation of Distance Education course (OMDE 601) of the MDE as recommended readings.

The Fifth EDEN Research Workshop on Researching and Promoting Access to Education and Training: The Role of Distance Education and E-Learning in Technology-Enhanced Environments was organized by EDEN in cooperation with the Centre National de l' Enseignement a Distance (CNED) in France. This workshop took place October 25–28, 2008 in Paris.

Again there were significant contributions from the MDE community of practice. If one includes all those involved for some time in the MDE, such MDE associates contributed two keynotes and four presentations. Altogether, close to 15 MDE team members were present and contributed in different ways: ranging from key note speeches, session chairs, and presenters of major papers or posters up to the MDE students presenting their experiences in so called "cracker-barrel" sessions.

Some of the research directly originated from within the MDE discussed the issue, to which extent one should enforce active participation in collaborative learning groups. The faculty presenting this research (Brindley et al., 2009*) had the experience of coteaching, which led to trust and common interest in becoming a community of inquiry, able to conduct a common research, albeit all three contributors are located in different countries (Canada, Germany, and the United States). The same applied for another team from the United States and Israel (Kurtz et al., 2004) who developed a joint research agenda as part of their shared MDE experience, albeit their research was aimed at surveying a wider international audience of online learners.

To give MDE students the opportunity to present at and be actively involved in an international conference remained part of the MDE knowledge management strategies: On occasion of this workshop two MDE students presented their experiences with the program in cracker-barrel sessions.†

The Sixth EDEN Research Workshop will be held in Budapest in October 2010. It is planned to mobilize the MDE community of practice to participate in full force again. The time allocated will permit forming research teams and beyond, serendipitously reflecting on practice, asking specific questions, and reporting some evidence-based findings at the conference. We hope to draw from these research

---

* Brindley, Blaschke and Walti: Creating Effective Collaborative Learning Groups in an Online Environment; the session was chaired by another MDE faculty, Gila Kurtz from Israel.

† Cracker-barrell sessions are short presentations where a person delivers repeatedly a short presentation (including a discussion about 15 minutes) to a changing conference audience moving from one table ("cracker barrel") to the other. According to the Merriam-Webster online dictionary, the term refers to the cracker barrel in country stores of the past, around which customers lounged for informal conversation. It is intended to underline the "friendly, homespun character" of the communication.

initiatives to publish a volume in the ASF Series to celebrate the 10th anniversary of the MDE in 2010.*

The lesson learned from conferencing is twofold: Preparing for a conference can trigger substantial additional efforts, thus advancing extraordinary opportunities for eliciting/generating new knowledge. Getting to know each other better by participating as a group contributes considerably to the constitution of a community of practice. In fact, the occasion of the conference also was used for convening a small MDE faculty meeting which set precedence for the EDEN Research Workshop to come.† In addition, the substantial presence of the MDE at a single conference arguably contributes optimally to project the program image internationally.

It can again be fairly argued that especially in three respects participating in the EDEN Research Workshop has proved its value: evaluating the role of the EDEN Research Workshop against the previous definition of knowledge management as capturing existing knowledge distributed within the organization; eliciting new knowledge from its members; and leveraging all this to improve the organization's performance. In terms of capturing knowledge and eliciting/generating new knowledge, much of the same arguments apply for the EDEN Workshops as for the ASF Series (see text to come). In fact, the EDEN Workshops defined a sort of rallying point that repeatedly triggered substantial academic efforts, which fed into the ASF Series and consequently into the MDE, be it as contributing to content or influencing procedures.

In terms of contributing to the formation of a *community of practice,* the whole package, working together to submit papers and participating as a group in a conference (which involves presenting together, or presenting to each other and listening to each other) allows forming a mutual understanding as persons, intellectuals, and researchers, from which, hopefully, trust emerges that moulds faculty, engaged in a common endeavor, to form a community in a less superficial meaning of the word.

The ASF Book Series on Distance Education

Possibly the most effective medium for *professional development* (as contributing to the *development of the profession*) was and still is the ASF Series. When applying our working definition of KM as capturing existing knowledge, eliciting new knowledge and leveraging it for improved performance, there is ample evidence that the ASF Series did all that.

A forerunner of the ASF Series, also closely associated with the MDE, merits attention: *The Final Report and Documentation of the Virtual Seminar for Professional*

---

* It is by accident that slot 10 in the ASF Series is still free. A volume was planned aimed at supporting a course (OMDE 626) within the program that later was merged (OMDE 625 and OMDE 626 were merged into DEMP 625), which rendered the original concept of the book obsolete.
† More on this under "Faculty Development."

Development in Distance Education (Bernath and Rubin, eds.), 1999). This publication is remarkable because it presents the complete transcript of the asynchronous communication between all 48 participants of the Virtual Seminar. It also succeeded in convening major experts in the field of distance education from various continents to test the waters of online teaching and learning and eventually influenced the syllabus for the MDE's portal course, the Foundations of Distance Education (OMDE 601).

Two concepts emerged in the context of the virtual seminar, which may be used here to illustrate reflective practice: Bernath's "ripple effect" and Fritsch's concept of the "witness learner," which eventually inspired Beaudoin's discussion of the "invisible learner" (Beaudoin, 2003, 2009). Bernath argued that the pace in asynchronous text-based conferencing is optimal for reflective dialogue. While turn-around times in traditional distance education were too long to be engaging, the pace of asynchronous discussion, with a response time close of around 24 hours, was short enough to keep up the motivational tension while allowing more time for reflection than the turn-taking of a face-to-face discussion: Posting a message seemed much like "throwing a stone into the water (the incoming messages) and creating ripples that expand outward in each recipient's head (pondering on the content of the message)" (Bernath and Rubin, 1999). Asynchronous conferencing, therefore, strikes the optimal balance between the spontaneity of a face-to-face discussion and the long return times, which prevented in traditional distance education any exchange which convincingly could pass as dialog or discussion.

Fritsch coined the concept of the "learning witness" in an evaluation of the virtual seminar when many participants in the virtual seminar reported that they profited a lot from the online seminar *in spite not having actively posted messages*. The term identifies an important potential of online learning (different from the usual situation of traditional distance education): that the learner can learn (as in a conventional face-to-face classroom) from observing other participants interaction with the teacher and among peers. Beaudoin, reviewing the "Final Report and Documentation of the Virtual Seminar ..." (which comprises Frisch's evaluation), was intrigued by this observation and later on published (in vol. 6 of the ASF Series) his own research findings on the "invisible learner."

Shifting the focus now to the ASF Series we do so from the vantage point of our definition of KM, professional development and reflective practice.* The treatment will not be strictly chronological but will begin with the volumes which best could illustrate the idea of "capturing the existing expertise" of the faculty involved, then focus on those volumes which best epitomize the concerted effort of the MDE as community of practice to generate new knowledge, and eventually comments on the later volumes which open up to the wider community of practice as represented, for instance, at the EDEN Research Workshops.

---

* For more detail on the ASF Series cf. the Annex.

Arguably no other Master of Distance Education is so well grounded in the theoretical canon of distance education as the MDE. One of the reasons is that a number of seminal contributors to this canon were involved in the MDE right from the beginning. Holmberg is one of these formative figures of the discipline. Both volumes 4 and 11, which he contributed, were aimed at updating his opus magnus (*Theory and Practice of Distance Education*, 1995). Holmberg's conceptualization of distance educations by its two *constituent elements* (content presentation and interaction) tallies nicely to the two aspects afforded by the *information* and *communication* technologies (ICT), one enhancing the sophistication of content presentation, one facilitating "responsive interaction at a distance." This convinces Holmberg that while acknowledging the enormous potential afforded by the new technologies his old conceptualization of the nature of distance education remains still valid.

Vol. 5 edited by Otto Peters on *Distance Education in Transition. New Trends and Challenges* is the "best seller" of the ASF Series and the internationally most widely consulted book of the series. The author addresses what was previously labeled as the "tectonic shift" in distance education. The volume includes detailed reflections of the opportunities afforded by the new technologies ("new digital spaces"), an elaborate reflection on the concepts of information and knowledge, as well as a reflection on the experience as visiting expert in the MDE. The volume was expanded in several editions. In the most recent forthcoming 5th edition, Peters will revisit his "industrialization theory" and comment on its lasting relevance.

Both volumes from Holmberg and Peters are required reading in the Foundations of Distance Education course (OMDE 601), and both authors are regularly participating as visiting experts in this course.

Volume 6, edited by Ulrich Bernath and Eugen Rubin, on *Reflections on Teaching and Learning in an Online Master's Program—A Case Study* is possibly the best illustration of the MDE as *community of practice*. It brings together MDE faculty, visiting experts (and indeed students), showing them as reflective practitioners in their field. In fact, producing the volume helped to turn this group of internationally distributed faculty into a community with a common purpose with respect to the MDE. The introductory Bernath and Rubin chapter gave the endeavor a history that became a reference source when the program applied for (and received) awards and accreditations. Beaudoin contributed a paper on the "invisible learner," which, as explained above, was sparked by Fritsch's concept of witness learning. Hülsmann, contributed two chapters, one on costs, which pointed out the different cost-structure of online learning and traditional distance education, and another one, which reflected on his experience in teaching online courses ("Texts that talk back"). A chapter on faculty support addressed the challenges experienced at this time of transformational change by distance educators testing the waters of online learning. Brindley et al. (2009) addressed this issue of high practical importance. (The chapter is seminal in the sense that its ideas are expanded in Volume 9.)

It is worth mentioning that the last section of the volume is dedicated to "voices of students" (Christine Walti, Brian F. Fox, Linda J. Smith, and Susanne Offenbartl) who describe and reflect upon their experiences in the program. All of the students contributing to this volume completed their degree and meanwhile hold important positions in the field of distance education. Encouraging them and giving them a platform for publication certainly helped them to make first important steps in their careers.

The volume nicely illustrates that professional development has to be read in two ways: as supporting the implementation of professional standards, as well as "professional development as development of the profession." The program, hence, had to be both innovative and experimental. This meant that faculty and program managers had to reflect on what they were doing and, at the same time, develop standards for a graduate program in distance education. While much of the curriculum is open to inspection (since it is accessible online) the volume was also meant to offer insights about the process, including critical reflections and, indeed, the emotional impact of developing and participating in such a project. The volume is also "recommended reading" in the *Foundations of Distance Education* (OMDE 601).

Greville Rumble, editor of Volume 7 on *Papers and Debates on the Economics and Costs of Distance and Online Learning,* more than most other distance educators, has theoretically appreciated the consequences of the impact of new technologies. His distinction of type A and type B technologies marked this impact.* Rumble has profoundly realized that any form of distance education fully exploiting the communicative capabilities facilitated by the new technologies (e.g., the virtual seminar approach afforded by online learning) comes with a different cost-structure and suggests a different instructional approach (Why design interactivity into the course material when you can wrap off-the shelf material—say, textbooks) in real dialog (in the form of online conferencing)? Rumble clearly appreciates that fully exploiting the communication capabilities will 'drive horses and carriages' through traditional distance teaching arrangements. More than others, Rumble identifies the trade-offs this has especially in terms of costs. Major parts of the volume are "required reading" in the *The Costs and Economics of Distance Education* (OMDE 606), and the editor contributes regularly to this course as visiting expert.

Volume 2 by Thomas Hülsmann on *The Costs of Open Learning: A Handbook* dates from research conducted at a time (second half of the 90s) when the online teaching format was still in an early and experimental stage. Though most of the cost figures are meanwhile dated 'The handbook' is still interesting from a methodological point of view. It finds that different technologies (print, radio, TV, etc.) differ significantly, albeit with large variations, in terms of cost of production per hour of students learning (cost/SLH). While most of the case studies look at traditional distance education formats, comparing the case studies on the OU and on

---

* His distinction of type A and type B technologies (Rumble, 2001/2004) were merely renamed by Hülsmann (2004) as type-i and type-c applications, in order to semantically link the two different sets of capabilities afforded by the new digital technologies with the respective letters in the ICT acronym.

the Virtual Seminar, the shift in terms of cost-structures induced by exploiting the affordances of online communication are all too visible. The volume is made available as "recommended reading" in the *The Costs and Economics of Distance Education* (OMDE 606, a course developed and regularly taught by TH as lead faculty).

Michael Beaudoin had been involved in DE for more than 20 years when he wrote Volume 8 on *Reflections on Research, Faculty and Leadership in Distance Education*. The volume is constructed to confront his two decades of experiences in traditional distance education with the more recent experiences of online teaching as MDE faculty member. Hence, the volume is constructed as publishing a distance educator's insights from the pre-Internet times and post-fixing to each chapter an epilogue written from the vantage point of his new experience as an online professor. This way Beaudoin addresses the changing research agenda, the new role of the professoriate, as well as emerging leadership issues in distance education. The volume is also "recommended reading" in the *The Management of Distance Education 2: Leadership in Distance Education* (OMDE 604; the course was developed and is regularly taught by MB as lead faculty).

Jane Brindley, Christine Walti, and Olaf Zawacki-Richter edited *Learner Support in Open, Distance and Online Learning Environments* (Volume 9), which is in the context of this article of particular interest because of the role of the volume within the MDE program development, and the contributions to the volume coming from the MDE faculty (including those contributors joining the MDE faculty only after the date of its publication).

The first item is dealt with quickly. Many of the papers for this volume had been initially prepared for the 4th EDEN Research Workshop. The workshop itself and the faculty meeting in its wake allowed extensive personal encounters and thus had a formative role in constituting the MDE faculty as a *community of practice*. The massive presence of the MDE at the Oldenburg EDEN Research Workshop even attracted new members to the MDE community. More importantly, the very fact of producing this volume gives credence to the importance the issue of learner and faculty support should receive within the program.

The volume also includes reprints of the keynote presentations to the EDEN Research Workshop in Oldenburg by Terry Anderson (research chair at Athabasca University and editor of IRRODL) and Nick Allen (former provost and chief academic officer at UMUC). These are available on DVD, attached to the book.

Volume 9 serves as required reading in Student Support in Distance Education and Training (OMDE 608), developed by Brindley and regularly taught by Brindley and Walti.

Volume 12 edited by Hilary Perraton, Bernadette Robinson, and Charlotte Creed on International Case Studies of Teacher Education at a Distance can be read to some extent as a reality check for those who view distance learning from the narrow vantage point of ICT-supported distance education. Though focussing on teacher education, the book provides a wide range of case studies from around the world. All chapters are similarly structured (covering country background, purpose, costs, and outcomes) which facilitates comparisons across quite different contexts. Volume 12 serves as recommended reading in Distance Education, Globalization and Development (DEMP 625) where Perraton has regularly served as visiting expert.

To sum up, it is worth emphasizing that all books of the ASF Series are now freely available as e-books under http://www.mde.uni-oldenburg.de/40574.html. This way, the series will be more widely (albeit selectively) used within the MDE program.

Evaluating the ASF Series against the previous definition of knowledge management as (1) capturing existing knowledge distributed within the organization; (2) eliciting new knowledge from its members; and (3) leveraging all this to improve the organization's performance, it can be fairly argued that in all three respects the ASF Series has proved its value.

i. *Capturing existing knowledge*: Many renowned experts have volunteered to use the platform offered by the ASF Series to report on their wide range of experiences (e.g., Holmberg, Peters, Rumble).

ii. *Eliciting new knowledge/generating new knowledge*: The tension produced by the tectonic shift between new online delivery format and a curriculum grounded in a canon of classical theory led to a number of major new contributions (e.g., Peters' discussion of the "new digital learning spaces," or Hülsmann's discussion of threaded discussions in "texts that talk back") or "nuggets" such as the "ripple effect," the "witness learner," the "invisible learner," type-i/type-c classification of digital technologies, and the portfolio as a tool for reflective learning, to name but a few. That many of the volumes were reviewed in major distance education journals and at least one volume has been translated in other languages amply demonstrate that the series has contributed to "professional development as development of the profession."

iii. *Leveraging all this to improve the organization's performance*: The primary goal of the MDE as a program is to form future managers in distance education. The ASF Series contributed in two ways to achieve its goals: by adding to content and by informing the process. Along these lines, most of the volumes serve as mandatory or recommended readings in at least one of the courses. Beyond adding to the corpus of readings and course material some ideas also informed the process. Making "visible participation" contributing to the grade emerged partially as a response to the discussion about lurkers (invisible learners) or witness learners and the role of articulating one's thoughts as essential for learning. The reflection on the portfolio both emerged from practice as it increasingly informed practice. There are secondary aims such as enhancing the visibility and the prestige of the program. That this objective was achieved can be gleaned from the various reviews of most of the volumes in many leading journals as well as from the fact that some of the volumes have been translated. The role of the series also helped the program to win a number of prestigious awards and accreditations (Sloan, 2003; UCEA, 2003, 2009; EFMD-CEL accreditation 2007).

Conclusion

In summary, unlike in many other discussions on knowledge management, we did not foreground technologies in this discussion as management tools. However, technology development plays a pivotal role since it is exactly the affordances induced by the new digital technologies (especially by their capability for responsive interaction at a distance) that produced the transformational situation, in which knowledge management as managing a community of reflective practitioners was possibly the best, possibly the only, management option. The MDE has distance education as the object of study while this object of study is undergoing transformation. Practice and theory had to co-evolve and feed into each other, creating a reenforcing loop.

We hope to have demonstrated that (1) the described faculty development measures, including face-to-face faculty meetings to strengthen the MDE as community of practice, (2) the use of the EDEN Research Workshops as forum to open to a wider community of practice, and (3) the ASF Series, served its purpose for knowledge management as defined for this paper.

Given that we have linked the above described approach to the tectonic shift towards ICT-supported distance education and e-learning, one may ask if the tectonic movement has not come to rest and is now well reflected in research and theory. To an increasing extent, we can now inform our practice by off-the-shelf theory rather than having to rely on our own reflective practice.

However, distance education is tied to technology. Paraphrasing Peters, one could say that "distance education is the most technology-supported mode of education." And the relentless pace of technological development makes sure that the "gales of creative distractions"* are not abating.

References

Beaudoin, M. (1999). Book Review: U. Bernath and E. Rubin (Eds.) (1999). Final Report and Documentation of the Virtual Seminar for Professional Development in Distance Education, Oldenburg: BIS-Verlag. In *Continuing Higher Education Review*, Vol. 63, 1999, pp. 158–162.

Beaudoin, M. (2003). Learning or Lurking? Tracking the "Invisible" Online Student. In U. Bernath and E. Rubin (Eds.) (2003), *Reflections on Teaching and Learning in an Online Master Program. A Case Study*. Oldenburg: BIS-Verlag. pp. 121–129.

---

* Schumpeter (1942).

Beaudoin, M. (2009). Reflections on Seeking the "Invisible" Online Learner (and Instructor). In U. Bernath, A. Szücs, A.Tait, and M. Vidal (Eds.) (2009). *Distance and E-Learning in Transition: Learning Innovation, Technology and Social Challenges.* London/Hoboken NJ: ISTE Ltd and John Wiley & Sons. pp. 529–542.

Bernath, U. and Hülsmann, T. (2002). Asynchronous discussions in virtual seminars: might they work? In: *Research and Policy in Open and Distance Learning.* Research Workshop Book. The Second Research Workshop of EDEN, University of Hildesheim, Germany, March 21–23, 2002, pp. 202–204. Budapest: EDEN Secretariat. [http://www.c3l.uni-oldenburg.de/literat/eden0203.pdf].

Bernath, U. and Rubin, E. (1998). A Virtual Seminar for International Professional Development in Distance Education, Universities in a Digital Era. Transformation, Innovation and Tradition. Roles and Perspectives of Open and Distance Learning. *Proceedings of the 7th European Distance Education Network (EDEN) Conference*, held at the University of Bologna, Italy, June 24–26, 1998 (Vol. 1, pp. 141–144). Budapest: EDEN.

Bernath, U. and Rubin, E. (Eds.) (1999). Final Report and Documentation of the Virtual Seminar for Professional Development in Distance Education. Oldenburg: BIS-Verlag. http://www.c3l.uni-oldenburg.de/publikationen/docum.htm.

Bernath, U. and Rubin, E. (Eds.) (1999). Final Report and Documentation of the Virtual Seminar for Professional Development in Distance Education—A Project within the AT&T Global Distance Learning Initiative sponsored by the AT&T Foundation and The International Council for Open and Distance Education (ICDE), Oldenburg: BIS-Verlag. http://www.c3l.uni-oldenburg.de/literat/docum.htm.

Bernath, U. and Rubin, E. (1999). An International Virtual Seminar for University Faculty and Administrators: Professional Development in Distance Education—A Successful Experiment and Future Directions. Paper presented to the 19th ICDE World Conference in Vienna, June 23, 1999. http://nova.umuc.edu/~erubin/icde99.html.

Bernath, U. and Rubin, E. (2001). Professional development in distance education—A successful experiment and future directions. In F. Lockwood and A. Gooley (Eds.), *Innovations in Open and Distance Learning, Successful Development of Online and Web-Based Learning* (pp. 213–223). London: Kogan Page. Retrieved January 5, 2010 from http://www.c3l.uni-oldenburg.de/literat/uligene.htm.

Bernath, U. and Vidal, M. (2007). The theories and the theorists: Why theory is important for research. *Distances et Savoirs*, 5(3), 427–458.

Bernath, U. and Szücs, A. (Eds.) (2004). Supporting the learner in distance education and e-learning. *Proceedings of the Third EDEN Research Workshop*, Carl von Ossietzky University of Oldenburg, Germany, March 4–6, 2004. http://www.c3l.uni-oldenburg. de/publikationen/eden.pdf.

Brindley, J.E., Zawacki, O., and Roberts, J. (2003). Support services for online faculty: The provider and the user perspectives. In U. Bernath and E. Rubin (eds.), *Reflections on Teaching and Learning in an Online Master Program. A Case Study.* Oldenburg: BIS-Verlag; (6), pp. 137–165 [http://www.c3l.uni-oldenburg.de/literat/bzr.pdf.

Brindley, J. E., Walti, C., and Blaschke, L. M. (June 2009). Creating Effective Collaborative Learning Groups in an Online Environment. In *The International Review of Research in Open and Distance Learning (IRRODL)*, Vol. 10(3). [http://www.irrodl.org/index.php/ irrodl/article/view/675/1271].

Dewey, J. (1933). *How We Think. A Restatement of the Relation of Reflective Thinking to the Educative Process.* Lexington.

Fritsch, H. (1999). Host contacted, waiting for reply. In U. Bernath and E. Rubin (Eds), *Final Report and Documentation of the Virtual Seminar for Professional Development in Distance Education*, Oldenburg: BIS-Verlag. pp. 355–378.

Holmberg, B. (1960). On the methods of teaching by correspondence. *Lunds universitetsaar-skrift* N.F.Avd. 1, Vol. 54 (2).

Holmberg, B. (2005). *The Evolution, Principles and Practices of Distance Education*, Oldenburg: BIS-Verlag.

Holmberg, B. (2007). Börje Holmberg on his theory of the empathetic teaching-learning conversation. In U. Bernath and M. Vidal, The theories and the theorists: Why theory is important for research. *Distances et Savoirs,* Vol. 5, No 3, pp. 431–433.

Hülsmann, T. (2008). Peters, Holmberg, Moore—a personal configuration. *Distances et Savoirs, 6*(3), 455–479.

Hülsmann, T. (2004). The two-pronged attack on learner support: Costs and the centrifugal forces of convergence. In U. Bernath and A. Szücz (Eds), Supporting the learner in distance education and e-learning. *Proceedings of the Third EDEN Research Workshop*, Carl von Ossietzky University of Oldenburg, Germany, March 4–6, 2004, Oldenburg: BIS-Verlag.

Hülsmann, T. (2009). Access and efficiency in the development of distance education and e-learning. In U. Bernath, A. Szücs, A. Tait, and M. Vidal (Eds), *Distance and E-Learning in Transition: Learning Innovation, Technology and Social Challenge*. London/Hoboken NJ: ISTE Ltd and John Wiley & Sons, pp. 119–140.

Kurtz, G., Beaudoin, M., and Sagee, R. (July 2004). From Campus to Web: The Changing Roles of Faculty from Classroom to Online Teaching, 28 pp. In *Journal of Educators Online*, Vol. 1(1) [http://www.thejeo.com/Archives/Volume1Number1/Kurtz%20Final.pdf].

MDE Program Self-Assessment Report for the EFMD CEL Accreditation (June 2006) http://www.c3l.uni-oldenburg.de/literat/EFMDfinalrevised.pdf.

Moore, M.G. (1973).Towards a theory of independent learning and teaching. In *Journal of Higher Education,* Vol. 44, pp. 661–679.

Moore, M.G. (2007). The theory of transactional distance (Chapter 8), In *Handbook of Distance Education*, 2nd ed. Mahwah NJ: Lawrence Erlbaum Associates.

Moore. M.G. and Kearsley, G. (2005). *Distance Education. A Systems View*, Belmont, CA: Wadsworth.

Peters, O. (2003). "Information" and "Knowledge"—On the semantic transformation of two central terms. In O. Peters, *Distance Education in Transition—New Trends and Challenges,* Oldenburg: BIS-Verlag, pp. 129–156.

Peters, O. (2010, 5th ed.). *Distance Education in Transition—Developments and Issues*, Oldenburg: BIS-Verlag.

Rumble, G. (2004). The costs of providing student support services (2001). In G. Rumble, *Papers and Debates on the Costs and Economics of Distance Education and Online Learning* (Vol. 7, pp. 163–174). Oldenburg: BIS-Verlag.

Schumpeter, J. A. (1942). *Capitalism, Socialism and Democracy.* New York: Harper & Brothers.

Wenger, E. 1998. *Communities of Practice.* Cambridge: Cambridge University Press.

Annex

The ASF book series on distance education under review (as far as we know) and in use as MDE textbooks.

Vol. 2: Hülsmann, T. (2000). *The Costs of Open Learning: A Handbook*, Oldenburg: BIS-Verlag. 165 pp.

Reviewed in *Open Learning*, Vol 16(3), 2001; *Open Praxis*, Vol. 1, 2002; *IRRODL*, Vol. 4(1), 2003; *The American Journal of Distance Education*, Vol. 19(3), 2005.

Recommended reading in OMDE606 Costs and Economics of Distance Education (http://www.mde.uni-oldenburg.de/download/course606.pdf); the former course title was: *The Management of Distance Education 1: Cost Analysis.*

Vol. 4: Holmberg, B. (2001; 2003 2nd ed.). *Distance Education in Essence. An Overview of Theory and Practice in the Early Twenty-first Century*, Oldenburg: BIS-Verlag. 113 pp.

Reviewed in *Open Learning*, Vol. 17(3), 2002; *DETC Memo* Sep/Oct 2002 (reprinted in *EADL Newsletter* 2002); *The American Journal of Distance Education*, Vol. 19(3), 2005.

Was required reading in OMDE601 *Foundations of Distance Education* Spring 2002 through Spring 2005; then replaced by **Vol. 11**.

Vol. 5: Peters, O. (2002; 2003 2nd; 2003 3rd; 2004 4th; 2010 5th ed.). Distance Education in Transition—Developments and Issues (up to 4th ed.: "New Trends and Challenges"), Oldenburg: BIS-Verlag. 1st ed. 181 pp.; 4th ed. 273 pp.

Translated into: Spanish by Universidad de Guadalajara in 2002, Portuguese by Editora Unisinos in 2003; the Chinese edition appeared as part of the *Series of Classic Works and Papers in Open and Distance Learning* edited by Prof. Zhang Demin, President of the Shanghai TV University and UNESCO Chair in Distance Education for East Asia.

Reviewed in *Open Learning*, Vol. 17(3), 2002; *IRRODL*, Vol. 4(2), 2003; *The American Journal of Distance Education*, Vol. 19(3), 2005.

Required reading in OMDE601 *Foundations of Distance Education* and at UBC/Monterrey's Master of Educational Technology (MET).

Vol. 6: Bernath, U. and Rubin, E. (Eds.) (2003). *Reflections on Teaching and Learning in an Online Master Program—A Case Study.* Oldenburg: BIS-Verlag. 295 pp.

Reviewed in *Open Learning*, Vol. 19(1), 2004; *IRRODL* Vol. 5(1), 2004; *The American Journal of Distance Education*, Vol. 19(3), 2005; *Distances et Savoirs*, Vol. 4(1), 2006.

Recommended reading in OMDE601 *Foundations of Distance Education* and at University of New Brunswick in Spring 2004.

Vol. 7: Rumble, G. (Ed.) (2004). *Papers and Debates on the Economics and Costs of Distance and Online Learning*, Oldenburg: BIS-Verlag. 192 pp.

Reviewed in IRRODL Vol 5(3), 2004; *Indian Journal of Open Learning*, Vol 14(2), 2005; *The American Journal of Distance Education*, Vol 19(3), 2005; *Distances et Savoirs*, Vol 4(1), 2006.

Required reading in OMDE606 Costs and Economics of Distance Education (http://www.mde.uni-oldenburg.de/download/course606.pdf); the former course title was: The Management of Distance Education 1: Cost Analysis.

Vol. 8: Beaudoin, M. (2004). *Reflections on Research, Faculty and Leadership in Distance Education*, Oldenburg: BIS-Verlag. 141 pp.

Won the Charles A. Wedemeyer Award in 2005 of UCEA's Distance Learning Community of Practice.

Reviewed in *IRRODL,* Vol 6(2), 2005.

Required reading in DEMP604 *Leadership in Distance Education.*

Vol. 9: Brindley, J. E.,Walti, C. and Zawacki-Richter, O. (Eds.)(2004). *Learner Support in Open, Distance and Online Learning Environments (+ DVD-Video).* 327 pp.

Reviewed in *Indian Journal of Open Learning,* Vol 14(1), 2005; IRRODL, Vol. 6(2), 2005; *The American Journal of Distance Education,* Vol. 19(3), 2005.

Required reading in OMDE608 Student Support in Distance Education and Training.

The DVD has been used in the "Web Course Design Community" at Stephen F. Austin State University (USA) in Fall 2005.

Vol. 11: Holmberg, B. (2005). *The Evolution, Principles and Practices of Distance Education,* Oldenburg: BIS-Verlag. 171 pp.

Won the price for the "Publication of the Year 2005" awarded by Forum DistancE-Learning (FDL).

Required reading in OMDE601 *Foundations of Distance Education* since Summer 2005 to date.

Vol. 12: Perraton, H., Robinson, B. and Creed, C. (Eds.) (2007). *International Case Studies of Teacher Education at a Distance,* Oldenburg: BIS-Verlag. 311 pp.

Vol. 13: Bernath, U. and Sangrà, A. (Eds.) (2007). Research on Competence Development in Online Distance Education and E-Learning: Selected Papers from the 4th EDEN Research Workshop in Castelldefels/Spain October 25–28, 2006, Oldenburg: BIS-Verlag. 262 pp.

The URL of the ASF Series: http://www.mde.uni-oldenburg.de/40574.html.

Chapter 15

Knowledge Management, E-Learning, and the Role of the Academic Library

Stephen Miller

Contents

Introduction

Academic libraries have a long and distinguished history of managing society's information and knowledge, and with the revolution in networked technology are continually growing and evolving their resources and services to meet the needs of a technologically sophisticated, well-connected, and geographically-distributed clientele. With the development of e-learning and e-scholarship, libraries have continued to serve the missions of their institutions by providing critical information resources, educational support, and services online at a distance: "Significant changes are taking place in the academic library in response to available technologies, the needs and wants of remote users, and the increasing popularity of distance and online learning" (Johnson and Magusin, 2005, p. 8).

This chapter will focus on the unique roles that academic libraries and librarians in e-learning environments can play in knowledge management initiatives, in contributing to knowledge management within the academic information infrastructure, and in implementing knowledge management practices and technology to enhance and improve their own organizations to better fulfill their missions in supporting scholarship and research. The intended audience of this chapter is e-learning administrators and practitioners in higher education, and it will also be a useful and informative overview for librarians and library administrators considering knowledge management initiatives. A basic understanding of the fundamentals of knowledge management theory and practices is assumed and is not covered in-depth.

Libraries for E-Learning

Fundamentally, "Libraries serve as a mechanism for making knowledge available in communities and organizations" (Lewis, 2007, p. 419). The choice of the word "knowledge" versus "information" is telling, for as will be discussed in this chapter, libraries not only manage tangible knowledge as recorded in books, online resources, documents, maps, photographs, and other materials, but are also facilitators of tacit knowledge through their educational activities and role in bringing people together. Libraries form a core part of the academic/scholarly information infrastructure, defined as "a collective term for the technical, social, and political framework that encompasses the people, technology, tools, and services used to facilitate the distributed, collaborative use of content over time and distance" (Borgmann, 2007, p. 19).

Brad Wheeler (2008) makes the point that academic endeavors prefixed with "e-" such as e-science, e-research, and e-scholarship, will, like the phenomenon of "e-business" in the 1990s, eventually lose their "e-" prefix as digital technologies become more firmly embedded in the activities of scholarship. Likewise, we should expect the concept of "e-learning" to eventually simply become "learning" as fully online and hybrid classrooms increasingly become the norm. The *Chronicle of Higher*

Education's recent analysis of trends and prediction of the shape of the university of 2020 suggests that with the rapid growth of online education, "the migration of most learning to computers may lead to a new kind of "dispersed university," with students working in their own homes. All teaching and monitoring of progress and quality would take place online" (Van Der Werf and Sabatier, 2009, p. 11).

Libraries for the support of such online and hybrid/blended learning and scholarship will likewise be increasingly based around digital collections and services offered digitally and from a distance. Over the past 50 years, academic libraries have embraced technology as a method of automating their operations, providing public access to collections, providing full-text resources through research databases and the Internet, and most recently beginning to develop transformative applications of technology to support scholarly communication, expand services, and create new tools for information discovery and access (Lynch, 2000). While most academic libraries will continue to maintain collections of physical materials for the foreseeable future (Arms, 2000), supporting e-learning requires the immediate access provided by online resources, as well as the infrastructure to quickly provide traditional paper-based materials in digital format to remote users. More significantly, libraries and librarians serve an important educational role in e-learning as both guides and educators, teaching students the skills necessary to navigate through today's often bewildering information environment: "The principal challenge of the electronic revolution is how to provide *guidance* to faculty members and students lost in the new universe of information" (Chodorow and Lyman, 2000, p. 70).

This shift from physical to digital and at the same time the growing demand for guidance and education is facing all libraries:

> The library of the future will be less a place where information is kept than a portal through which students and faculty will access the information resources of the world ... . [It] will have the daunting task of helping scholars discover what relevant information exists, anywhere in the world and in a variety of formats and media ... . [It] will be about access and knowledge management, not about ownership [of information]. (Hawkins, 2000, p. 153)

As e-learning continues to develop, the "digital," "virtual," or "online" library will increasingly be thought of as simply "the library." In fact, with the rapidly-growing centrality of digital materials and communications, even traditional campus libraries with large print-based collections are becoming more focused to serving "distant" users, even on their own campus:

> Online access to library resources has blurred the distinctions between main campus online users of library resources and distance learning online users ... . [On-campus] individuals function very much like distance learners and faculty in their online use of library resources and

require some of the same kinds of interactions with library personnel. (Association of College and Research Libraries, 2008, "Introduction: A Living Document," para. 1)

An important way that libraries and librarians are addressing these challenges, particularly in relation to online e-learning environments, is working to become more "diffuse" and embedded within the institution by cultivating relationships with faculty and serving as partners on committees and research teams, working to embed library services into course management systems and other e-learning systems, and collaborating widely with multiple stakeholders in building and managing collections and services (Lougee, 2002; Case, 2008). These and other approaches will be discussed further later in the chapter. Ultimately, just as the university is becoming more dispersed, the library will, also.

Standards for libraries for e-learning are defined by the Association of College and Research Libraries' *Standards for Distance Learning Library Services* (2008). These guidelines provide a philosophy for distance learning library services, including such principles as providing equivalent access to members of the distance learning community as provided to students and faculty in-person at the home campus, that direct human access to librarians and library services be available, that information literacy programs be made available, and that funding, management, and planning of the services be sufficient to adequately serve the distance learning population. Specific requirements detail the minimum components of supporting library programs for e-learning, including those of adequate fiscal support, personnel, collections and services, and facilities and equipment, as well as expectations for cooperation and collaboration, and assessment (Association of College and Research Libraries, 2008).

The University of Maryland University College's (UMUC) Information and Library Services serves as an example of a library designed primarily for e-learning, and meets the needs of students and faculty by providing a core collection of research databases that are carefully selected based on the needs of the curriculum. While the UMUC physical collection consists of only about 1,500 volumes and a small number of periodicals focusing on distance education and e-learning, the core of UMUC's online library collections consist of 120 research databases, which include extensive collections of e-books. These are enhanced by associated services such as metasearching and cross-linking technologies. Services such as electronic interlibrary loan from other libraries, with online delivery, electronic reserves in online classrooms, and borrowing from partner schools in the University System of Maryland and Affiliated Institutions (USMAI) Library Consortium provide just-in-time access to additional materials for teaching, research, and scholarship.

However, the fundamental mission of the UMUC library is by design an educational one, with the first of its three-part mission statement reading the mission of the library is "Educating students, faculty, and staff in the use of library and information resources and services, emphasizing the critical importance of information literacy knowledge and skills for success in today's information-rich world" (University of Maryland University College Information and Library Services, 2009). The second part of the library's mission focuses on the enormous importance of information literacy education and partnering with faculty to "promote and embed information literacy within the curriculum," followed by the third component of "developing and managing extensive online library resources and user-centered services for UMUC students, faculty, and staff worldwide" (University of Maryland University College Information and Library Services, 2009).

The library's mission statement was carefully crafted in order to shift focus from the common perception of the library as simply a place—a "warehouse" for books and information—to the library as an educator and partner in the e-learning process, while active collection-building and provision of critical services remains a critical and fundamental core task. In the e-learning and wider academic library environment, aligning the mission of the library with that of the institution is a critical strategic endeavor: "Academic libraries must find and articulate their roles in the current and future information ecology" (Lewis, 2007, p. 419). Further, "the ability to engage in the most fundamental way with the mission of a university will define the importance of academic librarianship in the future" (Dillon, 2008, pp. 53–54).

In support of this educational and e-learning focus, the library provides a vibrant student instruction program based on formalized learning outcomes and is provided through asynchronous and synchronous instruction in online (and to a smaller extent, face-to-face) classrooms. Additionally, the library manages a graduate-level library research skills course, which is required for all graduate students, in conjunction with UMUC's Graduate School of Management and Technology. Other instructional methods include online tutorials and video presentations and self-paced instructional resources. The library also conducts training and workshops for faculty, including a workshop on Google techniques and tools called *Google Universe*, which recognizes the need to educate users on the various information-seeking tools that they are actually using and how to get the best results from them, regardless of whether or not the tools or resources are provided by the library.

Roles for Libraries in Knowledge Management for E-Learning

Eight potential roles may be defined relating to knowledge management and libraries for e-learning. These certainly may not be the only knowledge management roles that e-learning libraries may be able to play, but this discussion should serve as a starting point for understanding these roles and the potential contributions of libraries for knowledge management. The roles are

1. Bringing the values and perspectives of librarianship to the table
2. Supporting digital scholarship and infrastructure
3. Serving as knowledge brokers/knowledge management agents
4. Building more participatory, diffuse library organizations
5. Developing and building awareness of tools for e-scholarship and knowledge management
6. Collecting and contributing data for analysis
7. Implementing internal knowledge management practices and processes to better fulfill the library's mission
8. Supporting the long-term preservation of knowledge

Bringing the Values and Perspectives of Librarianship to the Table

One of the most important resources that librarians can bring to the table for knowledge management projects in e-learning are a particular set of shared professional values and perspectives. These values, which are remarkably similar across the library profession throughout the world, are service, intellectual freedom, stewardship and preservation, equity of access, information literacy, privacy and confidentiality, respect and concern for intellectual property rights, and professional neutrality (Dole et al., 2000; Gorman, 2000; American Library Association, 1997, 2004). Although these values may be similar with those of other academic fields, the experience and professional culture of librarians, as well as the allied professions of archives and records management, can lend valuable insights.

Service—The service perspective is illustrated in the online environment by a concern with usability, findability of information, and ease of use of systems so that users can quickly locate what they are looking for, discover information resources and knowledge related to their interests, and ultimately be successful in their work. This focus is critical for the design and implementation of knowledge management processes and systems if they are to be effective and easy to use.

Intellectual freedom—Librarianship has deep concern with the free and unrestricted flow of knowledge and ideas (Gorman, 2000). A related value is professional neutrality, the separation of personal convictions and professional duties (American Library Association, 1997). As advocates for intellectual and academic freedom, librarians can help ensure that systems and processes allow for freedom of expression and the inclusion of many disparate points of view.

Stewardship and preservation—The stewardship perspective realizes that the preservation of culture depends on a complete and accurate historical record and the long-term preservation of knowledge and information (Gorman, 2000). In a world that is often focused on short or medium-term results and the use of information rather than its long-term safekeeping, librarians and archivists look at the long-term to ensure the continuity of access to information. In fact, because of this perspective,

… electronic records experts have argued for nearly two decades that archivists must be involved with records and record-keeping systems from the moment they are conceived, and they must work with systems designers and record creators to ensure the systems and their records meet record-keeping and long term preservation requirements. (Gilliand-Swetland, 2001, p. 95)

The same holds true for knowledge management processes and systems.

Equity of access—Related to the concept of intellectual freedom is the value of ensuring equitable access to information resources. Librarians work to ensure that information and knowledge resources are "readily, equally, and equitably accessible to all library users" (American Library Association, 2004). In the case of libraries and systems for distance e-learning, this perspective is mandated by professional standards which ensure that students, faculty, and staff associated with a higher education institution have equitable access to resources and services regardless of their physical locations (Association of College and Research Libraries, 2008). This perspective is likewise critical for successful distributed knowledge management systems and processes for e-learning.

Information literacy—Librarians work to educate students, faculty, and library users in general in the ability to recognize information needs and to locate, access, evaluate, and effectively and ethically use information, ensuring that they are information literate (Association of College and Research Libraries, 2000). In the knowledge management context, this educational perspective makes librarians aware of the need for individuals to recognize when knowledge is needed and how to locate, evaluate, and use knowledge in order to meet their goals and objectives, which can have a great impact on the planning of knowledge management systems and processes as well as the training of users, and implementing the cultural changes necessary for effective knowledge transfer to take place.

Privacy and confidentiality—"Informational privacy" is defined as "the right to control personal information and to hold our retrieval and use of information and recorded knowledge to ourselves, without such use being monitored by others" (Gorman, 2000, p. 144). As technology progresses, the access to and use of personal information, including trails of online information seeking behavior, becomes more and more of an ethical question. Librarians' deep professional awareness of privacy concerns and issues and practical experience with developing policies and systems that incorporate these values can help knowledge management teams to take such issues into account as knowledge management practices and systems are developed and implemented.

Intellectual property rights—Because of their role as information managers and providers, librarians are very concerned about intellectual property and copyright, and have long experience with the issues of copyright, particularly in relation to technology and the development of digital systems. Further, while librarians are concerned with respecting intellectual property, they realize that it is important and necessary to advocate for a balance between the rights of copyright holders and those of the user (American Library Association, 1997), particularly in educational settings. As with the other values, this experience and viewpoint is an important reason that librarians should be included in knowledge management activities.

Supporting Digital Scholarship and Infrastructure

Institutional repositories are an important way that many academic libraries have embraced knowledge management principles in seeking new ways to support scholarship and build the new academic information infrastructure. At its core, "a university-based institutional repository is a set of services that a university offers to the members of its community for the management and dissemination of digital materials created by the institution and its community members" (Lynch, 2003, "Defining Institutional Repositories," para. 1). A survey of libraries belonging to the Association of Research Libraries determined that libraries establish institutional repositories to bring together the institution's scholarship for preservation, free access, and enhanced visibility, with materials such as theses and dissertations, preprints, working papers, and published articles, conference presentations, and technical reports being most frequently included (Bailey et al., 2006). Such a repository is thus a service, rather than a particular software application or IT platform, that serves to collect the intellectual and scholarly resources created by an institution, make them broadly available, and preserve them for the future. The primary value of institutional repositories is realized in the "collocation, the interconnection, the archiving, and the preservation of the intellectual output of the institution" (Blythe and Chachra, 2005, p. 76). This intellectual output typically consists of articles such as preprints, working papers, copies of published articles, theses and dissertations, and other materials produced by faculty and students, but may also include research data sets, archival materials, reports, publications, presentations, and other documentation. Learning materials and learning objects, as well as multimedia resources, may also be included; however, such repositories normally do not have the functionality associated with a learning content management system or similar tool used for course development. As of early 2010, the University of Illinois OAI-PMH (a protocol that allows institutional repositories to share metadata about their contents) data provider registry lists 2,418 individual repositories (University of Illinois at Urbana-Champaign Grainger Engineering Library, 2010).

Such institutional repositories are typically based in academic libraries: "Running such an institutionally based, multidisciplinary repository is increasingly seen as a natural role for the libraries and archives of research and teaching organizations" (Smith et al., 2003, "Abstract"). Respondents to the afore mentioned Association of Research Libraries survey indicated that while IT and academic departments indicated interest in institutional repositories, libraries were the primary force in the creation of a repository (Bailey et al., 2006).

While IRs serve the traditional library roles of collecting, organizing, and making information available it is important for librarians to realize that such repositories are part of a broader knowledge management process. IRs must go beyond simple collections to realize greater value for the institution as part of the essential infrastructure to support scholarship and learning. IRs are understood to go beyond a simple catalog or database to fulfill a strategic role in scholarly communication (Lynch, 2003). The Association of Research Libraries suggests two ways this is possible: By allowing for greater control of an institution's scholarly products, thereby reducing the reliance on publishers and academic journals, and by serving to showcase the institution's quality and value in the eyes of its stakeholders (Crow, 2002).

Recent research indicates that users of institutional repositories are making use of them in ways that show repositories are being used as knowledge management tools. St. Jean et al. (2009) found that users of institutional repositories report that an important use is determining what kinds of research is going on at their own university, who is doing it, and what kinds of related works such as theses and dissertations have been done in the past. Faculty may use the repository to locate other faculty pursuing similar lines of research, and students may use it to determine what work has been done previously at the university in order to get ideas for dissertation or thesis topics, and even to locate possible members of their dissertation committees (St. Jean et al., 2009). The social and networking value of learning who was doing what kinds of research was recognized by users as an important knowledge management-related benefit of institutional repositories (St. Jean et al., 2009). Further, "interviewees mentioned that IR content had helped them to keep current in their area, to brainstorm, to structure their own writing, and to help their students," and that access to the raw data used in other's research was very helpful when captured in the repository (St. Jean et al., 2009, p. 14).

Such findings suggest very interesting future developments for institutional repositories in order to continue to increase their usefulness as knowledge management tools. Social networking functions to facilitate networking and collaboration, such as ratings and comments, are recommended by St. Jean et al. (2009). Additional social networking features, such as providing biographical and contact information for authors, would also be an important addition to facilitate communication and the building of networks. Unfortunately with existing institutional repositories, "faculty view IRs as only a place to deposit without seeing the full service potential of an IR" (Jantz and Wilson, 2008, p. 194). By capitalizing on the finding that users tend to use repositories in a social way versus simply an information search and retrieval way and building in more social networking features, libraries can increase the value and interest in institutional repositories, gaining more contributions while developing knowledge management systems that aid in making connections among faculty and students. These findings also suggest the need for the library to go beyond the simple collection, storage, and preservation of materials to become actively involved in the creation and production of institutional repository content as part of the scholarly knowledge management process.

As Branin (2009) notes, "what really matters is creating effective service models to fill ... the digital repository with the appropriate content," which requires a "much more proactive, flexible, knowledge management perspective and approach to designing the new service model in academic libraries" (para. 5).

Serving as Knowledge Brokers/ Knowledge Management Agents

Thomas Davenport and Laurence Prusak (1998) emphasize the important knowledge brokering role that librarians are well suited to play in knowledge management. By making connections and facilitating information sharing,

> ... librarians frequently act as covert knowledge brokers, suited by temperament and their role as information guides to the task of making people-to-people as well as people-to-text connections ... . [Because] corporate libraries often serve the whole organization, librarians are among the few employees who have contact with people from many departments. (Davenport and Prusak, 1998, p. 29)

The customer service orientation of librarians and their skills in researching and discovering information and knowledge give them a unique view of knowledge resources and needs within an organization, positing them to be excellent knowledge brokers: "Librarians [are] key players in creating efficient knowledge markets, in helping buyers and sellers find each other" (Davenport and Prusak, 1998, p. 29–30). This kind of interaction takes place daily in academic libraries, including those for e-learning where interactions are based around electronic communication:

> every time a student or faculty member asks a reference question and when bibliographic instruction takes place, mini-relationships are formed between the librarian and the faculty member or student... because responding to reference quests and providing instruction are two main components of an academic reference librarian's job, librarians and faculty are initiating these relationships on a daily basis. (Johnson and Magusin, 2005, p. 95)

The forming of these relationships are key to making the connections required for effective knowledge sharing.

It is important to recognize the role of librarians as active participants in and facilitators of communication processes, and not as simply collection-builders or keepers of information resources: "libraries becoming more deeply engaged in the creation and dissemination of knowledge and becoming essential collaborators with the other stakeholders in these actives" (Lougee, 2002, p. 1). Likewise, with knowledge management in general,

> too often, knowledge transfer has been confined to such concepts as improved access, electronic communication, document repositories and so forth… it is time for firms to shift their attention to the more human aspects – from access to attention, from velocity to viscosity, from documents to discussions. (Davenport and Prusak, 1998, p. 106)

Building more Participatory, Diffuse Library Organizations

David Lankes, Joanne Silverstein, Scott Nicholson, and Todd Marshall (2007) have developed a model along the lines of Davenport and Prusak's shift "from documents to discussions" (1998, p. 106), which focuses on the library as a facilitator of conversation. They state, "if libraries are in the knowledge business, they are also in the conversation business" (Lankes et al., 2007, p. 3). This kind of facilitation involves providing a wealth of knowledge as the building blocks for conversations to take place, storing the outcomes of conversations as recorded knowledge, through services and activities including teaching, participatory collection development, and public services, and increasingly by providing the infrastructure and services to more effectively facilitate conversations and knowledge sharing in the online environment (Lankes et al., 2007).

At the same time, "libraries are taking on far more *diffuse* roles within the campus community and beyond" and "[have] the potential to become more involved at all stages, and in all contexts, of knowledge creation, dissemination, and use" (Lougee, 2002, p. 1, 4). As Luce (2008) notes, "librarians must become part of the research process… library staff members need to 'go native' and embed themselves among the teams they support" (p. 48). The concept of the diffuse library, which is an involved collaborator and partner in the academic enterprise rather than a centralized information-storage and service location, fits neatly with the participatory library described by Lankes, Silverstein, Nicholson, and Marshall. Both concepts coincide with the views of Davenport and Prusak (2004), who envision the library as a "virtual information network" (p. 15) and information professionals as being embedded in the enterprise, assessing information needs, connecting knowledge holders, and emphasizing information use over control and ownership.

These models are useful because they help shift the emphasis away from libraries as storehouses of books and librarians as keepers of collections to the role of libraries and librarians as knowledge management agents within the academic information infrastructure.

Developing and Building Awareness of Tools for E-scholarship and Knowledge Management

The development of an online, Web-based information environment has affected academic libraries by breaking down traditional notions of the library as the sole "gateway to information" and holder of the university's complete store of information and knowledge. With the increasing availability of academic resources and tools on the Internet that are being used by faculty to share discipline-based knowledge and information, the library may be seen as one part of a widely dispersed infrastructure that may include university-based elements and Internet-based elements: "the reality of our information ecosystems today is that they are not closed systems but open ones: no university, for example, generates and controls all of the information that is important to its faculty, students, or staff" (Unsworth, 2008, p. 231). These external, Internet-based resources that are easily findable through Google and other search engines include articles, periodicals, and books, video and audio, discipline-based repositories such as arXiv.org, learning object repositories such as MERLOT, and the like. In addition information retrieval and networking tools such as blogs, wikis, RSS feeds, link managers, Twitter, and social networking sites are being used by faculty and students to share information and stay connected. Citation management and sharing tools such as Zotero, CiteULike, and Connotea have become important knowledge management tools for scholars and students to manage their resources and share them with others. BitApp, developed by the University of Wisconsin Madison Libraries, shows the potential of a knowledge management tool relying on pulling together distributed information sources to show the research interests of individuals and groups as well as trends in research interests, and to connect individuals with similar interests (Unsworth, 2008).

Concepts that have emerged in recent years such as "library 2.0," "shifted librarianship," and "blended librarianship," emphasize the need for librarians to be fluent and involved in the development and use of such tools. At the same time, as Koenig (2004) notes, there has been an absence of focus on user training and education in the successful use of knowledge management systems (and this can be extended to successfully using distributed knowledge management tools and developing a knowledge management perspective), and librarians are well placed to provide this support because of their extensive history with library instruction and information literacy education. In the higher education e-learning environment, maintaining knowledge of sites, technologies, discipline-based repositories, and other online tools that faculty and students are using can then lead into training and providing this information in individual interactions, presentations, online instruction, tutorials, and the like.

As an example, UMUC and other libraries have developed online tutorials for faculty on how to set up database alerts in order to receive current information on their disciplines. Similar educational resources could focus on keeping current with RSS feeds and related tools, discipline-based repositories and communication networks, and the use of social networking tools. Workshops on knowledge management and communication tools for faculty, such as UMUC's *Google Universe* workshop, can help make faculty aware of new tools that are available to them and help foster knowledge sharing.

A particular challenge for librarians in this role will be simply keeping up with the dramatic changes in technologies. The uneven usage and distribution of knowledge about them between different disciplines and communities of practice serves to further complicate this challenge. For instance, some academics feel that Facebook usage in their communities of practice has become too limited, and are preferring to now use Twitter feeds to keep up with news in their field, relevant articles, and preparing for professional conferences (Kim, 2010), while for other communities of practice Facebook may be a tool that has not even begun to be explored. However, by providing education and training in these kinds of tools, librarians stand to add incredible value for their communities by helping to facilitate more effective academic information and knowledge sharing.

Collecting and Contributing Data for Analysis

Libraries collect and manage a wide variety of data about their collections, interactions, patrons, and processes. This is much amplified by digital systems which record information about users and their movements and requests as they utilize library systems. Data collected by libraries include circulation data for traditional physical materials, Web site usage data and statistics, database login and usage figures, numbers of articles retrieved, numbers of reference questions and logs of electronic reference transactions, instruction sessions conducted and students reached, as well as other data. This information has long been used by libraries for purposes such as guiding collection development decisions and structuring services appropriately, and are even more important for these purposes in libraries for e-learning.

Because of the library profession's deep concern with privacy and confidentiality, and the effects of legislation such as the PATRIOT Act, most libraries are adverse to collecting and storing user information, particularly that which would connect a user to particular books or information and be used to track that patron's interests and intellectual activities, in potential conflict with the value of intellectual freedom. However, by contributing nonidentifying data about library users to both library-based and institutional knowledge management systems such as data warehouses and enterprise intelligence systems as they are implemented, significant knowledge, insights, and value can be created for the library and institution.

For example, data such as disciplinary affiliation, status as student/faculty/staff, and even the location of users can provide interesting insights when combined with other institutionally-held information. Questions that might be asked include "How does the use of the library affect student retention?" "Do students who are heavy users of electronic resources earn better grades?" Or, "Do faculty who use electronic reserves in their e-learning classrooms receive better ratings on course evaluations?"

These issues of data collection and sharing are, of course, ethically complex and must be carefully considered on a local basis. However, librarians should be open to exploring the potential uses of data due to the potential value that can be created for both the library and institution.

Implementing Knowledge Management Practices and Processes to Better Fulfill the Library's Mission

Libraries have used knowledge management techniques and practices to help improve communication in library operations and make the library more successful. A major aspect of this is internal knowledge management: "Knowledge management within libraries involves organizing and providing access to intangible resources that help librarians and administrators carry out their tasks more effectively and easily" (Jantz, 2001, p. 34). Secondly, the knowledge developed by librarians in the course of their work may be fed back to patrons providing an additional value-added information source for the library.

A major way that both of these aspects can be addressed is through management of reference knowledge developed through reference librarians' transactions with patrons. As Ganthi (2004) discusses, knowledge management systems for reference services help to systematically capture tacit knowledge of librarians, increase efficiency by allowing for quicker answers to questions, assist reference librarians in using and learning about the library's collections in the course of their work, and have a role in analysis of questions and for identifying needed resources for collection development. Such systems can also serve to increase communication within the library organization (Jantz, 2001), and are an important infrastructure component for the support of continual learning.

Another aspect of such systems is that by creating a public user interface to the system, library users can search the knowledgebase for answers to their questions without consulting a librarian (Ganthi, 2004). For e-learning applications in which library users work from a distance and may only use the library resources and never contact the library directly, having these kinds of "self-help" resources available for the users to find answers to their questions is especially important. Software platforms for managing virtual reference, such as QuestionPoint from OCLC, incorporate these kinds of knowledge management features as well as knowledge sharing and collaboration features.

It is important to note that knowledge management does not require a monolithic integrated system and may be implemented through practices and distributed tools. For example, as an approach to encourage knowledge sharing among reference librarians at UMUC is the presence of instant messaging clients on all librarian's desktops plus access to shared e-mail lists and blogs. Reference librarians often query individuals or the team for information needed to answer a particular question, or to gain input, seek help in deciphering a question, or have discussions about the best way of answering a question. This approach focuses not on a particular tool or technology, but an encouraged bias within the corporate culture towards information sharing and discussion within the team.

Another important way that librarians can make their knowledge of the library's resources explicit and available to a wide, distributed audience is though the development of subject and course guides. UMUC implemented the LibGuides product from Springshare to streamline the production and management of subject guides, which was also a shared knowledge management project with tangible benefits to the university community. This knowledge on a particular subject is often gained through the professional experience and the extended practice of answering reference questions, conducting research, or serving as a liaison for a particular subject area. According to library surveys and statistics, most users of the UMUC online library never consult a librarian, making this knowledge of appropriate resources available for a particular subject explicit and tangible was critical. In addition to librarians and library staff, faculty in UMUC departments were also contacted to obtain their feedback on the resources included, and changes were made based on this input. In this way the project reached beyond the scope of only the librarian's knowledge to include subject knowledge from the university departments. The availably of this knowledge in the form of subject guides allows many students and faculty to independently consult and make use of it.

UMUC created a unique implementation of LibGuides by integrating it with an existing electronic resource management system that was developed in-house using readily available database tools and programming languages. This system functions as a shared knowledgebase in which a resource can be entered once and cited in many guides. Since each resource has already been individually selected and reviewed by a librarian, the system also serves to provide awareness of vetted resources that are available for inclusion in subject guides. This makes the creation of new subject guides, including course-specific course guides, much easier because knowledge about UMUC's resources as well as Internet and physical book resources are captured and shared in a central repository.

For the internal management of electronic resources, a particular need in e-learning environments, libraries are also exploring the emerging trend towards electronic resource management systems. These systems are designed to organize the array of electronic resources that libraries provide, such as subscription research databases, and to centralize the management knowledge and information required throughout the life cycle of an electronic resource (Collins, 2005). These systems benefit libraries by providing "[a] central location for administrative e-resource data, display of resource advisories to patrons, access to license agreements by multiple people, ability to share information in a consortial environment, and assistance in defining and evaluating workflows" (Collins, 2008, p. 267). By providing a platform for centralizing knowledge formerly held tacitly by librarians, or in distributed files, and sharing that information with members of an internal team, or even external patrons in some cases, such systems are a good example of how a centralized knowledge management system can streamline processes and improve knowledge sharing.

Currently, as the field is still developing, the amount of labor and coordination involved tends to outweigh the benefits of these systems, however, librarians expect them to become critical and standard parts of a library's infrastructure over time (Collins, 2008). UMUC implemented some of these functions in the previously mentioned in-house system that centralized information about resources and contributes to the production of subject guides. After exploring the current state of commercial and open source systems, the library decided to streamline and improve the process of managing electronic resources using existing tools such as database applications and spreadsheets, rather than moving towards an integrated system at this time. As these systems represent important tools for internal knowledge management with great future potential, libraries should continue to follow developments in this emerging field.

Supporting the Long-Term Preservation of Knowledge

Given the closely held value of stewardship and preservation, librarians and their allied professions of archivists and records managers are uniquely suited to bring a long-term perspective to the development of knowledge management processes and systems for e-learning. This extends into such areas as systems design, where open data and metadata standards can make data easier to migrate as hardware and software systems become obsolete, and where distributed systems, multiple copies, and backups can help protect data for continued access. Digital libraries for e-learning, including repository and knowledge management systems that they may contain and manage, "must organize themselves to preserve the integrity of the works they manage for use over time by the individuals or communities that they support in the overall knowledge economy" (Waters, 2000, p. 196). This organization involves issues of technical infrastructure, maintaining effective discovery and retrieval processes over time, ongoing funding and support, and even copyright management to ensure that legal rights are in place to allow for effective storage and stewardship (Waters, 2000).

Anne J. Gilliland-Swetland (2001) describes the important and unique role that records play in knowledge management contexts: "It is critical to ensure that both electronic and traditional records are created and maintained in ways that maximize the knowledge and insight they can provide to the university and its members, while also ensuring that the university is not exposed to liability" (p. 95). The socially constructed nature of records and their organization capture knowledge of an organization's processes in tangible form, and "are expected to show how an organization carries out its business and makes decisions" (Gilliland-Swetland, 2001, p. 84). Focusing on the archives of a university as a function rather than as a particular physical place, archivists emphasize the importance of record-keeping within knowledge management practices and assist with the management of such records throughout their life cycle. (Gilliland-Swetland, 2001). These critical aspects of the information and knowledge life cycle should not be forgotten when implementing knowledge management practices, processes, and systems.

Conclusion

A recent study of university faculty and librarians confirmed that faculty researchers increasingly use materials found outside the library and that they "no longer feel a significant dependence on the library in their research process" (Housewright and Schonfeld, 2008, p. 30). Although faculty may use library collections and services in their work, these behind-the-scenes functions are typically invisible to faculty (Case, 2008). Further, "although librarians may still be providing significant value to their constituency, the value of their brand is decreasing" (Housewright and Schonfeld, 2008, p. 30). In e-learning, with faculty and students being widely distributed and the library becoming one node in the network of information used by faculty and students, this threat of invisibility is even more prominent as the library and its services may be simply taken for granted.

In order to combat these changes and increase the visibility of the library and the library's "brand value," Housewright and Schonfeld (2008) recommend that libraries "take steps to improve the value of their brand by offering more value-added services to raise their profile on campus" (p. 30). Providing leadership, partnering with faculty, administrators, IT professionals, and other stakeholders, and playing key roles in the development of knowledge management processes and solutions for e-learning in higher education as described in this chapter are important ways that libraries and librarians can be more visible and continue to add value to scholarship, research, and learning.

References

American Library Association. (1997). Code of Ethics of the American Library Association. Retrieved from http://www.ala.org/ala/aboutala/offices/oif/statementspols/codeofethics/codeethics.cfm.

American Library Association. (2004). Core Values of Librarianship. Retrieved from http://www.ala.org/ala/aboutala/offices/oif/statementspols/corevaluesstatement/corevalues.cfm.

Arms, W. Y. (2000). *Digital Libraries*. Boston, MA: MIT Press.

Association of College and Research Libraries. (2000). Information Literacy Competency Standards for Higher Education. Retrieved from http://www.ala.org/ala/mgrps/divs/acrl/standards/informationliteracycompetency.cfm.

Association of College and Research Libraries. (2008). Standards for Distance Learning Library Services. Retrieved from http://www.ala.org/ala/mgrps/divs/acrl/standards/guidelinesdistancelearning.cfm.

Bailey, C. W., Coombs, K., Emery, J., Mitchell, A., Morris, C., Simons, S., and Wright, R. (2006). SPEC Kit 292: Institutional Repositories. Washington, DC: Association of Research Libraries.

Blythe, E. and Chachra, V. (2005, September/October). The Value Proposition in Institutional Repositories. *Educause Review, 40*(5), 76–77. Retrieved from http://www.educause.edu/EDUCAUSE+Review/EDUCAUSEReviewMagazineVolume40/TheValuePropositioninInstituti/158011.

Borgman, C. L. (2007). *Scholarship in the Digital Age: Information, Infrastructure, and the Internet.* Cambridge, MA: The MIT Press.

Branin, J. J. (2009). Editorial: What we need is a knowledge management perspective. *College and Research Libraries, 70*(2), 104–105. Retrieved from http://www.ala.org/ala/mgrps/divs/acrl/publications/crljournal/2009/mar/editorial-3-09.cfm.

Case, M. M. (2008). Partners in knowledge creation: An expanded role for research libraries in the digital future. *Journal of Library Administration, 48*(2), 141–156. doi: 10.1080/01930820802231336.

Chodorow, S., and Lyman, P. (2000). The responsibilities of universities in the new information environment. In B. Hawkins (Ed.), *The Mirage of Continuity: Reconfiguring Academic Information Resources for the 21st Century* (pp. 61–78). Washington, DC: Council on Library and Information Resources and Association of American Universities.

Collins, M. (2005). Electronic resource management systems: Understanding the players and how to make the right choice for your library. *Serials Review, 31*(2), 125–140. doi: 10.1016/j.serrev.2005.02.005.

Collins, M. (2008). Electronic resource management systems (ERMS) review. *Serials Review, 34*(4), 267–299. doi: 10.1016/j.serrev.2008.09.011.

Crow, R. (2002). The Case for Institutional Repositories: A SPARC Position Paper. Washington, DC: The Scholarly Publishing and Academic Resources Coalition (SPARC). Retrieved from http://www.arl.org/sparc/bm~doc/ir_final_release_102.pdf.

Davenport, T. H., and Prusak, L. (1998). *Working Knowledge: How Organizations Manage What They Know.* Boston, MA: Harvard Business School Press.

Davenport, T. H., and Prusak, L. (2004). Blow up the corporate library. In H. Hobohm (Ed.), *Knowledge Management: Libraries and Librarians Taking up the Challenge* (pp. 11–19). Munich, Germany: K. G. Saur.

Dillon, A. (2008, August). Accelerating learning and discovery: Refining the role of academic librarians. In *No Brief Candle: Reconceiving Research Libraries for the 21st Century* (pp. 51–57). Washington, DC: Council on Library and Information Resources. Retrieved from http://www.clir.org/pubs/abstract/pub142abst.html.

Dole, W. V., Hurych, J. M., and Koehler, W. G. (2000). Values for librarians in the information age: An expanded examination. *Library Management, 21*(6), 285–297. Retrieved from http://info.emeraldinsight.com/products/journals/journals.htm?id=lm.

Gandhi, S. (2004). Knowledge management and reference services. *Journal of Academic Librarianship, 30*(5), 368–381. Retrieved from *www.elsevier.com/locate/jacalib.*

Gilliland-Swetland, A. J. (2001). Revaluing records: From risk management to enterprise management. In G. Bernbom (Ed.), *Information Alchemy: The Art and Science of Knowledge Management* (pp. 81–98). San Francisco, CA: Jossey-Bass.

Hawkins, B. L. (2000). The unsustainability of the traditional library and the threat to higher education. In B. Hawkins (Ed.), *The Mirage of Continuity: Reconfiguring Academic Information Resources for the 21st Century* (pp. 129–153). Washington, DC: Council on Library and Information Resources and Association of American Universities.

Housewright, R., and Schonfeld, R. (2008). Ithaka's 2006 Studies of Key Stakeholders in the Digital Transformation in Higher Education. New York: ITHAKA. Retrieved from http://www.ithaka.org/ithaka-s-r/research/Ithakas%202006%20Studies%20of%20 Key%20Stakeholders%20in%20the%20Digital%20Transformation%20in%20 Higher%20Education.pdf.

Jantz, R. (2001). Knowledge management in academic libraries: Special tools and processes to support information professionals. *Reference Services Review, 29*(1), 33–39. doi: 10.1108/00907320110366778.

Jantz, R. C., and Wilson, M. C. (2008). Institutional repositories: Faculty deposits, marketing, and the reform of scholarly communication. *Journal of Academic Librarianship, 34*(3), 186–195. doi: 10.1016/j.acalib.2008.03.014.

Johnson, K., and Magusin, E. (2005). *Exploring the Digital Library: A Guide for Online Teaching and Learning.* San Francisco, CA: Jossey-Bass.

Kim, J. (2010, January 3). Irrelevant Facebook. Retrieved from Inside Higher Ed Technology and Learning Blog at http://www.insidehighered.com/blogs/technology_and_learning/ irrelevant_facebook.

Koenig, M. E. D. (2004). Knowledge management, user education, and librarianship. In H. Hobohm (Ed.), *Knowledge Management: Libraries and Librarians Taking up the Challenge* (pp. 137–150). Munich, Germany: K. G. Saur.

Lankes, R. D., Silverstein, J. L., Nicholson, S., and Marshall, T. (2007, October). Participatory networks: The library as conversation. *Information Research, 12*(4). Retrieved from http://InformationR.net/ir/12-4/colis/colis05.html.

Lewis, D. W. (2007). A strategy for academic libraries in the first quarter of the 21st century. *College and Research Libraries, 68*(5), 418–434.

Lougee, W. P. (2002, August). *Diffuse Libraries: Emergent Roles for the Research Library in the Digital Age.* Washington, DC: Council on Library and Information Resources. Retrieved from http://www.clir.org/pubs/reports/pub108/contents.html.

Luce, R. E. (2008, August). A new value equation challenge: The emergence of eResearch and roles for research libraries. In *No Brief Candle: Reconceiving Research Libraries for the 21st Century* (pp. 42–50). Washington, DC: Council on Library and Information Resources. Retrieved from http://www.clir.org/pubs/abstract/pub142abst.html.

Lynch, C. (2000, January/February). From automation to transformation: Forty years of libraries and information technology in higher education. *EDUCAUSE Review, 35*(1), 60–68. Retrieved from http://net.educause.edu/ir/library/pdf/erm0018.pdf.

Lynch, C. A. (2003, February). Institutional repositories: Essential infrastructure for scholarship in the digital age. *ARL Bimonthly Report, 226.* Retrieved from http://www.arl.org/ resources/pubs/br/br226/br226ir.shtml.

Smith, M., Barton, M., Bass, M., Branschofsky, M., McClellan, G., Stuve, D., Walker, J. H. (2003, January). DSpace: An open source dynamic digital repository. *D-Lib Magazine, 9*(1). Retrieved from http://www.dlib.org/dlib/january03/smith/01smith.html.

St. Jean, B., Rieh, S. Y., Yakel, E., and Markey, K. (In press). Unheard voices: Institutional repository end-users. *College and Research Libraries*. Retrieved from http://www.ala. org/ala/mgrps/divs/acrl/publications/crljournal/preprints/crl-071.pdf.

Townley, C. T. (2001). Knowledge management and academic libraries. *College and Research Libraries, 62*(1), 44–55. Retrieved from http://www.ala.org/ala/mgrps/divs/acrl/publications/crljournal/2001/jan/townley.pdf.

University of Illinois at Urbana-Champaign Grainger Engineering Library. (2010). The University of Illinois OAI-PMH Data Provider Registry. Retrieved from http://gita. grainger.uiuc.edu/registry/searchform.asp.

University of Maryland University College Information and Library Services. Our Mission. Retrieved from http://www.umuc.edu/library/about.shtml.

Unsworth, J. (2008). University 2.0. In R. N. Katz (Ed.), *The Tower and the Cloud: Higher Education in the Age of Cloud Computing* (pp. 227–237). Boulder, CO: EDUCAUSE. Retrieved from http://www.educause.edu/thetowerandthecloud/PUB7202k.

Van Der Werf, M., and Sabatier, G. (2009, June). *The College of 2020: Students*. Washington, DC: Chronicle Research Services, Chronicle of Higher Education.

Waters, D. J. (2000). Steps toward a system of digital preservation: Some technological, political, and economic considerations. In B. Hawkins (Ed.), *The Mirage of Continuity: Reconfiguring Academic Information Resources for the 21st Century* (pp. 193–206). Washington, DC: Council on Library and Information Resources and Association of American Universities.

Wheeler, B. (2008) E-research is a fad: Scholarship 2.0, cyberinfrastructure, and IT governance. In R. N. Katz (Ed.), *The Tower and the Cloud: Higher Education in the Age of Cloud Computing* (pp. 108–117). Boulder, CO: EDUCAUSE. Retrieved from http://www.educause.edu/thetowerandthecloud/PUB7202k.

Chapter 16

Knowledge Management and Continuity of Operations: E-Learning as a Strategy in Disaster Prevention and Emergency Management

Claudine SchWeber

Contents

Introduction

- Can air traffic safety be maintained when almost 30% of the Air Traffic Controllers in the last three years were newly hired young people, replacing many retirees? (FAA 2008)
- Can educational institutions continue to operate when the physical plant is closed due to pandemic flu or massive disasters such as Hurricane Katrina?

Knowledge management "should stress the importance of passing on items of value to others" (Stern, 2010, p. 10). One strategy that enables the continuity of operations to prevent disasters or to manage during/after a disaster is the effective transfer of critical knowledge to varied stakeholders using e-learning and technological resources. Indeed, knowledge management can help to "capture, share, and leverage the knowledge of ... individuals before they retire" as well as those who need to manage operations during an emergency such as a national disaster (Liebowitz 2004, p2).

This chapter will explore the connections between continuity of operations, knowledge management, e-learning, and disaster prevention/emergency management in government and higher education sectors.

Continuity of Operations (COOP)

Continuity of operations is the overarching concept that includes business or academic continuity. COOP refers to an "institution's ability to maintain or restore its business ... when some circumstance threatens or disrupts normal operations ... ." (Pirani and Yanosky 2007, p. 2). This includes the need to ensure that "*essential functions* can continue during and after a disaster, including [preventing] interruption of *mission-critical services*, and the ability to [restore] *full functionality* as quickly as possible" (Root, p. 3; italics added). Business and government COOP have dealt with emergency management in several stages, whether the disaster was economic, environmental, or human-made (Root 2006; Curtis 2008).

Continuity of operations (COOP) has been a concern in the business community because retaining customers means survival and involves maintaining the availability and distribution of the product or services. A mid-2000 U.S. government report, for example, indicated that 40% of all companies that experienced a disaster did not reopen. A 2008 report conducted by the private sector suggested that the avian flu pandemic could result in 30–50% absenteeism (Curtis 2008, p. 38). In an environment where even brief interruptions could halt regular activities, "responding effectively to such circumstances can be the difference between a modest interruption and a severe blow to the institution's viability, providing powerful financial incentives to optimize [business continuity] readiness" (Pirani and Yanosky 2007, p. 1).

Continuity of operations applies not only to the private sector, but also to government and higher education. In the federal government, COOP is defined as "an effort within individual executive departments and agencies to ensure that Primary Mission Essential Functions (PMEFs) continue to be performed during a wide range of emergencies" (FEMA)* In education, academic continuity is the "process of maintaining continuity of learning in a crisis situation ... [such that] operations can be sustained which enable ... students to continue their studies the despite the disruption caused by the crisis" (AC).

As the cases below will exemplify, the use of technology and e-learning is an integral part of transferring the knowledge needed to prevent a disaster or to manage during and after such an emergency. In education, the *essential function* is to keep the learning process going by enabling access to faculty, students, and staff. For higher education, whether in the United States or France, teaching and learning are the "essential functions," which require transferring knowledge about the operation of "mission critical services" (such as course delivery, IT infrastructure, and access).

In the airline industry, the air traffic controllers' (ATC) essential function is "to move air traffic safely and efficiently ... [and] keep the airplanes moving" Federal Aviation Administration (FAA, 2008) thereby *preventing the interruption of mission-critical services.* The effective transfer of knowledge to the new generation of ATC employees is critical to avoid disaster. Effective COOP is closely linked to another important attribute: organizational resilience.

One outcome of continuity planning in business is a "design for resilience," which means that "an organization has internalized continuity management to the extent that all strategic decisions ... are made with a view towards making critical enabling processes resilient from the beginning" (Curtis 2008, p. 40). Since "an organization's resiliency is directly related to the effectiveness of its continuity capability ... its ability to perform its essential functions continuously" (FEMA), a knowledge management plan/process is critical for both disaster prevention and emergency management. Naturally, a plan that has been developed and tested before a disaster occurs is the optimal approach!

---

* The emergency management professional community labels the four phases as mitigation/ prevention; preparation; response; recovery. Comparable business terms would be analysis, planning, response and implementation, and resource recovery (Brazeau, p. 28). For the academic community planning, response, aftermath, and recovery represent the same ideas. Aftermath refers to the immediate period after the crisis has ceased (www.academiccontinuity.org). In the U.S. federal government, there are four phases to the continuity management cycle: plans and procedures; testing, training and exercises; evaluations, after-action reports, lessons learned; and development of corrective action plans (http://www.fema.gov/about/org/ ncp/coop/index.shtm#1).

Knowledge Management

"Knowledge management is the process of creating value from an organization's intangible assets [including] the ability to share and leverage knowledge internally and externally…" (Liebowitz 2004, p. 1). The process is said to involve four major areas: identifying and capturing the key knowledge areas that could be lost at severe risk to the organization; sharing/transferring the knowledge; internalizing and applying the knowledge within the organizational context; and the creation of knowledge that results in new products or services (Liebowitz 2004). For purposes of this discussion, which focuses on disaster prevention and management, emphasis will be on the first three areas.

E-Learning and Knowledge Management in Disaster Prevention and Emergency Management

Disaster Prevention

Preventing disaster was the intention of the French 2008 education plan, which feared large-scale consequences of a pandemic flu, resulting in a national plan for continuing of education using e-learning. A similar fear of disaster is a key concern of the Federal Aviation Administration (FAA) due to the loss of substantial numbers of retiring air traffic controllers. The influx of young entrants has involved serious considerations about knowledge transfer between generations.

In higher education, the most frequently identified components of an academic continuity system are communication; continuity of learning methods (such as e-learning, TV, radio); instructor and student readiness; and infrastructure support (AC components). France, which has a centralized national education system, launched a pandemic flu plan in 2008 dedicated to continuity of learning—*continuite pedagogiques*—that involved identification and sharing of key knowledge needed to be continued and the use of e-learning methods, their internalization and application among universities that are part of the digital environment (*universites numeriques*). For example, the plan was circulated by the French education ministry to education rectors and senior staff; processes such as e-learning and TV were the methods identified for learning continuation (depending on the existing operation of the university); students were to supply e-mail addresses upon application, to facilitate communication immediacy; instructor experience with digital learning was expected. The France education ministry, which has had a distance learning institution (CNED) since 1939 with the onset of World War II, had determined that educational learning was at risk if the flu's impact was extensive and identified the critical learning processes and infrastructure that would be needed, shared this information, and asked universities to internalize these processes into their organizational operation in readiness for action (personal e-mails, M. Vidal to author, July

10–15, 2008; Bourrel 2003). Some universities in the United States also developed plans, but given the localized structure of American education, the detail and dissemination varied substantially (UMD 2008; facultyFDU 2007).

In a different environment, effective knowledge transfer is a very high-stakes situation. The generational changes to the workforce among ATC presents significant potential dangers. At present, the Federal Aviation Administration (FAA) is reaching the required retirement age for large numbers of ATC who were hired as a cohort, en masse in 1981, to replace the 11,000 fired by President Regan after the failed strike of 13,000 controllers. (Poker 2010) The FAA projects a loss of 14,657 controllers in the decade between 2009–2018; almost 50% of these are the retirees. (FAA, 2008, Figure 4.1). In 2008, 14.2 % of the total (15,381) ATC were new hires; and 35% of these new hires were recent graduates of college training programs (FAA, 2008). The point is that a growing proportion of the new ATC are young people—in their 20s and 30s—while those about to retire or within a decade of retiring are in their 50s and 60s. In the airline safety environment it is really important to retain—"harvest"—their knowledge before the retiring employees' departure (Beasley et al., 2002). One might argue that the ability to effectively transfer the mission-critical knowledge, skills and abilities across generations is more than the keystone to continuity of operations; it is the difference between life and death for passengers and crew!

Among the challenges for the ATC is the transference of "tacit" knowledge, the information that is in people's heads learned over time and experience, rather than written down. Several authors have argued that "cross-generational biases inhibit tacit knowledge transfer … " (Liebowitz et al. 2007, p. 1133). How might this danger to air safety be averted? A recent doctoral dissertation examined several approaches to facilitating knowledge transfer between the experienced, older ATC and the new, younger entrants. The recommendations included the following: generational teaming; creation of systems for development, storage, and access of knowledge resources, such as development of computer simulations, gaming and information repositories, directories of experts and best practices; interactive frequently asked questions segments; rewards for knowledge sharing and development of repository data; development of high resolution simulations- and scenario-based tools that reflect actual conditions in the air, such as weather changes, aircraft cabin conditions; remote access to course materials, references, peers and faculty; development of onsite and remote "communities of practice" which could offer feedback and tutoring; computer-mediated meetings between new ATC and retired professionals; and establishment of connections between ATC and pilots (Poker 2009). Many of these suggestions go beyond the standard ways that knowledge was transferred in previous decades, which were onsite class sessions, written handbook, and face-to-face mentoring. Thus, the e-learning environment as a tool for knowledge transfer, which is so heavily recommended for the new generation, may be a challenge for the experienced air traffic controller. Indeed, the Federal Mediation and Conciliation Service (FMCS) conducted a training session in August 2010 on

"The Generational Mix in the Workplace: How to Bridge the Generation Gap for the Workplace" (e-mail to author, 1/21/2010).*

As these cases suggest, in today's economic and security challenged environment, knowledge transfer planning should be a core requirement for organizations if they want to prevent catastrophic knowledge loss or knowledge depletion (Beazley et al. 2002). E-learning approaches and tools make it easier and faster to take action.

Emergency Management (During/After a Disaster)

In the first decade of the 21st Century, we saw for the first time the possibility of continuing learning despite a natural disaster or even a short term war—using the power of technology enhanced education. In both the 2005 Hurricane Katrina disaster and the 2006 Israeli-Lebanon war, students at Xavier University in New Orleans and Empire State College's Lebanon campus respectively wanted to continue their education. For these institutions, the question was how could they respond to this desire for access fast enough to be of use and effective enough to maintain educational quality? Given the immediate dangers in their communities, distance/ e-learning was the only option.

Xavier University and Hurricane Katrina, 2005

Xavier University is a historically black and Catholic college in New Orleans, specializing in pharmacy, arts and sciences, and graduate programs in education and psychology; in 2005 there were approximately 3000 full-time students (SchWeber 2008).

Hurricane Katrina hit the Gulf Coast and New Orleans August 29, 2005 leaving thousands to be homeless or dead, and causing severe damage to buildings and the entire area within a three-day deluge. At Xavier, some buildings were destroyed, others filled with up to 6 feet of water resulting in mildew, toxic mold, and precarious structures. This meant that neither students, nor faculty or staff could access the facilities, and many scattered to other locations. Nonetheless, Xavier was able to recover sufficiently to re-open mid-January 2006 with 75% of the original fall enrollment. How did they do this?

---

* The workshop announcement starts with the following description: "All organizations are experiencing a new challenge these days. For the first time in history, there are four distinct generations in the workforce, each with different expectations, traits, characteristics, values, and work styles. This course is designed to help you meet the challenges of understanding how and why these differences manifest in the workplace today. This interactive two-day program will examine how you and your organization can bridge these generational gaps to best meet the needs of both organizations and employees, and how you can use this knowledge and understanding to enhance your organization" FMCS announcement, e-mail to cs January 21, 2010.

Xavier's recovery was due, in part, to two factors: First, about 40% of the returning spring semester students had enrolled in coursework at other campuses or online in fall 05; of these, one-third (418) took one or more courses through the Sloan Semester Program. This number was substantially more than at any other Louisiana or Mississippi institution. This continued connection with education, despite difficult circumstances, indicated a strong determination to learn within Xavier University. The online environment was so effective for the fall 2005 that the graduate education program was offered totally online during spring 2006, allowing the department and students sufficient time to reorganize for fall 2006. Second, Xavier was technologically prepared (SchWeber 2008).

The intent of the Sloan Semester was that online coursework would be an educational "bridge" for students in the affected areas who would take course(s) offered by a variety of institutions nationwide, which would be applied to their home campus. This would allow for educational continuity for the students, and give the hurricane-affected institutions time to reorganize. Course options were listed in the Southern Regional Education Board Web site. Eventually about 1700 students registered in 1345 courses offered free by 153 institutions (Sloan Semester, special report, 2006).

Xavier's technological back-up operation had several knowledge management ingredients: identification of the knowledge that would be needed to continue operations, information sharing with the university community, and application once the storm hit. This approach may have been due to the fact that XU's Vice President for IT, Catherine Lewis, had recently come from private industry where business continuity is not an unusual consideration. Thus, an emergency Web site in California had been established in May 2005, 3 months before the storm; back-up tapes were housed at a data storage facility rather than in a nearby building, as was the case with many institutions. A communication process was developed and implemented: XU's emergency Web site was activated when staff and students left the Xavier grounds a few days before the storm touched down. This provided basic information. In addition, back-up tapes, which had been housed at a data storage facility were collected, brought to, and eventually hosted by Xavier University in Cincinnati which enabled communication by Web site and e-mail. Alongside the activated emergency Web site, more dynamic outward communication was established. By mid-October 2005, and bi-weekly thereafter, the *University Newsletter* posted renovation details, photos of campus clean-up status, interviews with students "eager to return," progress towards the January 2006 re-opening, class schedules for the repeat fall semester, reports on fundraising and repair plans, details of registration procedures, cancelled courses, spring semester information, and more (SchWeber 2008).

Empire State College's Program in Lebanon

In the summer 2006, the Israel–Lebanon war was the impetus for academic continuity implementation. Empire State College (New York) quickly redesigned its onsite residency programs in Lebanon using multimedia and online technology to deal with the unexpected and dangerous environment by providing online courses for students impacted by the missiles and bombs, sharing information about the changes, and offering processes via e-mail, chat, and telephone.

The Lebanon Residency Program at Empire State College in New York State combined online and onsite instruction. The Lebanon program was part of the junior and senior years in a Bachelor of Science degree. The Empire State College (ESC) program served students at the American University of Technology in Halate and Tripoli and the American University of Science and Technology in Beirut and Zenle. Students from other Middle East institutions might also be enrolled. Concentrations included business, hotel management, marketing, information systems, and computer science. The program involved 18 week semesters, with a 10-day residency led by U.S.-based faculty on site in Lebanon once each semester. The remaining coursework was done online. Typically, there were 200–300 students and 20 faculty in each semester (SchWeber 2008).

When war broke out in the summer 2006, ESC realized that faculty could not travel to Lebanon for the fall residency. To enable the courses and learning to continue, ESC created a "virtual residency" using multimedia by videotaping the faculty, burning DVDs of the faculty lectures, and shipping the DVDs to the two Lebanese universities. Local students viewed the videos at the two partner institutions; those outside of Lebanon received individual copies. In-depth interaction was supported/supplemented by e-mail, chat, and telephone. The Lebanon program was able to continue in fall 2007 and beyond. The recovery from the war environment and the change from the onsite-residency model appears due to several factors: they quickly moved to work with their educational partners to establish a home base for the alternate learning mode (DVD); their experience with technology, in the form of online courses, meant students and faculty were comfortable with technology-based learning; this comfort also enabled the transformation of the face-to-face learning to DVD lectures by the instructors; they developed and implemented an effective communication system by using established channels and opening some new ones (Interview with Lebanon program director, cited in SchWeber 2008).

The disastrous situation which confronted both Xavier University and Empire State College in Lebanon exemplify the connection between knowledge management and e-learning that is possible during a crisis.

Knowledge Management, E-Learning, Continuity, and Organizational Resilience

The 21st century has presented us with challenges and opportunities: generational workforce changes and economic crises; natural disasters are challenges to business continuity of operations. New technological developments and tools offer opportunities for managing the challenges and being resilient in the face of continuing change.

Resilient organizations are those which can quickly and effectively anticipate or respond to changes that threaten the institution and the people. Several characteristics, adapted from research on individuals' survival from trauma, are associated with resiliency and knowledge management:

- Expand upon existing resources or obtain access to resources beyond those normally available (e.g., e-learning and technology tools; capturing and sharing effective practices as in the French pandemic plan; applying resources to the conditions on the ground, as Xavier University did)
- Practice *bricolage*, which is the ability to develop solutions out of existing conditions and being creative under pressure (e.g., identifying and leveraging knowledge within and among organizations, such as that done by Empire State College in Lebanon)
- Plan for or manage effectively in situations of uncertainty (identification and leveraging of experienced employee knowledge to new staff, as in the case of the air traffic controllers, including using e-learning applications) (Mallek 1998; Weick 1993).

While knowledge management has been discussed as a mechanism for continuity management, and e-learning/ technology are 21st century tools for facilitating that process, it is in the disaster prevention and emergency management area that its value is truly apparent. And although knowledge management has been seen as a way to mitigate the threat of losing productivity, profitability, and competitive advantage (Beazley et al. 2002), the greater value is the possibility of mitigating the loss of human capital (people) injured or dead in a disaster.

References

AC (Academic Continuity), http://www.academiccontinuity.org, retrieved 1/30/2010.

AC components (Academic Continuity components), http://www.academiccontinuity.org/node/288, retrieved 1/30/2010.

Beazley, H., Boenisch, J. and Harden, D. (2002), *Continuity Management: Preserving Corporate Knowledge and Productivity When Employees Leave*, John Wiley & Sons, New York.

Bourrel, J.R. (2003), *Les CNED ou les distances effaces: la Revue due Centre national d'enseignement a distance(CNED). Ministere de la jeunesse, de l'education nationale et de la recherche*, Paris. CNED.

Brazeau, P. (2008), "Holistic Protection," *Canadian Underwriter*, March pp. 26–28.

Curtis, G. (Feb/Mar 2008), "Beyond Disaster Recovery," *Directorship*, pp. 38–43.

facultyFDU (2007), Faculty quick-start guide: Preparing to continue instruction during an emergency (Fairleigh Dickinson University) http://fdu-coursecontinuity.wikispaces.com.

FAA (Federal Aviation Administration) (2008). *A Plan for the Future: The Federal Aviation Administration's 10-Year Strategy for the Air Traffic Control Workforce 2009–2018. (HQ-09833).* Washington, DC: Federal Aviation Administration Web site: http://www.faa.gov/airports_airtraffic/air_traffice/conroller_staffing/media/CWP_2009.pdf; http://www.faa.gov/about/office_org/headquarters_offices/ato/, retrieved 1/30/2010

FEMA (Federal Emergency Management Agency). Continuity of Operations Division http://www.fema.gov/about/org/ncp/coop/index.shtm#1. Retrieved 1/30/2010.

Liebowitz, J., N. Ayyavoo, H. Nguyen, D. Carran, and J. Simien (2007). Cross-generational knowledge flows in edge organizations. *Industrial Management & Data Systems*, Vol. 107 No. 8, pp. 1123–1153.

Liebowitz, J.(2004). Will knowledge management work in the government? *Electronic Government*, Vol. 1, No. 1, pp. 1–7.

Mallek, L. (Nov/Dec 1998). Putting organizational resilience to work, Industrial Management, Vol. 40, No. 6, pp. 8–13.

Pirani, J. A. and Yanosky, R. (March 29, 2007). Shelter from the Storm: IT and Business Continuity in Higher Education. http://www.educause.edu/ECAR/ResearchPublications/KeyFindings1165. Retrieved 1/31/2010.

Poker, F. (2009). Facilitating Continuity of Operations (COOP): The Transfer of Organizationally-Determined Essential Knowledge from "Baby Boomers" to "Generations X and Y" Air Traffic Controllers in the United States. Dissertation, University of Maryland University College.

Poker, F. (winter 2010). *Knowledge Transfer from Baby Boomers to Generations X and Y: Air Traffic Controllers in the United States. Perspectives on Work (Publication of the Labor and Employment Relations Association)*, Vol. 13, No. 2, pp. 25–28.

Root, D. (September 2006). Ensuring Business Continuity in Government (http://www.juniper.net/solutions/literature/white_papers/200203.pdf). Retrieved 7/ 25/ 2008.

SchWeber, C. (February 2008). Determined to learn: accessing education despite life-threatening disasters. *Journal of Asynchronous Learning Networks.* Vol 12, No 1, pp. 23–34.

Sloan Semester, special report (2006). www.sloan-c.org/publications/books/pdf/SloanSemester.pdf. Retrieved 1/30/2010.

Stern, S. (Jan 12, 2010). A Little Knowledge Is Deadly Dangerous. *Financial Times*, p. 10.

UMD (2008). Emergency Preparedness at the University of Maryland. www.umd.edu/emergencypreparedness/pandemic_flu/avfplan.cfm.

Weick, K. (Dec. 1993). The Collapse of Sensemaking in Organizations: The Mann Gulch Disaster. *Administrative Science Quarterly.* Vol. 38, No 4, pp. 628–652.

KM AND E-LEARNING: INDUSTRY PERSPECTIVES

Chapter 17

Knowledge Management (KM) and E-Learning (EL) Growth for Industry and University Outreach Activities via Capstone Projects: Case Studies and Future Trends

Joseph Betser

Contents

Introduction

Recent years have seen a tremendous growth in knowledge management (KM) affecting multiple disciplines [Liebowitz, 2009]. This chapter further focuses on KM and E-learning (EL; KM&EL) growth for industry and university collaboration via educational outreach capstone projects. Industry-to-university outreach is an important activity for the Aerospace Corporation (Aerospace) and Harvey Mudd College (HMC), as it enriches both education and industry. Such outreach activity directs student teams to working on current, relevant technical projects, at the same time affording industry the opportunity to engage emerging talent. Student projects are consistent with the [ABET 2020] vision, which mandates Capstone projects as part of required curriculum for engineering education by 2020. Aerospace and HMC have been engaged in a mutually beneficial relationship embodied in HMC's clinic program. HMC established the program decades ago, and it has grown over the years in recruiting industry sponsors and the number of annual projects to some 40 projects per year. HMC always believed that the practice of sound engineering does require practical education. This is accomplished by executing a statement of work that an industry sponsor and HMC agree upon and execute during the academic year. Each project consists of a team of four–six students, a faculty advisor, and a team of industry liaisons that oversees the project.

The Aerospace Corporate University Affiliates Program (CUAP)

Before describing our activities with Harvey Mudd College, it would be important to recognize the greater context in which these KM&EL activities are conducted. CUAP is an aerospace outreach program that creates collaborations among aerospace corporates and a multitude of universities. One strong motivation for Aerospace CUAP is the cross pollination fostered by their relationships. Aerospace keeps academia plugged in to industry advances, and academia keeps aerospace plugged into academic advances. Some of the universities participating in the Aerospace–CUAP program include HMC, Stanford, California Institute of Technology (CalTech), University of California–Los Angeles (UCLA), University of California–Berkeley (UCB), George Washington University (GWU), Georgia Institute of Technology (GeorgiaTech), University of California–Irvine (UCI), University of California–Santa Barbara (UCSB), University of Southern California (USC), Pennsylvania State University (PSU), California State University (CSU), and others. In addition to these more formal relationships, aerospace has various relationships with a host of other universities, including University of Maryland University College (UMUC), Massachusetts Institute of Technology (MIT), Princeton University, Columbia University, Stevens Institute of Technology, Air Force Institute of Technology (AFIT), Naval Postgraduate School (NPS), Johns Hopkins University (JHU), Purdue University, and many international universities via aerospace's participation in global professional activities and societies, such as IEEE (Institute for Electrical and Electronic Engineering), IFIP (International Federation on Information Processing), ACM (Association for Computing Machinery), American Institute of Aeronautics and Astronautics (AIAA), and multiple other affiliations. Another set of activities that engages aerospace with universities are the various joint projects between university and research agencies such as Defense Advanced Research Projects Agency (DARPA) and National Science Foundation (NSF). In the HMC CUAP case, in addition to the cross pollination discussed above, the interaction is much more intensive than with other CUAP relationships, as the HMC student teams provide aerospace with completed technical projects. Aerospace also participates in the education of the HMC students by providing oversight and technical advice during the execution of the projects.

STEM Talent Needs and the High Technology Industrial Base

Another important consideration for aerospace's involvement with universities, and in particular for the CUAP program, is our continual pursuit of talent in the enabling fields of science, technology, engineering, and mathematics (STEM). The NSF has published extensively regarding the short supply of STEM talent, and is making efforts [NSF, 2009] to address the need of the United States to grow STEM talent for the 21st century. The STEM supply shortfalls are growing and additional supply is coming under pressure, both because of emerging demand for STEM talent throughout the world, as well as because of declining interest in STEM careers within the United States among K-12 and college students. This situation requires proactive engagement with our universities, as the Baby Boomers rapidly approach retirement and high technology industry, and in particular the aerospace industry must replenish STEM talent from the Gen-X and Gen-Y demographics. Hence, as aerospace strives to provide a fresh supply of STEM talent for our industrial base, the CUAP program stands tall as one of our key tools to attract and retain STEM talent and keep the industry-based talent current.

The Harvey Mudd Clinic Program

The Harvey Mudd Clinic Program (HMC Clinic) is built on the notion that engineering, as well as applied sciences, requires the practice of the profession as part and parcel of the educational process. Hence, as early as the 1960s, HMC established the Engineering Clinic program, where engineering students go through a clinical program, very much like the education in which physicians engage as part of their formal training. The idea is that an engineer must practice the craft in a team setting, against a specific statement of work defined by a paying sponsor–client of HMC, and successfully execute that project over an entire academic year, in order to graduate and become an engineer. In later years, the clinic program was expanded to mathematics, physics, and computer science. Over the years that aerospace supported the HMC Clinic program, not only did Aerospace get a number of outstanding projects completed, but also the company afforded unprecedented access to some outstanding students. The Clinic format provides Aerospace 9 months of observation of the student's individual capabilities, as well as team performance. It has been an easy decision to approach promising students and attract them for employment consideration with aerospace. The students have had the same opportunity to evaluate aerospace as a prospective employer through the experience of working together with the Aerospace Liaison team. Hence, both the prospective candidates and prospective employer experience a "9-month interview" during which they assess future relationship opportunities. Once successfully recruited and hired, we find that the HMC Clinic alums perform exceptionally well in aerospace. These HMC Clinic alums know teamwork, they recognize how to perform for a customer, and they have good communication, presentation, and interpersonal skills, in addition to a very good technical education and core values.

Before we discuss in further detail the growth of the KM&EL component within the HMC Clinic framework, let us review some of the HMC Computer Science Clinics with which the author is directly involved.

Aerospace HMC CS Clinic Projects between 1993 and 2010

Some of the computer science clinic projects that aerospace sponsored over the past couple of decades include

1993–1994: Network Host MIB Implementation
1994–1995: Network Management by Delegation
1996–1997: Network-Enabled Vis5D
1997–1998: Network Intrusion Detection
1998–1999: Network Intrusion Detection Follow-on
1999–2000: Tools and Protocols for Intrusion Detection Systems
2000–2001: Implementing the IETF IDWG Intrusion Alert Protocol
2001–2002: Implementing an IDMEF Message Management Tool
2002–2003: Implementing the Interoperable IETF/IDWG/IDXP Protocol with Proxy/Tunnel Capability
2003–2004: Launch Range Countdown Clocks
2004–2005: Grid-Enabling the VISPERS Application
2005–2006: A Grid-Enabled Biometrics Identification Framework for Video Surveillance Applications
2006–2007: A Grid-Enabled Version of SOAP for the Aerospace Cluster and CDC Communities
2009–2010: Complex Event Processing of Telemetry Streams

As is evident from the above list, the projects covered a wide range of computer science topics. More specifically, these are by-and-large computer networking and distributed computing topics; we were actively working on the Internet even prior to the prevalence of Web browsers. Nevertheless, the network already afforded us convenient remote connectivity and a baseline KM&EL capability on all of these projects. As we shall present, the quality, bandwidth, and tool richness for KM&EL continually improved over the years. As early as 1993 we had good e-mail capability, combined with FTP (File Transfer Protocol) capability to transfer files remotely. Given that HMC and Aerospace are some 50 miles apart, frequent travel for face meetings was never a convenient option. Over time, weekly conference calls were also initiated. Typically three major face meetings a year are held at Aerospace, and at least four meetings at HMC. These meetings facilitate both the Aerospace and HMC team members to become acquainted with one another. Once those personal meetings take place, it becomes much easier to collaborate online and over the phone. Even our earlier projects dealt with the Internet Engineering Task Force [IETF]. The IETF is responsible for the global engineering of Internet standards. This is done by engineers all over the world, collectively contributing to Requests for Comments [IETF-RFCs]. The RFCs are available on the Internet itself, so all the world's Internet engineers can review the RFCs, contribute to the RFCs, and offer various reference implementations of emerging Internet standards. These reference implementations are used for interoperability testing conducted by IETF participants on real networks and real computers and devices. As a matter of fact, the IETF physically meets 3 times a year in various global locations. During these face meetings, the IETF engineers discuss the state of RFCs, and whether or not draft standards could be further elevated for each active RFC, among other topics. The governance of the IETF is one of the earliest examples of KM&EL community of practice, bringing together IETF engineers and communities (working groups) from all around the world, where more senior engineers sponsor and mentor more junior engineers in each IETF Area (Operation, Security, Routing, etc.). The RFCs are currently maintained online by the IETF, and are available to the public to read and contribute to.

Over the years, Aerospace and HMC have improved their ability to collaborate and track projects. This was done by introducing a Wiki for the Clinic projects. All project material was available to all Aerospace and HMC team members. Over time we increased the richness of the collaboration tools even further, including work breakdown structures, project milestone tools and other digital tools enabling tele-presence online collaboration.

In the following section, further details are reviewed for the technical aspects of the Aerospace HMC CS Clinic projects since 1993, the first year of the HMC CS Clinic program.

Detailed Review of KM&EL Aspects of the Aerospace HMC CS Clinic Projects

Described below in further detail are various projects led by Aerospace and HMC. Highlights of relevant KM&EL aspects of each annual project are presented. The subject matter of each project greatly affected KM&EL strategies that were employed throughout the various Aerospace HMC CS Clinic projects.

1993–1994: The Network Host MIB Implementation

The Clinic team executed a network management technology project. The team constructed a network monitoring system based on the Host MIB (Management Information Base) specification, RFC 1514 [Grillo and Waldbusser, 1993]. The Host MIB is a network data repository that allows the Simple Management Network Protocol (SNMP [Case et al., 1990]) to maintain and communicate network management attributes of host computers on the network. This project exposed the student team to the IETF engineering and standardization process, as well as to the KM&EL aspects associated with the authoring, editing, and enhancement of emerging Internet standards. One of the most novel aspects of the IETF standardization process is that it requires successful interoperability demonstrations, as well as broadening adoption of the standards and their implementations by the various Internet vendors. The magic of the Internet and its amazing operation and societal impacts is indebted to the core KM&EL process and protocols established by the IETF, which are successful to date, and are very likely to continue in success going forward.

1994–1995: Network Management by Delegation

In collaboration with Aerospace and Columbia University, the team supported a DARPA research project in Decentralized Network Management (DNM). An advanced, heretofore unimplemented, form of management called Management by Delegation (MbD) was studied for feasibility and a prototype was implemented by the student team. MbD allows network management tasks to be distributed among multiple hosts within the network, resulting in improved network performance (through parallelism), scalability (since all management tasks don't fall to a single host), and reliability (since there is no dependence on any one host). This was an opportunity to expose the student team to advanced research, as this was one of the first DARPA projects on DNM. Here we added collaboration across the United States, and worked closely with Prof. Y. Yemini's team at Columbia University on one of the most advanced ideas of the day. (Prof. Yemini is a leading researcher in computer networking.) This growth in KM&EL by distance learning from a research group across the country signaled a considerable leap in the understanding of the major forces and phenomena associated with the decentralization of network management, and control and intelligence functions. One of the earliest and most highly cited papers [Meyer et al., 1995] was authored by the Aerospace–HMC–Columbia team, and was presented at the International Symposium on Integrated Network Management (IFIP/IEEE IM 1995), which is still considered a seminal contribution in the enterprise management area. The HMC student team and the Aerospace team shared code with Columbia University, enhancements were written, and new concepts and KM&EL activities were created and shared with the global community, consisting of academic, commercial, and research stakeholders. In addition, these ideas were also shared with DARPA principal investigator (PI) communities during periodic PI meetings, as well as over Web sites, which were becoming more popular KM&EL vehicles at that time.

1996–1997: Network-Enabled Vis5D

The following project took on another aspect of networking and KM&EL. Aerospace and HMC were part of one of the fastest wide-area ATM (Asynchronous

Transfer Mode) network consortia in 1996, the ARC (ATM Research Consortium) being comprised of some dozen universities and research institutes in Southern California. The Aerospace HMC Clinic team developed a client–server library that enables Vis5d [SourceForge, Vis5D], a scientific visualization tool, to visualize data being streamed across an ATM network. Previously, the tool could only view data from a local file. The Clinic team was exposed to advanced graphics and visualization technologies that allowed 3D visualization in an immersive display technology such as ImmersaDesk [UIC, 1994]. Such advanced devices facilitate the visualization of advanced scientific, engineering, or medical data, and help the researchers develop new modalities of KM&EL for a number of high technology disciplines. The members of the team communicated the data and the tools via the ATM network as they were developed in each site. This enhanced the KM&EL of the students, as well as other members of the CS Clinic team at Aerospace and researchers at other ARC sites who were working on immersive display technologies. In addition, Aerospace conducted work with the Brain Aging Institute of the University of California–Irvine and UCLA. This allowed us to work on telemedicine applications very early, since MRI and SPECT images were reviewed by researchers at different organizations and network nodes over the ARC network.

1997–1998: Network Intrusion Detection (NID)

This project was inspired by DARPA intrusion detection research that was conducted in collaboration with Aerospace, University of California–Davis, Columbia University, and HMC. The growth in network ubiquity led to a corresponding growth in exposure to digital intrusions to the computer networks. For this first NID project, the team investigated ways by which to detect potentially harmful messages in a computer network, and then implemented two detection systems. One system uses software tools to collect information about the network and correlate message sequences with the suspicious circumstances under which they arise. The other system uses a custom packet snooping and de-multiplexing system to detect attacks. The KM associated with the NID field poses a unique challenge in that intrusion "exploits" program threats that exploit system vulnerabilities, and grow in number and sophistication even more rapidly than networks grow in size, speed, and reach. The KM&EL aspects of this include not only Aerospace, HMC, Columbia, and UCD, but also the NID community at large. This includes other DARPA Principal Investigators (PIs), other NID researchers throughout the world, IETF participants, and many more. We will see the growth in KM&EL of this field that is illustrated in the following several Aerospace HMC CS Clinic annual projects.

1998–1999: Network Intrusion Detection Follow-on

The field of NID has grown nearly as rapidly as our reliance upon computers and the need to keep their data secure. Unfortunately, current automated NID systems are inherently error-prone and inaccurate. The Aerospace HMC Clinic team tried to improve the accuracy of NID methods by using data correlation techniques to reduce false positives and to associate separate, seemingly harmless events with actual computer attacks. As we can see, the complexity associated with NID, and associated attack signatures grows exponentially with network growth. Not only does the number of NID signatures grow, but also as the networks become more complex, it becomes very difficult to trace and contain network attacks. Therefore, we felt that the KM&EL of NID signatures and strategies require an element of automation and decomposition, in order to enhance KM&EL by the computer systems themselves, as well as by the students and professionals who study NID.

1999–2000: Tools and Protocols for Network Intrusion Detection Systems

This project provided a further step in our KM&EL of the NID field. The growth of the Internet, and the subsequent growth in the number of corporate and institutional networks, as well as individual host computers, has resulted in an ever-increasing number of occurrences of network intrusions. The Aerospace HMC Clinic team performed research into existing intrusion detection tools and various strategies of fighting intrusions via the use of multiple intrusion detection systems. Since the NID field is so vast and its growth is very fast, we need to employ several KM&EL strategies. During this year, the team which was distributed among Aerospace, HMC, UC Davis, and Columbia studied a number of systems and built its knowledge of the state of the art of several NID technologies. Results were presented within the DARPA NID Program PI Meeting and, during further testing and discussion, it became increasingly clear that there was a compelling need to even further automate and decompose the problem in order to succeed in NID. This realization drove the next three annual CS Clinic projects, which markedly increased KM&EL within not only the DARPA team, but also within the Internet and the IETF communities and activities.

2000–2001: Implementing the IETF IDWG Intrusion Alert Protocol

This project addressed the challenge described above, focusing on IETF development of a new NID protocol. We decided to combine earlier IETF work that we had completed in the area of network management, and weave in some of our NID thoughts and ideas into the IETF to form the new Intrusion Detection Working Group (IDWG) of the IETF. The IDWG had been developing a common method of communicating NID events. This consisted of two parts, a transport protocol and a message format. In this project, the Clinic team assisted in the development, implementation, and evaluation of two proposed transport protocols. A small research company, Silicon Defense, was added to the development team, which also included UCD students and, as in other clinic projects, HMC students, Aerospace Liaison members, and faculty advisors. This resulted in intensive KM&EL activity, which helped propagate this knowledge into the global IETF community, within the security area. As the Internet "learns" to identify and communicate suspicious activities, more complex attacks could be parsed, understood, and effectively defeated.

2001–2002: Implementing an IDMEF Message Management Tool

This project incorporated additional information and feedback received from the IDWG activities, in order to focus on Intrusion Detection Message Exchange Format (IDMEF) [Betser et al., 2002], message creation, and handling, in order to help identify NID attacks. The Aerospace Corporation sponsored a series of projects described above, focusing on issues in intrusion detection in computer networks. The IDWG of the IETF was developing a common XML message format for communicating intrusion detection events, called IDMEF. The team designed and implemented a Web-accessible database-driven application to display, manage, and facilitate the manual correlation of IDMEF messages. The Web-based aspect of the work enhanced the KM&EL quality and intensity, as it was possible for anybody on the Web to see the results of the Clinic team results. Strong collaboration with Aerospace, Silicon Defense, and the IETF community invigorated effective KM&EL as our collective knowledge grew and others expanded on the development [Debar, Curry, and Feinstein, 2007].

2002–2003: Implementing the Interoperable IETF/ IDWG/IDXP Protocol with Proxy/Tunnel Capability

This project was the culmination of our NID work. It combined our work with DARPA, IETF, Silicon Defense, and HMC to develop an enhancement to the Intrusion Detection Exchange Protocol (IDXP). In the world of Intrusion Detection, there is a need for a common message format and transport protocol so that different organizations and network nodes can collaborate in order to defeat intrusion attacks. This allows for the easy correlation, display, and long-term storage of intrusion information. This year's project built upon the work of previous intrusion detection projects sponsored by The Aerospace Corporation. It provided for messages to securely pass through firewalls using a newly specified BEEP (Blocks Extensible Exchange Protocol) [New, 2001] profile called Tunnel. In summary, the six CS Clinics working on NID provided a continual growth in KM&EL, and expanded the state of the art and knowledge from an individual DARPA project to the global Internet and IETF community.

2003–2004: Launch Range Countdown Clocks

This CS Clinic project marked a new topic for Aerospace projects. Aerospace is tightly linked to computer networks and uses its knowledge to modernize the space launch ranges. Countdown clocks, a common tool of launch ranges, are used to synchronize and control the numerous and complex series of actions leading to the launch of a space vehicle or guided missile. However, countdown clocks rely on a standard for time distribution and synchronization that, in comparison to modern digital protocols, is anachronistic and needlessly restrictive. The Clinic team developed an entirely new standard for the management of range countdown clocks founded on modern and effective protocols, such as the Network Time Protocol (NTP) and the Hyper Text Transport Protocol (HTTP), which will improve both the accuracy and flexibility of countdown time services. KM&EL are enhanced in this project as time is communicated directly from the atomic clocks that provide the Global Positioning System (GPS) with world time. This knowledge is propagated to all elements within the launch range, teaching the operators an entirely new way to synchronize time. During this project an early version of a project Wiki was introduced. This Wiki was used to report project status, activities, and recent changes and developments to the team on all sites.

2004–2005: Grid-Enabling the VISPERS Application

This project began a series of clinics in the distributed processing area. The project addressed telemetry processing from space launch operations. Rockets are very noisy and vibrate quite violently. It is important to design launch vehicles and space vehicles to withstand the traumatic experience of launch into space orbit. This discipline is called Vibroacoustic analysis. Aerospace developed a number of tools to study this field. One such tool is VISPERS (Vibroacoustic Intelligent System for Prediction of Environments, Reliability, and Specifications). Figure 17.1 describes the VISPERS role within the analysis process. The team designed and implemented a version of waveform analysis tool, VAIL (VISPERS AI Lab) [Bentow et al., 2006], based on the "grid" highly-parallel computing paradigm, using the Globus toolkit. VAIL is part of a larger system that analyzes real-time sensor data to characterize the vibro-acoustic shock environment of launch vehicles. The team conducted a performance analysis of the grid-enabled tool, measured speedup, and analyzed communication bottlenecks. They also researched and surveyed the current state-of-the-art in grid computing tools and provided a study to facilitate future grid implementations by The Aerospace Corporation. There is a tremendous amount of knowledge associated with the vibro-acoustic field. The telemetry is analyzed and the information grows in quality and analytic capability. KM&EL is enhanced by a number of journal and conference publications [Bentow et al., 2006a,b] generated by this project, and shared with the grid-computing, enterprise management, and vibroacoustic communities.

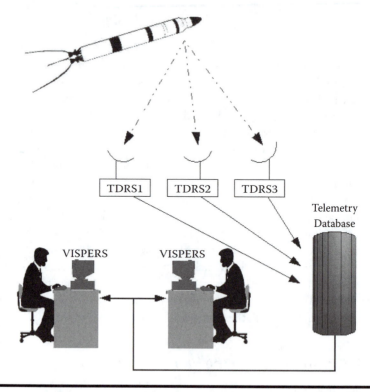

Figure 17.1   The VISPERS role within the vibroacoustic analysis process.

2005–2006: A Grid-Enabled Biometrics Identification Framework for Video Surveillance Applications

Another project that uses grid computing serves the biometrics discipline. This Clinic project addressed face recognition and grid computing with a framework for distributed biometric identification. ANUBIS, the Aerospace Networked Upgradeable Biometric Identification System, is a grid-enabled surveillance application that applies face recognition to video streams. ANUBIS utilizes Aerospace's Switchblade library, a Java framework for the distributed processing of streaming data, and a commercial toolkit, and is extensible to accommodate alternative biometric data schemes. During the execution of this project a more advanced Wiki was introduced by the Clinic team. All project data was captured within the Wiki, and easily tracked by all team members. This Wiki introduced more advanced project management tools, and helped the team work the schedule and the timeline, on top of the previous Wiki capabilities. KM&EL was enhanced as we were able to experiment with and integrate new technologies including pattern recognition and video streams from multiple geographic locations, and grid-enabled processing of high data rate video streams.

2006–2007: A Grid-Enabled Version of SOAP for the Aerospace Cluster and CDC Communities

The Clinic team created a platform-independent portal that enables a highly-parallel version of SOAP (Satellite Orbit Analysis Program, Figure 17.2) to be accessible to a wide community of users for the first time. Before, a user of the parallel version of SOAP would need to be conversant with UNIX commands and other technical aspects of grid computing. Using the team's portal, the power of grid-enabled SOAP is accessible through a simple Web interface. This project empowered every desktop user to use SOAP in a transparent way. Complicated interfaces were eliminated and simplified access enhances KM&EL for multiple users conducting Concept Design Center (CDC; Aerospace–CDC, 2001) design iterations. This expedited the design, analysis, and productivity within the CDC. The Aerospace CDC is a KM&EL facility, as it involves a team that can be distributed on the West Coast and East Coast. Team members from both coasts support a common concept design and collaborate remotely over the network. The availability of Cluster-SOAP capability to multiple desktops within the CDC in multiple locations enabled advanced KM&EL capabilities. The Aerospace HMC CS Clinic team engaged both CS and Engineering students and increased learning for all team members. These results were published in Barr et al. (2008).

2009–2010: Complex-Event Processing of Telemetry Streams

The Space Syndication Project (SSP) is under development at The Aerospace Corporation in support of net centric goals of the Department of Defense (DoD). For the DoD to move towards Net-centric information architecture, integration of new information filtering and fusion logic into the global data dissemination infrastructure must occur dynamically and immediately as needed. The SSP is realizing this goal by developing prototype services to enable transformation of data delivery systems into a global information ecosystem where every uploaded event processor results in new globally accessible information products. To demonstrate the potential of this infrastructure the SSP has developed an initial set of complex event processing programs and corresponding Web-based configuration clients and displays. To better illustrate the benefit of the SSP information infrastructure, a greater breadth and depth of applications must be developed. The Aerospace HMC clinic project will develop complex event processing applications with tangible benefits to our programs that demonstrate the full capabilities of the SSP infrastructure. This current CS Clinic project demonstrates advanced KM&EL in action. The product of the project will in turn provide up-to-date knowledge and continually educate the users with the changing state of the information. The project itself uses the Wiki, as well as the TRAC [TRAC] tool that allows the team to track progress, timelines, demonstrations, and

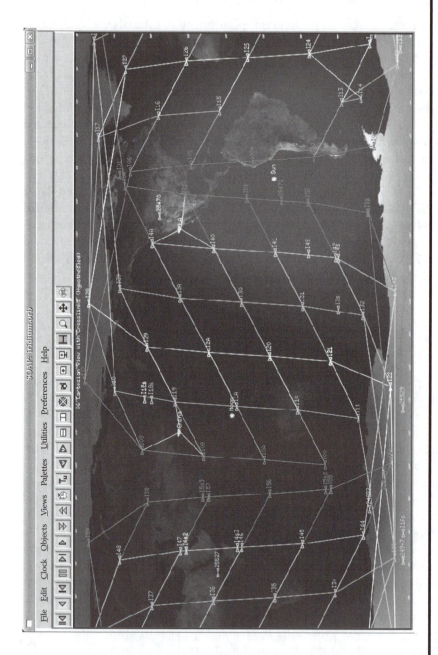

Figure 17.2   Sample output of the Aerospace SOAP program.

task breakdowns and schedules. In many ways this is the most advanced KM&EL Clinic project to date.

KM&EL Observations and Trends

Over the years, Aerospace and HMC engagement of advanced KM&EL has been on the rise. Early start was with online collaboration, which is the hallmark of the IETF. The actual subject matter of the work involved the use of RFCs in order to work on DNM and NID. The IETF has been in the forefront of online collaborations, as the development of the global Internet requires a very high degree of interoperability. Since the Internet technologies and standards are developed all over the world by multiple online contributors, the IETF developed the appropriate governance structure to accommodate online modifications to RFCs. Almost all the work is done as remote KM&EL by the contributors. Three times a year the IETF meets in person within various parts of the world. However the work between Aerospace and the HMC team depended on a considerable number of face meetings, interleaved with e-mail exchanges and teleconference calls. We also exchanged code and documents using primarily FTP in the early 1990s. Over the years projects advanced and engaged grid computing technologies, and the scope of the collaboration grew to the global supercomputing community.

Over time KM&EL was enhanced by adding Wikis in order to maintain a high level of semantic collaboration, and additional online tools and Web sites were incorporated. These included the Globus toolkit and the Global Grid Forum. In more recent years the use of Web-based project management tools such as TRAC was increased, as was the capability for high quality remote collaboration.

The HMC Clinic Advisory Committee (CAC) Governance

One of the interesting KM&EL activities that Aerospace took on over the years is a growing involvement with the HMC leadership and the CAC, to help guide the college with industry advice. The CAC reviews project outcomes, conducts feedback interviews with other sponsoring companies, and discusses new ideas for the HMC Clinic program. Some of the feedback is provided by Web-based survey tools such as Survey Monkey, but we also follow up with phone interviews with the sponsors. Multiple industry sponsors and stakeholders participate in the CAC, which allows for cross pollination and enhanced KM&EL from industry peers as well.

Global Clinic

One of the novel ideas that HMC and the CAC developed is that of the Global Clinic (GC). The GC expands the well proven idea of the HMC Clinic into other countries, creating collaborations on projects that span multiple countries across the globe. This is done with collaborating universities and industrial sponsors, which have operations in other countries. This is an exciting extension that takes KM&EL to a whole different level. The cross-pollination created by the interactions among the students from different countries adds an important dimension to the educational experience. The KM&EL collaboration tools, including Video Tele Conferencing (VTC), add interesting interactions and novel intercultural experiences as well. The KM&EL become even more effective for the GC projects due to the immersive experience in the beginning of the GC projects, during which students travel to the other countries and work together in a new environment. These initial face to face meetings enhance the remote collaboration later on within the project year, and KM&EL are thus further refined.

Engineering Visitors Committee

Aerospace was also invited to participate and chair the HMC Engineering Visitors Committee (EVC). The EVC works with the HMC Engineering leadership to set even more ambitious goals for Engineering and for KM&EL. The EVC consists of several senior individuals from industry, academia, and government. These individuals hold both e-mail discussions as well as face meetings in order to offer strategic advice to HMC. Aerospace recently participated in the ABET accreditation review for the department, during which the clinic program, as well as the GC program, received favorable feedback. Both programs are considered important mainstays of the education experience within HMC. New ways are continually sought by which to explore and grow KM&EL capabilities for clinic activities, as well as for other activities.

Future Trends, Communities, Social Networks, Semantic Networks, Wikipedia, Web 2.0, and Future Advanced Research

As Aerospace and HMC seek out future advances within the exciting area of KM&EL for capstone projects, it appears that there are limitless opportunities for advances in multiple areas. We anticipate tremendous growth in the areas of global communities of practice and communities of interest, and social networking technologies, as well as a number of Web 2.0 tools and technologies. These tools allow for even more intensive collaboration and crowd-sourcing of knowledge and information. With the advent of advanced search engines, Wikipedia-type knowledge repositories, advanced federated enterprise search, semantic webs, and Second Life, the sky is the limit!

Acknowledgments

This work would not have been possible without the support of the Aerospace Institute Corporate University Affiliates Program (CUAP), and the HMC Clinic program. In particular, special thanks are extended for the support of Wanda Austin, William Ballhaus, Rami Razouk, Zane Faught, William Krenz, David Evans, Marilee Wheaton, Sumner Matsunaga, Robert Frueholz, Michael Campbell, Carl Sunshine, Joseph Bannister, Alan Foonberg, Diana Johnson, Stewart Sutton, Mary Nichols, Samuel Osofsky Peggy Zweben, Stephen Lukasik, Maria Klawe, Ziyad Duron, Anthony Bright, Robert Keller, Michael Erlinger, Ran Liebeskind-Hadas, Giselle Betser, multiple Aerospace members of the technical staff, and many HMC students who participated in the program over the years.

References

Accreditation Board for Engineering and Technology, Vision for the Engineer of year 2020. "ABET 2020: Face the Future," http://www.abet.org/news_meetings.shtml.

The Aerospace Concept Design Center, conducts system engineering and architecture studies on space systems, http://www.aero.org/publications/crosslink/winter2001/01_sidebar2.html.

Barr, T., Byron, C., Duron, Z., Keller, R., Lickly, B., Nygaard, C., Roberts, K., AuYeung, M., Betser, J., Coggi, J., Davis, B., Lee, C., Stodden, D., and Thomas, M. "Grid-enabling orbital analysis and computationally intensive applications for a growing set of diversified users," *Proceedings of the 10th IEEE/IFIP Network Operations and Management Symposium,* pp. 615–629, Salvador, Brazil, April 2008, 2http://ieeexplore.ieee.org/xpls/abs_all.jsp?isnumber=4575087&arnumber=4575182&count=195&index=89&tag=1.

Bentow, B., Dodge, J., Homer, A., Moore, C., Keller, R., Presley, M., Davis, R., Seidel, J., Lee, C., and Betser, J, "Grid-enabling a vibroacoustic analysis application," *6th International Workshop on Grid Computing*, November 13–14, 2005, pp. 33–39.

Bentow, B., Dodge, J., Homer, A., Moore, C., Keller, R., Lee, C., Thomas, M., Seidel, J., Presley, M., Davis, R., and Betser, J., "Grid-enabling a vibroacoustic analysis toolkit," *International Journal of High Performance Computing and Networking*, 2006a.

Bentow, B., Dodge, J., Homer, A., Moore, C.D., Keller, R.M., Presley, M., Davis, R., Seidel, J., Lee, C., and Betser, J., "System management for grid-enabling a vibroacoustic analysis application," *Network Operations and Management Symposium*, 2006. NOMS 2006. 10th IEEE/IFIP, April 3–7, 2006b pp. 1–14, http://ieeexplore.ieee.org/search/wrapper.jsp?arnumber=1687615.

Betser, J., and Erlinger, M., "The challenges of advanced ATM applications", *Proc IEEE 3rd International Workshop on System Management*, Newport, RI, April 1998, http://www.computer.org/portal/web/csdl/doi/10.1109/IWSM.1998.668127.

Betser, J., Walther, A., Erlinger, M., Buchheim, T., Feinstein, B., Matthews, G., Pollock, R., and Levitt, K., "GlobalGuard: Creating the IETF-IDWG Intrusion Alert Protocol (IAP)," *Proc. of the 1st IEEE DARPA Information Survivability Conference and Exposition (DISEX)*, pp. 22–34, vol.1, Anaheim, CA, September 2001. http://ieeexplore.ieee.org/stamp/stamp.jsp?tp=&arnumber=932189&isnumber=20170&tag=1. http://ieeexplore.ieee.org/xpls/abs_all.jsp?arnumber=932189.

Betser, J., Walther A., Erlinger, M., Buchheim, T., Feinstein, B., and Matthews, G., "Creating the IETF IDWG Intrusion Detection Protocols IDMEF and IDXP," *Ground System Architectures Workshop*, March 2002, El Segundo, California. http://sunset.usc.edu/gsaw/gsaw2002/s5/erlinger.pdf.

Case, J., Fedor, M., Schoffstahl, M., and Davin, J., "The Simple Network Management Protocol (SNMP)," IETF RFC 1157, 1990. http://www.ietf.org/rfc/rfc1157.txt.

The Aerospace Institute (TAI), Corporate University Affiliates Program (CUAP) http://www.aero.org/news/newsitems/whatsinaface3-15-06.html.

Defense Advanced Research Agency. http://www.darpa.mil/.

Debar, H., Curry, D., and Feinstein, B., "The Intrusion Detection Message Exchange Format (IDMEF)," IETF RFC 4765, November 2007.

The Globus Alliance, http://www.globus.org/.

Grillo, P., and Waldbusser, S., "Host Resources MIB, IETF RFC 1514," September 1993, http://tools.ietf.org/html/rfc1514 Feinstein, B., Matthews, G., "Intrusion Detection Exchange Protocol (IDXP)", IETF RFC 4767, http://www.ietf.org/mail-archive/web/ietf-announce/current/msg03504.html.

Harvey Mudd College Clinic, http://www.cs.hmc.edu/clinic/info.

The Internet Engineering Task Force (IETF), http://www.ietf.org.

The IETF repository of Requests for Comments (RFCs), http://www.ietf.org/rfc.html.

Liebowitz, J., *Knowledge Retention: Strategies and Solutions*, CRC Press, Boca Raton, FL, 2009.

Meyer, K., Erlinger, M., Betser, J., Sunshine, C., Goldszmidt, G., and Yemini, Y., "Decentralizing Control and Intelligence in Network Management", *Proc 4th International Symposium on Integrated Network Management*, Santa Barbara, CA, May, 1995 (cited 95 times). http://citeseerx.ist.psu.edu/viewdoc/download?doi=10.1.1.30.4042&rep=rep1&type=pdf.

New, D. "The Tunnel Protocol" IETF draft, http://tools.ietf.org/html/draft-ietf-idwg-beep-tunnel-01.

National Science Foundation STEM Talent Expansion Program (STEP), http://www.nsf.gov/funding/pgm_summ.jsp?pims_id=5488 as well as many reports to Congress over the years, http://www.nsf.gov/pubs/2001/ceose2000rpt/congress_6.pdf.

Vis5D Visualization Tool, http://vis5d.sourceforge.net/.

Sutton, S., Betser, J. Hornickel, M., Gregorio M., Kern, J., Lincoln, C., and Crisostomo, J., The Aerospace Corporation case study, Book Chapter in *Knowledge Retention: Strategies and Solutions*, by Liebowitz, J., Ed., CRC Press, Boca Raton, FL, 2008, http://www.crcpress.com/product/isbn/9781420064650.

TRAC, http://trac.edgewall.org/.

University of Illinois, Chicago Immersadesk™ Immersive Visualization Station, http://www.evl.uic.edu/pape/CAVE/idesk/.

Chapter 18

Knowledge Management and Learning in Industry

Tim Howell

Contents

Knowledge management (KM) implementation is as diverse as the individuals and organizations that make up business, government, and education around the world. For this discussion, let us assume a mid-sized organization with resources to implement organizational and technology KM initiatives throughout the organization. This chapter focuses on personal knowledge involved in doing the work of a business and people-based tacit knowledge transfer for the purpose of promoting

323

continuous learning. We will explore overarching knowledge management principles, then get down in the trenches to work one-on-one with subject matter experts from the perspective of a knowledge management practitioner.

The Role of KM in Information, Knowledge, and Learning

KM objectives in a business environment are to sustain and improve organizational performance. "Knowledge abounds in our organizations but its existence does not guarantee its use" (Davenport and Prusak, 2000, p. 89). Successful KM practitioners understand the important role individual knowledge plays in achieving organizational performance objectives. KM practitioners also understand the difference between knowledge and information. The difference between knowledge and information must be clearly understood before defining people-based initiatives and selecting technology to support achieving performance expectations. Merriam-Webster Dictionary (2009) defines *knowledge* as "the fact or condition of knowing something with familiarity gained through experience or association; the range of one's information or understanding; the act or condition of having information or of being learned." *Information* is defined as "the communication or reception of knowledge or intelligence." In plain English, knowledge resides in each of us. It is the result of acquiring information through communication, study, or instruction. Why is understanding the difference between knowledge and information so important? Many companies simply role out Web-based tools with the expectation that these tools will provide resources to support their employee performance expectations. Tools alone rarely achieve real knowledge transfer. With this understanding under our caps, we can begin to select the people-based methods and technologies an organization may need to acquire information, share knowledge, and learn.

KM efforts often start with Information Technology initiatives to organize, codify, and archive information into searchable repositories. A good objective is to identify what information is needed (when, by whom, and in what form) to maximize efficient learning. Contextual search tools such as BING (Microsoft, 2009) or Invention Machine's, Goldfire Innovator (Invention Machine, 2009) help filter queries to a desired subject. An example search might start with the word *stock*. As the word is entered, BING suggests contextual adjectives ranging from stock trades and stock market to *Stockton Recorder*. The more contextual adjectives entered, the more specific the search results. A more sophisticated search tool would also suggest associative topics based on current or previous search topics. An example would be an Amazon.com (2009) search result suggesting readers who enjoyed Margaret Mitchell's *Gone with The Wind* also purchase *Scarlett,* its sequel.

As good as these search tools are, information repositories, sometimes falsely called a *knowledge base*, often fail to yield sustainable organizational knowledge growth (learning) without subject expert's insight on how best to find and apply information. In other words, it is difficult to find answers when one does not know what questions to ask. The "knowledge seeker" becomes disappointed with search results and stops using company information resources. The result is organizations struggle to realize value in information repositories alone that do not provide some form of self-help or live person guidance. Some commercial Web sites recognize this need for expert guidance by offering pop-up live chats with company experts. This is a step toward a richer person-to-person interaction. As technology advances, who knows? Someday we may all have a personal subject-matter expert avatar instructor (Second Life, 2009).

A holistic KM model includes both technology tools and people-to-people interactions. Why are people-to-people interactions important? The growth of one's subject knowledge is much richer when information is communicated with a wealth of experience from a subject matter expert. As an example, if you were traveling to an unfamiliar city, would you prefer a road map or a live tour guide with knowledge of the best travel routes, restaurants, hotels, and entertainment the city has to offer? My guess is you would learn more about the city with a tour guide. A holistic KM initiative encompasses people-based knowledge, knowledge steward-ship (the tour guide), information management tools, and a work environment that promotes continuous learning.

The knowledge management field is an umbrella that strives to integrate traditional disciplines common to core corporate operations. Mature KM initiatives involve all business functions with specific focus on business management, information technology, human resources, and training functions as core working resources. Business management establishes specific business objectives to guide information scope, retention, and distribution needs. In other words, what do employees need to know about the day-to-day internal and external business activities, business goals, industry marketplace, and advances in their specific work discipline? Information technology provides the communications infrastructure and works to streamline the accessibility and flow of information. Human resources, working with functional groups, identify personnel skills needs, and develop curriculum to enhance an individual's subject knowledge. Training, often a part of HR, designs instructional products to meet business learning needs. Employing all of these functional disciplines in concert helps to provide the right learning experiences at the right time to achieve organizational performance goals.

How Does Knowledge Management Serve Business-Learning Needs?

From a knowledge management perspective, achieving a work environment that encourages and supports free flow of the right information at the right time in the right format is an ideal goal. To achieve this goal, knowledge management practitioners work to first identify where individual knowledge is needed and, second, identify subject matter experts (SME) who can provide subject insight and learning guidance.

Historically, capture–index–share, a KM tenet, meant knowledge management practitioners facilitated face-to-face interactions only. As companies learn the value of converting stovepipe organizations into knowledge-sharing organizations, they have also adopted communication tools to assist and promote the *knowledge worker* environment. In recent years, broadband wireless networks and phone technologies have expanded access to one-to-one and many-to-many knowledge transactions, allowing virtual face-to-face communities of interest and social networking to develop. In the knowledge worker environment, subject matter experts are expected to be their organization's *knowledge stewards*. As the methods of promoting knowledge sharing evolve, the fundamental business need is still to learn. What is changing is the way knowledge seekers interact with knowledge sources, and how KM practitioners facilitate the flow of knowledge. Advances in communications technologies are accelerating access to knowledge workers who provide content for informal and formal training. KM practitioners still encourage experts to mentor others by sponsoring activities such as communities of practice, lunch-and-learn sessions, round table forums, how-to demonstrations, or work experience story telling. Now KM practitioners can include employees virtually from other work sites anywhere in the world.

To sustain and build on these KM-sponsored activities, KM practitioners work with functional teams to identify discipline knowledge stewards. Usually a seasoned employee or leader ("knowledge stewards") monitor their organization's learning needs. In this role, they network with other functional or discipline experts, maintain information repositories, mentor and sponsor new employees, lead discipline or industry learning sessions, and more. We are directly and indirectly in touch with each other more than ever through technology. Looking into the future, the challenge is to bring rich face-to-face interactions to virtual business networks such as LinkedIn (2009) and social networks like Facebook (2009).

Once learning needs are established, learning methods can be defined. In this stage, KM practitioners work with subject matter experts to define learning forums or partner with instructional design specialists to create more formal products from one-time training products up to full-discipline curriculum. Instructional design may range from instructor lead classes with tests and completion certificates to product use instructions delivered to a field rep's cell phone. Each learning method should be designed to serve unique business learning needs.

Working with Subject Matter Experts (SME)

Defining Learning Objectives First

KM activities are often concerned with preserving or preventing the loss of business knowledge. In this mode, focus is on who knows what and how we can capture what this person knows. Without defining learning objectives based on business needs first, the KM practitioner is unprepared to outline why the SME's knowledge is important and who will benefit from the knowledge-sharing effort. The SME's response will likely be "I know a lot about this subject, what would you like to know?" Being clear on specific learning needs helps the person organize their thoughts, gather materials, and focus on topics to be shared. It makes the job of recalling and expressing thoughts and ideas easier.

Finding the Right Subject Matter Expert

Many organizations have people who are looked to for answers. They are recognized because they have advanced training, years of experience, or are willing to research subjects to find experts or resources. These are the people who will contribute rich nuggets of knowledge to learning. How do you find these people? Start by asking coworkers and team leaders "Who is the go to person for this subject?" You will get different answers but generally, the majority of responses will point to a small handful of people. Once you have narrowed the field, do initial subject homework if you are not familiar or trained in the subject, and acquire a basic understanding of the field or discipline through self-study. This is your first impression for the expert and may define how successful you are in soliciting this person's help. Coworkers, the library, and Internet are great resources. This will prepare you to ask good leading questions, and use terms correctly and in the right context. Do not be afraid to say, "I don't know much about this subject, this is what I know, can you help explain so I can learn more"? Remember, if this is your first introduction and "sales pitch" to this person, having some subject knowledge will greatly increase the likelihood of successfully engaging with this person. Imagine how lively a conversation would be between two life-long *Star Trek* fans. They might recount story lines, exciting events, and mission triumphs. Now imagine how the conversation would be if one person does not know who Spock or James T. Kirk is and is not interested in futuristic space travel. You get the idea. It may not last very long and not much information would be exchanged.

In some cases, a manager may want to assign subject-knowledge-sharing tasks to a team member. This may help in facilitating an expert's contribution to a learning event or training products. Whether a person is assigned, volunteers, or has never shared subject knowledge, subject homework is still important to help you confirm this is the right person for the task. First ask, are you willing to share what you know with others? In many work environments today you are asking the person to be a benevolent knowledge donor. Ideally, time and money are allocated for knowledge sharing efforts, but many times these efforts are lunch-and-learn or after-hours' activities. The next question is what are the most important topics someone should know about this subject? Most SMEs are passionate about their work and have at least an idea of key must-know topics. These initial topics will help determine the form of information delivery and be the basis for organizing learning content. Then, discuss how the person will present their subject experience. Again, thinking about the business learning needs, can the expert be an instructor, participate in round-table discussions, be on call to answer questions, or write an e-learning script? There are many options but you and the expert should decide what method the expert is willing and able to accomplish. Not everyone is comfortable in front of a class or video camera. So select a method that you and the expert are comfortable with to clearly express verbally or in writing what the expert knows.

To illustrate the process of finding the right SME based on learning needs, here is a brief, real-life excerpt from the International Space Station (ISS) Design Knowledge Capture (DKC) project (Howell, 2009):

> The NASA ISS program office was concerned about losing 10 years of design knowledge. They needed to maintain a high level of trained flight support personnel who had first hand in-depth knowledge of all ISS components for its planned 30 years of on orbit operation. A small knowledge management team was assembled to find and interview design experts across a dozen contractors. The multimedia content would be used to develop training products for console operators in Houston and assembly support teams at the Cape Canaveral launch site. Multimedia presentations, how-to demonstrations, and round-table discussions, combined with supporting documentation, was also published in the NASA ISS DKC Web site.
>
> We established site coordinators at each contractor to help identify subject experts. Based on their recommendations, we solicited responses from a cross section of engineering and manufacturing program experts in multiple design disciplines including electrical, mechanical, software, and systems. We learned that involving program experts in the design of probing questions yielded richer, more detailed, how-does-it-work answers. These experts were also our first interview subjects. Interview, presentation, or demonstration recording methods were as unobtrusive as possible so the expert was not self-conscious or distracted by record-ing equipment. We respected individual's abilities and willingness to have sometimes very personal one-on-one discussions about their design development experiences. This approach yielded many "in their own words" expert knowledge nuggets not available in design docu-mentation. We learned that asking to video-record interviews made most people self-conscious and reluctant to discuss factual details for fear of making a mistake, so we assured each person they would have final review of their session and we would not publish until they were satisfied all details were correct. This put most people at ease and made them feel more involved in the process.
>
> The results of this and other knowledge capture activities was NASA University operations training for ISS systems console operators. The first class realized a 100% graduation success.

NASA is a very unique environment but the approach of identifying learning needs, then nurturing and coaching subject experts to incorporate their unique knowledge in training, can be successfully applied in any organization.

Subject Matter Experts—Introduction to Structured Knowledge Sharing

Most people contribute, without realizing, what they know every day through normal work responsibilities, project reviews, and even impromptu lunch-time conversations. Unstructured knowledge transfer is a healthy part of daily personal interactions in an organization. When the need is to formally transfer unique business knowledge from one person to another or one person to many, a KM practitioner needs to solicit that person's conscious assembly and delivery of what they know. Being asked to share what you are passionate about is great flattery to some, but met with suspicion or even fear by others. Everyone's willingness and ability to share their knowledge is based on their unique training, work life experiences, and motivation. Here are scenarios involving three kinds of contributors that KM practitioners will encounter when soliciting an expert's support to train others:

Eager contributors. Those who are secure in their position with the company or are experienced in mentoring others usually welcome the invitation and may even dive right into planning how they will share their experiences. This personality generally needs only delivery coaching or partnering with an instructional designer to develop a well-structured class or e-learning product. If the organization agrees, this person may be recruited to facilitate other SME knowledge transfer projects or ongoing knowledge stewardship assignments.

Reluctant contributors. The reticent person will require all the interpersonal skills you can muster. First, try to understand why the person is not interested. It may be the result of their work environment. The reasons may be more personal. Some people are shy or very often think what they know is not very important. This is more common than you would think. Most of us do not stop to take inventory of all we know. We apply skills and wisdom acquired over years of practicing our chosen trade without conscious thought so our daily work activities become common routines. In this case, try to explain that, as unimportant as this knowledge may seem, others in the company know much less about this subject and could benefit from learning from you. Again, have some knowledge, if not a working knowledge, of the subject. Know the business learning needs. Express interest in the subject. Point out specific topics the organization needs to learn to be more proficient and the overall benefit to the health of the company. Then explore participation options the person has to determine a working comfort zone. Options could range, for example, from writing how-to instructions or gathering their existing papers to recording a one-on-one conversation or participating in a moderated round-table discussion. Explore as many available options as possible until you settle on a working solution the person is most comfortable with.

Unwilling contributors. A more difficult scenario is the person who is concerned about giving away their unique abilities. They see their knowledge as their value to the company. If their unique knowledge is shared with others, they fear they will lose their job. This is a real fear for many in good economic times and obviously even more severe in bad times. As a KM practitioner, you most likely are not in a position to guarantee job security. However, it is important that you understand not only the current business environment but also this person's group dynamics before engaging in a discussion about sharing the very thing that is keeping them secure in their work. There are many reasons why a company would want to transfer unique business knowledge. They range from business growth to preserving retiring baby boomer's years of experience to name just two. For this example let's assume the company wants to increase the number of employees with this person's unique skills to balance work loads and expand into new product areas. Whatever the reason, be honest with the reasons for the knowledge capture request. It is very important to build trust, comradery, and empathy for the person's concerns. Explain how the person's knowledge will be used and who will benefit. Explore the same range of participation options discussed above to find a working comfort zone. In this scenario, more than the first two, to motivate you must inspire this person through examples of familiar coworker's successful KM projects, or company sponsored recognition and rewards programs.

If this approach is unsuccessful, try including coworkers in a collaborative project or positive support from the person's supervisor who could explain the company needs and why the person's expertise is valued. Be prepared to thank the person and move on if they continue to resist. Remember, sharing knowledge requires the person's *ability and willingness* to communicate their tacit knowledge experiences.

Designing SME Questions

The purpose of designing SME questions is to establish the relevance of a person's knowledge to business learning needs and then to help someone recall and organize their thoughts and information. Questions should first lead the person from a general overview of their background to establish their credibility and subject background to put the subject in context. Next, questions should be specific to elicit as many facts and examples as possible. Ask subject experts to help design subject-specific questions they would ask a peer. They are probably in the best position to know what is most important. The questions need to be specific to business operational, administrative, or technical learning needs. It helps to start with a question template that can be customized to the specific subject. Here is an excerpt from an engineering SME interview example:

1. Please describe your involvement with the XXXX effort, including your number of years on the project.

2. Describe the hardware/software, first in layman's terms without technical jargon and acronyms, then using any terms you wish.
3. What were some of the earliest design concepts of the hardware/software during the evolution of the XXXX activities?
4. Please give us a functional and physical description of the XXXX hardware/software as it has evolved into the current version.
5. What do you remember as the defining or guiding principle(s) for the hardware/software?
   a. In the early days of development
   b. More recently
6. What were the major hurdles that had to be overcome to complete the design?
7. Are there any problems that came up more than once? If so, what were they?
8. What were the key "lessons learned" from the development and testing of this hardware/software?
9. What were some key decision points that were encountered along the way, what were the options considered, and why did you choose the path you did and reject the other options?
10. What improvements or upgrades would you suggest for the hardware/software and what benefits would be obtained if these were implemented?
11. If you had it all to do over again, what changes would you make in procedures, materials, etc.? Why? Put another way, how would you advise someone just starting out on a similar type of XXXX project to proceed differently?
12. What is the worst thing imaginable that could happen to the hardware/software? How can this be avoided? What would be the best way to handle it if it happened?
17. Who are some of the most qualified people to diagnose problems with the XXXX? Most qualified to repair them?
18. Can you recommend additional resources on the XXXX such as engineering or scientific papers or relevant reports?
19. Would you be available to consult in the future?
20. Are there any questions that we should have asked you that we did not?

Capturing SME Knowledge

As discussed earlier, the ideal work environment is one where the organization is able to self-manage its knowledge needs through knowledge stewards or self-guided learning. Often the genesis of this ideal environment is the practice of soliciting experts to be mentors and training content providers. Here are three methods of providing learning content for formal or informal training:

Interviews. Interviews can be in the form of questionnaires, audio, or video recordings. The content of questionnaires can provide the text of classroom or e-learning training. Recorded interviews can be one-on-one or group interviews. Often group interviews, either peer-to-peer or interviewer to group yields much richer knowledge nuggets. One person often helps another recall facts or event details. Sometimes group interviews break into point counter point debate, which results in new information discoveries. Like a questionnaire response, this type of multimedia content can also be used as classroom or e-learning content with the added benefit of seeing and hearing an experts anecdotal stories.

Presentations and demonstrations. Presentations should not be limited to or by PowerPoint charts. Charts add visual information and structure to the presentation but should be used, as in an interview, to prompt the presenter to elaborate on his or her unique experiences, thought processes, or decision-making. Another form of presentation is story telling. A well-presented story is rich with first hand experiences that illustrate events, personal interactions and decisions in context of the events, and successes and failures. Like any good story, there should be a beginning, middle, and end.

Collaborative discussion. This form of knowledge capture can consist of peer-to-peer debate, problem solving, or simple round-table discussion. The objective is to provide experts a forum to explore concepts, propose alternate thinking on an existing business initiative, or discuss the merits of a successful business practice. Consider opening this type of discussion to the entire organization to introduce more junior points of view, questions, and possibly new information. Like the first two capture formats, the objective is to solicit the best current information from the best minds your organization has to offer for the benefit of the entire organization.

Incorporating SME Content in Instructional Design

Translating a person's unique knowledge into usable information another person can acquire and then apply to their work is what knowledge transfer is all about. Planning how to deliver an expert's information is as important as capturing it. As discussed earlier, identifying learning needs first will help an expert, a KM practitioner, and an instructional designer focus on the right knowledge to capture and share.

In e-learning formats, indexing training content is particularly important for quick subject search, remediation, and learning retention. In this learning environment, no one wants to sit through a 2-hour video interview to get to the information they need. For these reasons, partnering an expert with an instructional designer can help clarify learning objectives and guide best-delivery format and software tools decisions. Not every expert is a teacher. If the intent is to provide classroom training, an instructional designer can coach an expert on how to set learning expectations, organize classroom presentations, and design tests.

Information, Knowledge, Learning—Completing the Cycle

Learning styles are various approaches or ways of learning (LdPride, 2009). It is commonly believed that most people favor some particular method of interacting with, taking in, and processing information. Educating methods are chosen that are presumed to allow that individual to learn best. Learning styles range from Kolb's experiential learning (Kolb, 1984) to passive lecture. Finding that items presented both visually and verbally are better remembered gave rise to a dual-coding theory, first proposed by Allan Paivio (1971) and later applied to multimedia by Richard Mayer (2001). Mayer has shown learners are better able to transfer their learning, given multimodal instruction.

A good learning experience occurs when one can see, hear, and read at the same time. This is sometimes called the "3D effect" of learning. What you see may be body language or expression. You hear voice inflection. Reading gives you the details that substantiate the verbal or visual information. Each sensory experience reinforces the others. Studies have shown this type of learning experience improves retention significantly for most students. When a recognized subject matter expert is added to the equation in classroom or e-learning methods, they bring credibility to concepts and facts presented. They can provide real life examples to illustrate practical application of concepts and facts. This helps put abstract ideas and relationships in context more quickly and provides guidance for the student's own decision-making.

Web-based, multimedia e-learning has opened new learning avenues for business. These technologies help bridge time and distance to bring experts to students. In business, e-learning can provide just-in-time training 24 hours a day, 7 days a week. A more far reaching example is the International Space Station design and maintenance e-learning products uploaded to the astronauts on orbit. In turn, astronauts regularly transmit back what they have learned performing experiments in near zero gravity as they orbit the earth. This is an example of a work environment that encourages (requires) and supports free flow of information where students are also teachers. It also illustrates how people in any business organization can teach each other through strategic knowledge stewardship and applied learning initiatives.

Knowledge Management and Learning

The practice of partnering knowledge management practitioners, business management, and human resources to identify learning needs and connect subject experts with knowledge seekers fosters an environment of continuous learning opportunities. This strategy helps to maintain organizational performance in the face of inevitable organizational flux due to business, economic, or personnel changes. E-learning extends this objective to stabilize and improve performance by capturing and preserving subject matter expert knowledge in a portable format to be accessed anytime, anywhere when subject experts may not be available. Whether online video lectures such as MIT Open CourseWare (2009) or interactive language training provided by RosettaStone (2009), e-learning is an integral part of holistic KM initiatives designed to achieve work environments that encourage and support free flow of the right information at the right time to sustain and improve business performance.

References

Amazon.com. (2009). Retrieved November 15, 2009, from http://www.amazon.com.

Davenport, H., and Prusak, L. (2000). *Working Knowledge.* Boston: Harvard Business School Press.

Facebook. (2009) Retrieved November 15, 2009, from http://www.facebook.com.

Howell, T. (2009). In Their Own Words: Preserving International Space Station Knowledge. NASA ASK, Issue 36. Retrieved December 10, 2009, from http://askmagazine.nasa.gov/issues/36/index36.html.

Invention Machine. (2009). Retrieved November 15, 2009, from http://www.invention-machine.com/ProductsServices.aspx?id=50.

Kolb, D. (1984). *Experiential Learning: Experience as the Source of Learning and Development.* Englewood Cliffs, NJ: Prentice-Hall.

LdPride. (2009). What are Learning Styles? Retrieved December 15, 2009, from http://www.ldpride.net.

LinkedIn. (2009). Retrieved December 15, 2009, from http://www.linkedin.com/.

Mayer, R. (2001). *Multimedia Learning.* New York: Cambridge University Press.

Merriam-Webster Online Dictionary. (2009). Definitions retrieved November 15, 2009, from http://www.merriam-webster.com/dictionary.

Microsoft. (2009). Retrieved November 15, 2009, from http://www.bing.com/?scope=web&mkt=en-US&FORM=MSNH11.

MIT OpenCourseWare. (2009). Retrieved December 15, 2009, from http://ocw.mit.edu/OcwWeb/web/courses/courses/index.htm.

Paivio, A. (1971). *Imagery and Verbal Processes.* New York: Holt, Rinehart, and Winston.

RosettaStone. (2009). Retrieved November 30, 2009, from http://www.rosettastone.com/.

Second Life. (2009). Retrieved November 30, 2009, from http://secondlife.com/?lang=en-US.

Chapter 19

Virtual Leaders: Born or Made?

Mary Key and Donna J. Dennis

Contents

Distance matters. An effective leader who has regular face-to-face contact with employees might not be as effective in cyberspace. Good conventional leadership skills are necessary but not sufficient to lead others at a distance. Therefore, it's alarming how few organizations offer any special development for virtual leaders—especially in light of some of the recent findings. Data on virtual distance shows that when it is managed properly, positive results can be significant in areas such as trust, innovation, job satisfcation, on-time and on-budget performance, and helping behaviors (Lojeski, 2010).

Perhaps the assumption is that good leaders should just know how to transfer their skills to a virtual environment—as if they were "born" rather than "made." For example, a Society for Human Resource Management study focused on the development of virtual leaders and reported that 80% of the respondents stated that special training was "not at all" a priority for virtual leaders. Over 60% of the respondents went on to say that their organizations provided no specific training for either the virtual team leader or virtual team members (Rosen et al., 2006).

A similar finding occurred in a large survey conducted by the Human Resources Institute (HRI), now the Institute for Corporate Productivity (i4cp), and commissioned by the American Management Association. It asked respondents to allocate 100 points to various characteristics that support strategy execution. The highest-ranked characteristic was "openness to change" and the lowest was "virtual management" (AMA/HRI, 2005).

So, the good news is that leading virtually is on the radar screen; the bad news is that it isn't a priority. This could turn out to be major problem. Additional research conducted by i4cp clearly shows that the ability to foster innovation is one of the top characteristics of leaders, both today and, especially, in the future. Yet, there is mounting evidence that innovation and working stand virtually at odds with each other. A study on "virtual distance" and innovation as applied to virtual teams at 17 organizations indicates that virtual distance has a significant and negative relationship to innovation (Lojeski et al., 2006).

"Virtual distance" in this study was defined as both perceived and physical distance, highlighting the point that leading virtually is often a blend of virtual and face-to-face interactions. What seems to matter here is the perception of distance between leaders and those who are supposed to be following them. With so many organizations setting innovation as a goal for a competitive advantage, additional attention needs to be paid to how to enhance innovation virtually. One clear way is to minimize the perception of distance and take time to focus on stimulating and reinforcing innovation.

Innovative practices generated virtually, need to be captured or they become lost knowledge. Unfortunately, organizations still don't place a priority on knowledge retention and transfer. Experts have gone to great lengths to develop and articulate best-in-class strategies for organizations to follow. But while knowledge retention is an acknowledged talent management strategy, it is not widely practiced in most organizations; in fact it seems to be more of an afterthought (DeLong, 2004; Liebowitz, 2007; Liebowitz, 2009). In a 2009 survey conducted by i4cp, only 21% of the respondents participating rated their organizations as retaining knowledge "pretty or very well." Almost 80% (78.8%) of the respondents reported that they didn't retain knowledge well or only moderately well. So with almost 80% of organizations setting themselves up for a significant drain of business wisdom, innovation will decrease. Interestingly, the remaining 20% in the i4cp study who stated that their organizations retain knowledge "pretty well" or "very well" showed a direct correlation with higher market performance (market share, profitability, revenue growth, and customer satisfaction) (i4cp, 2008). Clearly, strong consideration needs to be given to capturing innovative processes and practices when they occur virtually and otherwise.

If innovation is enhanced by reducing the perception of distance, then how do you accomplish that? What is different about leading virtually? Distance impacts a leader's ability to collaborate, communicate, reach common goals, build community and connectedness, manage conflict, and coach. Recent research (Siebdrat et al., 2009) shows that dispersed teams can actually outperform groups that are collocated. To succeed, however, the authors conclude that virtual collaboration must be managed in specific ways. To get to higher levels of performance, virtual leaders need to work harder at relating to follower needs and aspirations in order to have the same level of positive impact that they would if collocated (Howell et al., 2005).

Broken down to its simplest form, virtual leaders need to be competent in three broad areas: technology, task, and relationship. First, considering technology, virtual leaders need to be able to use available technologies well. Technologies are, after all, a double-edged sword. Video conferences, online chats, instant messages, polling, e-mail, the use of avatars, social media, and other forms of communication can be powerful tools and can accelerate the development of rapport among strangers. However, integrating these forms of communication to enhance effectiveness isn't easy, especially if you consider differences in communication styles, cultures, and expertise among the virtual team members.

Managing technology in a virtual environment is complex. Consider teams that are dispersed over more than three contiguous time zones, or team members whose native language is different from the majority of other team members, or team members who do not have equal access to electronic communication and collaboration technology.

Virtual leaders not only use technology well, but also select appropriate technology for the team's work. They do this while accommodating the special needs of team members. Over-reliance on e-mail is common in today's work environment, but can be particularly damaging in virtual work. Alternatives like instant messaging and wikis should also be integrated into the leader's tool kit. Utilizing a shared space is often more efficient and avoids conflict from misunderstood e-mail. Virtual leaders set standards for the use of technology on the team. The best leaders form agreements within the team for response time with e-mail and voice mail.

Virtual leaders set standards for knowledge sharing. Nearly every virtual team is focused on the problem of effective knowledge sharing. Each member of the team brings significant expertise in some areas but noticeably less knowledge in others. Many organizations have developed a role called chief knowledge officer (CKO) to pay attention to the processes and support systems that virtual teams rely on. The CKO can assess whether the team has the necessary resources and tools to ensure successful collaborative results in terms of communication tools. Knowledge sharing and knowledge management in general need to be part of the way an organization works as an ongoing set of processes and not viewed as a project. Building a culture that captures, retains, and manages knowledge is critical to effective virtual leadership.

The best virtual leaders are especially vigilant in task-related competencies. These competencies include setting up work coordination processes, team agreements or norms, clarifying roles and responsibilities, setting goals, measuring milestones, and following up. Setting aside the time to lay a strong foundation for the team is time-consuming and yet pays off in the long run. Teams with a high level of task-related processes outperform teams with a low level. The more dispersed the team is, the more important it is to excel in this competency. Teams with high dispersion find using formal team charters, rules of engagement, and group rooms where goals can be posted for all to see to be useful tools that allow work to be done more easily. When work is ongoing and consistent, trust is built. Accountability also gives a sense of fairness in how standards are applied so trust can be accelerated because team members perceive that despite the distance, the playing rules are the same.

In their study on collaboration and team behavior at 15 multinational companies, Gratton and Erickson (2007) found that diversity among virtual team members can initially be a deterrent to collaboration; the greater the number of strangers on the team from different backgrounds, the less likely team members will share knowledge or show other collaborative behavior. The researchers conclude that although teams that are "large, virtual, diverse, and composed of highly educated specialists" are increasingly critical to complex projects, these same factors stand in the way of getting things done and being effective in getting along (p. 102).

In another study (Earley and Gibson, 2002), it was found that heterogeneous teams (teams comprising members from different cultures) do become more effective than their homogeneous counterparts. But there is a time lag of approximately 17 weeks due to a lack of shared understanding of communication strategies in the early stages. The amount of communication that is deemed to be appropriate within work contexts varies according to the cultural norms of each country. Cultures vary according to the amount of context that communicators have in each situation. Getting the right frequency and detail of communication is difficult. What is perceived as overcommunication in some cultures can be perceived as undercommunication in others. This data points to another aspect of what's different in virtual team leadership and why virtual team leaders work harder to achieve success.

Virtual leaders need to be competent in the socioemotional or relationship side of virtual team leadership. Increasing cohesion, trust, and a sense of connectedness are critical drivers of success. Specifically, virtual teams that have processes that increase the levels of mutual support, member effort, work coordination, balance of member contributions, and task-related communications consistently outperformed other teams with lower levels (Siebdrat et al., 2009). Team spirit in virtual teams is especially difficult to achieve. However, team engagement can make a big difference when conflicts surface on how issues get resolved and on how the team moves forward. Clearly, one difference in virtual work is the need for individual team members to assume accountability for key processes such as providing mutual support, communication, and coordination.

Perceived distance can lead to a higher level of distrust, and trust is among the core building blocks for high-performance leadership (Reina and Reina, 2006). In the absence of familiar visual cues, conversations become harder to decode and trust-building becomes a tougher challenge. A lack of trust can also result in communication problems, which are often compounded by differences in language backgrounds among global teams (Manning, 2003). Yet, having diverse global teams working on complex business issues is often critical to success because varying views and backgrounds can offer new ideas and innovations that like-minded teams can't produce.

It's difficult to "perfect" virtual leadership in today's environment where preparing virtual leaders is not usually a priority and where the technological and market environment is changing rapidly. But organizations can rest assured that working virtually is on the upswing. So, helping leaders apply best practices in this area will help separate the best companies from the rest. What are some ways that organizations can develop virtual leadership? The remainder of this chapter will focus on what leaders and organizations can do to build virtual leadership as a core competency.

Developing Virtual Leadership Competencies

Developing top-notch virtual leaders often requires good planning, as well as developmental support and practice. Leadership development programs should include segments on how any given leadership skill or practice can be applied virtually. However, given that many organizations don't have formal programs of this sort, leaders often don't get the necessary training and support. Getting started can be a daunting task.

One effective way to start is by assessing where you are in terms of the three meta virtual leadership competencies: technology, task, and relationship.

Technology Competencies

List the technology your team currently uses. Are you matching the electronic technology to the needs of your team? Do you model good use of the technology and have you developed agreements about response time and when not to use e-mail? Does training need to be provided on how to use the technology available? Often leaders answer that "yes," the training is available through e-learning. Experience confirms that some degree of "required-ness" is essential to get people on board and, further, that leaders establish a link between business needs and desired outcomes. Leaders set the tone by clarifying expectations, and participants set the pace at which they engage with the e-learning.

Task-Related Competencies

List what agreements the team has for communication and other work processes. Are you and team members following your processes? Are team members clear about their roles and responsibilities? Do they know the goals of the team and individuals on the team? Is there open discussion to improve processes? Are best practices and critical processes being captured so that new members don't have to reinvent or take time to ferret out needed knowledge? How is knowledge being managed?

Relationship-Related Competencies

List what you have done to build relationships and a sense of team spirit or engagement with the team. Rate where team trust is on a scale from 1–5; (5 is great and 1 is not). Do all team members know that you expect them to build positive relationships with other team members? How do you communicate your expectations and provide feedback? Have you established communication guidelines or "rules of engagement"? Do you set aside time routinely to connect with each team member? Do you respond quickly when team members need assistance with conflicts? Do you actively build your knowledge of other cultures? Do all team members feel included? What is the level of comfort team members have in sharing information and ideas with each other?

To make this assessment more helpful ask the team members for their input. This could take the form of a meeting dedicated to a "team check-up" discussion, or a more formalized questionnaire that could be posted or sent via e-mail. Review results with the team and solicit suggestions for improving areas that offer opportunity for improvement. In addition you can solicit best practices and tips from other virtual leaders. Use a knowledge management system to begin to create a place where new leaders can go to get help and share ideas.

Tips and Best Practices

Leaders who show that they are particularly skillful in managing performance with virtual teams should be involved in the development of other managers who might be struggling with virtual team practices. Perhaps they could conduct a Webinar or podcast to share their perspective and ideas.

Another starting point might be the development of communities of practice where leaders who have had some successes with virtual leadership share what has worked and what hasn't with other managers. The community becomes an internal think tank of sorts for what can be applied and what might be avoided when leading virtually. It's also important to capture the tacit knowledge generated by the community and make it available for ongoing management development. Retaining valuable information on internal practices and actively sharing it leads to competency development and culture change.

Evidence indicates that a culture of collaboration is a key factor in the performance of teams and organizations. If virtual teams made up of diverse members are less likely to collaborate and in turn perform at higher levels, what are some of the things that leaders need to do to bridge this gap? First, leaders need to be conscious of how to build trust and collaboration and infuse it into the culture of their teams—and ultimately the organization as a whole.

Research on communication and trust in virtual teams suggests that to facilitate trust early on in the team's existence, team members need to focus on social communication as well as task-related communication. In one large study, an analysis of e-mails exchanged for different teams during the first two weeks of the team's formation found that the highest performing teams largely communicated about nontask things such as hobbies, families, etc.—in other words, the best teams spent time on sharing social things about one another (Jarvenpaa and Leidner, 1999). In addition, messages in the best teams showed enthusiasm and optimism. Best practices for building trust in virtual environments includes taking individual responsibility to build a relationship with each person on the team; this means engaging in social conversation, providing timely responses, forewarning team members of upcoming absences, and providing quality responses to requests for information. Research on how virtual teams can collaborate faster and work more effectively shows that by involving or "seeding" clusters of team members who have worked effectively in the past, you can accelerate the movement of a team to higher levels of performance (Gratton and Erickson, 2007).

High performing teams set up procedures that support achieving the tasks they are accountable for. The use of richer media (voice and video communications in particular) helps when establishing and building virtual relationships. Effective communication tools such as instant messaging help team members to avoid misinterpreting the actions of their colleagues and gives a less formal way of getting to know each other. The best teams have learned that "silence" or nonresponse to communication (e-mail, voice mail, etc.) can be very damaging to virtual team effectiveness as it leads individuals to misattribute explanations for the silence.

In addition to social communication, virtual team leaders facilitate cognitive trust building at the outset by sharing information about each team member's accomplishments, experience, competence, and integrity. To further relationship building, consider socialization strategies such as virtual coffee breaks/online chat rooms, and social conferencing via video or telephone. Another strategy to increase trust and relationship building is to provide guidelines for communicating within multicultural teams. For example, in some cultures, the use of "feeling words" can be confusing and team members have been known to spend hours trying to figure out the meaning of messages sent when the sender expresses how they feel about a certain next step. Clarification of what you are communicating, why, and what action, if any, you want the receiver to take is essential to communicating effectively.

Creating a collaborative culture requires scrutinizing the work environment to make sure that collaborative behavior gets rewarded and behaviors that waylay collaboration get extinguished. A simple way to initiate this thinking is to devote time in virtual meetings to involve team members in defining what's collaborative and what's not. For example, team members can get started by addressing three simple questions:

1. What behavior is not collaborative?
2. What will we be saying and doing with each other if we are displaying collaboration?
3. What will we be saying and doing with our internal and external customers if we are displaying collaboration?

After collecting the behaviors that the team members have targeted, use them to define the ground rules or "how" the virtual team agrees to behave. Those team members that model the agreed-upon interaction behaviors should be rewarded and recognized for their collaboration while those that don't should experience consequences. Just as project results and milestones or the "what" of performance should be celebrated, collaboration or the "how" should be as well.

When possible, at the onset of forming a virtual team, leaders can build trust by taking time to conduct interviews with each team member one on one to get to know them and their motivations. It's important to remember to set a mutually convenient time for each party and be sensitive to time zones. When it's time to recognize a job well done, the leaders will be able to personalize the recognition because they know something about the team member and have taken the time to better understand what's motivating to them. Also, virtual leaders can build trust the tried-and-true way: by showing consistency and doing what they promise they'll do.

If you have a budget to bring your virtual team together to meet in person and for training it will facilitate developing trust more quickly. If this is not possible, use of richer media-like voice and video in initial stages of a project will speed up relationship building (Kandola, 2006). Research shows that it's often more effective to bring team members together for a team-building session after they've begun to work together so they have a context for the training (Zigurs, 2003). It's useful for leaders to develop a communications plan that reflects the frequency and types of communication. And since ongoing feedback can be more difficult in a virtual environment, it makes sense to develop a calendar for regular coaching and performance feedback.

Because team members within the same culture and across cultures have different communication styles and needs, virtual leaders might also want to use a communication style assessment that gives the team members feedback on how they like to communicate and how they like to be communicated with. Effective virtual leaders make themselves available across time zones and plan regular virtual team meetings for progress reports, updates, milestones, recognition, and brainstorming (Mullich, 2005).

Coaching and mentoring programs support collaborative behavior. Coaching virtually brings its own set of challenges. However, technology can assist so that the managers and team members can see each other as they discuss performance expectations and feedback. Some organizations have instituted peer coaching programs where peers support each other's development and performance on projects. If teams are large, peer coaching to improve team results may be a useful, low-cost alternative.

Being able to spur innovation is especially important for such leaders. To build innovation into the process, they can designate a specific time to focus on innovation during meetings and then implement new ideas in real time. This can be an effective way to show an openness to ideas and approaches. When appropriate, innovation can be reinforced by illustrating the impact it's had on the work at hand.

At SRI International, a think tank that has produced innovations for over 60 years, they created something called the *virtual watering hole*. A "watering hole" is a multidisciplinary, collaborative environment where participants come together virtually to improve their value propositions and create more customer value. In an SRI watering hole, you might hear elevator pitches and innovation plans where participants give feedback on how to make the value propositions more accurate, crisp, and comprehensive (Carlson and Wilmot, 2006). What SRI learned is that innovations require a synthesis of many ideas to succeed, including the new product or service, enabling technologies or capabilities, barriers to entry from competitors, a compelling business model, and essential partnerships. They live by a belief that, "only by regularly tapping into the genius of the extended team will new, high-value innovations be created rapidly enough to keep up with the exponential economy" (Carlson and Wilmot, 2006).

In the end the question of whether virtual leaders are born or made is—yes! Many authors have addressed this question for traditional leadership. John Gardner in his book titled *On Leadership*, noted "Many dismiss the subject with the confident assertion that 'leaders are born not made.' Nonsense! Most of what leaders have that enables them to lead is learned. Leadership is not a mysterious activity… And the capacity to perform those tasks is widely distributed in the population" (p. xix).

Achieving high levels of performance virtually can be learned. Organizations need to pay more attention to how they teach leaders to apply their skills in virtual environments and to create awareness that the virtual environment requires additional thinking, skills, application, and transfer. Utilization of knowledge management systems to pass on learning will speed up the learning process and ensure that knowledge management and transfer become part of the organization's culture. With planning and attention, virtual leadership can become a core competency of your organization and an asset for the future.

References

American Management Association and Human Resource Institute (AMA/HRI). *Leading into the Future: A Global Study of Leadership: 2005–2015*, 2005.

Carlson, C. and Wilmot, W. (2006). *Innovation*, Random House, Inc. New York.

DeLong, D. (2004). *Lost Knowledge*. Oxford: Oxford University Press.

Gardner, J. (1990). *On Leadership*. The Free Press, New York.

Gratton, L. and Erickson, T. (2007). Ways to Build Collaborative Teams. *Harvard Business Review*, November, 101–109.

Institute for Corporate Productivity (i4cp). (2008). *Knowledge Retention Survey.* Retrieved from http://www.i4cp.com.

Jarvenpaa,S. and Leidner, D. (1999). Communication and Trust in Global Virtual Teams, *Organization and Science,* June, Vol. 10, Issue 6, 791–815.

Kandola, P. (2006). The Psychology of Effective Business Communication in Geographically Dispersed Teams, September. Sourced from the internet, January 2010, http://www.cisco.com/cisco/web/UK/pdfs/Cisco_Psychology_report.pdf.

Liebowitz, J. (2009). *Knowledge Retention: Strategies and Solutions.* New York: Auerbach.

Liebowitz, J. (2007). *Social Networking: The Essence of Innovation.* Lanham, MD: Scarecrow Press.

Lojeski, K.S. (2010). *Leading the Virtual Workforce,* John Wiley & Sons, Hoboken, NJ.

Lojeski, K.S., Reilly, R., and Dominick, P. (2006). The role of virtual distance in innovation and success. *Proceedings of the 39th Hawaii International Conference on Systems Sciences.* Los Alamitos, CA: IEEE.

Manning, T.T. (2003). Leadership across cultures: Attachment style influences. *Journal of Leadership and Organizational Studies, 9*(3), 20–30.

Mullich, J. (2005, June 16). Making your team stronger by bridging "virtual distance." *CIO Insight.*

Reina, D.S., and Reina, M.L. (2006). *Trust and Betrayal in the Workplace.* San Francisco, CA: Berrett-Koehler.

Rosen, B., Furst, S., and Blackburn, R. (2006, Summer). Training for virtual teams: An investigation of current practices and future needs. *Human Resources Management,* 235–236.

Siebdrat, F., Hoegl, M., and Ernst, H. (2009). How to manage virtual teams. *MIT Sloan Management Review,* Summer, Cambridge, MA.

Zigurs, I. (2003). Leadership in virtual teams: Oxymoron or opportunity? *Organizational Dynamics, 31*(4), 339–351.

Index